Breaking the Surface

BREAKING THE SURFACE

An Art/Archaeology of Prehistoric Architecture

DOUG BAILEY

OXFORD
UNIVERSITY PRESS

OXFORD
UNIVERSITY PRESS

Oxford University Press is a department of the University of Oxford.
It furthers the University's objective of excellence in research, scholarship,
and education by publishing worldwide. Oxford is a registered trade mark
of Oxford University Press in the UK and in certain other countries

Published in the United States of America by Oxford University Press
198 Madison Avenue, New York, NY 10016, United States of America

CIP data is on file at the Library of Congress.

9780190611873 (cloth)
9780190611880 (paper)

9 8 7 6 5 4 3 2 1
Paperback printed by Webcom, Inc., Canada
Hardback printed by Bridgeport National Bindery, Inc.,
United States of America

For Alasdair and Michael

Contents

Preface

THIS IS A book about holes. I referred to it as *The Holes Book* when speaking to apparently interested colleagues, clearly uneasy students, and politely un-impressed friends and relatives. They wanted to hear more about the excava-tions that we were part of in southern Romania, in a village called Măgura. There, we were opening and studying a site that contained examples of Europe's earliest architectural form, the pit-house or pit-hut. When people asked about that fieldwork, I tried to explain what we were doing, what we were finding at these sites, and what the sites meant in terms of the grand narrative of human history, particularly with reference to the transition to a fully sedentary life that marked the Neolithic (6500–3500 cal. B.C.). In these conversations, I started to hear myself talk about the pit-houses less as build-ings and more as holes sliced into the ground. The more I tried to describe what these sites were, the more I felt the first ticklings of the inescapable itch of an idea: if we were going to get to the bottom of our Neolithic pit-hut site in Romania, then maybe we would be better off thinking of them not as architec-ture, but as holes cut into a surface (i.e., the ground). I had very little idea what this might mean. It was still many months before I would discover that other academics and scientists for some time had been building a robust body of research and thinking about holes: about what they were, and about the con-sequences that a hole had on its diggers, users, and fillers. At a similar level of ignorance, I had little idea that a series of modern and contemporary artists had been making work by making holes since well before I had been born.

I scratched that itch. In an earlier project (Bailey 2005b), I had let my at-tentions be distracted in a similar way. In that work, I had wondered what might happen if we stepped away from goddess and cultic interpretations of Neolithic figurines, and I had sought value far from traditional archaeological typologies and means of explanation. There I had found relief in research about miniaturization, about three-dimensionality, about touch, about the rhetorics of illusion and representational absence, and about the politics of visual representation. In my new work on digging pits in the ground in Romania I let my curiosity take me in several unrelated directions: to the philosophy of holes, to the visual perception of concave shapes, to the diversity of ways that different communities spoke and thought about cutting or breaking an object, and to understandings of what defines a surface and what is the significance when that surface is the ground upon which we walk.

I started to see holes everywhere, particularly in the prehistoric past, but also as a primary process and method by which we uncover the past (i.e., excavation through digging into the ground). With no respect to research sampling strategies or to complete coverage of periods, or even of any one period, I poured myself into the holes of two British sites: The Middle Bronze Age Wilsford Shaft and the Neolithic causewayed enclosure at Etton. Wilsford had fascinated me since I had used it as a case study in one of the first classes I had taught as a Junior Lecturer (the class was about Later Bronze Age Britain) at Cardiff University. Etton was a different type of site, but also well excavated, analyzed, and published (Pryor 1998). It was also a key site in one of archaeology's hotter debates of the 1990s and 2000s (i.e., structured deposition).

At the same time as I was picking apart the excavation records of Wilsford and Etton, I ventured into the studios and galleries, interviews and letters of artists whose methods of work and thought were the cutting of surfaces. I returned to Gordon Matta-Clark, an artist whose thoughts about "an.architecture" and anti-archaeology had inspired me in my earlier work on late Neolithic villages (Bailey 2005a). Next, I dove into the cut canvases of the Italian, postwar artist Lucio Fontana. Then, I agitated myself with Ron Athey's 1990s performance works on the body; on pain; and on sexuality, AIDS, and HIV.

There are other places that my exploration could have taken me: other artists; other prehistoric, historic, and contemporary archaeological sites; other parts of the humanities, sciences, and social sciences (one that still nags at me is a study of why dogs dig holes: Odendaal 1997). In all of these deep interrogations of hole cutting, however, the more I learned, and the farther my expeditions took me, the more I realized that there was no simple, contained, understanding of making holes today or in the recent past, in the art world, in the laboratory of behavioral scientists, or of the consequences that doing so had on the people who did the cutting, digging, and surface breaking. Each new example of hole-making that I encountered convinced me that the same was true of our 8000-year-old pit-houses in Romania; no one explanation or interpretation would do them justice. Two options faced me: (1) step back into the standard (and wholly valuable) archaeological treatment of field-sites and the objects that come from them—dig, analyze, interpret or (2) work the holes in the ground at Măgura into a set of correspondences and reactions with the non-archaeological manifestations of hole-making that I had been learning about.

I went for the second option. The result is this book. As you move through it, you will find that it is not a traditional research monograph, clearly not an excavation report (though I ask that it be accepted as my scientific account for our seasons of fieldwork at Măgura). My aim has come to be to make something new, unexpected, and open-ended with these fragments, examples, artifacts, art works, philosophies, and modern discoveries about people and what they do and think when they cut holes into surfaces. As such, the book vibrates from prehistory to the late twentieth century, from finely tuned philosophic debate to a teenager in his bedroom cutting himself as an act of emotional relief, from archaeology to art and beyond. Making holes in surfaces affects what we think and do. The inter-texts that come after chapters 3 and 6 and before the appendix are attempts to bring this into play, and the layouts of the title pages for the book's chapter are another: the book attempts to prove that holes matter by doing and showing this happening, not merely by writing academic prose.

But the title of this book is not *The Holes Book*. The final title and its clarity come thanks to an anonymous reviewer's suggestion and to the editorial team at Oxford University Press who suggested *Breaking the Surface*. While *Breaking the Surface* is a much finer label, the book was always been and remains concerned with holes. In fact, the project itself disappeared into several huge holes, and for several extended periods of time no one (including me) could figure out what had happened to it or where it had ended up. Such is the power of holes. At the beginning (more years ago than I am willing to admit), I won a sabbatical grant from the Arts and Humanities Research Board (Award Reference: AH/F003064/1). And yes it was that long ago; not only a time when the AHRB still existed but also a time when an academic based in the UK could get a grant to cover enough teaching and administrative work to clear the time necessary to shape a book project.

I spent that sabbatical year at Stanford's Archaeology Center, and by the end of twelve months, I had completed detailed and deep research on pithouse sites from four great prehistoric and historic cultures. Before I could shape those half-finished chapters into a coherent manuscript, however, an (only partially) unexpected though particularly craterous hole appeared in the road ahead. I tumbled in and spent the next three years chairing the Anthropology Department at San Francisco State University. I have a feeling that Cardiff may still wonder where I went, and why I didn't come back. After three years of chairing the department at SFSU, I climbed out of that hole and opened up my files and notes for this book. Almost immediately I fell into another uncharted crevice that had opened without warning under my feet. This new hole sucked me down into a project comparing material that I had some understanding of (Neolithic figurines) with objects and a world that I had only the barest of knowledge (Japanese Jōmon dogū).

While in that hole, I curated an exhibition at a museum of art (The Sainsbury Centre for Visual Arts), produced an accompanying book (Bailey et al. 2010), and absorbed (with great pleasure) a wholly unexpected body of knowledge of the prehistory of Japan and of its modern food, culture, people, and landscape. Two years later, I climbed out of that hole and stood again on the surface. I realized that during my time in these two holes my thinking about pit-houses at Măgura had shifted dramatically. My perspective had moved. The horizon was not where I had remembered it to be. Those half-finished sabbatical chapters appeared much less satisfactory than they once had seemed. I restarted, refocused, found a publisher willing to take on a more experimental work, and produced the work that you are now reading. To get here has required help from many places and many people.

The list of friends and colleagues who deserve thanks is long. In Romania, I learned much from Dr. Pavel (Cristi) Mirea, of the Teleorman Regional Museum of History; Cristi knows so much more than I will ever know about the prehistory of Eastern Europe, and in particular about the Neolithic in the region in which sits the Southern Romania Archaeological Project. Much of what I have written about in this book started with (very) early morning conversations on site at Măgura and very late evenings in his museum laboratory in Alexandria. The buzz of fieldwork and a team of highly skilled individuals trying to put together an 8000-year-old past energized the discussions about pit-houses and what they were (and were not). To members of that team, I offer deep thanks: Radian Andreescu, Adrian Bălășescu, Amy Bogaard, Costel Haită, Mark Macklin, Amelia Pannett, Valentin Radu, and Laurens Thissen. The anchor of our work at Măgura was the Department of Archaeology at Cardiff University; Măgura would not have happened without Steve Mill's acute mind and drive.

In total, sabbatical support and institutional backup has came from four places: Cardiff University and my students and colleagues there; the Stanford Archaeology Center (especially Ian Hodder, Lynn Meskell, and Barb Voss, but also Peter Blank and Stanford's Bowes Art and Architecture Library); the Norwegian Academy of Sciences and my colleagues at the Centre for Advanced Study (Hein Bjerck, Vigdis Broch-Due, Mats Burström, Caitlin DeSilvey, Alfredo González-Ruibal, Tim LeCain, Saphinaz-Amal Naguib, Thora Péturs-dóttir, Chris Witmore); and the Anthropology Department at San Francisco State (Peter Biella, Mark Griffin, Sahar Khoury, Martha Lincoln, Jim Quesada, Meredith Reifschneider, Cindy Wilczak, and the students of my graduate seminars and classes on The Origins and on Art and Visual Archaeology).

Success and accuracy in working across the book's range of disciplines, artists, and excavations could not have come without the generosity and advice from many people, friends newly made and colleagues long ago met: Martin Bell, Katarina Botić, Joanna Brück, Sev Fowles, Charly French, Pia Gottschaller, Tim Insoll, Dominic Johnson, Ian Kuijt, Kornelija Minichreiter, Joshua Pollard, and Francis Pryor. Many improvements on my thinking have come from comments I was grateful to receive at seminars and conference sessions where I tested ideas included here. For inviting me to speak at their institutions or in their conference sessions, thanks are due to Peter Biehl, Brian Boyd, Andy Cochrane, Zoe Crossland, Dan Hicks, Simon Kaner, Stephanie Langin-Hooper, Becky Martin, John Robb, Nicole Rousmaniere, Ian Russell, and Anita Synnestvedt,

At Oxford University Press, I have benefited from the support of Sarah Pirovitz, Abigail Johnson, and Stefan Vranka, as well as Gwen Colvin and Rene Carman. OUP dominates archaeological publication in a way that Cambridge did in the 1980s and Routledge did in the decade or so after that. I am proud to be part of the OUP team. The comments from the anonymous reviewers of my book prospectus and the final manuscript focused my thinking, tightened my argument, forced me to delete weaknesses that I was blind to, and made the resulting text far superior to what I had thought was satisfactory. Putting together the book required contributions from many individuals in many places, whether they were producing line-art (Svetlana Matskevich), or helping me to find images or clear rights for the reproduction: Meghan Brown (Art Resource); J'Aimee Cronin (Artists Rights Society); David Dawson (Wiltshire Museum); Annie Bartholomew, Anita Duquette, Elizabeth Sussman (Whitney Museum); Mai Pham (Bridgeman Images); Maria Villa (Fondazione Lucio Fontana); and John Wareham (Star Tribune in Minnesota). At times, I was overwhelmed by the generosity of artists, photographers, and artists' estates and galleries who offered digital files of their prints and granted me the right to use them: the Gagosian Gallery (and Sara Womble) for images of Chris Burden's 1971 *Shoot*; Anthony McCall (and Lauren Nickou) for images of his 1973 *Line Describing Cone*; Catherine Opie (and Jose Luis G. Lopez at Regen Projects) and Dona Ann McAdams for photographs of Ron Athey and of his 1994 performances; ORLAN for images of her surgery performances; Marc Petitjean for his images of Gordon Matta-Clark's 1975 *Conical Intersect*; and to Edward Ashbee, son of the late Paul Ashbee, for rights to use the Wilsford Shaft illustrations.

Finally, there is a core group of friends and supporters who must bear some responsibility for *Breaking the Surface* because of the influence that they have had both on the work particular to this book project, but also more widely on my thinking about the limits of archaeology. I write all of my work in reflection to my late father, who taught me more about research and work than anyone else could have. To my mother, now in her tenth decade, who still reminds me of the difference between the use of "farther" and "further" and with whom I continue to battle over the use of commas, semicolons, and colons; she may be the only person who has read every word of everything that I have ever written; much love to her. To Meg, who saw my thinking about holes emerge, who challenged me in so many ways, and who expanded my life, I offer the deepest respect and retain fondest memories. Full appreciation to Michelle, who opened my world to contemporary art and beyond, and whom I hold with great respect and admiration. For Maggie, who revealed the wonders of Hidden Beach and showed me a world beyond, I reserve the deepest warmth.

On a level of intellectual inspiration, four people continue to affect my thinking and my approach to work. The first is Mike Pearson whose creative output at the edges and across the disciplines and practices of performance, performance research, archaeology, ethnology, and beyond continues to make me think in new ways: a great friend and an inspiration. Second is Bjørnar Olsen who saw the beginnings of this book project and then has become one of my closest and most trusted friends. Bjørnar's work has always inspired me through example and through its precise intellectual rigor and experimental risks.

Two other people have shaped my work and my career, and both have had significant impact on *Breaking the Surface* and it is to each of them that I dedicate this book. Of these, the first, Michael Shanks, I had met when I was finishing my PhD. He had finished or was finishing or was on some other track at Cambridge on which most of the rest of us were not. Later Michael changed my life by inviting me to spend a sabbatical year (2001) in his lab at Stanford; I returned for another sabbatical (in 2007), providentially sharing lab space with Bjørnar Olsen. I am in Michael's debt for two things. In bringing me to Stanford, he made available a set of resources (intellectual, social, cultural) that I had not had access to before. Those sabbatical years changed the way I thought about archaeology, about research and writing, and about life. The second debt I have to Michael is for his *Experiencing the Past* (Shanks 1992). Though much neglected, and certainly less studied than the books that Michael wrote with Chris Tilley (Shanks and Tilley 1987a, 1987b), *Experiencing* was a radical experiment in archaeological thinking and publication. It bears rereading today.

Matching the impact of Michael on my work is the support and mentorship I have received from Alasdair Whittle. In 1993, I took up my first job as a university-based archaeologist; it was as sabbatical replacement for Alasdair. After the sabbatical job finished, I managed to hustle my way into a series of subsequent jobs in the department at Cardiff. While Alasdair supported my efforts to stay employed and in Cardiff, his greatest contribution to me (as it has been to many others) has been an unending series of conversations, advice, criticisms, and provocations about every aspect of being an academic, being an archaeologist, being an author, being a grant-winner, and staying sane in the process. To both Alasdair and to Michael, this book is one attempt to thank you for your help and support.

Chapter 1

Cutting Pit-houses

FUNCTI⃝ DEPOSITION,
QUESTIONS NOT ASKED

OUR EXCAVATION TEAM was scraping the bottom layers of the pit-house; the fill was much darker at this depth and there were many more, though much smaller, fragments of pottery, but few other artifacts. Laurens had walked over. He looked down at Ben scooping soil into a plastic sample bag. I handed him the large pottery fragment of a red-painted footed-base (Figure 1.1). We had called him over to look at it. He felt the weight of it in his hand. Solid. Heavy.

"Early Criş. Pedestal base of dish. Red slip ware. Massive. Heavy. Half a kilo? More? Edges reworked. Used again for something else. Big dish. Sexy stuff. Any more of this?"

Laurens turned the base fragment over and traced his index finger along the straight edges of the deep cross-shaped incision that someone had cut out of the surface of the bottom of the pot 8000 years ago. I handed Laurens a similarly sized fragment of a second pedestal base that we had found earlier in the afternoon a little higher in the stratigraphy of the same pit-house. This second base-fragment was made of the same, slick-coated, red-painted pottery. Laurens bent down and looked through the bags of material that had come from the pit, carefully labeled and lined up, ready to be taken to the lab at the museum. He asked for the rest of the sherds from these two pots. We said there were none. Radian arrived, looked at one of the bases, smiled, and spread his hands in explanation: "It's part of the ritual foundation deposit of the pit-house." He handed the base back to Laurens, turned, and walked back to the finds tent.

Măgura

It was late summer in 2003 and we were near the end of a long season of excavating Neolithic pit-houses at a Criş, Dudeşti, and Vădastra Culture

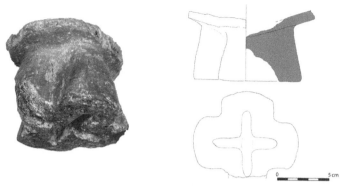

FIGURE I.I Top, bottom, and side view of ceramic pedestal base fragment, Criş Culture (6000–5700 cal. B.C.), from Complex 13, Măgura-Buduiasca, Romania; scale: diameter 12 cm, height: 10 cm. Photo copyright D. W. Bailey.

FIGURE I.2 Excavations at Măgura-Buduiasca, view to the east of Sondages 20 (near) and 19 (far). Photo copyright D. W. Bailey.

site in the village of Măgura (Buduiasca) in southern Romania, just north of Alexandria, the county capital (Figure 1.2). The project was a big one, a collaboration among The Romanian National Museum, the local Regional Museum of Teleorman County, and Cardiff University. Our aim was to broaden and refine current understandings of the transition when prehistoric people shifted from living in mobile hunting and gathering groups to settling in village residential communities of plant cultivators and animal breeders: the transition that Gordon Childe had termed the Neolithic Revolution over eighty years ago. While Childe (1925) defined much of that revolution in economic terms (i.e., the shift to cultivation of wheat and barley and the breeding of sheep, goat, pig, and cattle), an important component of the transition was the settling down of people into semipermanent and then permanent huts and houses, camps, and villages.

Our project focused on the first phase of this settling down (in local culture-historical terminology, the Criş Culture, or Starčevo-Criş, or Starčevo, or Körös Cultures) at a site where we had located a series of pit-houses. Pit-houses, pit-huts, pit-dwellings, earth-cabins, semi-subterranean houses[1]—the terminology varied, but the concept was the same: it was the origin, in southeast and central Europe, of a settled, residential lifestyle. The pit-houses that we had already excavated and the one that contained the pedestal bases that Laurens had identified and Radian had interpreted were good examples of pit-houses from this region of southern Romania. Indeed they were similar to pit-houses from other regions of Romania and from other regions of southeastern and central Europe.

Though early Neolithic pit-houses varied in size, experts agreed that they shared a set of characteristics: pit-houses were dug into the surface of the ground (between 0.25 and 1.5 m in depth); their floorplans were irregular in shape, though usually oval; they were roofed with light-weight coverings made of saplings covered with branches and boughs and perhaps animal skins; their roofs were supported by timber posts placed into shallow holes in the pit-house floors; ovens and hearths kept occupants warm and cooked their food; floors were made of hard-packed soils; flint and polished stone tools were used and stored in particular areas of the pit-house; pottery was used and kept in them; eventually, people abandoned the pit-houses and often filled them with trash or other debris. Residence in pit-houses was understood to have been short- to medium-term: perhaps as much as several years, maybe as little as a single season. It was likely that people may have used them as longer-term occupational base camps from which they ventured to find raw materials, to plant foods, or to hunt. Regardless, archaeologists both local and foreign understood pit-houses as evidence of an important shift toward sedentary living.

Early sedentism took this form in many parts of these regions, particularly in the temperate areas from northern Bulgaria and further northward through Romania and beyond and to the west, in Serbia and on into central Europe proper. In southern regions, though pit-houses were also present, people living at these times (from 6000 cal B.C.) had also built more permanent, larger structures at ground level; archaeologists better understood these and more securely interpreted them as the first houses and villages of European prehistory.

That evening at Măgura, we talked at dinner and later in the lab at the museum about the pedestal bases that we had found that day and about their place in the lower levels of the pit-house we were digging. Where were the rest of the sherds from these two, fine-ware pots? We turned over Radian's suggestion about rituals and foundation deposits. We struggled to find evidence either for or against his proposal. We talked about the other finds from the pit-house and then from the other pit-houses we had excavated. Two of us argued about the postholes that we had identified around the edge of one of the other pit-houses at the site and which we had plotted in pencil onto our site-plans as the locations of posts to support a roof. Were they really postholes, or were they just the holes left by rodents (prehistoric or modern, it didn't matter) that had burrowed down and into the pits long after people had moved away? If they weren't postholes, then the pit-houses had probably not had roofs. If this were the case, then what kind of structures would they have been?

Amy reported that her processing of the macro-botanical remains of samples taken from the pit-houses had produced very few cereal grains or any evidence of the cultivation of plants such as wheat or barley; she had found no preserved remains of wood that might have been used as fuel in the hearths or ovens. Perhaps they used dung, she suggested, to provide warmth. Cristi pulled out a box of carefully bagged and tagged human bone that we had found at the bottom of some of the pit-houses. He and Cătălin laid out each of the plastic bags on the lab table. There were no complete skeletons, not even any articulated bones from a single individual: just scrappy fragments, some bits of skull, other fragments of long bone, a few teeth. Cristi and Pompillia poured out tiny coffee cups of țuica distilled by Florin's uncle; the bottle stood on the table among the finds' bags.

The more evidence that we pulled together, the less clear became our vision of what these pit-houses were. Meli flipped through her notes and drawings, making a quick inventory of flint tools and cores from the pit-houses; she saw no good evidence for any knapping events in or near the pit-houses, though noted a possible but unusual correlation between Criş phase flaked tools and plant harvesting. Steve opened his laptop and showed us three-dimensional plots of the pit-houses that we had finished excavating: similar shapes, similar depths, but strange forms. Did people really live in these holes cut down into the ground? Mark and Ruth walked in to the lab. Mark summarized initial thoughts for a geomorphological history of the valley; he surprised us with his observation that the river valley had changed a great deal, not only in the millennia since people had lived in these pit-houses but also in very short periods of time while those people were in this valley. The trickling "river" that we walked across to get to the site each day used to run at the other side of the valley and, at that time, had rushed at speed and with erosive power. We pressed Ruth to tell us her thoughts about the numerous fist-sized lumps of hard, white material that we had pulled out of many of the pit-houses and which formed a harder geologic layer down below the prehistoric alluvium and into which the pit-house buildings had been dug.

Adrian and Vali arrived from Bucureşti. They offered preliminary thoughts about the animal remains excavated from the pit-houses. The animal bone from Măgura and from their analyses of contemporary sites in southern Romania revealed a trend in the animals that people were eating. At the time that people had lived at Măgura, pig made up a relatively constant, but small, proportion of the diet; sheep and goat had become less and less important, while cattle grew in significance and dominated the pit-house fauna. Were these people cattle farmers, staying in one place for long periods of time, or was it better to think of them as herders, moving with the animals, perhaps with the seasons, maybe staying in some places for longer periods or time, in other places for shorter ones? Handing his empty cup to Steve for a refill, Costel added thoughts from his work on the microscopic sequences of the soils and sediments that had filled the pit-houses after they had gone out of use. He was puzzled by the absence of wood ash in his microscopic study of the soils and sediments from the pit-houses. It matched the absence of wood fragments from Amy's flotation analysis of macro-botanicals.

Radian sat in the corner, shrugged his shoulders, and deferred to the specialists whenever the conversation stopped at him. After he left, we talked longer into the night. What started to become clear from that session in Cristi's lab was that none of us was particularly comfortable classifying the features that we were digging at Măgura as pit-houses. The more that we excavated, the more material we analyzed, indeed the longer that we talked about the site and questioned the traditionally accepted interpretation of these pits as pit-houses, the less certain we were that we knew what we were digging. We shared the same concerns, though the feeling was not unanimous; a few more experienced team members argued for the emergence of Neolithic sedentism at the site (Figure 1.3). Satisfied with this status quo understanding, I noted that these colleagues were not part of the team that spent all day, each day on site; they had not dug down into the pit-houses, felt the soils get darker with depth, and they had not been part of the never-ending on-site discussions through which we struggled to understand what had happened here 8000 years ago.

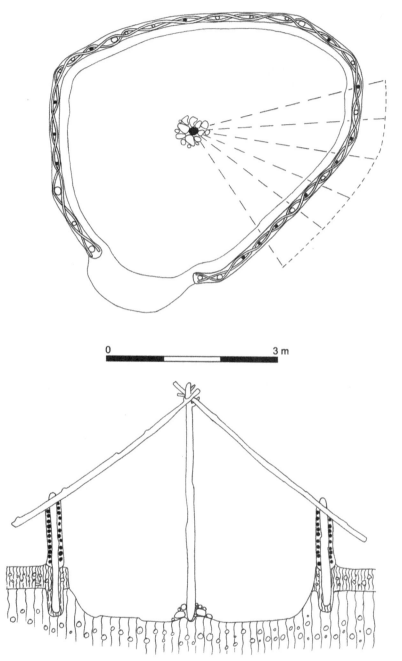

FIGURE 1.3 Traditional view of sedentism and pit-houses. Image copyright D. W. Bailey.

What to Do? Măgura in Its Context

At Măgura we were pushing the methods and the evidence as hard as we could, and even with that, we had unanswered questions. What are these pit-houses? Is it even accurate to call them pit-houses? What to do? Standard archaeological practice dictated that we place our work and emerging results into the local regional sequences and draw analogies with other similar sites. At the closest geographic range, there were few (if any) early Neolithic pit-house sites in Teleorman County that had been excavated recently and where a rigorous attention to precision in recovery allowed for critical thinking and new interpretative perspectives. Contemporary sites from the region are several, including current work at adjacent Măgura-Bordul lui moş Ivănuş (Balasse et al. 2013; Mirea 2005, as well as less recent work at Băieşti and Târgşoru-Vechi (Comşa 1959: 180; Popescu et al. 1961: 631–632; Teodorescu 1963: 251–264), Dulceanca (Comşa 1994: 13–39), and Bungetu (Tudor and Chichideanu 1977) (Figure 1.4). A review of the publications of these excavations yielded solid, if traditional, presentations of the material and interpretations of the sites: they were villages or camps of pit-houses, evidence of people settling down.

Following standard methods of searching for the function and meaning of the pit-houses at Măgura, the next step was to find a site from the same period, with comparative social and cultural references, and which had been recently excavated and published. Here we were better served, and though there are several sites to choose from, the one selected for more detailed discussion here is located in Croatia: the Starčevo Culture site at Galovo—Slavonksi Brod—where excavation had started in the late 1990s led by Dr. Kornelija Minichreiter of the Institute of Archaeology in Zagreb (Minichreiter 2007a).

Galovo—Slavonski Brod

Galovo is an early Neolithic pit-house settlement dating to the beginning of the Starčevo Culture (Linear A phase). Starting in 1996, excavations at Galovo identified three phases of Neolithic activity, dating to 6100–5700, 5760–5630, and 5300–5000 cal B.C. The excavators refer to the site as a "completely preserved early Neolithic farming settlement" of pit-dwellings (Minichreiter 2007a: 33) consisting of pits that functioned as residences (e.g., Pits 37, 64/107, 153); burials (e.g., Pits 9 and 15); ritual spaces (Pit 41); working places (e.g., Pits 205, 207, and 291); areas for the production of stone tools, pottery, and textiles; as well as pits that had combinations of different functions (Pit 9). Other features of note at Galovo are "cult structures" (Minichreiter 2007a: 37), and evidence for the physical separation of ritual from domestic space. While each of the pit-

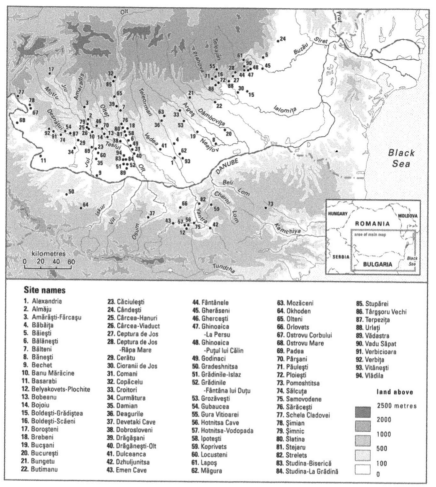

Site names

1. Alexandria	23. Căciuleşti	44. Fântânele	63. Mozăceni	85. Stupărei
2. Almăju	24. Cândeşti	45. Gherăseni	64. Okhoden	86. Târgşoru Vechi
3. Amărăşti-Fârcaşu	25. Cârcea-Hanuri	46. Ghercești	65. Olteni	87. Terpeziţa
4. Băbăiţa	26. Cârcea-Viaduct	47. Ghinoaica	66. Orlovets	88. Urlaţi
5. Băiești	27. Ceptura de Jos	-La Persu	67. Ostrovu Corbului	89. Vădastra
6. Bălăneşti	28. Ceptura de Jos	48. Ghinoaica	68. Ostrovu Mare	90. Vadu Săpat
7. Bălteni	-Râpa Mare	-Puţul lui Călin	69. Padea	91. Verbicioara
8. Băneşti	29. Cerătu	49. Godinaci	70. Pârşani	92. Verbiţa
9. Bechet	30. Cioranii de Jos	50. Gradeshnitsa	71. Păuleşti	93. Vităneşti
10. Banu Mărăcine	31. Comani	51. Grădinile-Islaz	72. Ploieşti	94. Vlădila
11. Basarabi	32. Copăcelu	52. Grădinile	73. Pomoshtitsa	
12. Belyakovets-Plochite	33. Croitori	-Fântâna lui Duţu	74. Sălcuţa	**land above**
13. Bobeanu	34. Curmătura	53. Grozăveşti	75. Samovodene	
14. Bojoiu	35. Damian	54. Gubaucea	76. Sărăceşti	2500 metres
15. Boldeşti-Grădiştea	36. Deagurile	55. Gura Vitioarei	77. Schela Cladovei	2000
16. Boldeşti-Scăeni	37. Devetaki Cave	56. Hotnitsa Cave	78. Şimian	
17. Boroşteni	38. Dobrosloveni	57. Hotnitsa-Vodopada	79. Şimnic	1000
18. Brebeni	39. Drăgăşani	58. Ipoteşti	80. Slatina	500
19. Bucşani	40. Drăgăneşti-Olt	59. Koprivets	81. Stejaru	
20. Bucureşti	41. Dulceanca	60. Locusteni	82. Strelets	100
21. Bungetu	42. Dzhuljunitsa	61. Lapoş	83. Studina-Biserică	0
22. Butimanu	43. Emen Cave	62. Măgura	84. Studina-La Grădină	

FIGURE 1.4 Map of early Neolithic sites in the vicinity of Măgura-Buduiasca. Image copyright Pavel Mirea; image used with permission.

houses at Galovo has comparative value for our work on Măgura, here detail is provided on three of the earliest pits at the site (Pits 9, 205, and 207).

Pit 9

For the initial phase of human activity at the site the excavators have identified ritual features: wooden crescent-shaped fences enclosing a space 12 m diameter and sets of large posts possibly used to support dead bodies for excarnation (Minichreiter 2007a: 61, 63, 75). Pit 9 measured 15 × 5 m and had been dug to a depth of 1.0 m below the prehistoric ground surface; the presence of postholes in the floor of the pit argues that the pit-house was roofed. Termed in the excavation report a "large pit house," Pit 9 was surrounded by crescent-shaped fences made of wooden posts (Minichreiter 2007a: 63) and contained the remains of three skeletons and two "ritual kilns" (Minichreiter 2007a: 63; 2007b: 28).

Consisting of three internal spaces, Pit-house 9 had an entrance on its eastern side. In the pit's central space was a concentration of pottery (fourteen fine and coarse-ware vessels: bowls and footed-bowls), a fragment of a "sacrificial table" (Minichreiter 2007a: 63), animal bones, four stone adzes, and three axes. The excavators suggest that in this central part of the pit people "resided" after entering the pit-house and having carried out ritual feasts (Minichreiter 2007a: 63). Down into the floor of this central space, people had made a "cult burial" of a cattle horn (Figure 1.5) (Minichreiter 2007a: 63; Bronić and Minichreiter 2007: 715; Minichreiter and Botić 2010: 110, figures 1 and 2, plates 1 and 4).

In the northern internal space of Pit 9,

FIGURE 1.5 Cult burial of cattle horn in Pit-house 9 at Galovo—Slavonksi Brod, Croatia; view to the southeast. Image copyright Kornelija Minichreiter; image used with permission.

excavators found the skeletons of a man and a woman, two elongated kilns, and a small fireplace. The kilns had been built along the eastern and western walls of the pit with their openings oriented to the outside of the pit-house proper. Though shaped like pottery kilns, these kilns had been built with a wood and wicker armature (thus distinct from the clay ball construction used in other Galovo pottery kilns), had thin walls, and had been used infrequently (Minichreiter 2007a: 63, 65). On the interior floor of the northern kiln, the builders had pressed into the surface the figure of a circle and a rectangle. The presence of this figure, the kilns' positions in the pit-house, and their infrequent use prompted the excavators to identify their use as ritual (Minichreiter 2007a: 65). To the southwest of the southernmost kiln was a small fireplace that has been interpreted as the "symbolic representation of a home hearth" (Minichreiter 2007a: 65).

The skeletons in Pit 9 were placed in the area between the two kilns. The male skeleton, the head of which was only represented by a few bones of the skull, was a forty- to fifty-year-old, and the people who buried him in pit-house 9 had covered his body with soil, pottery sherds, and flint debris (Minichreiter and Botić 2010: 111). The other skeleton (of a woman, thirty-five to forty years old) did not have its head, and was covered with a similar mixture of soil, pottery, and flint. Where the woman's head would have been, excavators found a large concentration of pottery and burnt animal bones (Minichreiter and Botić 2010: 112).

In the southern part of Pit 9, a third skeleton had been placed: a twenty-five- to thirty-year-old male, also without it head (Minichreiter 2007a: 63). With the individual were pottery vessels, animal bones, stone tools, and a lump of ochre; all was covered with pieces of fired clay (Minichreiter and Botić 2010: 113). A miniature ceramic "altar" (modeled in the shape of an animal "bearing a small sacrificial vessel" on its back) was found 0.15 m above the skeleton (Minichreiter 2007a: 63). Based on the contents of the pit, it is most probable that Pit 9 started as a residential pit, or perhaps a working pit, and was only later used as a burial pit (personal communication, August 2016 Katarina Botić).

Pits 205 and 207

Pits 205 and 207 are different from Pit 9, though they are from the same early phase of the site; together, 205 and 207 probably formed a single, contemporaneous structure (Minichreiter 2007b: 27) (Figure 1.6). A pottery kiln (257) was built between Pits 205 and 207. Referred to by the excavators both as a "work-pit" and as a "pit-house" (Minichreiter 2007b: 23, 27), Pit 205 was 7 × 5 m in plan, 1.0 m deep, and had a two-step entrance to the northeast (Minichreiter 2007a: 53) (Figure 1.7). The pit-house consisted of two separate areas, one to the north and one to the south. In the northern area were three spaces: a small area (0.75–1.25 m), perhaps a storage space or shelf behind a loom to the north (marked by thirty fired-clay loom-weights); a small space (1.40 × 1.0 m) in front of an ash-producing oven dug into the floor of the pit-house; and a central area where excavators found a group of coarse- and fine-ware pottery, bone tools, two polished stone axes, and an "idol" resembling a sealing stamp (or *pintadera*) with a zigzag pattern on its base (Minichreiter 2007a: 53n16).

In the southern part of Pit-house 205 were three separate working spaces: a shelf (0.80 × 1.20 m) used for drying clay vessels before firing (Minichreiter 2007a: 53), a walking surface (3.0 × 1.5 m) with a small niche (0.7 × 1.1 m) attached and raised 0.40 m above the floor that probably functioned as a seat or a shelf, and a slightly lower floor surface (1.2 × 1.2 m) in front of a large pottery kiln where someone could have stood while working (Minichreiter 2007a: 53). The excavators interpreted the shape and interior space of 205 as a pit-house organized in a practical and rational way "to satisfy the requirements of performing diverse activities such as ... firing of clay vessels and production of textiles" (Minichreiter 2007a: 53).

Pit 207 contained a similar range of features and spatially distributed activity areas. Described as a "working pit-dwelling" and a "work pit-house," Pit 207

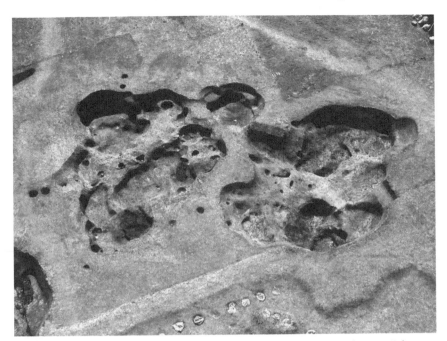

FIGURE 1.6 Aerial view of Pit-houses 205 (left) and 207 (right) at Galovo—Slavonksi Brod, Croatia; view to the southeast. Scale: distance across both pits is c. 14 m. Photograph copyright Kornelija Minichreiter; image used with permission.

measured 7 × 6 m and had been dug down 0.6 m into the Neolithic ground level (Figure 1.8). In addition to a bread oven in the west-central part of the pit, and a hearth in a shallow pit in the northwest of the pit-house's interior (along its western side), the pit-house consisted of three other separate, small, working zones. On the eastern side was an elongated pit (0.2 m deep) containing animal bones, including a cattle vertebra and a sheep mandible. Along the northeast and northwest interior edges of the pit-house, as well as along the southern edge, small niches mark out space where people would have sat while they worked; here were found pieces of worked animal bone and a triangular bone awl that was probably used for sewing leather (Minichreiter 2007a: 53, 55). In the southern part of Pit-house 207, a shallow pit marks out a specially detached working zone (1.8 × 1.5 m) where were found part of a bone awl and other pieces of animal bone. The entrance to the pit-house was on its eastern side and led down and into the largest "room" (1.6 × 2.4 m) (Minichreiter 2007a: 53).

Pit-house Function at Galovo

Galovo Pits 9, 205, and 207 illustrate a range of activities, from death, burial, and feasting to leatherworking, textile production, and pottery firing. Other pits at

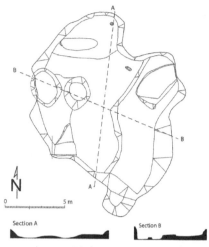

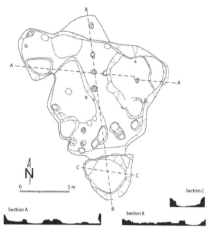

FIGURE 1.7 Pit-house (or "working-pit") 205 at Galovo—Slavonksi Brod, Croatia. Image copyright Kornelija Minichreiter; image used with permission.

FIGURE 1.8 Working Pit-dwelling (or "work pit-house") 207 at Galovo—Slavonski Brod, Croatia. Image copyright Kornelija Minichreiter; Kornelija Minichreiter.

Galovo contain evidence for other activities. Pit 291, for example, contained over one thousand flint artifacts: from well-used cores, to (retouched and unretouched) blades, as well as bladelets, borers, a drill, and primary flakes from knapping (i.e., with cortex on them), and even a blade that could be refitted back to its origin core. Also present were four fragments of polished stone tools (axes and adzes), and a grinding stone (Minichreiter and Botić 2010: 109; Minichreiter 2008). Indeed, many pits at Galovo contained large numbers of flaked stone. On the other hand, Pit 37, from the site's latest phase, contained few artifacts at all and is understood to have been a "sleeping room" (Bronić and Minichreiter 2007: 715).

The excavators base their interpretation of a Galovo pit-dwelling's functions on the shape of the pits and the contents found within them. They understand pits with little material in them to be residential; those with particular types of debris at their base (e.g., bone or flint) are working pits (personal communication, Katarina Botić, August 2016). Most of the pits at the site were filled in with rubbish at the end of their primary uses or soon afterward. Some pits—Pit 9 is a good example—probably had several different, perhaps successive, functions: first residential, then working, and finally funerary and ritual. As another example, Pit 64/107 was both a residential and a working pit.

A longer discussion could follow here debating the method and inherent assumptions entailed in trying to read the function of a pit-house (at Galovo

MAIN ENTRANCE

FIGURE 1.9 Reconstruction drawing of residential Pit-dwelling 10 at early Neolithic Zadubravlje, Croatia. Image copyright Mijenko Gregi; image used with permission of Kornelija Minichreiter.

or at any other contemporary pit-house sites in central and southeastern Europe). Is shape a relevant determinate? Are objects recovered in the pits found in situ or are they in secondary or tertiary contexts? Regardless of that debate and its results, there is common agreement across the local literature and in the institutions, museums, and field projects that these pits were pit-houses. Even when their contents suggest particular sets of activities or acts of deposition (flaked stone tool production or disposal of the deceased), or specialists create illustrations or refer to them, they do so as dwellings or houses (Figure 1.9).[2] Could we assume that the pits that we were digging at Măgura had similar functions to those at Galovo? Were they residential, working, or burial pits?

Longer Interpretive Contexts

The most accurate summary for Galovo is that its pit-houses contained evidence of many different activities that people undertook in the early Neolithic. While the Galovo excavations and publications offered insight into possible interpretations of the Măgura pit-houses, does other interpretive work exist that would help us to connect our excavation in southern Romania with that in Croatia? While some of our initial questions about the function of the Măgura pit-houses were finding answers, also evident and starting to emerge along the way were new questions that perplexed us (e.g., why did people do the things that they did in pits that they had dug into the ground?). One view that was finding focus in our thinking was a sense that generalizations based on form and contents that identified the features at Măgura and at Galovo as houses might well be misplaced, and even if proved to be correct, they failed to push deeper into why people living 8000 years ago in these places thought it appropriate to make and use pit-houses (residential or working or burial or a combination) in the ways and forms that they did.

Our investigations went a step further (back in time), and asked broader questions. What lies at the deeper academic base of understanding these Neolithic pit features (at Galovo, at Măgura, and across the region) as residential? What is the source of the longer interpretive tradition that identifies them as houses? One place to begin is with late nineteenth- and early twentieth-century works that shaped the ways that archaeology developed as a discipline and as it has been practiced in the study of European prehistory. A second set of sources is the more recent, late twentieth-century interpretive syntheses of the European Neolithic.[3]

Lewis Henry Morgan and Gordon Childe

In his highly influential (though now mostly unreferenced) 1877 volume, *Ancient Society or Researches in the Lines of Human Progress from Savagery through Barbarism to Civilization*, the American railway attorney and proto-ethnographer Lewis Henry Morgan (1818–1881) laid down many of the fundamental premises of a cultural historical approach to the study of the past: that is, the approach that continues to dominate prehistoric archaeology in eastern and central Europe. Listing inventions, discoveries, and primary institutions through which humankind had progressed from savagery first to barbarism and them to civilization, Morgan included "house life and architecture" (Morgan 1877: 12).[4] "House architecture," he argued, provides the researcher with a strong indicator of a people's position in the progress from savagery to civilization: "Its growth can be traced from the hut of the savage, through the communal houses of the barbarians, to the house of the single family of civilized nations" (Morgan 1877: 13).

Though he held that "successive arts of subsistence" (Morgan 1877: 16) are the most valuable ways to distinguish successive "ethnical periods" of human progress, Morgan emphasized the importance of a community's house construction technology. Thus, in the Western Hemisphere, Morgan identified the use of adobe brick and stone in house building as a sign of the shift from Lower Status (or Older Period) to Middle Status (or Middle Period) of Barbarism. In addition Morgan saw the domestication of animals and cultivation (aided by irrigation) as further parts of the transition, and that the use of pottery was a sign of the transition to Lower Barbarism (Morgan 1877: 17). According to Morgan's scheme, therefore, the phase of human development in which ancient people lived in huts (i.e., the periods of Savagery and the Lower Period of Barbarism) was one in which "we shall have approached quite near the infantile period of man's existence.... In a condition so absolutely primitive, man is seen to be but only a child in the scale of humanity... in a word, he stands at the bottom of the scale" (Morgan 1877: 38). For Morgan, therefore, a people's architecture was directly related to their position along his "ethnical" progression: people living in pits were, literally, savages.

Morgan's work had influence, most notably through Marx and Engels's writings, but also to European prehistory through the work of Gordon Childe (1892–1957). Childe's 1929 book *The Danube in Prehistory* influenced generations of thinkers and fieldworkers in European prehistory. For Childe "house form" was one of the critical, identifiable "types of remains" that made an archaeological culture, or in his precise 1929 terms, "a people" (Childe 1929: vi). In his argument, Childe notes the presence of "pit-dwellings" in the Palaeolithic of southeast Germany (Childe 1929: 18), before focusing on the Neolithic in the early excavation at Vinča in Serbia, where Vasić had uncovered "oval pit-dwellings" in the form of "half-subterranean huts" (Childe 1929: 26–27). Indeed in Miloje Vasić's 1936 publication of the site, the excavator included a photograph in which he posed four of his local workmen lying down in a pit-house as an illustration of the structure's capacity and function (Vasić 1936) (Figure 1.10a and b).

Looking to the north, Childe then reviewed his Danubian I Culture (e.g., at Lissdorf in central Germany and Grossgartach in southern Germany) (Figure 1.11a and b), noting the presence of "huts" formed of irregular oval depressions often with hearths, and ash and "refuse" in them; he regarded some of the pit-dwellings as "genuine habitations," and claimed that "despite the cramped and unsanitary life that they would impose, the pit-dwellings are warm and easily constructed" (Childe 1929: 43). Childe continues, transferring terminology and meaning from twentieth-century Western society onto prehistory; thus, the pit-huts at Grossgartach have "a porch in front and two 'rooms'" (Childe 1929: 57). Childe makes similar references in passing to "huts" on the Upper Maros (at Marosvásárhely, modern Romanian Târgu Mureş) (Childe 1929: 104), in Poland (at Jordansmühl) (Childe 1929: 124), in the Oder-March-Vistula in his Walternienburg-Bernburg Culture group (Childe 1929: 135), in the Rhine Valley in the Michelsberg Culture (Childe 1929: 181), as well as in early Bronze Age contexts, as in the Aunjetitiz Culture in Bohemia, Silesia, Thuringia, Moravia, and lower Austria (Childe 1929: 227).

FIGURE I.IOa *Zemynitse* [Pit-house] M at Vinča. Image after Vasić 1936: plate 3.

Reading *Danube*, however, one senses that Childe did not fully believe some of these identifications of pit-huts and pit-houses: in referring to "pit-dwellings" in his Period II at Lengyel (Childe 1929: 88), Childe questions the excavator's interpretation as dwellings of the shallow oval pits (2 × 1 × 1.5 m deep) and the "ashes and kitchen refuse" at Erösd as dwellings (Childe 1929: 98).

Stuart Piggott and Ruth Tringham

In his synthesis of prehistoric and ancient European societies, both in his own monograph (Piggott 1965), and in collaboration with Graham Clark (Clarke and Piggott 1965), architecture (let alone pit-dwellings as an autonomous topic) was not a central concern for Stuart Piggott. Economy was paramount for social development; the built environment took second stage, often relegated to a consequence of the emergence of settled agricultural living. Referring to early farming communities, Piggott and Clarke put it this way: "the early development in such societies of the architectural skills required for the erection of monumental and permanent buildings, such as temples and palaces, is eloquent evidence of an enlarged time perspective, for those buildings were made to last beyond a single lifespan and were intended for the conduct of ceremonies and traditions similarly conceived as permanent" (Clarke and Piggott 1965: 158).

FIGURE 1.10b Zemynitse [Pit-house] M at Vinča. Image after Vasić 1936: plates 6–7.

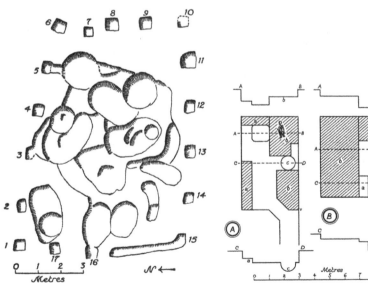

FIGURE 1.11a Gordon Childe's reconstructions of pit-huts at Lissdorf, Germany (after Childe 1929: figure 23).

FIGURE 1.11b Gordon Childe's reconstructions of pit-huts at Grossgartach, Germany (after Childe 1929: figure 29).

When pits and pit-dwellings do appear in Piggott's work and in his collaboration with Clarke, they do so in the contexts of pre-agricultural, Palaeolithic, or Mesolithic cultural and economic landscapes. Thus, writing about post-glacial hunter-gatherers at Tannstock in southern Germany, Schötz in Switzerland, and Farnham in England, Piggott refers to the "huts marked by roughly oval hollows" (Piggott 1965: 33). For the east European and Russian sites of Kostenki and Avdeevo, he describes mammoth hunters living in "encampments or villages of houses" partly dug down into the subsoil (Piggott 1965: 30) (Figure 1.12). For Natufian structures at 'Eynan and Nahal Oren, Piggott mentions (in passing) their open "settlements of oval or circular houses up to about 25 feet diameter, partly sunk in the ground" (Piggott 1965: 40). Piggott and Clarke discuss the "oval houses scooped out of the ground" at the early hunting sites of Siberian Mat'ta and Buret' (Clarke and Piggott 1965: 98–99), and the structures at Upper Palaeolithic Dolní Věstonice in the Czech Republic: "all that remain... are the floor, sunk to some extent into the sub-soil; deeper hollows used possibly for storage" (Clarke and Piggott 1965: 76). They refer to modern mobile communities in their understanding of mobile hunter-gathers, specifically the Eskimo [sic] use of winter structures as permanent and "made up of earth-houses" or snow structures (Clarke and Piggott 1965: 128). If anything, the perspective one recognizes in these works is back through time, away from settlement agriculture and toward the mobile hunter-gathering or Palaeolithic societies.

Steering away from the long wake of Childe and Piggott's contributions, Ruth Tringham's 1971 *Hunters, Fishers, and Farmers of Eastern Europe 6000–3000 BC* became a classic late twentieth-century synthesis of the Neolithic in the region and provided much-needed detail about the Neolithic in southeastern Europe. While, like Piggott and Clarke, much of her discussion focused on economic and material culture (particularly the transition to farming, styles of pottery, and lithic technique), Tringham also reviewed the range of early habitation and pit-structures. Writing about the Mesolithic in the Czech Republic, she describes pits with hearths in or near them and with postholes around them, as at Tašovice (Tringham 1971: 41): "This would suggest that some of the pits were used as habitations with a light wooden or skin superstructure," before advising readers not to interpret all pits on contemporary sites as dwelling places (Tringham 1971: 41). Considering Soroki in Moldova, Tringham notes the local interpretation as "semi-subterranean dwellings" used in the winter or autumn for the shallow ovoid pits at Soroki II and their contents of hearths and stone-working areas. She argues, however, that there is no evidence for postholes, and she thus qualifies the dwelling interpretation as an "assumption" (Tringham 1971: 47–48). In her review of the later phases of the earliest food producers, Tringham moves straight to discussions of the

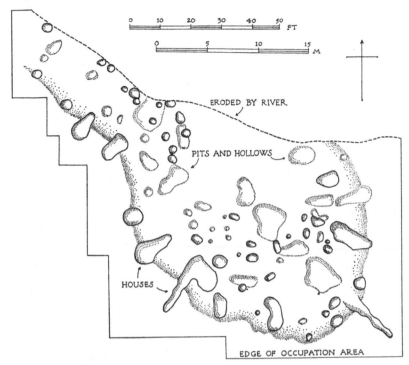

FIGURE 1.12 Stuart Piggott's reconstruction of the plan from Avdeevo, Russia (after Piggott 1965: figure 3).

construction techniques for surface-level buildings (mud-bricks and wattle-and-daub) (Tringham 1971: 71–72) before cautioning against seeing pits as habitation: "From the absence of any traces of a superstructure over the pits or habitation floor within them, it seems unlikely that any of the pits were lived it" (Tringham 1971: 86).

Whittle and Souvatzi

In his end-of-the-century synthesis of the European Neolithic, Alasdair Whittle refers to "so-called pit-dwellings," which he reports "are often assumed to be the principal form of habitation" in Serbia, in the area of Starčevo culture communities (Whittle 1996: 48). Whittle mentions the "small pit-dwellings" in northeastern Bulgaria (Whittle 1996: 49), in early phases at Sesklo and Achilleion in Greece (Whittle 1996: 53), in northeastern Bulgaria (Whittle 1996: 77), across the Hungarian Plain (Whittle 1996: 84), and in the Linear Pottery Culture north of the Carpathians (Whittle 1996: 85), before noting the *"fonds de cabane"* or *"capanne"* at Abruzzo in east-central Italy (Whittle 1996: 323). Pit-dwellings (and other manifestations of a built environment) imply mobility of people and limited investment in building structures that would have lasted longer (Whittle 1996: 52). The use of scare quotes and the phrase "so-called pit-dwellings" reveal, in Whittle, the same lack of belief in dwelling as function as noted for Childe and Tringham.

In his fieldwork at Neolithic Ecsegfalva in Hungary, Whittle examined an early Neolithic Körös Culture site in detail and with a host of modern interdisciplinary specialists and analyses (Whittle 2007). While the goal of the Ecsegfalva project was not primarily keyed to the study of pits or pit-houses, the site contained pit-features and these received the team's full attention. Most striking (and unlike earlier discussions), however, is that in the project's final publication, the discussion was less about identifying the particular function or meaning of a pit-feature, than it was about the acts of the digging and filling of the pits. About the larger pit at the site, Whittle writes: "to build a house, you must first dig. Digging makes that place, that house-to-be. At the end of the house the house-hole should be filled, to bury past lives and to restore to the earth what belongs to the earth" (Whittle 2007: 999). Even here, though, the default is to refer to these features as houses, and even here these comments are included in an offering of "Other ways of telling" positioned outside of the main text in a special section (almost an epilogue of the main excavation report) under the chapter title, "Homage to János Banner" (Whittle 2007: 753).

In her overview of houses and households in Neolithic Greece, *A Social Archaeology of Households in Neolithic Greece: An Anthropological Approach*, Stella Souvatzi reviews the architectural evidence from sites in central and western Greek Macedonia (Souvatzi 2007). She writes of the late fifth millennium cal B.C. phase at Stavroupolis as a "camp of elliptical pit-dwellings" 4 × 6 m in size and having areas for storage and hearths with ovens located outside (Souvatzi 2007: 166, figure 6.7), and of similar features at Thermi and Makriyalos I. At Makriyalos II, she refers to a particularly deep "dwelling pit" that had a staircase leading down into it, potentially with basement cellars and wooden floors (Souvatzi 2007: 167). For Achilleion she notes large pits with plastered floors, "suggesting pit dwellings" (Souvatzi 2007: 169), and at Mandra she notes that the three early phases consisted of mostly pit-dwellings (Souvatzi 2007: 171). For Nea Makri in central Greece, she notes the appearance (late in the sequence: Phase 4, the Middle Neolithic) of "pit-buildings" coexisting with more substantial mud-brick buildings (Souvatzi 2007: 172). In her detailed and authoritative review of houses in Neolithic Greece, Souvatzi emphasizes the variety in form and date of pit-dwellings, though she remains content in using the term.

Significantly, Souvatzi reserves discussion of several unusual pit features for a section toward the end of her book, under a subheading "communal social and ritual structures" (Souvatzi 2007: 216–222, figures 7.1–7.4). The first example she discusses is a "communal subterranean" building at Promachonas-Topolniča I on the Greek-Bulgarian border (Souvatzi 2007: 216-20). The structure is large, deep, has repeatedly rebuilt clay floors, and contains many cattle *bucrania*, horns of rams, bulls and deer, large numbers of serving, storage, and cooking vessels, anthropomorphic figurines, house models, tools, ornaments, grinding stones, and animal bones. The layers of stones, reeds, and branches that separated individual layers of these materials had been burned. The site's excavators relate this pit feature to communal rituals during which people consumed food and offered objects (Koukouli-Chrysanthaki et al. 2005: 101), one assumes to deities or to the natural world or the earth itself. Souvatzi suggests that this pit and its contents document collective actions of discard and destruction of material that followed shared ritual guidelines, intended to rebalance a communal ethos in the face of emerging social differentiation (Souvatzi 2007: 219–220).

As a second example of an unusual pit feature, Souvatzi offers one from late sixth-millennium B.C. Makriyalos I (Souvatzi 2007: 220): a large (30 × 15 m and up to 1.4 m deep) "pit-feature" that contained large numbers of pottery fragments, animal bones, cereal grains, grinding stones, burned clay fragments, which were deposited over a short period of time. The excavators and Souvatzi read the feature and the material as evidence for communal activities of feasting and conspicuous consumption intended to strengthen relationships at local or regional levels (Souvatzi 2007: 220). A large and deep pit feature from early fifth millennium cal B.C. Makriyalos II receives similar interpretation (Souvatzi 2007: 220–221). In these two examples, Souvatzi distinguishes nonresidential from residential uses of pits at Neolithic sites, and suggests that the standard reading of pits as houses may not be fully appropriate in all contexts.

Summary

Reviewing work stretching from Morgan's later nineteenth-century writing to Whittle and Souvatzi's recent anthropologically fueled thoughts, we find the origins for the received interpretation of Neolithic pits, like those at Măgura, as houses or dwellings or, at least as having residential function, as identified at Galovo. Also of note, however, are the cautions advised by Tringham and Whittle in reaction to archaeologists' continuing assumptions that these features were indeed dwellings. Even here though, these cautions are not accompanied by concentrated, critical discussion of what parts of the authors' senses and definitions are unsupportable. Even in her broadening of the discussion to include her unusual pits and potential social actions of protest, Souvatzi retains the more general use of the term "pit-house" and its accompanying inference of residence and sedentism.

These syntheses, from the early work of Morgan and Childe through the overviews of Tringham and Whittle, set the tone (and the vocabulary) for generations of archaeologists in the field, in the classrooms, and in publication. It would be possible, as a next step, to review excavation reports and interpretations of Neolithic pit-houses across central and southern Europe; such a project would require a book of its own. One could review, for example, Haskel Greenfield and Tina Jongsma's helpful work at Foeni-Salaş in southwestern Romania and their arguments for the correlation of pit-houses at that early Neolithic "settlement" (their term) with mobile pastoral economies (Greenfield and Jongsma 2008). In doing so, we would find their explicit definition-by-checklist of what qualifies a pit as a "living structure" (Greenfield and Jongsma 2008: 115).[5] For Greenfield and Jongsma, a pit-house has the following characteristics: evidence that it was covered (i.e., posts to support a roof); a definable shape (particularly with vertical sides); remains of a "hump" of soil around its circumference (to keep out rain wash); material in situ on the floor; and a soil bench around the edge (Greenfield and Jongsma 2008: 115). Greenfield and Jongsma conclude that the people at Foeni-Salaş had a "relatively mobile settlement system, with relatively short-term occupations of structures" and that they lived in "pit-houses" representing individual "households" consisting of a nuclear or small extended family (Greenfield and Jongsma 2008: 125). Greenfield and Jongsma offer discussion of value, reviewing archaeological and ethnographic work on pit-dwelling communities beyond the Neolithic of central and southeastern Europe. In their work at another early Neolithic site (Blagotin), Greenfield and Jongsma expand their earlier discussions, and consolidate their conclusions about the residential functions of pit-houses (Greenfield and Jongsma 2014).

Building a New Approach to Neolithic Architecture

In my own earlier publications about the built environment in the Southeast European Neolithic, I viewed pit-houses as a stage in the development of people's attachment to the land; I drew social and political inferences from the shape and size of structures, and I focused on the spatial arrangements of clusters of pit-houses in contemporaneous phases of villages or camps (Bailey 1999a, 1999b, 2000: 39–62). I argued that the marking out of space by building a structure was one way of inhabiting a place, by physically displaying occupation and possession of location. Similarly, I stressed that pit-houses were temporary, small, constrained built environments, and thus were distinct from other structures that were built on top of the ground surface and which became more frequent as the Neolithic proceeded.

I noted that pit-houses were small and physically constrained, and thus that many of people's activities at the time would have happened outside of these structures. Finally, I identified the rather haphazard, or at least not clearly organized, distribution of pit-houses at any one site; where a pattern was evident, I understood it in terms of the consequent effects on relations and communications between the people living in each pit-house: working outside of buildings in shared and more open spaces collaborating on small-scale or more widely spread projects (e.g., hunting and gathering). A major inference was that group actions and their arrangements would have been flexible, adjustable, and of relatively short-term duration.

In hindsight I can now see that the approach I followed was comparative, between pit-houses and what (in the main) came later: physically more substantial constructions that were not only larger, of a different shape (rectilinear), but also made of more durable materials. I assumed (without support) that pit-houses were houses-made-in-the-ground and that an understanding of their function or meaning would come from contrasting them with what came next: the more substantial surface-level buildings. In those writings, I focused most closely on the consequences that would have resulted from different physical and social arrangements of people, places, and things. I was not interested in (read, I ignored) questions about the original actions that created the pit that was used (either immediately or at some later time) as a possible shelter or workspace, and which I and others were complacent to define as a pit-hut.

One fashion in archaeological thinking at the time (mainly the mid-1980s) was to map floor-plans and village distributions of buildings in terms of depth analysis as a proxy for private and public spaces (Foster 1989; Bailey 1990; Chapman 1990) following the work of Bill Hillier and Julienne Hanson (1984), or to see the precise repetition of a later, new floor plan precisely aligned on top of an earlier, older one (Bailey 1990, 1996, 1999). When I offered my attempt at an alternative (Bailey 2005a), it was to use the language and conceits of minimalist art, such as serial repetition, and the irreducible essence of the geometrically shaped surface-level building in my suggestion that houses were not all that important to the people moving into, out of, and around them, at least in the economic, cultural, technological, or spiritual terms that archaeologists normally focus on.

Least valuable were my simplistic readings of pit-houses as architectural features: that people had made these structures as buildings that they used for short-term occupation (i.e., that they were houses or huts). In this I followed the traditional, functionalist explanations for these features as outlined in the paragraphs above. The only attention I paid to the construction of the pit-house was to note that they were not particularly deep and that sometimes their individual locations took advantage of natural hollows and "co-opted" readily available natural materials. Even here, though, I was thinking more about the energy and time invested in the making of structures and less (or more honestly, not at all) about any significance of digging or breaking the surface of the ground.

Other Ways of Thinking About Pits and Pit-features: Deposition

This book explores other ways to think about the features that we commonly call pit-houses, pit-dwellings, pit-huts, or earth-cabins. As noted above, the focus of so much previous and current work has been on the house, hut, dwelling, and cabin. A major exception has been the work of archaeologists who have concentrated on the acts by which people placed material into pits and pit-houses: deposition. Picked up by John Chapman (Chapman 2000b, 2000c) from the broader debate in the study of British prehistory about structured deposition (Richards and Thomas 1984; Thomas 1991, 1999) and applied to the Neolithic of southeastern Europe, this alternative has opened up important new thinking about the artifacts and materials that archaeologists find in pit-houses. As I will suggest, however, for all of its original thinking, the deposition approach has ignored one of the most significant actions and processes inherent in pit-houses: the acts of breaking the surface of the ground in the digging of the pit. This book takes up those actions and processes in detail, and before we begin that journey, it is useful to examine the deposition approach to pits, and to recognize that though it did much to stimulate new thinking, it missed important parts of the phenomenon of pits and pit-houses.

John Chapman

One of the more provocative treatments of the Neolithic pits of the southeast European Neolithic is John Chapman's discussion of pits, life cycles, ancestors, and deposition (Chapman 2000b). Chapman questions the received explanation of pit functions as dwellings or houses. He focuses on the materials placed in pits and the socially embedded meanings and consequences that those pit deposits may have had. His conclusion is that traditional equations of pits with dwellings are mistaken, and that "large, irregular pits were used as working areas for a range of activities" (Chapman 2000b: 87). Indeed, his suggestions gain traction in the context of sites such as Galovo, noted above.

To begin his re-evaluation, Chapman distinguished between pits that were "foundation deposits" and those that were "open-air" pits.[6] Chapman argues that in foundation deposits, people exchanged "material remains with the ancestral earth," particularly clearly in the placement of infants or children in small pits under the floors of Neolithic buildings (Chapman 2000b: 66). In foundation deposits, Chapman identifies a "linkage of persons at one end of the life-cycle to provide regeneration and fertility to structures and, perhaps, the social relationships making up new households at the start of a new life-cycle. The newly dead were interred in material which, in some cases, comprised virgin soil…while, in other cases, symbolizing the ancestral matrix to which all will eventually return" (Chapman 2000b: 68). For Chapman, people used the recently deceased as a connection between the ancestors and the "future life-cycle of dwelling houses" (Chapman 2000b: 69). Distinct from foundation pits are the open-air pits, which are not found under building floors but at a distance from structures. Often, open-air pits contain large numbers of objects of particular materials in specific associations (Chapman 2000b: 69).

Significantly, Chapman conceives of pits in terms of life cycles; archaeologists excavate merely the last stage of that life cycle. The contents of a pit (as excavated, at least) only refer to the end of its use. From this, Chapman identifies the digging of the pit as its labor and delivery (Chapman 2000b: 64): the original "excavation of a bounded area (its 'birth')" created a new structure (the pit) as well as a mass of material, some natural and some cultural, at least in cases where digging cut into soils containing objects abandoned, discarded, lost or deposited in earlier times (Chapman 2000b: 64). The pit's life consists of the filling of that newly created structure: "the lifetime of a pit is measured…by the extent to which it has become full" (Chapman 2000b: 64). And to complete the cycle, ultimately, the "death of the pit is marked by the complete refilling of its form, rendering the land surface whole again and sealing the earlier deposits so as to make them once more invisible" (Chapman 2000b: 64).

To dig a pit, in Chapman's vision, is first to cut into the soil, perhaps accessing the past, then to remove material from the soil, and, eventually to replace it in specific ways with current cultured material (Chapman 2000b: 64). Most important for Chapman are the practices by which people deposited objects into the holes that they had dug into the ground. The primary theme of Chapman's article is deposition, specifically the "deliberate structured deposition" of objects as a significant social practice within a community (Chapman 2000b: 61); for him, the majority of material that has been excavated from Neolithic sites "has been subject to structured deposition" (Chapman 2000b: 63).

Structured Deposition

For an understanding of the pit-houses at Măgura, and in the region as a whole in the Neolithic, the issues that Chapman raises are important; they move us away from the assumption that pits were dwellings, and they draw down our attention to the objects in the pits and the actions and consequences of placing them there. Chapman's arguments follow from a larger debate around the concept of structured deposition as introduced to archaeology by Colin Richards and Julian Thomas (1984), and subsequently as elaborated by Thomas (1991, 1999) and others, such as Josh Pollard (2001).

Chapman found inspiration in a larger debate around the concept of structured deposition in archaeology, particularly the seminal work of Julian Thomas, first with Colin Richards (Richards and Thomas 1984), and then as taken forward and expanded by Thomas himself as part of single-authored treatments on the British Neolithic (Thomas 1991: 56–78; 1999: 62–88). Recent comment by Josh Pollard (2001, 2008) has refined the thesis, and Duncan Garrow has written an excellent historical critique of the concept (Garrow 2012).[7] The original argument of Richards and Thomas held that people of the southern British Neolithic intentionally selected and deposited particular materials and objects (specifically lithics, pottery, and animal bone) in pits that they had dug into the ground: further, that archaeologists can detect certain "structural qualities" in the patterns of these deposited materials. The authors of the original 1984 paper termed this pattern "structured deposition" (Richards and Thomas 1984: 189).

At the core of Richards and Thomas's argument was their carefully documented observation that certain deposits of material at the Neolithic henge monument at Durrington Walls, in southern Britain, exhibited "a degree of formality" that could not be explained as utilitarian: "when the material was deposited, it was done in a particular manner, obeying certain rules which were important to the actors involved" (Richards and Thomas 1984: 215). At Durrington Walls, therefore, one could identify distinct patterns in the materials placed in the Southern and Northern Circles, in the enclosure ditch, in the Midden, and in the Platform (the latter now seen more carefully as a house of some sort): specifically with respect to Grooved Ware pottery, the quantities of flaked stone tools, the portions of animal bodies, and the particular animal species included. At Durrington and at other contemporary henge sites, Thomas identified "contrasts and oppositions" in the ways that materials were put into the ground in particular places, and he repeated the conclusion that these patterns were "formal and structured" (Thomas 1991: 81); for Thomas these patterns revealed a non-hierarchic ordering of the differentiation among objects and materials, best defined as "segregated correspondences" (Thomas 1991: 68–69).

In these broader monograph-length analyses of the British Neolithic (Thomas 1991, 1999), Thomas expanded the original concept, paying particular attention to the many pits that people (both then and now) dug on British Neolithic sites. Thomas cautioned against the assumption that Neolithic pits shared function or meaning with pits from other periods of British prehistory, most particularly the local Iron Age. While archaeologists confidently interpreted the latter as facilities for storing foodstuffs such as grain (Clarke et al. 1960), Thomas showed that Neolithic pits were distinctly different.

Unlike the Iron Age examples, Neolithic pits were shallow in depth, bowl- (and not flat-) bottomed, and had straight sides that had little, if any, signs of weathering or erosion, and which contained homogenous fills that suggested back-filling without delay (Thomas 1991: 59–60). Furthermore, the plant remains present in Neolithic pits were often burned and a mixture of different wild species: not what one would expect of a storage facility (i.e., monocrops of domestics such as wheat or barley) (Thomas 1991: 60). Thomas suggested that the fills of the Neolithic pits contained materials, the combinations and conditions of which would have been out of place in a domestic deposit or in other casual, daily, disposal of rubbish (Thomas 1999): high proportions of (frequently unbroken) flaked stone tools compared to flaked stone waste, flaked projectile points, axes made of flaked and ground stone, stone mace-heads, bone pins, engraved stone plaques, uncommon and well decorated pottery vessels, human bone, and animal bone from high meat-yielding joints (Thomas 1991: 57, 60, 61).

The patterns were clear. Neolithic British pit-fillings did not make sense in terms of food storage or rubbish; pit contents were records of something else altogether. Examining patterns in a range of different Neolithic sites, particularly the ditches of causewayed enclosures, but also henges, hoards, long barrows, and wet places, Thomas found similarities in records of artifact types and their placements. He concluded that the making of these deposits was "governed by a common set of ideas" through "the digging of pits and ditches, and their refilling, presumably with symbolically charged items and substances" (Thomas 1991: 66). Of what these acts were symbolic was another matter, though Thomas suggested that the depositional acts themselves may best be understood as if they were a resource that people in the Neolithic could manipulate, for example, in order to impose an oriented pattern on the landscape (Thomas 1991: 66).

Refining Structured Deposition

In later writings, Thomas and others have refined the concept of structured deposition. Josh Pollard has suggested that at some British Neolithic sites where the quantities of material are large, and thus probably linked to the later stages of the site's use-life, the structured deposits record formal acts that people played out as they abandoned the site (Pollard 2001: 323). As Pollard puts it, the depositions into pits "could have taken on the performative qualities of any ritual, mediating between different stages in the lives of people, places and objects" (Pollard 2001: 323). For Thomas, the materials and artifacts would have provided people with potential contrasts that they could have drawn attention to as necessary to take advantage of "general principles" and "put together through an improvisatory practice...as outcome of creative play or *bricolage*" (Thomas 1999: 78–79).

Pollard pushes forward this more flexible sense of structured deposition, noting that Thomas had never intended the patterns that he and Richards detected to imply a formulaic and inclusive universal set of rules governing material arrangements (Pollard 2001, 2008; Thomas 1991: 81). Pollard focuses on the aesthetic qualities of deposition as a practice and as a process for which skill, judgment, interpretation, and inventiveness would have been essential (Pollard 2001: 316). Here, there is less room for the rule-bound dictate of formal structures. Acts of deposition were individual performances that followed proficiencies in "assembling and crafting" material and action, and which found guidance in the inherent qualities of the objects involved as well as in relation to symbolic principles (Pollard 2001 322).

Pollard sees the objects in these pits and ditches as formal burials of transformed materials that people treated in special ways relative to their conceptions of renewal and regeneration. Pollard suggests a connection with processes of the postmortem excarnation of the human body and the subsequent burial of the dead, a practice well documented in the British Neolithic (Pollard 2001: 323; Thomas 1991: 136; Whittle 1991). Pollard emphasizes the material and the potency that some objects may have acquired through daily engagements with people, places, animals, and other things (Pollard 2001: 323). Pollard suggests that the objects deposited were selectively gathered, and thus that the acts of collecting objects for deposition were foci for the construction and reinforcement of memory: the agency of objects rested in part in their service as mnemonic devices (Pollard 2001: 323).

Basing his argument on work at the Windmill Hill Neolithic causewayed enclosure, Pollard further dissolves the rigidity of Richards and Thomas' original proposal for rules and structural guides. At Windmill Hill, Pollard sees general principles in action, but also individual invention and performative practice that differs among the individual segments of the enclosure ditch there (Pollard 2001: 322). Pollard writes of an "aesthetics of deposition" (Pollard 2001: 328) and suggests that practices of deposition were neither tightly bound by rules, nor completely without pattern. Picking up on Thomas's reference to invention and *bricolage*, Pollard contends that deposits and depositions are best described as performances with individual acts taking place in different settings, with ranges of motives and outcomes (Pollard 2001: 328). In this sense, combinations of actions and materials created new articulations and relationships that extended beyond the limits of the act or object itself. As Pollard argues, these deposits produced what Howard Morphy had called "successful theatre" (Morphy 1992: 204) and thus which stimulated the necessary sensory response required for particular ritual (Pollard 2001: 329–330).

The Elephant in the Structured Deposit: Digging the Pit

The structured deposition proposal therefore identifies formally orchestrated deposits of selected materials and artifacts that people placed in holes that they had dug into the ground (i.e., pits for posts, segments of ditches in enclosures, holes under the floors of huts) and concludes that such deposits are significations and ascriptions of meaning, memory, and performance: "objects are part of a material 'language,' and through structured sets of association, separation, and linkage in deposition construct contextually specific statements" (Pollard 2001: 316). As is clear, and as Pollard notes, the structured deposition approach successfully moved discussion away from simplistic proposals of the meaning of an assemblage of objects in a pit; the debate significantly retooled the dialogue with a vocabulary of relations between people and material culture, with particular, precise comment on the agency of artifacts, how objects may represent meaning, and the ways that meaning may be embedded, created, and contested in materials and performance (Pollard 2001: 317).

Having respect for the power of the structured deposition argument and a full recognition of the positive impact it has had, particularly in British prehistoric archaeology, it is important to recognize what is absent from that discussion. With its attention to object, materiality, performance, and memory, the structured deposition perspective devotes little attention (at least of matching intellectual vigor) to the creation of the physical context in which the deposit takes place: the digging of the posthole, the cutting of the enclosure ditch-segment, the making of the pit by perforating the surface of the ground. Do these preliminary events of digging, cutting, and perforating have less or no significance? Indeed is it even appropriate to consider them as preliminary? Are digging, cutting, and perforating perhaps important acts and performances on their own, potentially unrelated to the later, secondary performative actions of placing flint, pottery, and bone into them? Does the making of the pit have significance that is unrelated to structured deposition, and if so, then has much (perhaps all) of the vigorous discussion of that topic occluded another act or set of actions of significance in the British Neolithic? From these questions emerges the possibility that the cutting of the ground (i.e., the making of the pit or ditch segment) may have had its own, independent sets of references, meanings, and engagements with what it meant to live in the world of the Neolithic, both in Britain and in central and southeastern Europe.

On Digging Ground as "Ground"

Attention to the actions and consequences of digging of pits and ditches into which deposits were placed (regardless of how one wishes to read those deposits: structured or otherwise) is fleeting. Thomas suggests that for the late Neolithic settlement at Durrington Walls, house construction came, on the one hand, after the excavation of "borrow pits" dug to extract raw materials for wall daub and floor plaster, and, on the other hand before the digging of "decommissioning pits" that cut through house floors at the end of the structure's use-life (Thomas 2012: 2). Thomas sees these digging events as "pit episodes" that segmented time with important household events (Thomas 2012: 2). But why pits? Why digging into the ground? What consequences and potential meanings might the acts of cutting the ground have had?

As the beginning of an answer, Thomas suggests that placing specific objects in the ground in particular places may have played a role for mobile Neolithic communities as "the fixing of the evidence of domesticity in the landscape [and] may have been a means of domesticating the wild" (Thomas 1991: 76). Perhaps this was the case, but why? What was it about the ground, and about the placing of materials into that ground, that would have made that possible? Thomas suggests that pit-deposits were one of the ways in which people created, re-created, and contested the identities of place, and that the first deposits were merely representations of events that occurred at a particular place (Thomas 1999: 72–73). But why the ground? Might we benefit by focusing on the ground that is cut as Ground, an entity of more significant ontological essence? What did Ground (as a metaphysical entity) mean to those people? How did such a Ground sit within (or literally under and around) those people's understandings of what and who they were, living in their worlds: indeed, of what that world was? Thomas hints at the potential when he writes that by digging pits and placing objects in them, people brought meaning to places, fixing a connection between people and a place (Thomas 1999: 87; Pollard 2001: 323).

More potent comments about digging ground/Ground are available, though usually they are little more than passing comments made in longer discussions of other matters. Thus, in their examination of isolated pits in the Scottish Neolithic, Kenneth Brophy and Gordon Noble suggest that the initial act of breaking the ground may have been significant: the ground that was broken was "important ground" (Brophy and Noble 2012: 74). In his original treatment, Thomas suggested that if placing objects in pits was part of a Neolithic fixing of place, then the digging of the pit itself may have been part of a process of transformation (Thomas 1991: 76). Later, in his discussion of the bluestones at Stonehenge, Thomas isolates the digging of the topsoil out of the ground in order to make a place for the stone to sit in, by writing of it in terms of "presenting component parts of the landscape in unfamiliar ways, putting its substance on view and enabling entry into the earth itself" (Thomas 1999: 178). Thomas identifies the significance of the role played by the action of digging-into-the earth as the principal attribute in common with Neolithic pits and ditches (Thomas 1999: 83).

With these isolated and underdeveloped comments, we get glimpses of deeper dimensions of the actions carried out: digging pits is of the Ground and of the earth. What did earth mean to people excavating a hole to seat a stone? In the concluding chapter to his 1999 *Understanding the Neolithic* (a rewriting of his 1991 *Rethinking the Neolithic*), Thomas gets closer to the issue, proposing that putting things together in the ground may provide a "statement about the nature of certain metaphysical relationships," and that "depositional practice was a means of using the material world in order to create meaning" (Thomas 1999: 224). By the later Neolithic, he continues, the digging and filling of a pit may have been seen as an event in itself (Thomas 1999: 224–225).

Thomas notes that the British Neolithic is culturally distinct in term of people's digging into the earth to create pits and ditches, particularly when understood in the contexts of the transportation and shaping of timber and stone to build structures (Thomas 1999: 35). Brophy and Noble push this on, questioning which was more important, digging the pits or putting objects

into them; they suggest that interpretative foci on ritual may not provide satisfactory understandings of what pits were and what they meant (Brophy and
Noble 2012: 74). Amelia Pannett fuels the discussion, suggesting that the act
of pit-digging may have been more important than the materials deposited
(Pannett 2012: 142). Pollard suggests that when we observe the "neatness of
form and execution" of the making of the pit, we see significance of the acts of
digging as processes of "crafting" and "sculpting": that people made the pits
themselves with aesthetic qualities (Pollard 2001: 325).

What is made of the digging and the ground, therefore, is a matter largely
ignored (a proverbial elephant in the pit of the structured deposition debate); few
experts (either of the British Neolithic of other periods or regions) have opened
up discussions into it. Tantalizingly, Thomas suggests that a post placed in a
pit may mediate between earth and air, hidden and visible (Thomas 1999: 83),
though even here the emphasis rests on the post and not the pit or the ground.
Discussing deposits made at henges, he hints that people's conceptions of
the world may have invoked distinctions between above and below ground
(Thomas 1999: 85). Elsewhere, he conceives of a distinction between the
above- and below-ground in terms of threshold, the crossing of which held
local significance in creating durable traces of memory (Thomas 1999: 72).
In his vision of the types of symbolic resources that may have come into
play with the digging of pits, Thomas writes of "opening of holes in the
earth," as something more complex and nuanced than "digging pits" (Thomas
1999: 77).

Tim Darvill provides one of the richest stimuli for deeper thought. Writing
about the Neolithic of the Isle of Man and the pits, pit-clusters, and earth shafts
there, Darvill sees those pits as "land-cuts" where "strange things happened and
where sights, sounds, smells, and extra-sensory perceptions mingled the ghosts
of the past with actions of the present and the sounds of the underground rattled
through their imaginations" (Darvill 2012: 40). Benjamin Edwards tempts us
with provocative thoughts in his discussion of Neolithic Northumberland: pits
(even without posts in them) affect people's perceptions of space (Edwards 2012:
95). In his work at Ecsegfalva in Hungary, Whittle suggests that "pits would
have been dug not only to provide material for house construction but also to
claim and tame the place in question; living in that place then took place, and
when the time of the place came to at least a temporary end, material from the
house or structure was returned to the earth" (Whittle 2007: 731). More forcefully, Whittle writes that the flow of daily life contained "the respect shown for
the earth by digging pits into it and eventually returning its material to them"
(Whittle 2007: 745), and the "demonstrable connections" that people had with

the earth (Whittle 2007: 748). Huge are the potentials in each of these brief, side-comments on the significance of breaking the surface of the ground by digging. None of the authors, however, take the discussion forward. We are left hanging. As if over a hole cut into the surface of the ground.

Gamble, Locales, and Rituals of Attaching-to

One other direction in which to look for traditional inspiration for our exploration of the Măgura pit-houses is backward through time, into the Upper Palaeolithic. Indeed one wonders that if the practice of Neolithic pit-houses grade through time in either direction, then it may most likely be back into the Palaeolithic; pit-houses might best be seen as the tapering off of a behavior better understood in the debates about human behavior, material culture, and environment that populate Palaeolithic research. To this point, Clive Gamble's treatment of the European Palaeolithic and his engagement with the Upper Palaeolithic pit-dwellings at the Moravian sites of Dolní-Věstonice and Pavlov are of particular value (Gamble 1999).

At the core of Gamble's wider approach is a rethinking of the Palaeolithic in terms of locales and regions (Gamble 1999: 65–80; Gamble 1998). Gamble defines locales as encounters, gatherings, social encounters, and places: "locales, rather than sites, are where interaction took place and is preserved" (Gamble 1998: 68). Encounters are an individual's interaction with animals, plants, and other people where the paths of the person and the others intersect (Gamble 1999: 69). Gatherings are performances among portable resources such as people's bodies, food, stone, and other materials; gatherings and their attendant interactions can be preserved in objects, for example, such as hearths (Gamble 1999: 71). Locales, however, are "where social life is performed, where attention occurs" (Gamble 1999: 76), and where activities of attending and attention are essential mechanisms (Gamble 1999: 413).

Locales may be a better way to think about the features and traces of activity that we usually call pit-huts or pit-dwellings. Gatherings are enduring locales; they are the encounters that have survived (Gamble 1999: 71). Furthermore, Gamble distinguishes gatherings from social occasions; the latter are the contexts for a performance that is established by objects disembodied from the people involved. Often social occasions involve architecture (Gamble 1999: 71), and always provide a focus for performance and social life (Gamble 1999: 393).

With this way of thinking, and following Lewis Binford's work on the Mask Site (Binford 1983 [1978]: 291), Gamble suggests that we should not limit

our understanding of a Palaeolithic hunting watch-camp to a functional identification of hunting and resource procurement activities. Rather we should
think about the interactions of the people at the camp: for example, activities
directed in the main to reducing boredom (Gamble 1999: 74). Gamble's use
of locale recalibrates the way we see the prehistoric past and moves us a considerable way past the uncomplicated direct reading of artifacts that produces
anecdotal claims for function: the pit is a house, a working area, a burial, a
ritual space. It also pushes us beyond the focus on deposition (e.g., the contents of the pit reveal its sociopolitical function and meaning). Might we be
better served to think of pits and pit-houses in these terms, particularly as
locales, and not in functional vocabularies?

Gamble's survey of Palaeolithic Europe briefly touches on examples of sites
with pits-houses in his discussion of the later Upper Palaeolithic (post–30,000
years ago) and the pit-structures at Dolní Věstonice and Pavlov in southern
Moravia in the Czech Republic (Gamble 1999: 387–401). The original excavators described these as semi-subterranean huts (Klíma 1954, 1963, 1983).
In his treatment, Gamble redefines the traditionally termed pit-houses in
terms of actions of attachment that work to constitute a locale as a place.
He identifies the features at sites like Dolní Věstonice and Pavlov as the rituals
of "attaching-to" social gatherings (Gamble 1999: 399). The huts were "part of
the attaching ritual to the locale. They provided it with that sense of place as
the gestures which were used both to create and to recreate its history and
continuing significance for the people" (Gamble 1999: 401). The actions
of making the huts "invest locales with physical structures and associated
temporal rhythms for cultural performance and future action" (Gamble 1999:
387). Specifically, "the repeated act of digging at Dolní Věstonice-Pavlov is
further evidence for the character of the rituals of attaching and detaching
associated with place. Ochre had been dug from the ground. Digging was also
the primary rhythm, the sequence of gestures in a *chaîne opératoire*…which
created the forms of the hut platforms" (Gamble 1999: 414). Of note, Gamble
mentions (though, again, only in passing) that the ground would have been
a boundary between what was below and the surface of the ground "where
action occurred" (Gamble 1999: 414).

An initial benefit of Gamble's approach (e.g., especially in his deployment
of the term locale), is that we can dispense with the loaded (heteronormative,
industrialized) qualifying terms "house," "dwelling," "hut," and even of "settlement" or "camp." These terms have over-homogenized and reified the prehistoric actions and gestures of early Neolithic sites such as Galovo, Măgura, and
before Gamble's reassessment, of Dolní Věstonice and Pavlov. At a broader
scale, this standard terminology has dogged pit-structures in the literature

and in the field; hence the frequent use of italics or "scare quotes" in publications, both in the syntheses of Tringham and Whittle and the site-specific publications of Greenfield and Jongsma. Furthermore, thinking about the pit-houses at Măgura from Gamble's attaching-to and locale perspectives encourages us to consider what has not previously been seen as important or central to those features: the intimate or publicly shared acts and gestures of digging or of filling and not of the objects themselves and of whatever potential functional (or depositionally structural) information we might read from those objects. For Gamble the attaching-to ritual of digging was a fundamental action of defining places (as at Dolní Věstonice-Pavlov) as locales (Gamble 1999: 415).

It may be best for us to think of the features at Măgura as social occasions, the pits themselves as "artifacts that represent gestures which continue to live even though they are no longer animated by use or direct association with an individual" (Gamble 1999: 415). Perhaps it would help if we focused our efforts on seeing the actions of making the pit (i.e., in its digging), and if we thought with what Gamble calls an action of attachment: digging a hole into the ground as an act of attaching-to. It may not matter what happens in that hole: deposition of objects, use for shelter, filling upon abandonment may all be irrelevant, or at best, secondary and epiphenomenal. Finally, Gamble's approach allows us to see digging, depositing, and filling (indeed even our twentieth-century excavation of objects of archaeological interest) each as potentially equal actions of encounter and attention-focusing machines.

The Questions and Structure of This Book: Art, Archaeology, and Art/Archaeology

From the discussion so far, it is clear that so much work on pits and pit-houses has focused on deposition and the filling of holes cut into the ground, particularly through the debates around structured deposition, but more generally through the widespread (almost universal) equation of pit contents with pit function. Little work has focused on what may be an equally (indeed, perhaps even more) important action, gesture, and movement: digging into the surface of the ground. This book takes as central the focus on digging and breaking the surface of the ground, though in doing so, it points its lens in unusual directions, and ventures beyond the frames of traditional archaeological practice and thinking.

One aim of this book is to probe new understandings of a specific archaeological feature and concept: the pit-house. A second aim is to investigate a different type of exploration about these themes, in this case as redefined above: digging and breaking the surface of the ground. The approach pursued in the pages that follow wanders far from the edges of the marked trail we normally follow in archaeological method, theory, and interpretation. In this introductory chapter, I have stayed on that trail, with my eyes down or straight ahead only, blinkers tightly tied to prevent wayward glimpses: hence the review of sites that are contemporary with Măgura, the review of interpretive or synthetic accounts of pit-houses and pits in the relevant archaeological literature, and the attention to the structured deposition debate.

As the reader will soon see, my efforts to see (in the full sense of that action) Neolithic pit-houses have little to do with the Neolithic or with pit-houses, or even, necessarily, with archaeology as traditionally understood. Another book could have (and perhaps should have) assembled a comprehensive collection of examples of pit-houses from southern Romania, from the wider region of southeastern Europe in the Neolithic, from other regions from the same period, and then from other regions and other periods ranging from prehistory, through antiquity, and on into the historic and contemporary archaeological and ethnographic present. Such an account might even find great value in looking at nonhuman primate nesting behavior in such an approach. I would applaud such an effort, and I would look forward to reading the results and conclusions reached. I have taken a different path, and the writing of this book is part of that journey.

Art/Archaeology

In the chapters that follow, I attempt to work in a different space, outside of archaeology. In the examples, studies, arguments, and agitants that I have included, the reader will find attention to contemporary and modern art, to philosophy, to the psychology of human visual perception, to linguistic anthropology, and to a social anthropology of grounded-ness. While I have found relevance in many disparate areas of thought and action, I have found particular inspiration in the work of art practitioners (e.g., Gordon Matta-Clark, Lucio Fontana, and Ron Athey). Having noted that, be aware that my approach is not one of art history or even of the ways that archaeologists have co-opted the interpretation of art (prehistoric, ancient, or modern) or of artistic art practice. Thus, just as this book is not primarily archaeological, it is also not primarily about artists, art movements, or the art historical. Just as it is outside of archaeology, the discussions in the chapters that follow also are outside of art history and art practice.

At its core, this book is an attempt to work in the space of art/archaeology (see Bailey 2014, 2017a, 2017b). As such the primary goal is not to provide answers, but to provoke new questions and explore the shadows of their consequences. In this sense this book lurches over and beyond the edges of open-ended creation. While a major thrust of art/archaeology is political, the work laid out in the pages that follow asks the reader (and the excavator, museum visitor, gallery viewer, art collector, art student, and archaeology student alike) to work through a series of otherwise unconnected works, analyses, observations, and provocations. There is no simple answer at the end of the book, or even on the last page of each chapter. The project is about questions. As such it turns away from the core of most academic work and the academicians' belief that we can make authoritative conclusions.

Art/archaeology follows three processes: disarticulation, repurposing, and disruption. In many ways it is an applied archaeology that takes objects from the past, as well as the products of archaeological work (e.g., field reports, section drawings, finds' photographs, laboratory results) and breaks them from their (pre)historic contexts. This disarticulation severs the ties between the artifact and its chronologic, cultural, or technologic contexts. It finds inspiration in discussions of the archaeology of the contemporary past in this sense: ordering of time and chronology fade. Once separated from its past, the artifact or monument becomes available for the archaeologist, or the artist, or the art/archaeologist to use as if it were a raw material to be deployed in the creation of a new work, perhaps archaeological, but more forcefully in a new context, a new place, and a new set of debates that rest in the world in which we live and work. This re-purposing liberates the materials of the past; they are now like the acrylic inside the tube that the artist squeezes onto his palette or the block of granite that she takes from the quarry and shapes with rough chisel. At the core of an art/archaeology is the creative act: to make something new from the raw materials mined by the archaeologist and the historian.

As an attempt at an art/archaeology, this book follows closely the principles of disruption and repurposing: pit-houses are pulled from their context and used to make a broader argument about the actions and consequences of cutting surfaces. So also do I exploit (as raw materials) the works of the three modern and contemporary artists selected. The final process (disruption) is less easily manifest. While some art/archaeology projects make work that explicitly targets a clear social or political problem (social alienation, house-less-ness, racism), this book aims to disrupt the way that we think about the past (any past) and the ways that we should engage with that past. Should archaeology take as its primary goal the representation of human actions in the past? This book argues that the answer is no, and, even here, we would have to assume that we can agree on what "representation" might mean in a critical archaeology. Thus the book itself is a creative act, built with a group of disarticulated objects, sites, works, and debates, which I repurpose to argue against closed archaeological interpretation. In the book's organization and (at times) sharp juxtapositioning of one raw material with another, in the unexplained injection of the three inter-texts that follow chapters 3, 6, and the appendix, as well as in the disruptions of both the chapter title pages and the chapter headers, I attempt to work though the three processes of an art/archaeology and to make a work that steps over the trench-wall of the archaeological excavation and the restraining rope of the art gallery.

Why These Agitants?

Each chapter that follows consists of a stimulating agitant (closely described and interrogated) that I believe helps us to think in new ways not only about what people were doing at Măgura 8000 years ago but also that makes us think anew about other places, peoples, and actions: most particularly about our own perceptions of big themes, such as landscape, other worlds, perspective, our engaged living in this world. None of the agitants that make up this book are connected to Măgura, or even to the Neolithic of southeastern Europe. I propose no thread of analogy. Though I have included archaeological examples (e.g., the chapters on Etton and Wilsford), I do not pretend that there is any direct link between those sites and the Neolithic Romanian work that prompted this project. Most clearly unconnected with the past of Măgura are the book's other components (e.g., discussions of linguistic anthropology, philosophy, and visual perception). Most of those discussions are rooted in our modern world and, from a traditional perspective, have nothing to do with either art or archaeology.

The strategy followed here is of juxtapositioning: to place together otherwise unrelated and unconnected elements in ways that provoke unexpected thoughts and engagement. The results are unplanned, unexpected, and unevaluated; they rest with the reader. Following a similar strategy, I approached the traditional presentation of prehistoric anthropomorphic figurines in museums in *Unearthed* (Bailey et al. 2010): I juxtaposed prehistoric figurines from southeastern Europe and prehistoric dogū from Jōmon Japan both with each other and with unconnected historic, modern, and contemporary images and objects. The project succeeded in book form, but failed in the project's installations in the galleries of the Sainsbury Centre for Visual Arts. In the book, images of dogū and figurines were present, as were short texts hinting at interpretations of major thinkers on the topic, and radically inappropriate and unexpected texts, images, and artwork. In the exhibition, the authorities prohibited the mixing of the non-archaeological with the prehistory. The

SCVA demoted Barbie dolls and her friends to inferior, exterior displays, cautiously prevented from cheapening the figurines and dogū. In a parallel way the editors at OUP declined to "cut" holes in the pages of chapters 4 and 7 by placing blank discs of empty, white (holed) space on top of parts of the descriptive text. The intention had been to disrupt the rather stale and standard presentations of the sites of Wilsford and Etton, and to make this book a more vital example of art/archaeology. OUP kept their publishing toes well within the lines of the archaeological and the traditional.

In *Unearthed*, powerful was the inclusion of images (and some texts) into the pages of the book that juxtaposed the unexpected and unconnected. Thus, the infrequent images of figurines and dogū were interrupted and sidelined by short texts on what might be key themes (e.g., miniaturization, portrait, *bonsai*, children's doll play, stereotyping, the penis, cropping, Disneyland, the gaze), by contemporary artists' new work made in response to the artifacts on display (my own and Kuwashima Tsunaki's photographs, Shaun Caton's pastel-on-paper drawings and free-verse poems, Nickolas Muray's images of his lover Frida Kahlo, Anthony Gormley's *Field*, Claude Heath's *Venus*), by contemporary artist's works on (un)related themes (Michael Ashkin's tabletop landscapes, Marc Quinn's *Blood Head*, Jonah Samson's *Fucking*, Miklos Gaál's tilt-shift photography, Slinkachu's miniatures, André Kertész's *Distortions*, Hans Bellmer's *Doll*); by uses of figurines and dogū in non-archaeological contexts (collector's images, manga cells); and by other unrelated and "inappropriate" materials (Barbie dolls, Bild-Lilli dolls, Paradise Yamamoto's erotic bonsai). That book offered no authority-narrative to guide the reader/viewer, no table of contents or index offered structure or approach, and no chapters of positioning context or background scholarship prepared the reader.

The decisions of which agitants to include in the present book and how to position them follow the same logic as did the choices for *Unearthed*. Core themes emerged for the Sainsbury project (miniaturization, body, nudity, representation-as-subversion); so also for this book (cutting, digging, holes, ground). There is no limit to the number or range of possible agitants that could have been chosen for this book. The decisions could have delivered other objects, sites, materials, and analyses. If someone else were to take on this project, her decisions would be different, and the conversation would head in another direction. Having made those decisions, however, it became important to investigate each agitant in detail, and not to slip over one or another in passing with a paragraph of discussion, a suggestion of possible relevance, and a string of citations for the reader to do the deeper work themselves: preferred here is a denser, richer, thicker archaeology.

The decision to work through each agitant at this level of detail follows a commitment to balance the scale of scholarly intent to the scale of the evidence and to the shapes of the interpretation and explanation required. This book is about digging holes into the ground of a landscape 8000 years ago in what is now Romania. In real time, those prehistoric actions and gestures of digging occurred at the pace of embodied action. Deliberate. Detailed. Slow. Muscle by muscle. Calorie burned by burned calorie. The agitants administered here, when you turn over the next page, are present in equal detail and pace: not of interpretive synthesis but of life-pace. If archaeologists claim to talk and write about people in the 8000-year-old past at the level of intention, consequence, belief, worldview, and meaning, then we need to ground our work at the same tight scale of intimate knowing. That scale is several dimensions of degree finer than the ones with which we started our work at Măgura: the broad generalizations about sedentism or the Neolithic Revolution or culture historical phasing.

Chapter 2

Cutting Skin

RON ATHEY'S *4 SCENES* (A.D. 1994)

The Cut

ON THE EVENING of March 5, 1994, on the stage of Patrick's Cabaret, at 506 East 24th Street in south Minneapolis, Minnesota, Ron Athey, a thirty-four-year-old HIV-positive, white man leaned over a half-naked African American, and made twelve cuts into the man's back with a scalpel.[1] The pattern of cuts was precise and planned: three sets of parallel, triple lines and a broad triangle (Figure 2.1). As the scalpel perforated the brown skin, the cuts revealed white subdermal tissue in the openings of the body's surface. Blood filled the holes made by the scalpel and then ran down the black man's back. Athey blotted the blood with paper towels. Assistants took the towels, butterfly-clipped them onto a cord that ran out into the spectators, and wound the bloody towels over the aisles of audience space. In the background a soundtrack played dark-wave industrial music.

In the performance, the black man is Divinity Fudge (the alter ego or *scene persona* of Darryl Carlton). The cuts made into his back were part of a four-minute scene called *The Human Printing Press*, one of several pieces of a larger work titled *Excepted Rites Transformation* that Athey performed at Patrick's Cabaret that night. These Minneapolis excerpts were four sections of a larger Athey production, *4 Scenes in a Harsh Life*, which he had performed earlier that year: three times at the Highways Performance Space in Santa Monica, once at the Los Angeles Theatre Center, and three times at a club event (Johnson 2013a: 74).

At the Patrick's Cabaret performance, *The Human Printing Press* began with Athey, dressed in overalls and a red baseball cap, in character as Steakhouse Motherfucker: a blue-collar worker relaxing in a strip club after his factory shift. Wearing high heels, a fluffy wig, evening gloves, and a pink bikini, Darryl Carlton (as Divinity Fudge) appeared on stage as a drag queen

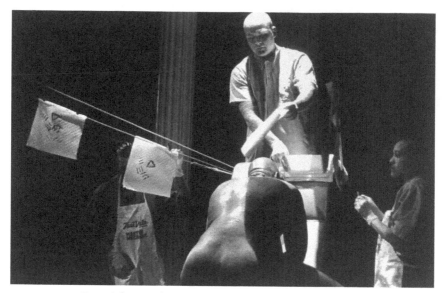

FIGURE 2.1 Ron Athey and Divinity Fudge in *Human Printing Press*, PS 122 (1994). Photo copyright Dona Ann McAdams; image used with permission.

dancing in a dress made of colored balloons. Steakhouse Motherfucker popped Fudge's dress-balloons with a cigar that he then extinguished on Fudge's buttock. Actors playing fellow factory workers grabbed and stripped Fudge who sat on a bench so that his back faced the audience; at that point, Athey, as Steakhouse Motherfucker, cut into the skin of Divinity Fudge's back.

The Human Printing Press was the second of four scenes in the Minneapolis version of *4 Scenes in a Harsh Life*. The evening at Patrick's Cabaret had begun with an introduction by John Killacky, then the curator of performing arts at Minnesota's Walker Center, the institution sponsoring the performance. In the longer version of the performance, next came a preamble to the show by Athey, dressed as a woman evangelist in religious clothing of the late nineteenth and early twentieth centuries. He spoke to the audience about his childhood fascination with religious fanaticism, particularly with the stigmata; Athey had cut his and his sister's hands with a razor blade when they were children (Young 2005: 108). In the performance, Athey stands in a pulpit next to a naked transgender person named Pigpen (representing St. Sebastian), whose skin (on her arms, legs, and the sides of her body) had been pierced with a dozen arrows (Shank 2002: 222). In the show, Athey pulls out the arrows.

FIGURE 2.2 Ron Athey pierces the cheeks of three company members in the "Dagger Wedding" scene of *4 Scenes in a Harsh Life* (1994), PS 122, New York. Photo copyright Dona Ann McAdams; image used with permission.

The next scene in Minneapolis was *The Human Printing Press* where Athey, as Steakhouse Motherfucker cuts Divinity Fudge. Following *The Human Printing Press* came a scene titled *Suicide Bed* in which Athey gouged his scalp with a spinal needle while a soundtrack of his voice recounts his ongoing battle with drug addiction and describes a dream he once had in which he was covered head to toe in black tattoos, and was levitating and which had helped Athey transcend his dependencies (Johnson 2013a: 67–68). In this scene, Athey's shoulders and chest are exposed and reveal freshly acquired tattoos, his skin healing from the tattooists' punctures. While Athey speaks, the audience sees images of thirty hypodermic needles inserted in a neat geometric pattern along an outstretched arm. On stage, Athey uses white sheets to mop up the blood that is running from the cuts he makes to his scalp with criss-crossed needles (Johnson 2013a: 68). Athey removes the needles from his scalp and blood runs down his face. Divinity Fudge rubs the blood over Athey's face and head and then washes it off.

In the next (final) scene of the Minneapolis performance, Athey appears in a conventional businessman's suit and glasses and officiates at a wedding of three individuals whom Athey calls "daggers" (Figure 2.2). The brides are naked but for loincloths; they have dozens of bells attached by needles to their chests, breasts, backs, and legs. Male drummers provide a beat, the brides dance, and the bouncing bells make their skin bleed at their points of attachment. Men and women scream. Athey talks of his childhood, of people speaking in tongues, of episodes of religious ecstasy, of turning away from his religious heritage, of his drug addiction, and of finding salvation in self-flagellation (Shank 2002: 223–224). Athey takes off his clothes, unbinds two of the brides (who had been wrapped in white fabric), and pierces their cheeks with metal spears. Preaching from a pulpit, Athey declares, "There are so many ways to say Hallelujah" (Shank 2002: 224).

The Minneapolis staging of the excerpts from *4 Scenes in a Harsh Life* lasted close to an hour. After the performance, about a quarter of the audience stayed for a twenty-minute discussion and question-and-answer session chaired by the Walker's John Killacky (Johnson 2013a). Athey and the other participants spoke of the performance and of their roles in it. Darryl Carlton (Divinity Fudge) talked of the scarification as a traditional practice among African cultures (Abbe 1994a); others answered technical questions about cutting and perforating skin (Johnson 2013a: 68).

Consequence

Three weeks after the performance, the local newspaper, *The Minnesota Star Tribune*, ran an article about the show, written by a *Star Tribune* staffer, the local art critic Mary Abbe (Abbe 1994a) (Figure 2.3). The front-page article led with the report that one of the people attending the show had made an informal complaint to Minnesota state health officials about the performance, specifically about the bloody paper towels, the fact that they had been suspended over the heads of members of the audience, and the concern that the spectators could have contracted AIDS if blood had dripped on them. Abbe reports that the Walker had taken appropriate precautions, and that the state health organization agreed.

In her article, Mary Abbe described the performance, paying special attention to *The Human Printing Press* scene, and using mildly sensationalized language (Young 2005: 106): "the performer *sliced* an abstract

FIGURE 2.3 Mary Abbe (2007). Image Tom Wallace, copyright *Star Tribune* (Minneapolis); used with permission.

design into the flesh of another man, *mopped up* his blood with towels and sent them *winging* above the audience on revolving clotheslines" (Abbe 1994a as cited in Young 2005: 106 with Young's emphases). Abbe describes Athey as "knife-wielding." The article included quotes from audience members, including the one who had complained about the show (Jim Berenson, a local sculptor and flight attendant for Northwest Airlines). Berenson said that he had had no idea what he was in for, and recalled that "at least one member of the audience fainted" (Abbe 1994a), that others left as the performance unfolded, and that people knocked over chairs to get out from under the clothes lines from which hung the blood-patterned paper towels (events that, in fact, never happened). Berenson told Abbe that the performance had disgusted him, that he would have left (but did not because he could not reach an exit), and that he had later phoned to complain to the health departments of the City of Minneapolis and Hennepin County.

Abbe's *Star Tribune* article also included responses from Walker Center officials, including Kathy Halbreich, and John Killacky, both of whom defended the performance and detailed the health and safety precautions that the Walker had taken. Abbe also included statements from Rich Danila, a supervisor of the AIDS epidemiology unit at the Health Department, who stated that having reviewed the steps taken at the performance, he did not believe that the audience had been placed in any danger. As Dennis Yelkin, one of the spectators put it, and as quoted by Abbe, "I was shaking, perspiring, nauseated.... But I have to add that I thought it was a...legitimate performance, as weird and horrible as it sounds" (Abbe 1994a: 1A).

Five days after her first article, Mary Abbe wrote a follow-up (Abbe 1994b) reporting the Walker's reaction to the public's concern as reported in her original article. In this second article, Abbe described the atmosphere of danger and fear over the performance by comparing it to a restaurant that served people toxic blowfish without warning them of the possible, potentially fatal, side effects. Abbe wrote that she and "most people in this country" (Abbe 1994b) find mutilation to be a horror, and she complains that the Walker should not have endorsed a performance that included it. Calling the Patrick's Cabaret show "grotesque," she protests that even though the Walker had warned spectators that the performance included erotic torture and techniques of bondage and discipline, it should have warned them that Athey would be "cutting someone up" (Abbe 1994b: 1E). She writes of Athey's "slicing and piercing" (Abbe 1994b: 1E), and includes comments from other audience members, one a professor of art history, the other a member of the Knights of Leather (a local gay and lesbian group); the former found no problem with the show; the latter [*sic*] phoned the newspaper to complain and to report that people had walked out of the show.

To her credit, in her second article, Abbe places Athey's work in the context of 1930s French avant-garde playwright, poet, and actor Antonin Artaud, and other European and American performers of the 1960s and of more recent date, such as Chris Burden. She also presents a wider range of responses to the performance and to the potential danger of the blood-print paper towels, reporting that though some thought that they would drip blood onto the spectators and fall apart, others saw them as "almost dry, like art prints" (Abbe 1994b: 1E). The final analogy that Abbe offers, however, is local and disparaging: she compares Athey's performance to the early 1990s' Jim Rose Circus' Mr. Lifto and the Torture King, whose act included piercing his tongue with a wire coat hanger, dangling weights from his pierced ears, and lifting heavy objects attached to his nipple rings. In a final condescending comment, Abbe suggests that the Walker directors' strong, defensive reaction to the original criticism of the Athey show was as if Clarence Thomas had defended himself against accusations of sexual harassment by calling his critics racists.

National Response

Two days later, *The Washington Post* published an article about the performance and about the reactions it had stimulated, and raised the broader issue of federal funding for the arts in the United States (Trescott 1994). The Walker Center was a recipient of funds from the National Endowment for the Arts (NEA) and had made $150 available to Athey as a contribution to the travel costs associated with the performance at Patrick's Cabaret. The *Post* quoted a member of the audience (Anna Sales, a nurse practitioner and research assistant at the University of Minnesota) who thought that the "ritual aspects were quite wonderful" (Trescott 1994: C1). In addition, the *Post* published comments both from the then-chairwoman of the NEA (Jane Alexander) who echoed local reports that appropriate precautions had been taken during the performance, and from the executive director of the National Association of Artists Organizations (Helen Brunner) who supported the funding of difficult, potentially offensive art.

The following week, the *Minnesota Star Tribune* ran a third piece about the reactions to the Athey performance (Robles 1994). In it, Jennifer Robles, one of the paper's editorial writers, defended the Walker against the criticisms highlighted by Abbe and some members of the audience. Robles focused on Athey's intention to use "scarification rituals" to examine the ways that art-practice can investigate AIDS as a form of martyrdom (Robles 1994: 21A). In addition, Robles pointed out that, paradoxically, Abbe's articles have given unplanned publicity to Athey's performance, and that the (now) national discussion of the show could be seen as a second and wider "assault" on the sensibilities of people who neither attended the Minneapolis performance nor wanted to know about Athey and his work. She writes about the special power that art possesses to trouble, worry, and fascinate people. She corrects the more sensationalized comments made by Abbe in her articles (e.g., the amount of blood that was released, the danger of contracting HIV), and she reminds readers of the outcry over the 1990 exhibition of Robert Mapplethorpe's work at the Cincinnati Contemporary Arts Center (and the eventual acquittal of its director, Dennis Barrie, of obscenity charges). Robles also warns (presciently) that the type of conflict between "official taste and artistic vision" which the Athey furor was whipping up may induce significant and damaging threats to arts funding at a national level.

Congressional Response

When word of the Athey performance and the local reaction reached the United States Congress, members there roused dormant attacks on federal funding of the arts. In response, Jane Alexander (chair of the NEA) wrote to each member of Congress noting that the original *Minnesota Star Tribune* reports of the performance had included errors, specifically about blood dripping on the audience (Gelfand 1994), errors in reporting due in part to Mary Abbe's absence from the performance. As Abbe admitted in a July article in the *Minnesota Star Tribune*, she had not attended the performance at Patrick's Cabaret; she learned of the show two weeks after it had been staged, from a third party who herself had overheard a conversation about it at a Minneapolis hair salon (Abbe 1994c).

Other press coverage included articles in the *Boston Globe* (cited in Abbe 1994c) condemning the use of federal funds for the show that it termed an abomination, and the *Los Angeles Times* (cited in Abbe 1994b) calling the debate a minor scandal. Martin Mawyer, then-president of The Christian Action Network also attacked the NEA funding; the network sent a letter to its followers declaring a taxpayers' war, asking Network members to sign and send preprinted certificates to members of Congress that read "As a voter and taxpayer in your district, I want you to know that I am sickened and outraged that my tax funds were spent on this NEA 'Blood Production.' I have repeatedly expressed my request to you and others in Congress to DEFUND and ABOLISH this rogue agency that wastes millions and offends millions" (BCFE 1994).

Later that summer, Mr. Mawyer mounted a public exhibit at the Radisson Riverfront Hotel in Augusta, Georgia, as part of a Christian Action Network meeting there, intending to influence Senator Max Cleland, a Democrat representing that state. The exhibit included images of Athey's work. In discussion with local reporters, Mawyer stated that Athey "takes a needle, stabs it in the back of an HIV-positive performer, drips the blood onto a cloth, takes the cloth and drapes it over the audience and shakes it" (Augusta Chronicle 1997). In a similar vein, right-wing televangelist Pat Robertson condemned Athey on his nationally syndicated television show *The 700 Club*, and mailed out posters depicting Athey as the antichrist (Sandahl 2001: 58; Johnson 2013a: 72).

In Congress, the charge of the outraged was led by Senators Robert Byrd (a Democrat from West Virginia and chairman of the subcommittee that oversees the NEA) and Don Nickles (a Republican representing Oklahoma and the ranking minority member of the subcommittee). At one point in the debate Representative Robert Dornan (Republican from Southern California) shouted that the NEA chairwoman had defended Athey's performance and what Senator Clifford Sterns had called his "slopping around of AIDS-infected blood" (Killacky 2014). When Senator Jesse Helms (Republican from North Carolina) made his pitch to defund the NEA, he brought to the lectern a life-sized photograph of Athey in his role as St. Sebastian covered with blood (Johnson 2013a: 78).[2]

Athey's Minneapolis cutting of Carlton's back and the use of the resulting blood to make patterns on paper towels had become one of the main arguments used by conservatives in Congress to reduce (or potentially defund) the NEA. Though an original proposal (by Representative Spencer Bachus, Republican from North Carolina) to cut NEA funding by 53 percent was defeated (as was a second and a third proposal to cut it by 42 percent or 5 percent, respectively) (Johnson 2013a: 83), Congress's final agreement was to cut funding to the NEA by $3.4 million (or 2 percent). Athey's performance (and the original mistaken and sensationalized reporting of it) was the heavy ammunition used to assault support for the arts at a national level.

On July 25, 1994, Abbe wrote a third article for the *Minnesota Star Tribune*, reporting on Congress' decision about NEA funding, with detail about the grants for the 1995 funding cycle made to Minnesota applicants, including the Walker Center (Abbe 1994c). In her report, Abbe refers to Athey's Minneapolis performance as "a body-piercing and bondage event." She reports comments made the previous week by Buddy Ferguson (public information officer at the Health Department in Minneapolis) who stated that if the department had been asked to evaluate the methods and procedures for handling blood, it would not have endorsed the original performance (Abbe 1994c).

International Response

Athey performed *4 Scenes in a Harsh Life* in London (July 1994) and New York (October 1994). In both places, sponsors took extra precautions in the wake of the fallout from the Minneapolis show. At Performance Space 122 in New York, funding was secured from private donors only, a registered nurse was present, and a more detailed warning was presented to potential audience members who were asked to sign a release and to waive their right to make any legal or civil claims (Shank 2002: 224). When the Institute of Contemporary Art in London (ICA) considered presenting *4 Scenes*, it asked its lawyers to assess the institution's legal position (Keidan 1995: 64); the result was that the ICA asked Athey to drop several key scenes from the performance.

The problem that the ICA faced related to British law and the show's acts of scarification and piercing (Keidan 1995: 64). Under UK law, anyone deliberately injuring another (regardless of whether or not consent had been given) was guilty of actual bodily harm. According to Lois Keidan, then director of Live Arts at the ICA, the Institute's worries about presenting the performance, however, were not of legal action, but of the potential damage to the institution's financial lifelines: they feared the loss of membership dues from potentially outraged Institution subscribers and the possible effect on rental fees for the use of ICA facilities to host public and private events (Keidan 1995: 65). For the London performance, therefore, the Human Printing Press was shown as a video in an otherwise live show (Myers 1995: 62). In addition, the scene in which the skin of Athey's head was pierced by a crown of thorns was replaced by a "pre-pierced body double," and the cheek-piercing of the *Wedding Ceremony* was replaced with another ritual act, in which the performers pierced their own cheeks (Keidan 1995: 65).

Relevance and Context of *4 Scenes in a Harsh Life* for Măgura

How does Athey's work and the reactions that it caused help us understand the 8000-year-old pit-huts at Măgura? What relevance is there in late twentieth-century performance and extreme body art for a more sophisticated engagement with the built environment of the early and middle Neolithic? I suggest that the answers are found in the particular mechanisms and conceits Athey used in *4 Scenes in a Harsh Life*, as well as in the effects that they had on the members of the audience seated at Patrick's Cabaret, and on the journalists, commentators, and politicians not present at the show. Also relevant is the disjuncture between Athey's (or the Walker's) original intentions in staging the performance and the reactions and the different understandings that so many took from what happened on stage.

Part of Athey's intention is found in his personal, medical, and political positions, each set tightly in the mid-1990s AIDS epidemic, in Athey's own status (and his burden) of being an HIV-positive survivor, and in particular events of his childhood. Additionally relevant is the connection that Athey established between the performers of 4 *Scenes* and the members of the audience. Of particular importance is the extreme excess of Athey's work: using otherwise unfamiliar materials and behaviors that are normally outlawed, taboo, or hidden from public view, and with which he makes emotional connection with audience members to invoke them to action. Finally (and here is the articulation with the other agitants and examples in this book), part of the impact of what Athey does and the effects that it has derives from the actions of breaking surfaces, of cutting, of perforation, and of making holes; in this case, most specifically, the cutting of Divinity Fudge's back and the various perforations of the other performers' skins.

Athey's Background and Intentions

Ron Athey (b. 1961) grew up in a devout Pentecostal family; he was often in church, attending revivals, or listening to his grandmother's predictions that he was the Second Coming of Christ (Figure 2.4). Athey's use of religious symbolism in his performance work (particularly fables of martyrdom, sacrifice, and the stigmata) has deep roots in his boyhood (Young 2005: 107). As a teenager, Athey moved away from Pentecostalism, came out as gay, and struggled with addiction to heroin in his twenties (Young 2005: 107). He tried to kill himself several times and was diagnosed as HIV-positive when he was in his twenties (Young 2005: 107). Emerging as an artist first in the underground punk club scene in Los Angeles, performing with Rozz Williams as *Premature Ejaculation*, as well as acting as a central performer in an LA revue at Club FUCK!, Athey worked to expand sadomasochism in art and performance venues (Jones 2013: 167). In much of his performance work, Athey recounted the experiences and consequences of his childhood, that his work thus maintained a "frission of autobiography and of the real (i.e., that this is his life, this really happened to him)" (Young 2005: 110).

As his work emerged and matured, Athey focused increasingly on sexual acts, bodily functions, disease, and death (Johnson 2008), giving particular priority to three interconnected concerns of the late twentieth and early twenty-first centuries: sexuality, religion, and the wound (Johnson 2013b: 14). As he told Julie Myers, "I have a history now that dates back to as early as you have an instinct to cut something. The family religion I was raised in, I was

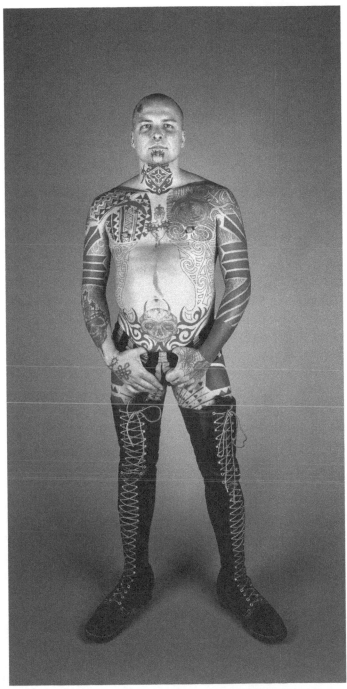

FIGURE 2.4 Catherine Opie, *Ron Athey* (1994) Chromogenic print 60 × 30 inches (152.4 × 76.2 cm). © Catherine Opie, Courtesy Regen Projects, Los Angeles; image used with permission.

taught to see people with stigmata. And I also had experiences where I'd cut my sister's finger with a razor blade just to see the blood come out. It was one of my earliest memories. I think we were both in diapers. I just wanted to see what was inside. It's such a fascination with physiology. What's going on inside of us and why" (Myers 1995: 60).

Athey's work is political, connected to the body in a brute and direct way: "in my performances, sex acts are used to make statements about politics, identity, and physical boundaries" (Athey 1997: 71, cited in Doyle 2013: 126). Individual performances emerged as Athey wrestled with philosophical queries, and as he worked through the issues in the process of planning, particularly in the performance of the work (Johnson 2008: 510). While some inspiration for the topics and symbols he employs loops back to the absurdity of his child-hood experiences, much stimulation comes from later dream images remembered and written down upon waking (or immediately after hypnosis sessions) (Johnson 2008: 512).

When he introduced the show at Patrick's Cabaret in Minneapolis, the Walker Center's John Killacky was explicit in informing the audience that the work they were about to witness was a response to the then-current public phobia about AIDS and homosexuality (Johnson 2013a: 72): thus, *Excepted Rites Transformation* and its larger source performance, *4 Scenes*, must be understood primarily in light of the AIDS epidemic of the 1980s and mid-1990s (Johnson 2013b: 26). Bruce has shown that *Excepted Rites Transformation, 4 Scenes*, and Athey's other blood-works were essential parts of the processes though which people came to terms both with the fears, hostility, and prejudices that were directed at HIV-positive people and people with AIDS, and with the broader panic, hysteria, and homophobia that dominated popular and political culture at the time (Bruce 2013: 122). For Athey, in a more personal sense, his works, most especially *4 Scenes*, are his attempts to answer the difficult questions that he asked himself at this point in his life as an HIV-positive survivor. How does he move forward in his life in the light of the death of his friends? How does he deal with his own sickness (Johnson 2013b: 26)? How does he come to terms with his own survival in the wake of the deaths of so many others?

Athey on 4 Scenes *and His Own Work*

At a 1995 panel discussion at the ICA in London, Athey spoke about his use of Darryl Carlton's blood in the Minneapolis performance, saying that in sending the blood of a gay man (literally "homosexual blood") over the heads of the audience he was playing on people's fears of the body and of disease, both of which he understood were powerful sources for homophobia

(ICA Panel 1995: 66; cited in Shank 2002: 224). Athey understood *4 Scenes* as his attempt to explain his own childhood: "the arrogance of being chosen by God [i.e., the prophecy of his grandmother that he had been chosen to evangelize], and the pain of being unloved and of active self-destruction" (Athey 2013: 106). Through the work's different scenes, Athey examines working-class sexism, drug addiction, suicide attempts, prophetic dream images, leather daddy/boy role-playing, and nontraditional weddings. In doing so, he looks for the drive that would lead someone to go to a strip club or channel the voice of God (Athey 2013: 106). His work is full with questions; the performance is his means to seek answers. In all of this, Athey's work is an extension of his life (Young 2005: 109), and the questions it asks are the queries that he has about his particular position in homophobic America and in his specific personal sexual, religious, and personal history.

As Athey suggested during the ICA panel discussion, his work investigates the impact that personal fetishism has on one's sanity, where fetishism is taken as a mantra and obsession (Figure 2.5). In *4 Scenes*, he combines tattooing, scarification, and primitive ritual with leather, white weddings, and evangelism (Athey n.d.; cited in Shank 2002: 224), while acknowledging the role of self-destruction in his and others' lives. Athey was looking for a way to express the roles that self-hatred and self-destruction have played in his life, "what it is like to feel so hopeless you try to take your own life" (Royce 1994). As Athey put it, his works are "parallel to doing penance...something inherently spiritual...that makes it a ritual. It is like a public ritual" (Myers 1995: 61).

FIGURE 2.5 Catherine Opie, *Ron Athey/Pearl Necklace* (from Trojan Whore) (2000) Polaroid 110 × 41 inches (279.4 × 104.1 cm). © Catherine Opie, Courtesy Regen Projects, Los Angeles; image used with permission.

The Body

The body is central to Athey's performances, particularly as a target for what many see as abuse and savagery. He wounds the body's flesh to disrupt our perceptions and understandings of the very object (the body) and actions (otherwise illegal or private acts) undertaken. The aim is to rupture the accepted procedures and materials that society uses to construct its subjective definition and moral judgment of individuals, particularly gay men (Johnson 2013b: 122). The body is the essential site for these disruptions, with representations of sexually expressive masculine and feminine bodies focusing attention on cross-gendered relationships (Jones 2013: 168). As such, often Athey's works focus on the body of a person who has endured and survived, just as Athey has survived when many of his friends have not: that is, survival of trauma though suffering (Young 2005: 110).

Much of Athey's work transgresses, challenges, and transcends boundaries. The physical boundaries of the body are perforated. He cuts skin. He spills blood (Johnson 2013b: 10). Athey pushes against the boundaries of his own body, of the bodies of those he performs with (Lunch 2013: 143), and of the audiences' perceptions of what are the appropriate limits to the territory of both the performers' and the audience's own bodies. In this, the works challenge the accepted nature of visions of corporeality. Athey's transformations of the body are intentionally unsettling: needles go in, blood comes out; matter, fluids that are supposed to be inside are released, exposed, and disseminated beyond the sacred limit of the skin (Young 2005: 109) through the actions of penetration, perforation, and cutting. The confusion of exterior and interior, the physical dislocation of the natural positions of substance and fluid, and the puncture of the boundary between inside and out (i.e., the perforation of the skin) cause powerful, unavoidable reactions for the viewer: nausea, discomfort, anxiety, fear (Young 2005: 109).

Athey pushes his own body to the edge and beyond. In what the audience often sees as extreme acts of pain (or torture), Athey tests the control that he has over his own body (Opie 2013: 143). The performances are equally intense for the audience and for artist. Athey has spoken of feeling suicidal after a three- or four-night run of shows, of the difficulty of bringing himself back to the reality of the standard world in the wake of intense experience. Particularly relevant is the real-time condition of each individual performance. He cannot rehearse the shows; he must work each one at full throttle and affect: "It takes a couple of days. Sometimes it takes a couple of weeks before I can watch the tapes [of the shows]" (Myers 1995: 61).

Athey's work on the body and its boundaries is cultural work in the face of the crisis of the body at his own personal level (as an HIV-positive man), of the body in general (as the constructed conception of corporeality that we all share), and of the body politic (Gund 2013: 55). The engagement with AIDS is charged and confrontational. Where AIDS destroys and betrays the bodies of the infected individual, Athey's performances are precise and controlled; his works are organized responses to the disorganized disease that destroys the body (Gund 2013: 56).

In all of this, Athey challenges the accepted sanctity of the body, especially as that assumed purity plays out through traditional religious and moral codes and practices (Johnson 2008: 509). In using the body in inappropriate ways (many would say ab-using and mis-using it), Athey disrupts and breaks open the standard functions of the body as it normally rests in cultural, social, and biological definition (Heathfield 2013: 210) (Figure 2.6). Athey requisitions the body and uses it as a shifting medium for joy and for pain as well as for his own rebirth and transformation (Heathfield 2013: 220). He crosses long-respected lines of what is acceptable, rational, and aesthetically pleasing (Johnson 2013b: 10). The work bullies artistic production and consumption across borders of pain, crisis, and physical disruption, and, in doing so challenges (and dispenses with) the sanctity that human flesh traditionally possesses in modern Western society as normally derived from religious, cultural, and legal logics. The effort aims to activate emotion in order to upend these existing belief systems (Jones 2013: 171).

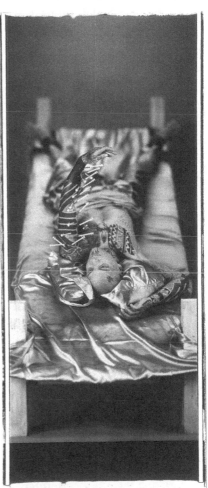

FIGURE 2.6 Catherine Opie, *Ron Athey/Suicide Bed* Polaroid 110 × 41 inches (279.4 × 104.1 cm) Polaroid 110 × 41 inches (279.4 × 104.1 cm). © Catherine Opie, Courtesy Regen Projects, Los Angeles; image used with permission.

The Audience: Connection, Generosity, and Bearing Witness

A critical part of Athey's performances is the connection established between the audience, on the one hand, and the performers, bodies, acts, fluids, and the props of the show. His work brings the audience into the moment of the excessive acts he carries out on stage. Audience members are made present at a crime scene; they are there (Young 2005: 110) whether they like it or not. While some may claim that Athey's intention is to shock, it is possible that the intention is better defined in terms of generosity: Athey wants the extreme character of his actions to work as acts of giving. The results are shared, live experiences on stage, intended to cause physical responses in the spectators to the same degree as of the performers (Johnson 2008: 511).

Alison Young has called this the "forensic autobiography" of Athey's work; in enacting injury to himself, Athey makes each member of the audience a witness to the act as it is committed (Young 2005: 110). Of the blood on the paper towels sent out over the heads of the spectators, Athey is saying, "Here is the wound, here is the evidence of the wound coming by" (Myers 1995: 61). Audience members are made to watch blood flowing, and to witness the physical response to pain without the safe distance normally provided by representation or reproduction or by the traditional separation of performance and theater spectator. There can be no question or uncertainty. It is happening. It involves actual injury. The blood is real. The skin is cut, perforated (Young 2005: 116), and opened up to reveal what is beneath, what is within, what is otherwise hidden and out of sight. As Athey says, "I cannot fake cutting" (quoted in Royce 1994). This is no stage trick, sleight of hand, or special effects.

Thus, 4 Scenes invokes audience members into a forensic relationship with the artists and with the artists' injuries (Young 2005: 107). The suffering that Athey experiences on stage is deflected onto the spectator (Young 2005: 110); Athey creates and inhabits a space in which the spectator must suffer as well (Young 2005: 110). He distributes (in that sense of generosity) the suffering out to the audience, even beyond seeing, hearing, and smelling something at a distance. He sends a physical, tangible part of the suffering into (or in 4 Scenes, above) the audience. The objective is to force the people sitting in Patrick's Cabaret to endure the same physical experiences that Athey, Darryl Carlton, and the other performers endure and suffer (Young 2005: 109). In this way, Athey sees the paper towel blots of blood from Carlton's back as a direct connection of audience-to-performance (Athey cited in Trescott 1994).

Athey's aim is to make the spectator aware that he or she is implicated in the demands of watching what Athey does to his own body and to the bodies of others, and to make those spectators accept and experience the suffering as their responsibilities for watching (Young 2005: 110). Athey's work implicates the audience into the production of the performance (Heathfield 2013: 209). The audience reaction to their enforced participation is complex and multiple. The spectator inhabits a place of sensory and emotive paradox and continuous ambivalence, "at the same time expressing dread and delight, pain and pleasure" (Heathfield 2013: 210).

Upsetting the Audience

Some of the most powerful results of Athey's performances are the distress and disruption they cause their audiences, both those present and those who learn of the work from media accounts or word of mouth. How do these works upset people? What makes them disturbing? And what are the consequences of these effects? Amelia Jones has written at length and with insight about this, focusing on Athey's work in the deeper struggles over the role of emotion in art (Jones 2013). Jones argues that Athey's work (like other artists' work from the 1960s onward) aims to erase the separation of emotion and logic that had been common to modernist art traditions (Jones 2013: 164). Reviewing bodywork by Yoko Ono (*Cut Piece*, 1964–1965), Carolee Schneeman (*Interior Scroll*, 1975), Adrian Piper (*Calling Cards*, 1986–1990), Lorraine O'Grady (*Mlle Bourgeoise Noire*, 1980–1983), and Karen Finley (*Memento Mori*, 1992), Jones shows how these artists used their bodies (and the audiences' perceptions of bodies) in their art in order to connect powerfully with their audiences' emotions (Jones 2013: 165). Crucially, the connection was established through emotional attachment and a provocation to repulsion (Jones 2013: 164).

Jones argues that Athey's work follows this longer, post-1960s tradition. Works like *4 Scenes* have a specific and peculiar power to mobilize forbidden feelings in audience members and to activate pathos among them (Jones 2013: 177). As we watch Athey's work, we must confront our own feelings of extreme discomfort and acute physical pain. Other current body-incisive performance work functions in similar ways. In a vibrant description of the French artist ORLAN (b. 1947), Allucquére Rosanne (Sandy) Stone speaks of the "entranced revulsion" of the audience that ORLAN achieves with her body cuts: "to hold them in thrall and still have them puking on their shoes" (Stone 1996: 43) (Figure 2.7). Among her many works, ORLAN is perhaps best known for *Reincarnation of Saint-Orlan* (beginning in 1990), in which plastic surgeons reconfigure ORLAN's face while the artist remains conscious, reads poetry, and records the surgery/performance for live broadcast and reproduction. In both ORLAN's and Athey's work, the entranced revulsion comes from the extreme discomfort and pain experienced on stage and then given to the audience to share.

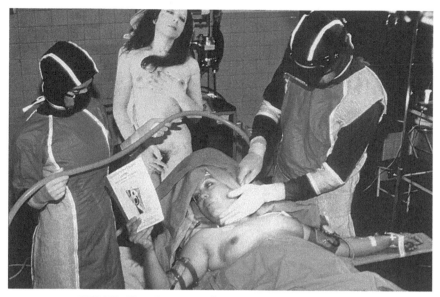

FIGURE 2.7 ORLAN, *First Surgery Performance* (1990). Image copyright ORLAN; image used with permission.

The Role of Fear

What is it about Athey's work that upsets the audience? One answer is fear. Cutting into the skin of the performer, pushing metal spikes through his cheeks, inserting hypodermic needles into her scalp, using fishing wire to sew bells into the skins of the dancers' torsos are all acts that scare the audience. One source of this fear is a vicarious recognition of the pain being inflicted onto another person in a shared space (i.e., the theater, Patrick's Cabaret), a space that has been united, in the case of *4 Scenes*, through the distribution of blood-blotted paper towels. When we watch and hear the pain of another person on stage, we remember our own fragility as physical beings in the world (Jones 2013: 161). Much of Athey's performance confronts and exploits the character of pain (Jones 2013: 174). His body suffers through his own and his fellow performers' actions. These acts frighten the audiences (both those present and absent), because causing pain breaks the existing, shared rules of behavior that are normally enshrined in legal, ethical, and moral code. Society has allocated pain-causing behavior to a category of unacceptable, unsafe, or illegal action. Public nudity. Sexual acts. Bloodletting. Combine the acts' unsafe and illegal statuses with a dose of a lifestyle and sexual preference that make many Americans uncomfortable (and about which a significant number remain militantly opposed to) and the resulting cocktail is strongly infused with fear, outrage, and volatile reaction.

Athey's work is about feelings (Jones 2013: 152): how his body feels; how the audience feels about what they are watching happen to other people's bodies; and how the audience feels about their own bodies. A result of Athey's injection of fear and pain into his work is that the audience cannot avoid taking a share in these feelings. Athey has taken away any route to avoidance. His work insists upon reaction, particularly on bodily reaction, and especially on emotional reaction: discomfort, fear, sadness, but also love, longing, and joy (Jones 2013: 167). The audience cannot avoid taking a role in the performance and in the application of pain to the performers' bodies: one can empathize, one can disprove; one can be angry and disgusted; one can revel in it and enjoy (Jones 2013: 174); but, one cannot avoid giving meaning to what is happening, to the sounds, images, and smells (Jones 2013: 156).

From Spectator to Witness

The intense emotional response that the audience has with the work, with the performers, and with those watching, listening, smelling, and cringing, shifts the audience's status from that of spectator to one of witness (Jones 2013: 158; Doyle 2013). Athey puts the audience into the work: the blood-damp paper towels over their heads, the otherwise intimate, hidden fluids, sounds, and acts transform what started as a public space into a shared private one (or at least it makes us rethink the boundaries of our private and public spaces). The audience is in the work through their relational experiences of the emotions activated, released, and stimulated by what Athey and his team are doing. As witnesses, members of the audience occupy a more politicized relationship to the performers, to their fellow witnesses, and to the world beyond the limits of the performance (Jones 2013: 177).

In her comparison of Athey's work with other performance artists who intentionally injure themselves, Alison Young sees the spectation of injury-being-made as a forensic event (Young 2005: 17). In Athey's pain-infliction work, Young sees the same conceits at work as in the work of body artists like Chris Burden (b. 1946) (Figure 2.8): in *Shoot* (1971), Burden had an assistant fire a bullet into his left arm; in *Transfixed* (1974), Burden was nailed to the back of a Volkswagen Beetle; in *Through the Night Softly* (1973), he crawled, mostly naked, through fifty feet of broken glass; in *Doorway to Heaven* (1973), he pushed two live electric wires into his chest until they crossed, exploded, and burned him; and in *Prelude to 220 or 110* (1971), Burden lay bolted with copper bands to a concrete floor near buckets of water that had live electricity cables in them (any viewer could have spilled the water and electrocuted him).

As the viewer of the injury watches the bullet being fired into Burden's arm, the buckets of electrified water sitting by him strapped to the floor, or Athey cutting Carlton's back, the viewer who had been spectator becomes witness: as the spectator becomes witness, the injury becomes testimony (Young 2005: 17). In this sense, the injury makes those watching the cut made

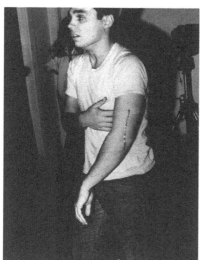

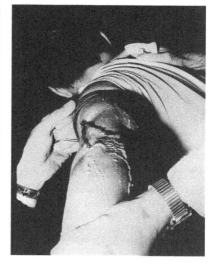

FIGURE 2.8 Chris Burden, *Shoot* (November 19, 1971), "At 7.45 p.m. I was shot in the left arm by a friend. The bullet was a copper jacket 22 long rifle. My friend was standing about fifteen feet from me": upper left, No. 8; upper right, No. 9; lower left, No. 2; lower right, No. 4. Images © Chris Burden. Images courtesy of The Chris Burden Estate and Gagosian.

or the pain caused acquire the status of witnesses as if they stood before a jury or judge (Young 2005: 110). In these ways, viewers are made complicit in a crime scene; their own pain and fear sit within the ethical implications of the cut, of the penetration, and of the bloodletting (Young 2005: 110). To inflict the injury in the performance is to invoke the member of the audience (Young 2005: 107). Athey's goal is to make the person who is watching aware of the implications of watching and of a responsibility for watching; Young argues that the viewer (now made witness) experiences this responsibility in terms of suffering (Young 2005: 110).

The manner in which the fear and pain are shared between performer and audience is important: via visual, aural, physical excess. In his discussion of Athey's work, Dominic Johnson focuses on the ways that the pursuit of excess leads to a more explosive performance that disturbs the stable traditions of existing cultural codes and cultural practice (Johnson 2010: 3). Finding reference in the work and writings of French intellectual Georges Bataille (1897–1962) (e.g. Bataille 1930), Johnson illuminates the roles that mutilation, body-cutting, and body destruction can have in fragmenting an individual's homogeneity, particularly when a part of a person is projected outside oneself (Johnson 2010: 6).

One of the effects of Athey's excessive performances is the delayed response that the audience may feel. Just as it takes Athey time after successive performances to come back to reality (as he says, even weeks before he can watch the tapes), so also does bearing witness to the performances cause a similar dynamic lag in the viewer's responses: "Something that I've come to expect

FIGURE 2.9 Catherine Opie, Ron Athey/ Human Printing Press w/Darryl Carlton (from *4 Scenes*) (2000) Polaroid, 110 × 41 inches (279.4 × 104.1 cm). © Catherine Opie, Courtesy Regen Projects, Los Angeles.

is that most people don't know how they feel for twenty-four hours.... And then, later, often when they get back home, they can't stop thinking about it all night. They seem to formulate their opinions over the next twenty-four, forty-eight hours. I think that's good, it's not just like 'yeah' clap at the end and do a couple of bows" (Myers 1995: 60).

Athey's work is political, but not only in the most obvious sense as played out in the mass media and Congressional moral wrangling that followed the Minneapolis show. Jones suggests that the work ignites a flame of political aware-ness that emerges out of the "tender and uncomfortable sadness, fear, love, long-ing and joy" to which Athey's work opens the viewer (now made witness) (Jones 2013: 158). Furthermore, as an assumedly unintentional result, 4 Scenes provided politicians and others with a powerful object with which to spur fear and homophobia among the general public (Jones 2013: 168) (Figure 2.9).

Relevance to Măgura

And what about the pit-houses of Măgura? At the simplest level, the value of Ron Athey's work for the topic of this book could be twofold. The first is that digging a hole (perforating the surface of the ground) in the Neolithic of Măgura is as if it were a performance in its creation, life, and function, and in the ways that people interpret and engage that hole and the acts of its re-dig-ging today, as well as those original actions 8000 years ago. The second con-nection might be between the surface of the ground and the skin of the body: that people digging, using, watching, bearing witness to that hole 8000 years ago held the surface of the ground in their minds, spirits, and lives in much the same way as the people of most modern, Western, industrialized commu-nities hold the human body and its skin today.

The contention made here is that by thinking of our excavated pit-houses in southern Romania through the work of Ron Athey (and particularly of his 4 Scenes in a Harsh Life and its excerpted 1994 performance in Minneapolis) we find a rich, unexpected, and previously hidden connection with the life-ways of that place at that time. The connection of body surface to ground surface forms part of the discussion in chapter 9, and was the subject of a recent alternative format publication (Bailey 2013). In the following paragraphs, I explore the cor-respondences of hole digging to performance, particularly as activated by Athey's 4 Scenes.

Măgura as Performance

To work through the correspondence of performance requires that we think about the Măgura pits though the same set of agents, materials, actions, intentions, and consequences (planned and not) that we thought with when we wrestled with, enjoyed, cringed (or perhaps did all three things) over Athey's scenes, particularly *The Human Printing Press*. In particular, value comes from thinking about the Măgura pits in the following connections: the performer as cutter and digger; the audience(s) as spectator and witness implicated to action and the real-time emotional authenticity of excessive action; the visible and opaque intentions and consequences of the actions carried out; the remnant effects of ephemera and missing data; and, finally, the unavoidability of unresolved questions.

Performer/Cutter/Digger

If Athey/Motherfucker is the cutter of Carlton/Fudge's back, then who was the digger of the Măgura pits? Who perforated the ground? Did he or she have special status, special skills, and experiences? Was access to the action of cutting the earth restricted? If so, why, to whom, and by whom? At first these questions appear simple. Some readers will already have the answers: the Neolithic people, the pre-Indo-Europeans, the inhabitants of Măgura. If we step beyond the straightforward, anecdotal (and thus limited) truths of these answers, we may discover an alternative, fertile field to work within. Lois Keidan writes that Ron Athey and artists like him are mystical beings of the modern world, that we need them to help us comprehend and negotiate the complicities of our times and the difficult issues within them, that they prevent us from hiding from "darker truths" (Keidan 1995: 65).

I suggest that it is highly likely that the pit-diggers at Măgura did the same thing. The man, or woman, or group may well have worked in ways that helped people understand the complexities and darknesses of life 8000 years ago. We are heuristically flexible and open-minded enough to widely acknowledge, at the same level of chronological remove that David Lewis-Williams has argued (Lewis-Williams 2002), that 35000 years ago, the Upper Palaeolithic cave art of southwestern France and northeastern Spain worked within a system of beliefs and actions by which special community members moved through the membrane of cave walls into and out of this mortal and that spiritual world. I contend that we would gain much by accepting that people deep in European prehistory (as at Măgura) understood the surface of the ground as another boundary or threshold.

If that were the case, then the perforation of that boundary would have been significant at a fundamental, perhaps even subconscious level. We are faced with a new question: "what did the ground mean to people in the Neolithic?" It is significant that this is a period of time and a group of people who were compounding great interest in cutting the ground and placing materials below ground surface: inhumation of articulated, breathless, immobile bodies; deposition of special objects (skulls, pots, waste materials); and the insertion of the bases of wooden posts and building foundations into holes cut through the surface of the ground.

I suggest that it is equally significant that through a range of other actions these same communities understood the ground, what is under it, and what comes from it as central to much of their essence of living: the extraction of materials to be worked into objects of significance (flint, clay, copper, gold); the collection of materials essential to life (water from springs); the managed intrusion into and magical transformation through the ground's energies (root foods, cereal, and wild plants). All of these (inter)actions, and their products, promote Ground and what is within and below it to a status of supernatural, perhaps even mystical and dangerous, but certainly powerful, essence.

New questions emerge. We want to know if just anyone could cut the ground, at any time, in any manner, in front of just any watchers, for just any reason without a series of (now) potentially unrecoverable consequences, and without first obtaining specific legal, cultural, spiritual, or ethical permissions. I contend that decisions about who could cut open the ground were significant, and that some individuals (or groups) would have had either preferential access or, even, sole rights to do so. In a not-dissimilar way, we recognize that not just anyone has the right agreed to by their community (or the skills necessary) to cut open the skin of the human body, in any auditorium/theater/hospital, with any tool, in front of any audience, for any reason, without a similarly weighty set of preparations, permissions, and consequences.

Audience/Spectator/Witness/Excess/Fear

I want to know more about the audience watching the diggers/performers cutting into the surface of the ground at Măgura. It is highly likely that in that audience people would have reacted, complained, reported to others, cringed, scandalized those acts of cutting and perforating the surface of the ground. As archaeologists, we seldom allow ourselves to imagine people who watched activities that we usually dismiss as mundane (such as digging a pit) in the Neolithic (Figure 2.10). Usually we offer a generic and limp reconstruction that does not extend beyond formal description. Athey's work forces us to see the members of the audience, and to probe their statuses and reactions.

Even here, thinking about Măgura with Athey's work in mind takes us farther than just gluing two-dimensional cutouts of people onto the landscape of southern Romania. It is more than merely inserting spectators. Vitally, it is a turn from spectator to witness, and from observation to testimony. Those bearing witness were implicated into the action and had a responsibility in the same way as the individual audience members at Patrick's Cabaret bore witness and testimony to the cutting of Darryl Carlton's back. The dirt and

FIGURE 2.10 Excavations at Măgura-Buduiasca, view to the west of Sondages 21 (near) and 20. Photo copyright D. W. Bailey.

stones, once extracted, had roles to play in concurrent and subsequent activities. It may have been the case that it had similar meanings and powers as did the blood blotted on the paper towels hoisted out over the audience. It is highly likely that the dirt and stones and roots implicated the Măgura audience to witness bearing testimony. Those witnesses would have had statuses of differences within that small group watching, but also separate from their larger communities. If there was public outrage and debate, would they have been complicit in it? I sense that their presence and witnessing would have created a shared space (intimate and private or public and exposed) within which were connected the diggers and those who would testify to the perforation of the ground. It is probably that here is where we will find the significance of the blocks of white calcium carbonate in so many of the lower strata of the Măgura pits: down to and into which they dug, and of which they pulled out and handed to those watching or set at their feet.

It is also possible that fear faced this 6000 cal. B.C. audience. It is likely that the cutting of the ground would have upset them, or at least some of them. How could that be? The answer may most easily be found in thinking about the potential powers and essences that pieces of the undersurface would have brought with them when they crossed the boundary of the ground and spilled out, over the feet of those watching and digging, onto their hands. There would have been manifest distress in the act of rupturing a surface that, according to accepted code, moral, and practice, was normally kept complete and whole. Possibly it was a fear about what they felt and understood: specifically with what was lurking under the surface. The digging into the ground may well have had specific and peculiar power to mobilize forbidden feelings. We are forced to consider what were these feelings and understandings.

It is also likely that the cut interfered. The opening up of what was otherwise kept closed could well have threatened powerful and vital essences of life at Măgura in the same way that Athey's perforation of the skin on Carlton's back released (in frightening ways) the liquid essence of his living, homosexual body. It is possible that the fear was activated in the Măgura witnesses because the diggers interfered with and threatened the same sort of living entity or raw materials that were in and of the ground and upon which people relied for spiritual and nutritional survival. The rupture of the surface may have threatened the source of water. The opening of the ground may have threatened the home of root foods, or the worlds of rodents, reptiles, and insects, all of which must have had particular (and to us probably never to be known) significances and values to those bearing witness. It would not be surprising to find that it was frightening to witness and be complicit in a violation of the undersurface, subcutaneous strata where also existed the granite that formed grinding stones, where existed flint and chert that held cutting edges, where existed copper and gold that transformed identities, from where came the unexplainable and miraculous energies that poked up though the ground contained in plant stems, nuts, berries, seeds, and fruits. In these ways pain and fear could have accompanied that 6000 cal. B.C. breaking of the surface.

It is also possible that the threat was deeper still. The danger that they risked may have been connected directly to the very senses of being and sanity of the audience bearing witness as if to a crime that threatened the stability of life. It could have been a fear that lurked and rested and was hidden within a normally intangible, invisible zone. Perhaps the audience (and the diggers) only felt the fears and dangers of that dark zone in brief passing, perhaps as nothing more than a subtle displeasure and unbalancing. It is highly likely that those reactions (of both digger and witness) were not unlike the ones experienced by Athey and his audiences: the cutting of the ground may have touched deeply hidden and long repressed exposures to earlier pains and fears. We are faced with new questions about what might have been the Măgura correspondences to Athey's sexuality, childhood religious encounters, homosexuality, and guilt.

What was excessive about the Măgura holes and particularly of the cuts and cutting that formed them? Cutting the ground (and Carlton's skin) was a departure from custom and reason. It invoked emotion in ways that were not normally allowed, and it overstepped the authorities and permissions in ways that were violent and extravagant. The undersurface was not the place of daily life in Măgura; to open and enter it was excessive and dangerous conduct that violated decency and the moralities of behavior. To do so was to create an instance of outrage beyond what was necessary in life: to cut the Măgura ground and open it as Athey had cut and opened the skin of Carlton's back. Today we see the cutting of the earth, even as we excavate the site and again cut the ground, without reaction to the excessive, to the outrageous and violent because, in our modern worldviews (not only of archaeologists but also of strip-miner, deep-plower, optical cable-layer), we have become sanitized to the pain and emotion that comes from cutting the ground. At the other end of the analogy, we sit in the audience at Patrick's Cabaret; we react to the excess because we have not been sanitized of the emotion or to the cutting of the human flesh and the release of what is within (blood).[3] It follows that the cutting of the 6000 cal. b.c. ground challenged the accepted sanctity of the earth's surface. The breaking of that surface would have fragmented the homogeneity of that ground. Digging those holes disrupted and broke open the standard functions of the ground as it normally rested (at that time) in its cultural, social, and biological definitions.

For Athey, there is no way for him to fake what he does in his performances; he cannot counterfeit the cutting of the skin. In fact, a portion of the power and impact of his cuttings comes from this authenticity of actions, the spilling of the blood, and the sounds of the acts and the actors. He breaks the surface of the skin in real time and with real affect. He must fully commit himself, his knife, and Darryl Carlton to the cut of the skin: he pushes the sharp edge of the scalpel blade through the surface layer of Carlton's black skin, down into the white tissue, releasing red blood. At Măgura, the diggers would have had to fully commit in the same way; there was no way to fake it. They had to swing or push the antler mattock or scapula shovel or stone axe-adze through the vegetation and into the surface of the ground: first hard, then softer and moister underneath. Eventually they would have reached a different stratum (harder, crumbling, white, calcareous) chunks of which they pulled up out of the under surface, and placed on the ground above at the edge of the hole.

The skin is opened, the blood runs; the ground surface is perforated, the crumbling topsoils and carbonates are opened to the air. For both Athey and Măgura, to cut and to dig were actions of authenticity, the proof of which rested both in the connection of the witnesses to the acts and in the release of the materials (blood and calcareous white) out of their standard positions (below the skin and the ground). The strength of the reactions and testimony comes from these transgressive acts and these displacements.

Intentions/Consequences/Visibility/Ephemera

If Athey's audiences are implicated to participate and bear witness and in many ways are invoked to action, what is the corresponding implication and invocation for the Măgura audience and witness? The implication may not have been immediate, and may not have been consciously felt, but may have simmered in thoughts, feelings, and prejudices that unintentionally directed other Măgura actions and speech. The invocation may have been manifest (or hidden) in what happened above ground; after 6000 cal. B.C. in this (and other, similar periods and regions) an above-ground built environment emerged in the classic architecture of the southeast European Neolithic: wattle-and-daub, post-framed, roofed, walled buildings that were, almost without exception, tangibly linked, rooted physically into the undersurface via post-holes and foundation trenches that were cut into the surface of the ground.

The invocation may have been manifest (or hidden) in what happened below surface: in the increasing role played by the act of putting seeds into the ground, and then of bearing witness to vegetal extraction of mystical, unexplainable powers that produced wheats, barleys, and pulses, the seeds that were eaten (the act of eating itself transgressing yet more boundaries), and that were to become such a vital element in negotiations of subsistence, property, territory, and power in the millennia that followed. Equally, this is evident in actions of below-surface deposition, clear in new relationships coming into being between people, objects, and what is below: the placement of people or objects and of valuable (and valueless materials and material culture) into the below surface, such as the rise of inhumation of the deceased in pits in houses and villages and then in cemeteries.

Finally, the conversation of Măgura with Athey's performances can be worked through the reactions that the audiences have both to Athey's cutting and to Măgura's digging. Not only would audience/witness reactions have been strong, emotional, unexpected, or unpredictable, but, also, some of the most powerful reactions may have been experienced by absent audiences (i.e., those who saw neither the scalpel pierce the black skin nor the antler perforate the ground). If Athey's performance caused effect, than it was greatest in the pages of *The Washington Post*, the proceedings of the United States Congress, the legal offices of the ICA in London, and even in a hair salon in downtown Minneapolis. The effect of cutting the Măgura ground might have been greatest not among those who were present, but in those who were not there, but to whom stories and reports of the cutting and digging were represented, both at that near time, in that local place, but also in other places at those and at other times in that and other locations. The reactions may have been strongest and the consequences heaviest well away from the pits of Măgura.

Unavoidable Unresolved Questions

Athey makes performance works. What do they mean? Eight thousand years ago, people dug holes in the ground at Măgura. Why? Athey's works function in specific contexts and debates. He states his original intentions, what it meant to him, what he wanted to achieve: to engage and provoke discussion about sexuality, religion, wounds, homophobia, the AIDS crisis. The Walker Center (and indirectly the NEA) invited and sponsored that work; their remit was to promote, support, and exhibit artistic work for the local community. Patrick's Cabaret functioned as a venue, took in gate receipts, provided seats and stage. The work was one part of the Fifth Annual Minneapolis LGBT Film Festival (Johnson 2013a: 66). The woman sitting at the Minneapolis hairdresser, talking to her stylist about a weirdo art show that had taken place several weeks earlier, and which she did not attend, and who a friend of the *Times Tribune* contributor, Mary Abbe, overheard, that woman wanted a shampoo-and-set. Mary Abbe wanted to write a column for any number of reasons (pay, prestige, reputation, or deeper, unrealized and perhaps repressed feelings about the Walker Center where she had once been the public information director). The woman complaining to her stylist may have wanted to inform, educate, complain, and project a personal moral position. All of these reactions and readings and consequences of the performance of *4 Scenes* in Minneapolis are equally alive and legitimate. Some may come into and out of currency with different contexts, times, and places, but all are alive.

The holes that they dug at Măgura may well have served as shelters, as places to knap flint or bury garbage, as places to defecate and urinate. Each digger probably came to the physical actions of digging the hole from different personal positions, desires, needs, displeasures, and discomforts. Each probably had different understandings about the holes they dug and used. Performance and pit-house emerged from undoubtedly clear intentions and from perceptions of function and of need at several levels, though there may have been a primary one for each: art event; house pit. Beyond these primary anecdotal understandings of function rest more complicated, ephemeral, and less easily identifiable consequences and contingent results. It is in these latter, deeper, murkier, mainly intangible (and unrecoverable, and unrecordable) realms that both Athey's cuts and Măgura's diggings find their richest meanings.

Both for Athey and for those who bear witness to his work, and particularly for those at distance from his performances (i.e., the overwhelming majority of people who have reacted to, protested, decried, and written about them—that includes this writer), the impact and effect are significant. For all participants (actors, audience, witness, moral crusaders) a basic, common shared effect may have run deep under any of these more obvious and more easily traced aims and consequences. Regardless of intention or political party line, for all participants, cutting the skin and perforating the surface of the ground are transcendent. To cut/dig is to cross over and go beyond, to break boundaries of acknowledged forms: the earth and the body. To cut/dig is to see what is inside and otherwise out of sight. To cut/dig is to take all participants to other places: into the calcareous undersurface and into the oozing subcutaneous tissue and fluids. While the other intentions, aims, and consequences of cutting/digging are not unimportant (and to many they will remain the reason for, the intention of, and the meaning of cutting and digging—that is, to disgust, to provoke, to get rid of waste products, to bury the dead), it is this deep connection that is at greatest work here; it has the strongest, most lasting, and broadest-reaching effect. Paradoxically, there is little or no trace of this impact; it is intangible, ephemeral, unrecorded, invisible, unpredictable, ghostlike, perhaps not even barely recognized, despite its location at the core the actions of cutting/digging. If it takes any form, then this impact is of a shift in atmosphere and essence of how one is and how one subconsciously knows how it is to be.

If this is the case, then the most important part of both the Athey performance and the Măgura pit-digging is not present (now and was not clearly present then), is never recoverable, has left no trace, and cannot be recorded or measured. In every sense of that delicious term, our understanding of pit-digging, like long-perished organic materials from poorly preserved archaeological strata, will always remain fugitive. If that is the case, then both performance researcher and archaeologist are faced with two options: to abandon all effort to study, to engage, and to work with each analyst's chosen topic of study, or to embrace the reality of that absence and immeasurability and to move into new territory, itself unsure and frightening. The latter option is the course taken in this book, and in a broader effort to look beyond the (rational, standard, professional, ethical, and wholly respectable) practices, methods, and intentions of the analytic work that we do when we wrestle with human behavior of 8000 years ago.

Chapter 3

Cutting Holes

PHILOSOPHY AND PSYCHOLOGY

THE DISCUSSION OF Ron Athey's performance work and the significance of ground, skin, and the actions of cutting the surfaces of both released our understandings of what happened 8000 years ago at Măgura from traditional archaeological discourse. We can push further by recognizing that when those people cut the Măgura ground in the way that they did, and when Athey cut the skin of Darryl Carlton, the results were holes made into surfaces. If the Măgura pit-houses are holes made into the surface of the ground, then what is it about their ontological status as holes that might expand our thinking about these places and those actions? Initially, both holes and surfaces appear to be simple and easily understood entities. When we think in more detail about holes, about how we might define them, and about what might be the consequences of creating holes, however, we encounter a rich set of debates and discussions that further complicates our understandings of Neolithic pit-houses.

As it turns out, holes are curious beings, and thinking about them opens unanticipated and at times bewildering lines of thought. A significant literature on the philosophy and psychology of holes exists, and it is to these discussions that this chapter turns, particularly to the recognition that holes are paradoxes that are difficult (perhaps impossible) to define, and as shapes that have disproportionate advantages in attracting human visual attention. As we will see, examination of a philosophy of holes demands the examination of a philosophy of surfaces, and when we recognize that we can think of holes as concavities, we see that concave shapes have unusual and unexpected priorities in human visual perception. This chapter establishes correspondences between holes as pits dug into the ground through an examination of the definitions and statuses of holes and surfaces and of the perceptual consequences of concave shapes; as a result, the discussion broadens the connections made in the previous chapter's examination of skin and ground cutting.

The Philosophy of Holes

In their seminal work *Holes and Other Superficialities* (1994) and in later writing (2004, 2012) the analytical metaphysician Roberto Casati and the philosopher Achille Varzi provide a rich discussion of the definitions and significances of holes. Casati and Varzi argue that holes have shape, size, and location (2012), and that in terms of topological and morphological classification, the broader category "holes" includes the following categories of forms and actions (Figure 3.1): a depression in a surface (i.e., one that lacks edges and does not penetrate that surface) (Casati and Varzi 1994: 40); a superficial hollow (i.e., deeper than a depression, marked clearly by edges resting on a surface, but also not penetrating that surface) (Casati and Varzi 1994: 40–41); a perforating tunnel (i.e., penetrating a surface completely so that a background, or some other surface, is visible) (Casati and Varzi 1994: 54); and an internal cavity (i.e., a space marked by no edges on the surface and not fully penetrating the surface) (Casati and Varzi 1994: 39–40). They draw a further distinction between digging and deformation (Figure 3.2). In these senses and through their definitions, holes are "spatiotemporal particulars," and as Casati and Varzi tell us, we can find holes, measure them, and recognize their differences and similarities to an extent that classification is possible.

Making Holes

To come into being in the world, holes depend on basic creative operations: digging, cutting, pressing, and perforating, as well as (potentially), filling, though, as we will see below, this last action is of secondary importance. To make certain types of holes (e.g., tunnels and cavities) requires a removal of matter from an object (Casati and Varzi 1994: 17). At the most basic level, a hole is nothing more significant than the byproduct of some other action. One can make a hole by digging, by furrowing (i.e., an action of greater affect than

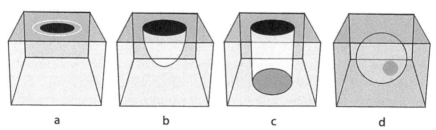

a   b   c   d

FIGURE 3.1 Hole variations: (a) depression; (b) hollow; (c) tunnel; (d) cavity (redrawn by Sveta Matskevich after Casati and Varzi 1994, figures 4.1, 10.1).

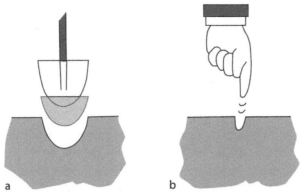

FIGURE 3.2 Hole variations: (a) digging and (b) deformation (redrawn by Sveta Matskevich after Casati and Varzi 1994, figures 4.1, 10.1).

grooving), by drilling, by carving, or by gouging (Casati and Varzi 1994: 141). The simplest of these processes is the continuous deformation of an object's surface through the application of pressure: a relatively simple process that requires neither cutting nor perforation nor penetration of the surface (Casati and Varzi 1994: 141). Alternatively, one can make a hole by piercing, punching, and puncturing a surface; such actions cut a surface but do not remove material. When an action penetrates beyond the full depth of the surface material, the result becomes a tunnel through that surface. As Casati and Varzi suggest, the creation of a hole of this sort begins with the making of a hollow that descends down into the body of the surface, and it is only at the very end of the process, through the "magic moment of perforation" that a hole comes into existence, and in doing so changes fundamentally the topology of the object so holed with a tunnel (Casati and Varzi 1994: 142).

Surfaces

Regardless of the creative action applied to make a hole or how one defines diverse categories of holes, the thing most central to the ontology of holes is a surface; holes depend on surfaces for their existence. There are the surfaces into which a hole is made, and there are surfaces that are brought into being during the creation of a hole. Thus, Casati and Varzi suggest that holes have skins: the part of the hole's host (i.e., the surface) that is shared by the hole where the newly created hole comes into contact and has pressed down or displaced material of the surface (Casati and Varzi 1994: 7). One makes a hole into a surface, and the result is a new surface that lines the new material boundary marked by the hole.

In a similar vein, Marco Bertamini and Camilla Croucher (2003: 52) define a hole as a contour that encloses an object. Perhaps at the most basic level, one can define holes, as Bertamini does (2006: 884), as a missing piece of a surface. In this sense, a hole is a discontinuity in the surface of some material object (Casati and Varzi 1994: 11). If this is the case, then to understand holes and their significances requires a knowledge of surfaces. In fact, Casati and Varzi argue that holes are superficial dependents; holes do not exist and cannot act without a surface. Part of the conundrum of definition that a hole presents is the recognition that a hole finds its definition always in terms of something else (Casati and Varzi 1994: 6, 16; 2012). No hole can exist on its own (Casati and Varzi 1994: 18–19). As with Casati and Varzi, Kurt Tucholsky (1930) and Bertamini (2006: 890n4) have argued that holes are ontologically parasitic. A hole requires an object to host it. They are always in something else and cannot exist on their own (Casati and Varzi 1994, 2012). That host is the surface.

Surfaces have importance beyond the definition of holes; they play a primary role in human visual systems (e.g., Lappin and Craft 2000; Nakayama et al. 1995; Nakayama and Shimojo 1992). However, surfaces (like holes) are not as simple as they first appear, and they avoid our attempts at easy definition. For Avrum Stroll, a surface is that aspect of people's everyday lives by which we organize and structure the worlds around us (Stroll 1988: 12). The more we examine the characteristics and positions of surfaces, the more unstable and insecure their statuses become.

To which object does the surface of a boundary belong? The answer is never clear or easy. Surfaces appear to always be boundaries, marking off the world in various ways, always separating two objects or two spaces, yet, surfaces never appear to have material form or any essential properties (Stroll 1988: 189–194). Does the boundary between two objects exist as its own entity? Stroll offers the troubling example of the contact of the air and water of a lake (Stroll 1988: 28) (Figure 3.3). He suggests that one may state that the surface of the water is rough, but one doesn't usually (ever?) say that the air is rough in the same situation. Why is this the case, particularly if the boundary between the air and the water is one and the same? How can one side of the boundary be rough, but the other not be anything? The question that results is important: does the air have a surface?

Stroll exposes us to the problematic position of surfaces when we see them meeting in boundaries. Perhaps certain elements of the world do not have surfaces or at least only trouble us when we try to locate, define, and describe their surfaces. Stroll argues that some things (living human beings and most

FIGURE 3.3 Carol Highsmith, *Water and Air: Clouds over Inks Lake* (2014); image reproduced with permission from The Lyda Hill Texas Collection of Photographs, America Project, Library of Congress, Prints and Photographs Division.

large animals, clouds, trees) do not have surfaces (Stroll 1988: 33–35): clouds are not dense enough, trees are too irregular (thus, we talk of the surfaces of parts of trees such as bark or leaves), people and large animals are amorphous and mobile (they have skins and it is these that have surfaces) (Stroll 1988: 188). Other objects lack rigidity and solidity and prevent talk of their surfaces: wigs, cotton candy, and wild grasses (Stroll 1988: 35). Even more important, Stroll suggests that surfaces affect our knowledge of our worlds. They block our perceptions of objects (Stroll 1988: 13): of what is below, behind, and within. Surfaces are particularly confusing when one thinks about the powerful roles that they play in making and marking boundaries.

The relationship of hole-to-surface is important and reciprocal. Not only are surfaces essential for holes, but holes create surfaces; when one makes a hole, one also creates a new surface along the boundaries of the hole (i.e., the lining or the skin) (Casati and Varzi 1994: 152). Perhaps an entity that does not normally appear to us to have a surface only obtains its surface once that surface is holed. Like holes, surfaces are entities that do not normally exist by themselves (Stroll 1988: 184); they are outermost or uppermost, and easily visible, but they are not identical to the whole object of which they are the face (Stroll 1988: 185).

In his *Ecological Approach to Visual Perception* (1979), James Gibson defines the ecological reality of the world and distinguishes his ecological approach from a geometric one, and in doing so offers a "nomenclature for surface layout" that allows study of perception and behavior (1979: chapter 3). A world understood in terms of surfaces (and not in terms of lines, as in abstract geometry) is a world of meaning. Gibson sees surfaces as distinct from (geometric) planes: the former are colored, opaque, textured, and substantial. Where two surfaces meet, an edge or a corner results, and the "reference" surface for all other surfaces in our world is the ground. Gibson employs surface as the critical component in his nomenclature. In his words, surfaces are "where most of the action is" (Gibson 1979: 23).

In his critique of Gibson, Tim Ingold (Ingold 2007), suggests that one turn away from the consideration of matter, and toward substances and media and the surfaces between them (Ingold 2007: 14). Ingold argues that we see the world (and objects within it) practically experienced and not as identifiable, measureable, or able to be fixed (Ingold 2007: 14). He suggests that the surface of the land (for example) is not a boundary, but "a vaguely defined zone of admixture and intermingling" (Ingold 2008: 8), and that it is in this intermediate zone that life is lived (Ingold 2008: 8). Ingold argues not for surfaces as boundaries but from the position that the environment is made of openings and ways through, but not of insides or outsides (Ingold 2008: 12).

The potential for ambiguity is strong with any examination of holes, of surfaces, and of their articulations. As Stephen Palmer has written about holes in terms of enclosure (1999: 286), the status and ontology of the contour of the enclosing object create a paradox for definition. The contour belongs either to the surrounding area, or to the hole, or to both. If one cannot determine that the contour belongs to either the surrounding area or the hole, then the remaining option is that it belongs to both. If this is the case, then the resulting ambiguity (perhaps impossibility) threatens our rational thoughts about objects and our measured ability to perceive reality: how can something (the boundary) be two things (surface and hole) at the same time? The solution is not to choose one or the other shape as owning the boundary; let them belong to both and let both belong to it. The solution is to recognize that boundaries between shapes, places, worlds, and holes and surfaces possess powerful, undefined (and perhaps undefinable) statuses, powers, and potentials, and strongly affect how we see and experience the world in ways that are open to potentially dangerous and unsettling uses and abuses. These powers of boundaries (and of surface and holes, perhaps) come from their uncomfortable positions that deny clear definition and understanding.

Filling Holes

Surprisingly, particularly for archaeologists, the existence of a hole does not depend upon the identity of the material, matter, stuff, objects, people, or anything else that might be inside the hole (i.e., its filling) (Casati and Varzi 1994: 2) (Figure 3.4). While it is true that one of the essential properties of a hole is its ability to be filled (Casati and Varzi 1994: 56), and thus, in Gibson's terms holes afford filling (Gibson 1979), it is also true that filling (as act) and filling (as object) are not primary to the ontology of a hole. The filling of holes is of secondary importance, and any subsequent acts of filling (important though they may be for other, subsequent uses or understandings of the hole) only come into play once the hole has been created, once it has been deemed to exist.

Casati and Varzi (2012) make this point in writing that the hole's filling is the hole's guest. In doing so, these authors clearly represent the relationship between a hole and any contents it may eventually possess; the fill, though potentially important for other discussions (e.g., of actions of use), does not define the hole; it only informs on a later act or set of acts. We are mistaken to connect those later acts to the significance of creating a hole. Too desparately, we grasp for function and intention and, in doing so, collapse together the vital space between the hole (as alteration of surface and boundary) and its

FIGURE 3.4 Conservators piecing fragmented jar back together in the Pottery Conservation Laboratory of the Archaeological Area of Akrotiri, Santorini. Image http://creativecommons.org/licenses/by/2.0 (accessed July 15, 2017).

secondary use (as object in life). This state of affairs confounds the archaeological mind; an archaeology of holes (in the sense of pits and pit-houses, for
example) usually limits itself to an examination of the material that is excavated from the hole and restricts itself to an attempt to retro-construct the
taphonomic sequences by which those materials were placed into the hole:
Harris Matrices, micromorphological analyses, taphonomic reconstructions.

The discussion in this chapter moves us out of traditional territories of
analysis and into one in which I promote, as paramount, the creation and
essence of a hole, and where we leave for others the need to unravel what happens after a hole is created. To this we could refer to the debates over structured deposition by Thomas, Richards, Pollard, Garrow, Chapman, and others
as detailed in chapter 1. To be sure, thought about those secondary events and
actions (which gravitate toward holes) will take account of other, equally, important properties of holes: for example, their abilities to constrain the movement of anything that is placed within them. Holes keep objects in place, and
hinder the movements of other objects on the surface into which the hole has
been established (Casati and Varzi 1994: 116). For some, such as Bertamini,
this process of enclosure is the essential criterion for a hole's definition
(Bertamini 2006: 884). There is nothing incorrect with this, but it is a discussion that is secondary to the focus of this chapter: the status and affect of
holes.

To finish the discussion of the importance of the contents of a hole, let us
recognize that to fill a hole is to destroy it (Casati and Varzi 1994: 151). The
specific condition of the material filling of the hole determines the degree of
hole destruction: whether destruction is partial or complete. If the fill material
is identical to the material of the surface into which the hole has been cut,
then the hole is truly destroyed: it disappears. On the other hand, if the material that fills the hole is distinct in its composition from the material of the
surface, then the hole survives, even though it has been filled and appears to
have disappeared.

Do Holes Exist?

Lively philosophical debate has focused on the existential status of a hole: does
a hole exist as a material body? David and Stephanie Lewis argue that holes
are actual physical things (though a special class of thing) that exist as material objects; they suggest that though a hole may be empty, it is physically
manifest in the tangible reality of its lining, and that the only issue requiring
discussion concerns the choice of terminology that we should use to describe
holes (Lewis and Lewis 1970). More suspiciously, Bertamini and Croucher

ask whether or not holes actually exist in and of themselves (Bertamini and Croucher 2003). In their seminal work on the broader topic of the human visual recognition of shapes, Donald Hoffman and Whitman Richards define holes as negative parts (Hoffman and Richards 1984: 85). Similarly, Casati and Varzi suggest that holes are "as-if" entities, are fictions (Casati and Varzi 1994, 2012), and thus are not real things at all. Stephen Palmer pushes the discussion in another direction; he suggests that holes may indeed exist, but the problem is that we do not know how to recognize their shape, because, at their core, holes are figures that describe other shapes (Palmer 1999: 286).

Casati and Varzi (2012) identify the conundra that complicate attempts to determine whether or not a hole exists. Because the matter that makes up a hole (that which is inside the hole) is absent (it has been removed though the actions of creating the hole), we cannot, as is normal with any other material object (and in archaeological discourse), refer to the hole's composition in order to define it. Nothing is available for us to refer to or to identity with. A hole is not stone, clay, bone, wattle-and-daub, pisé, mud-brick, antler, charcoal, copper, plastic, silicon, or any another material; it is neither organic nor inorganic. It, just, is not. But it also, just, is. Thus, if we try to identify a hole in terms of its material of composition, we face a first conundrum of definition, and we are defeated by it.

Another attempt to define a hole is to refer to the matter that makes up the host of the hole (the stuff around it, the surface that the hole was cut into), and which one hopes would define the hole. Here we face a different problem. On the one hand, the dirt, cement, wood, brass, bone, or fired clay that constitute the surface in which the hole resides, are physically, palpably, manifest. They exist. We can see them, touch them, feel them, describe them, and measure them. On the other hand, and here is the problem, that host (silt, clay, chalk, soil, sediment, gravel, ash, dung, loam, loess, peat; organic or inorganic) can vary almost infinitely with time and place. Though that host can be of many different compositions and materials in many different places, at each place of different material, one can find something that is the same: the hole. Therefore, the second conundrum of definition is that if we rely on the hole's host as the primary reference for its definition, then we have nothing secure with which to proceed: the hole is not the surface into which it had been cut.

Casati and Varzi offer a third conundrum of hole definition: the problem of disconnection that follows the making of multiple holes in one surface (Casati and Varzi 2004, 2012). In their example, someone punches a hole in a card, then punches a second hole in the same card, and then asks, how many holes are there (Figure 3.5)? Clearly, there are two perforations, but are there two holes? Are they separate things, or are they two different parts of the same

FIGURE 3.5 Card with two holes cut through it. Photo copyright D. W. Bailey.

thing, where that thing is something best understood as the holing-of-the-card? It is not unusual for a single object to have two or more, disconnected parts. Casati and Varzi offer examples: the lowercase letter *i*, a pencil that has been broken in half, a bikini. One could add to the trouble by asking what would be the status of two (or more holes) cut through the same surface, such as the ground or a wall in a house. Are they disconnected elements of one thing, or are they two (or more) separate entities? There is no easy or correct answer (Casati and Varzi 2004: 26). In summary then, when we encounter a hole and its contents, its surroundings, and its curious status as both multiple and unique, we struggle, indeed we fail, to fully (or with any confidence) iden-tify or define a hole (Casati and Varzi 2012).

Emerging from this discussion is an understanding that holes have a special, powerful, ontological status; they exist but are not real objects (Bertamini and Croucher 2003). Holes are slippery, elusive entities (Casati and Varzi 1994: 1). For Jacob Feldman and Manish Singh (Feldman and Singh 2005), holes are "special things." Holes are ambiguous; they appear to be phenomenological entities that have a shape of their own, but they are actually just empty space (Palmer 1999: 286). There exists a separate, not insubstantial, literature on the status of holes in terms of figure and ground, though this is specifically rele-vant to two-dimensionality. In that literature, Rolf Nelson and Stephen Palmer (Nelson and Palmer 2001: 1213) note that we can recognize a two-dimensional image of an object in front of a background as either a hole (the object is cutting through the surface of the background), or as an object sitting in front of (but not perforating the background) (see also Palmer 1999). The three-dimensional world is perceptually richer and prevents such ambiguity from taking hold; the addition of depth secures our recognition of either hole or front matter.

Beyond the Conundra

One solution to the conundra of definition, as Stephen Palmer and Irvin Rock suggest, is to understand that holes are "uniform connected regions," and that these are the initial units of perceptual organization (Palmer and Rock 1994). Alternatively, Andrew Wake and his colleagues argue that holes are best understood as regions of space-time, specifically regions of space-time that are located at certain discontinuities in the surfaces of material objects (Wake et al. 2007: 373). The argument they make is for a third way; holes are neither physical entities/objects (as the Lewises suggested), nor are they a special, slippery type of entity (as Casati and Varzi concluded) (Wake et al. 2007: 376). Rather, Wake's team argues that holes are simply different regions of space-time, and as such are less mysterious (at least in terms of philosophy) than other authors believe them to be.

Another alternative comes from Phillip Meadows (2011). He suggests that holes are not particulars at all, and that we are mistaken in our attempts to understand them as such. Meadows argues that holes are best understood as properties or relations. In a discussion about which fundamental ontological category holes belong to, Meadows argues that holes are not objects, nor are they objective. One of the criteria of objects is that they bear properties, and that properties are ways of being; they are the ways that objects are (after J. Levinson 1978). For Meadows, holes are properties or relations among the parts of the host. As a consequence, holes give rise to metaphysical puzzles, because they present problems (as noted by almost all of the authors discussed above) about where and how we should fit holes into an ontology. As Meadows notes, one cannot put a thing or an object into a property or into a relation: "The hole is the spatial relation between parts of the object" (Meadows 2011: 315). Holes are not things but they affect objects and people and places; holes do things; they state relationships in spatiotemporal and other, perhaps, metaphysical terms and worlds.

Holes Disrupt

While it is not certain that holes exist (though my money is on Meadows' conception that they are relations and properties, and on Wake's team's idea that they are regions of space-time), it is clear that holes interrupt, disrupt, and alter our perspectives on parts of our world that clearly do exist (ground, land, territory) (Casati and Varzi 1994: 153), as well as on almost everything in that world (people, animals, objects, and actions). Holes are but one type of discontinuity in a surface; others include bumps, ridges, grooves, dents, and corners (Casati and Varzi 1994: 13), or in Gibson's thinking "wrinkles" that include convexities and concavities (Gibson 1979: 33). Indeed, the first act of making a hole is to create some fissure in a surface, and then to isolate and remove a part of that surface material: holes, thus, begin though fissuration (Casati and Varzi 1994: 152).

An essential consequence of making a hole is that to do so, one imposes a detour to movement: the path along the surface leading from one side of a hole to another is always made longer because of the intrusion of the hole (Casati and Varzi 1994: 174) (Figure 3.6). Holes disrupt surfaces and thus disrupt movement. The hole is in the way; making a hole restructures the surface of the object holed. When an object, like the surface of the ground, acquires a hole, that object is changed (Bertamini and Croucher 2003: figure 1.2), and that change has consequences for people living on that surface, and for how they understand their lives through their connection with that object. In making a hole, and restructuring the existing surface, something new (i.e., a surrounded area) has been created (Nelson and Palmer 2001).

FIGURE 3.6 *Bridge Washout.* Image courtesy National Archives, photo no. 311-MAD-47761.

As Casati and Varzi suggest, holes are to space what pauses are to time (Casati and Varzi 1994: 186); they insert a gap where one was not originally present. Gaps invite filling, obstruct progress, create tension, and disrupt continuity. A hole is a disturbance. A hole disturbs the surface of the object that it cuts into, and thus it disturbs all of the connections and meanings that that surface (and that object) has for the people who know it and exist with it, within it, on it, or now, literally through it. While the disturbance can be significant, there is no reason that the consequences of the act of disturbance need be conscious and readily recognized by the people concerned, either at the time of the hole's insertion or afterward. Critically, the disturbance in the surface caused by its being holed may have significant impacts on people's perceptions and on the day-to-day living that those people never realize.

Summary of the Philosophy of Holes

In summary, the following observations about holes have importance: holes are byproducts of creative actions (e.g., cutting and perforating); holes have special ontological status; a hole is ambiguous; no hole can exist on its own; a hole is parasitic to its host; that host is usually a surface; a hole is an as-if entity, a fiction, and a negative part; a hole is a region of space-time; a hole is a property or a relation (and not an object); holes depend on surfaces/objects for their existence; holes disrupt and alter perspectives; a hole is a discontinuity and a detour; an object/surface holed is an object/surface fundamentally changed; secondary acts, such filling, are of secondary importance to the essence of a hole; and to fill a hole is to destroy it. A consequence of these observations is that if we redefine pit-houses, as at Măgura, as holes, then we will have opened up new territory for thought and understanding of these prehistoric entities.

Shape Recognition: The Visual Advantage of Holes (aka Concavities)

The previous section reviewed debate over whether or not holes exist, and suggested that holes are paradoxes that disturb, disrupt, and transform host objects and, in turn, alter people's perceptions and interactions with objects (and surfaces). From the discussion that follows emerge intriguing realizations about the effects that holes have on human perception. In this discussion of the psychology of visual perception, holes are defined as concave shapes, or concavities, on and in surfaces and objects. As it turns out, human vision reacts to concavities in particular ways, and though there are areas of debate and some dissent, the majority of work has shown that concavities have an advantage over other shapes in terms of attracting our visual, perceptive attention (e.g., Barenholtz et al. 2003; Barenholtz and Feldman 2006).

In the psychology of the human visual system, important research has focused on shape recognition: the visual identification of an object using only its morphology. Research has examined the ways that shapes are mentally represented and, in particular, has identified those aspects of shape that are unusually important and, thus, preferentially emphasized in human perception. At the base of this work is the understanding that the human visual system makes more explicit some information (e.g., brightness, length, shape) than it does others (Cohen et al. 2005: 313). In terms of possessing information for the description of shape representation, curved shapes (or the curvature along a contour) rate particularly highly (Alhazen 1030 [1989]; Attneave 1954; Singh and Fulvio 2005; De Winter and Wagemans 2004; Norman et al. 2001; Wolfe et al. 1992; Feldman and Singh 2005).

In a series of experiments on the psychology of visual representation, Elan Barenholtz and his colleagues documented important differences in the ways that people react to subtle changes in the shapes of objects (Barenholtz et al. 2003). In one study, Barenholtz's team presented to each of their human subjects sets of images of two-dimensional shapes, and asked the subjects if the shapes were the same or different. In the experiment, subjects saw a series of images in rapid succession: a fixation point (i.e., a cross in the center of the display screen); an irregular geometric base shape; a "mask" (i.e., a visual spacer to clear the previous image for the subject's mind); the same irregular geometric base shape or the same base shape, but with a slight modification made to it; and another "mask" (Figure 3.7). The modification that the team made to the outline of the original base shape was limited to either the addition or removal of a convex or a concave portion (Figure 3.8). In summary, subjects saw one shape, then they saw a second shape, and then the team asked subjects if the second shape was the same or different from the first one.

The results were surprising. Subjects showed significantly greater accuracy in recognizing the presence of a shape change if the modification was the addition or removal of a concave portion of the shape's outline (Barenholtz et al. 2003: 7). When the change was concave, the subjects accurately noted the alteration 70.83 percent of the time; when the change to the original base shape was convex, accuracy was only 36.94 percent (Figure 3.9).[1] Barenholtz and his team concluded that our minds perceptually represent concave sections of a contour in significantly different ways than when they

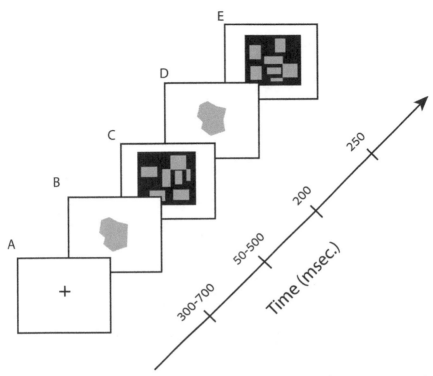

FIGURE 3.7 Sequence of images shown to subjects in visual perception experiments (after Barenholtz et al. 2003: figure 2).

represent convex shapes (Barenholtz et al. 2003: 8). Additional work by the Barenholtz team and other teams has supported these results (Barenholtz and Feldman, 2003; Bertamini and Farrant, 2005; Cohen et al. 2005; Vandekerckhove et al. 2007; Hulleman et al. 2000; Barenholtz et al. 2003) and have revealed the complexity of the processes (Bertamini and Farrant 2005; Bertamini 2008).

Experiments by Johann Hulleman and his colleagues (Hulleman et al. 2000) and by Jeremy Wolf and Sara Bennett (Wolfe and Bennett 1997) have shown that concave features "pop out" in search tasks in a visual field when that field also contains convex shapes, but that convex shapes do not behave in the same way (Hulleman et al. 2000) when they share a field with concave shapes (Figure 3.10). These experiments defined "pop out" as an increase in efficiency and speed of search by a test subject. Hulleman's team argued that in visual shape perception, "concave cusps" (i.e., a curve that points into the object and not into the background) play an important role in the way that humans assess

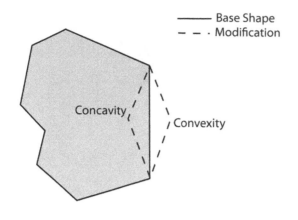

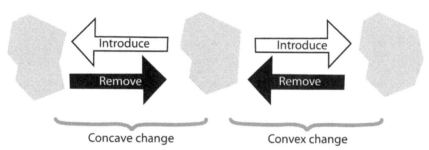

FIGURE 3.8 Concave and convex shapes introduced and removed (Barenholtz et al. 2003: figure 1 a).

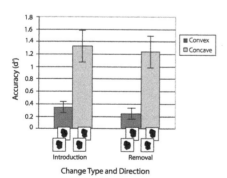

FIGURE 3.9 Bar chart showing results of experiments by Barenholtz and colleagues: mean performance as a function of change type (convex vs. concave) and change direction (introduction vs. removal) (redrawn by Sveta Matskevich after Barenholtz et al. 2003: figure 3).

and determine the structure of an object, and that when we process visual stimuli, we do so for concave shapes differently than we do for other shapes (Hulleman et al. 2000: 162). The experiments that the team ran measured the time that a subject's eye and brain took to search for a convex and for a concave shape. The results showed that there was a clear difference in subject reaction time depending on which shape they were shown: searches for concave shapes were more efficient (i.e., they took less time) (Hulleman et al. 2000: 165).

FIGURE 3.10 Holes popping out (after Wolfe and Bennett 1997: figure 8).

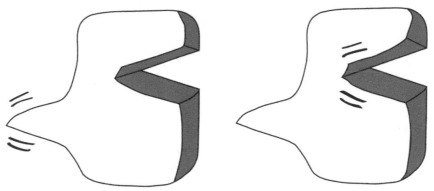

FIGURE 3.11 Three-dimensional concavity study results (after Barenholtz and Feldman 2006: figure 6B).

Much of the work on the perception of concavity has investigated either the differences in the human reaction to concave and convex visual stimuli, or in the specific effects that convex shapes have on perception. Hulleman and his team (Hulleman et al. 2000; Hulleman and Olivers 2007) have shown that in visual-search tasks, our minds locate concave shapes more efficiently than they locate convex ones. For their part, Joachim Vandekerckhove and his colleagues investigated Barenholtz's original results on the sensitivity of concavities, but examined the use of wire stimuli (in addition to the shape outlines—or "silhouettes"—used in Barenholtz's work), and examined the potential importance of the condition of the concave shapes (i.e., angled versus smoothed vertices) (Vandekerckhove et al. 2007). Their experiments showed that concavities have a perceptual advantage when the concavity is smooth-sided (as well as the sharp-angled and straight-edged, as Barenholtz had shown: Figure 3.11), and they suggested that the concavity effect may indicate a global processing of shape external to local contexts (Vandekerckhove et al. 2007: 1259).

Why Do People Locate Concavities More Efficiently and More Quickly?

Why does the human visual system prefer concavities? Hoffman and Richards (1984) suggest that concavity is important for defining the parts of an object, and that this gives special status to concave shapes: concave vertices of a shape play a role in the way that the mind parses that shape (Hoffman and Richards 1984; Bertamini 2001). Bertamini (2001: 1308) suggests that the reason rests in the fact that a convex shape has only one shape (the contour as a whole), while a concave shape has more than one part: sections of a contour joined by vertices. In the visual search event, it is the multipart character of the concavity that attracts the eye (Bertamini 2001: 1308).

Hulleman (et al. 2000) and Glyn Humphreys and Hermann Müller (2000) suggest that there are "specific detectors of concavities" in the human brain and visual processing, and that this is the main reason that the human visual system searches for concave shapes more efficiently and accurately (Bertamini 2001: 1308). Barenholtz and Feldman (2003, 2006: 540) suggest that there exists an "articulating-concavity bias" in human visual perception; perhaps the human visual system has an inherent preference for concave shapes. Elias Cohen and his team note earlier work on monkeys' cortexes, "where neurons are found to display differential sensitivity to either convex or to concave extrema of curvature" (Pasupathy and Connor 1999, 2001).

Vandekerckhove and his colleagues reviewed existing attempts to explain the differential perceptions and the preference for concavity, and showed that research fell into two distinct camps (Vandekerckhove et al. 2007: 1253). In one, the localist explanation holds that concavities carry more information than do convexities because they occur less frequently in the visual world than do convexities (see discussion in Feldman and Singh 2005; see Resnikoff 1985). Thus, because they carry more information, they are more easily and quickly located by the human visual system. The other, globalist, account holds that concavities are more easily and more quickly detected because of the important roles that they play in the way that parts make up larger shapes (see De Winter and Wagemans 2006; Keane et al. 2003; Koenderink 1984). Thus, concavities connect different parts of shapes or objects more often than do convexities, and thus they play a more pivotal role in an object's existence. In assessing and comparing the localist and the globalist explanations, the Vandekerckhove team concluded that this rigid localist/globalist dichotomy of explanation is unhelpful, and that future work should consider how the two perspectives may combine and interact in helping to explain the privileged position that convex shapes hold in visual recognition (Vandekerckhove et al. 2007: 1259).

Another possible explanation is that when we take in visual information, our minds seek boundaries. If this is the case, concavities (i.e., holes) draw us to them because concavities mark out boundaries. Following Hoffman and Richards (1984) and Hoffman and Singh (1997), Barenholtz and Feldman remind us that concavities (when understood as a series of contour points that make up a negative curve) are normally perceived as boundaries between parts of a shape (Barenholtz and Feldman 2006: 532). As Elias Cohen and his colleagues argue, concavities are important representationally "not because they are the basic units of shape representations, but because they help to delineate the basic units from each other" (Cohen et al. 2005: 319). As suggested above in the discussion of the relations between holes and surfaces, boundaries are uneasy beings.

If concavities (i.e., holes) define boundaries between perceived parts, then it may well be that we perceive concavities (i.e., holes) as boundaries between worlds or realities. In making a hole in a surface, therefore, one defines (or at least unintentionally draws attention to) the boundary between two parts (or regions, worlds, or realities) that otherwise might not have come into perceptual existence. It is possible that this is why we bury the dead in holes cut into the surface of the ground. Conversely, it is possible that the inverse also is of importance to our subconscious sensing of the world. I contend that, in many different parts of the world in many different periods, people may have considered earth and stone barrows, tell settlements, pyramids, and megalithic monuments as things that are still of the world in which we exist (and which do not engage boundaries between worlds/parts). Similarly, when people placed the deceased in a barrow of dirt and rocks placed on the surface of the ground (thus making a convex shape), the result was that those deceased individuals remained in their world; they were not deemed to have crossed over a boundary. The consequence then is that when people placed a body in a pit that they had dug into the surface of the ground, they moved that body into another world, a world across a boundary, a world in which we do not dwell.

The Other Side: Convexity as a Preferred Visual Search Target

In a recent report of new experiments into visual search preference for concavity, Barenholtz noted studies that have argued that in some situations, it is convex shapes (and not concavities) that have representational advantages

(Bertamini 2001; Gibson 1994; Hulleman and Olivers 2007). The argument is that the differences in search and location speeds are factors of the number of tasks required, including the judgment of position and the detection of symmetry when seeing a shape or object. For example, Marco Bertamini's investigation of the ways in which people visually judge the position of a shape showed that his subject-observers were more accurate in judging the position of a convex shape than when they judged the position of a concave one (Bertamini 2001: 1295). Bertamini concluded that in terms of recognizing a shape, being convex and not concave is of importance for a shape. Regardless of the primacy of convex or concave shapes in their representational attraction to the human eye, the significant fact remains that human perception does not treat concave and convex shapes in the same way. Thus to make a hole (i.e., to make a concavity) has significance (as yet, not fully understood) for the way that we see our world around us, particularly the ground.

Summary: Perception of Concavities/Holes

In summary, the following observations about human visual perception of concavities (i.e., holes) are important: in terms of perception, holes can be seen as concave shapes; the human visual system reacts differently to concave and convex shapes; the human visual system detects changes in a shape more accurately and more efficiently when the change is the addition or removal of a concave element; the human visual system locates concave shapes more quickly that it does convex shapes; in visual searches, concave shapes "pop out," and convex shapes do not; concave shape perceptual preference may be a factor of the amount of visual information carried by a concavity, and of the role that a concavity plays in a multipart shape; the positions of concave shapes as boundaries within and between shapes may be a factor of the perceptual preference for concavities; perceptual preference for concave shapes may be a global effect, or a human perceptual bias (perhaps seen in nonhuman primates), and not linked to local contextual information and conditions; and a minority of research argues that convexities possess a perceptual preference in the human visual system.

Relevance to Măgura

Do these discussions of the philosophy of holes and the visual perceptual psychology of concavities have any relevance to the Măgura pit-houses? Isn't it enough for us to say, "These are holes that people dug into the ground 8000 years ago"? Do we gain anything from wandering through the debates and discussions over the existence of holes as material or immaterial? Did those people who dug those holes 8000 years ago on the terrace in the Vedea Valley participate in some nuanced philosophical debate over the essence of holes? These questions are legitimate, but they miss a deeper level of significance of action that we need to address.

What type of holes was made at Măgura 8000 years ago? Were they hollows, perforating tunnels, or internal cavities? If we look again at the stratigraphy, we see the evidence in a new light. I contend that, in terms of the philosophy of holes, it is significant that holes that these pits were dug down into reached the white calcium carbonate layer (Figure 3.12). In perforating the brown and black surface soils, and entering the harder white stratum below, the Neolithic diggers made a hole in the true sense that Casati and Varzi term a perforated tunnel. If we understand holes to be concavities constructed into the surface of the ground, then the results of Barenholtz's work suggest further significances for our understanding of the pits that people dug into the ground 8000 years ago in southern Romania (and throughout the region in the Neolithic).

No direct connection exists between the philosophical debates over the ontological status of holes and surfaces, the potential of concavities as visual

FIGURE 3.12 Excavations at Măgura-Buduiasca uncovering the white calcium carbonate sub-layer in Sondage 21, view to the west. Photo copyright D. W. Bailey.

attractors, on the one hand, and the cutting of the ground at Măgura, on the other. Rather, the value of the philosophical and psychological research finds its currency in our broader attempt to explore the unrecorded and untraceable significances of digging into the ground, removing dirt, and thus making holes. Holes matter. As paradoxes of being (do they exist or not?), they bring into being sites of questioning and imbalance. As disruptions into otherwise continuous surfaces (upon which they depend, philosophically and physically), they insert fissures into otherwise coherent realities. As attractors of our visual attentions, they offer higher levels of significance. What happens with, around, in, and through holes derives otherwise unrecognized significance and power. The actions of making holes carry these energies fueled by paradox, disruption, and attraction. The actions of putting objects into holes share that flow, those energies, and their disruption. The actions carried out in holes absorb and ride that energy. The actions of filling that hole maintain consequences of significance. Because of the power that comes with breaking the surface in the act of making a hole (of digging a pit at Măgura), all actions, objects, and engagements with that hole/pit take on a particular essence. The contents (or the hole-makers, hole-users, or hole-fillers) on their own may not matter; their association with hole-making and the time-space of the hole is where their meaning and significance rest.

Conclusions

Thinking about the Măgura pit-houses through the philosophy of holes and surfaces seeds new questions and allows us to draw fresh inferences about what happened when people dug those holes and about the consequences of those actions. If pits-understood-as-holes are ambiguous, then digging them unsettled what had otherwise been agreed and accepted. If a pit-as-hole cannot exist on its own, then the action of making (and also of using, filling, and abandoning) that pit-as-hole implicates the surface of the ground into which the pit/hole was cut. If a pit-as-hole is a negative, fictive thing (an "as if"), then breaking the ground surface by digging a hole introduces an alternative to the real, nonfictive, landscape on which day-to-day life was played out. If a pit-as-hole is not an object, but a relation or property, then cutting a hole into the ground surface challenges, manipulates, transforms, and contests the previously active relationships that had been played out over that grounded landscape. If a pit-as-hole disrupts and alters perspectives that people had of the grounded landscape of living, then the making of that hole likely altered the ways in which people saw their position in the reality of their daily lives, lived out on the surfaces of existence. If a pit-as-hole is a discontinuity and a detour, then breaking the surface of the ground in this way would have broken the continuity of the surface reality of living in that place at that time and would have inserted a detour not only in physical, phenomenological space but also in the metaphysical space of being in that world. If a pit-as-hole fundamentally changes the character, essence, and energy of the surface into which it cuts, then that pit would have significantly altered the part of the physical world that those people used as referent to being present, positioned, linked to, and separated from others, and to their physical, natural, social, and political environments. If the filling of the pit-as-hole is of secondary (or tertiary) significance to the place of that pit in those lived landscapes, then the majority (in most cases, all) of how we pretend to study, interpret, and explain pit-houses is naive and blinkered.

Furthermore, thinking about the Măgura pit-houses through the psychology of visual perception of convexities cultivates growth from the seeds sown by a philosophy of holes. If people respond differently to pits-understood-as-convexities than they do to other human constructions and natural objects, then these pits would have afforded different responses from people making and seeing them, as well as differences in the particular uses and comprehensions that people would have had of them. If pits-as-convexities are more easily and quickly received into human visual perception, then their making and all that happened to them, in them, and around them would have had priority in the positioning of how people saw and valued the world in which they lived. If pits-as-convexities "pop-out" of their natural and constructed backgrounds, then those pits would have taken on preferentially greater significance as context and place for actions, events, depositions, and meanings than would have other, alternatively shaped contours of those worlds. If pits-as-convexities carried more visual information than did other (shaped) parts of the landscaped world, then those pits would have been particularly powerful and spacious, conceptual and physical archives for locating actions, objects, and events in the worlds of the people who dug and moved into, out of, and around them. If pits-as-convexities were particularly equipped as boundaries within and between surfaces, contours, and worlds, then those pits would have been powerfully sited to partitioning off one world from the next, and, perhaps more significantly, of providing specific locations for the movement between those worlds.

At Măgura, therefore, pits-as-holes-and-as-convexities would have worked actively as humanly constructed points in the lived-upon land at which received reality was established, contested, severed, transformed, disrupted, and broken. The consequent atmosphere of ambiguity, paradox, and conundrum would have charged the acts of breaking of the ground surface with these pits with particular and potentially dangerous, volatile energies and potentials. What happened at Măgura, both in the breaking of the ground surface in this particular way, and in the eventual uses of those breaks in the land surface at secondary and tertiary remove, would have held local significance that far outstrips our traditional understandings and ways of studying and explaining them as pit-houses, pit-huts, or places of structured deposition. If fact, the conditions outlined in this chapter provide powerful passages toward knowing more nuanced understandings of why people felt it appropriate to live in, flake stone in, sleep in, bury the dead in, and place particularly selected objects in specially followed patterns of deposition. The power of the pit is in its digging and in its condition of being a hole in a surface that attracted our perceptual (and spiritual) attentions.

Inter-text

er 4

Cutting Deep

BRONZE AGE (1470–1290 CAL. B.C.)

The Cut

Five and a half thousand years ago, on a low chalk plain of what is now southern England, a group of people cut through the surface of the ground, probably using cattle scapula shovels and deer antler picks. Once they had broken the surface of the ground, they dug down; they placed the turves and soil that they removed in a circle around the hole. They built that circle into a bank of flattened top and battered sides (Ashbee 1989e: 26, fig 21:1). As they dug, they cut through a shallow layer of dark black topsoil, and then soils and sediments that had been mixed by many millennia of seasonal cycles of freezing and thawing; finally they cut down into the visually, tactilely distinct white chalk below (Ashbee et al. 1989c: 4).

Cutting down into the chalk, they made a circular hole wide enough across for an adult to lie down without bending his or her knees. They deepened the hole in short episodes of digging and removing dirt and chalk. Diggers cut into the chalk, driving in their antler picks, then pounding the antler burrs with a rock hammer (Ashbee 1989e: 33) (Figure 4.1). To make their picks, they collected antler shed from mature red deer, and then hardened the soft, raw antlers by storing them to cure until needed (Ashbee 1989e: 33). The antler picks worked well to remove the chalk and the occasional nodule of flint that ran in seams through the white material. As they dug, the diggers roughly shaped the hole into what we would recognize as a cylinder, running perpendicular to the ground surface. As they dug, they removed the waste, tossing it or carrying it up to the ground level above.

At a depth where the starting ground surface was level with one of the digger's foreheads as she stood, the excavators cut the sides of the hole smooth, dressing them to the vertical with a bronze axe (Ashbee 1989e: 33). In some places they straightened the wall with upright strokes, bringing the axe

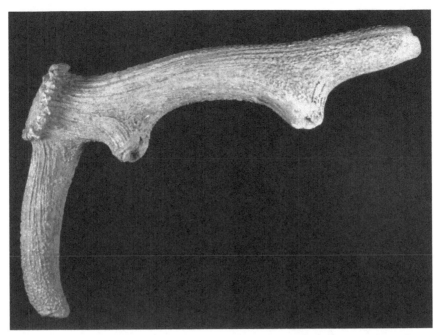

FIGURE 4.1 Antler pick from Woodhenge, Durrington, Wiltshire (400 mm long, 240 mm wide, 75 mm high). Photo Wiltshire Museum, Devizes, used with permission.

straight down against the surface left rough by the antler picks. In other places, a digger swung his axe from the side, smoothing the surface with horizontal cuts (Figure 4.2). Another digger made her stroke at an angle, dressing the surface with diagonal blows (Ashbee 1989e: 34–35). Most frequently, they straightened the walls by using the flat face of the bronze edge; occasionally, they cut the chalk with the axe-blade's pointed corner tip (Ashbee 1989e: 34–35).

Once they had finished smoothing the walls of this first meter and a half of the hole, the diggers took up their

FIGURE 4.2 Wilsford Shaft: axe cut marks—vertical, upright, horizontal, diagonal. Image copyright Edward Ashbee; used with permission.

antler picks again, and dug down, starting a new section, swinging their tools, prying out chunks of the white chalk and clearing them to the top of the

FIGURE 4.3 Wilsford Shaft: broken flint nodule in the wall. Image copyright Edward Ashbee; used with permission.

hole. Up on the ground surface, others added this newly excavated material to the bank running around the hole's mouth. Section after section, they dug straight down into the ground.

At the juncture where a higher section met the next lower one, at the place where the smoothed walls of the upper segment met the smoothed walls of the deeper section, one of the diggers would clean the ragged join between the sections with her pick (Ashbee 1989e: 33). Often, the diggers found raw nodules of flint in the chalk; they gathered these with the chalk debris and hoisted them to the surface. Sometimes as they cut the vertical wall of the hole, their picks bounced off of a flint nodule sticking out from the smoothed surface of the wall. If the nodule was too large to remove without damaging the wall's dressed surface, a digger would smash the flint flush with the wall, so that the vertical surface remained straight and uninterrupted (Ashbee 1989e: 33, fig. 35) (Figure 4.3). The men and women cutting the hole kept the diameter of the cylinder a constant size: just large enough so that if one of them lay down on his back with his head touching one wall, his toes would just reach the wall opposite. They dug with effort, but also with caution and care, keeping the sides of each successive section true to vertical.

In some places, they made mistakes and mis-cut, taking the line of the wall out of true. When they reached a depth at which the diggers were so far below the ground surface that three of them would have had to have stood on top of the shoulders of the digger below to reach the surface, they lost control of the wall's verticality. To correct, they cut back deeply into the wall with their antler picks and brought the shaft into true again. Which one of them realized the error? Did they argue? Did someone take the blame? Did one of them lose his or her place in the hole? Were some of the diggers more accurate with their axes then others? Did the more experienced teach the others? Did some not want to learn or listen? Did someone not pay attention? Was one of the axes less useful or easy to handle?

Having righted that first major mistake, the diggers cut straight again, taking extra care. After cutting a new section, however, the diggers veered off the vertical again. Was it the same digger who had let the earlier section slip out of true? Was someone new in the hole, someone without the other's experience, or had one of the diggers been given a second chance? Did they argue about the need for the hole to have walls this true to the vertical? Regardless, the error again forced the diggers to take the time and make the extra effort to cut the wall back to plumb. Problems continued. The sides of the next section of cutting were smooth, but they did not run vertical. Another episode of corrective cutting followed, bringing the sides of the deepening hole back to the vertical (Ashbee 1989e: 32). The diggers had more success with the next section: they cut the chalk straight and smooth. No repairs were needed.

On its own, each section was just deep enough so that when standing on the floor of the hole, one of the diggers could reach up with the hands above his head and touch the smoothed walls of the previous section. They dug deeper. This next, new section was out of true, and they spent more time cutting the top and bottom of the wall back to the vertical. By now the diggers were deep below the ground surface: if four diggers could have made a human ladder (with one standing at the bottom and the other three standing on the shoulders of the digger below), then the person at the top would just about have been able to reach up and rest his hand on the surface of the ground at the mouth of the hole. At this depth, diggers moved into and out of the shaft using ropes and baskets, just as they removed chalk and debris from the hole. The next section that they dug was straight, and the transition to the section below that (a shorter one; 1.5 m) also was smooth and trouble free. After this, mistakes started again. The next section badly lost its line and the diggers had to cut deep into the slanting wall to pull it back to vertical.

They never finished the next section they started cutting; after half of the depth it should have reached, the diggers stopped (Figure 4.4). They left the walls ragged and the bottom uneven. A blow from a digger's pick sliced into the chalk, and opened a fissure from which water started seeping into the hole (Ashbee 1989e: 33). This final section was never straightened or completed; they left the walls out of vertical, and they left the bottom unflattened. They did not dress the antler-picked walls with their metal axes. They stopped digging.

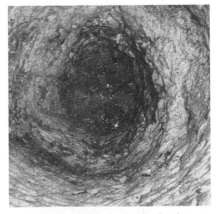

FIGURE 4.4 Wilsford Shaft: dug to the bottom. Image copyright Edward Ashbee; used with permission.

By the time they struck the last blows of antler pick against chalk wall and scooped the debris into a basket and hoisted it up to the top, that last digger was standing with wet feet deep below the ground surface: a depth equal to the heights of fifteen adult diggers standing one on the shoulders of the next. With the water flowing into the shaft at its base, further digging was impossible. Was that digger content? Was she frustrated? Was this what they all had wanted to happen? Was the person standing at the bottom scared? Would she brag about it to those waiting on the surface up above, standing in the daylight? What did she think, getting wet down below, out of sight, in the damp dark?

Interpreting Wilsford: Function or Ritual?

The 1960s excavators of this deep shaft at Wilsford and their successors paid much attention to determining the function of the hole. Was it a well? Was it a place where ritual or special ceremonies took place? The authors of the final report disagree over the function (Ashbee 1989a; Bell 1989): one prefers a functional explanation (the hole was a well); another argues for a ceremonial use (the hole was place of special deposits). Some analysts interpret the finds dug out of the hole as incidental accumulation and argue that the shaft went out of use when water flooded its lowest part. Indeed the latter suggestion finds support in the unfinished state of the final few dozen centimeters of the shaft: the angle of the digging on one of the shaft's side, the smaller diameter, the undressed pick marks. Some interpreters point to the evidence for animal-related activities near the shaft to suggest that the shaft functioned as a well; indeed remains of wooden buckets at the base support this interpretation.

The Contents of the Hole

The excavation report (Ashbee et al. 1989d) provides a detailed presentation and discussion of the methods of excavation and of the material uncovered by the teams that worked at the site between 1960 and 1962.[1] Interested readers will find there the excavation materials and debate between Paul Ashbee and Martin Bell. A full synthesis of the materials recovered in sequence as excavated is included in the appendix at the end of this book.

As is more fully represented in the appendix, excavation tracked the recovery of materials in five generally distinct parts (Figure 4.5): an uppermost, most recent, filling of a funnel-shaped cone, with little archaeological material;

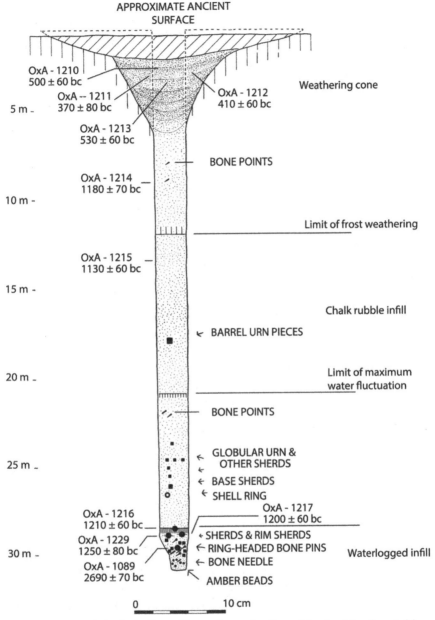

APPROXIMATE ANCIENT
SURFACE

OxA - 1210
500 ± 60 bc

OxA -- 1211
370 ± 80 bc

OxA - 1212
410 ± 60 bc

Weathering cone

5 m

OxA - 1213
530 ± 60 bc

BONE POINTS

OxA - 1214
1180 ± 70 bc

10 m

Limit of frost weathering

OxA - 1215
1130 ± 60 bc

15 m

Chalk rubble infill

BARREL URN PIECES

20 m

Limit of maximum
water fluctuation

BONE POINTS

25 m

← GLOBULAR URN &
    OTHER SHERDS
← BASE SHERDS
← SHELL RING

OxA - 1216
1210 ± 60 bc

OxA - 1217
1200 ± 60 bc

OxA - 1229
1250 ± 80 bc

← SHERDS & RIM SHERDS
← RING-HEADED BONE PINS
← BONE NEEDLE

Waterlogged infill

30 m

OxA - 1089
2690 ± 70 bc

← AMBER BEADS

0   10 cm

FIGURE 4.5 Wilsford Shaft profile (redrawn by Sveta Matskevich after Ashbee
et al. 1989a, figures 7, 8, 64).

below that, a section (from 1–3.5 m in depth) with few finds; below that, a section (from 3.4–12 m) that had remained open to weathering for some time and which contained more finds; below that, a lower section (from 12–21 m) that contained a similar number and range of finds; and a lowest section (below 21 m) that contained the greatest amount of material in the best state of preservation. Human bone was found in very low numbers and never in articulation. The director of the original excavation (Paul Ashbee) and the coordinator of the project that completed the post-excavation analysis and brought the results to publication (Martin Bell) interpreted the site in significantly different ways.

The Shaft as Well

Martin Bell makes a strong and clear argument that Wilsford functioned as a well that people used in the Middle Bronze Age to water livestock (Bell 1989: 128–133; see also Bradley 1975: 50; Osborne 1969: 564). Bell builds a wide base for his conclusion with a detailed reconstruction of the character of the land, environment, and climate of the Bronze Age terrain around the site. He points to a range of convincing evidence, arguing that the landscape around the shaft was grazed grassland, probably with the same grassland plants (such as *Festuca ovina/rubra* or *Carex humilis*) that are found on the chalklands in modern times (Robinson 1989: 88). In addition he adds the insect evidence (particularly the beetle remains), the presence of grass taxa among the pollen, the presence of grassland fungi (puffballs), the presence of bird species characteristic of open downlands (the skylark), and the presence of toads, frogs, pygmy shrews, and field voles, all of which suggest longer grasses nearby.

Based on Caroline Grigson's analysis, the evidence of aborted and neonatal lambs (Grigson 1989: 107) suggests that sheep-breeding (or at least birthing) took place near the shaft. In addition, the presence of beetles of the genera *Geotrupes, Aphodius,* and *Onthophagus* suggests a local environment in which herbivore dung was present (Osborne 1989: 97). The argument for animal herding is strong. Present as well is evidence for the planting of crops. In addition to cereal taxa among the pollen, the charred seeds of barley, emmer wheat, and flax suggest that part of the landscape was under cultivation (Robinson 1989). Using evidence of mollusc species/taxa and sediment character (the presence of *aeolian* silts), Bell reconstructs an environment at Wilsford that is drier than the present one in which the modern diggers excavated the shaft.

Bell argues that the faunal remains found in the shaft (the lambs and the small vertebrates) are accidental inclusions: they simple fell in. He notes that the human bone found in the upper section of the shaft has provided dates that place it 800 years after the original shaft cutting and the activities represented in the lowest finds. Bell contends that the shaft was not part of a settlement or the focus of sustained or significant human activity that might have been linked specifically to the location of the hole. He notes the difference between the types of artifacts found in the shaft and the types of artifacts found in deposits in contemporary settlement sites or wells: the Wilsford material lacks the variety of finds that characterize those other sites and it does not contain evidence for significant crop activity (i.e., few cereal seeds and little crop-processing waste).

While there is little evidence that the shaft was part of a settlement, the analysis of the beetle remains (particularly an abundance of furniture beetle, *Anobium punctatum*, which requires dry seasoned wood) suggests that a wooden structure stood at the top of the shaft in prehistory (Osborne 1989: 97). Based on the abundant presence of beetle species associated with stored food (i.e., *Ptinus fur*) and particularly of dry materials such as granary waste or stored animal food (i.e., *Stegobium paniceum*), Bell argues that the structure at the top of the shaft was perhaps a barn containing stored food.

Bringing all of this well-disciplined evidence together, Bell concludes that Wilsford functioned as a well for watering livestock that grazed the land around the shaft, and that there was a wooden building at the top of the shaft in which people stored animal feed. The recognition that the most common artifacts from the bottom of the shaft were tools that were used to bring water to the surface and to give it to animals (i.e., buckets and rope, plus a scoop) supports this argument (Figure 4.6). As a stimulus for digging the well, Bell suggests a prehistoric population expansion and a coincident, more intensive arable and pastoral land-use in a landscape where the limited availability of water had prevented expansion in earlier periods.

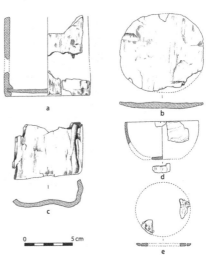

FIGURE 4.6 Wilsford Shaft: buckets, rope, scoop (redrawn by Sveta Matskevich after Ashbee et al. 1989a, figure 51).

The Shaft as Ritual

In an alternative interpretation of the hole at Wilsford, Paul Ashbee has argued (as have others: Piggott 1973, Ross 1968) that the site had a ritual function.[2] Ashbee relies on a review of comparable shaft-sites in the UK and Europe, on an assessment of the effort required to make the shaft, on the types of artifacts and animal bone found in the shaft, and on the position of Wilsford in the nearby Stonehenge landscape. Arguing against the proposal that Wilsford was a well, Ashbee suggests that it would have made more sense to move animals to the River Avon (3 km to the southeast) than to dig a hole in the chalk to a depth of 30 m. He suggests that the shaft did indeed fill with water, and that this is what some (such as Bell) might expect of a well. Ashbee's interpretation of the presence of water in the shaft, however, is that the hole was sunk for non-utilitarian reasons and that it had to be abandoned after its diggers unexpectedly struck the water-bearing fissure (Ashbee 1989a: 137).

Ashbee suggests that no more than two people could have worked at the same time in the shaft, perhaps with one person digging with a pick or an axe and the other filling baskets with rubble and sending them up to the surface (Ashbee 1989a: 134). Additional estimates and calculations propose that the diggers could have removed 76.2 kg of material per hour and that at this rate, the complete digging of the shaft would have taken 3,300 hours or 420 eight-hour days of work (Ashbee 1989a: 134). In addition to the time thus calculated to dig the shaft, Ashbee adds time for the removal and dumping of the chalk from the shaft, the construction of the bank at the surface, as well as the shaping of the walls of the shaft with axes and measuring and making plumb the direction of the diameter of the hole as it was being dug. A final estimate is offered for the time needed to dig the hole: a year's work by ten people (Ashbee 1989a: 134). The manner of cutting the shaft is also important. The attention to carefully dressing the walls of the shaft as the diggers deepened it, meter by meter, with broad-bladed axes suggests to Ashbee an attention to detail that would have been unnecessary in constructing a well for purely utilitarian purposes (Ashbee 1989a: 137). In addition, Ashbee suggests that particular members of communities were closely involved with the planning and digging of this shaft and others, and that these individuals "could not be other than the precursors of the Druids" (Ashbee 1989a: 134).

Ashbee makes comparisons with other shaft sites in the UK and continental Europe. He refers to the three shafts (the deepest reached 36 m) at Holzhausen *Viereckschanze*, a quadrilateral earthwork enclosure of late La Tene date (late Iron Age) in southern Germany (Schwarz 1960, 1962, 1975). Ashbee draws attention to the presence of a vertical timber placed in the bottom of one of the Holzhausen shafts and the presence around its base of traces of organic compounds and the late Bronze Age loomweights that were found in its fill (Ashbee 1989a: 134); he suggests that this is evidence for a formal deposit (Ashbee 1989a: 137). In addition Ashbee refers to shaft sites from various periods of British prehistory, as at Maumbury Rings (late Neolithic; 2900–2200 cal. B.C.) where a series of shafts had been sunk to depths of up to 10.5 m in the bank of a henge monument (Bradley 1975), at Canon Hill in Berkshire (Bradley et al. 1978), and at Eaton Heath, Norwich (Wainright 1973).

To strengthen his case, Ashbee looks to Celtic iconography, myths, and literature, as well as to the classical world of the ancient Mediterranean (Ashbee 1989a: 134), noting that "it has not always been possible to reconcile the contents of the majority of these shafts with material considerations. This has led to the belief that they had a ritual function" (Ashbee 1989a: 134). Ashbee introduces evidence (in his terms "oblique support") to back up his interpretation, referring first to possible connections between shafts and springs and lakes into which votive offerings were made. References come from the literature of Irish myth (e.g., the *Cath Maighe Tuireadh* [The Battle of Magh Tuireadh] and its accounts of warriors being thrown into a well over which spells were cast), and from scenes on Celtic metalwork (e.g., the Gundestrup cauldron [Late La Tène, 200 B.C.–A.D. 300] and scenes depicted on it of victims thrust down a shaft).

Next, Ashbee discusses classical references to the role of pits and shafts in ritual and religious activities: the cover of the *mundus* in Italian cities and in the Palatine, Pausanias' description of priests' rites performed over pits at Titane in Sicyonia, Philstratus' discussion of ceremonies performed in the "hollow earth," and Homer's references to *bothroi* (garbage pits) as connections to the underworld and as appropriate features into which to make offerings. Furthermore, Ashbee emphasizes the location of the shaft in the Stonehenge landscape, suggesting that the shaft may have been sunk in connection with or response to particular phases of alteration of the Stonehenge monument, specifically the dismantling and removal of a timber-framed component at the site, marked by the empty Y- and Z-holes (Ashbee 1989a: 135).

For additional support, Ashbee turns to the shaft contents, particularly the wooden artifacts, animal bones, and the large amounts of "amorphous organic material" (Ashbee 1989a: 135). The presence of these materials in the shaft inspired first thoughts that the shaft had a ritual significance (Ashbee 1963), a view that found support (or at least repetition) from others (Piggott 1965: 232; 1973: 383; 1975: 89; 1978: 50; Ross 1967: 25–26; 1968: 257; Coles and Harding 1979: 263; Megaw and Simpson 1979: 27; Burl 1981: 205–206).

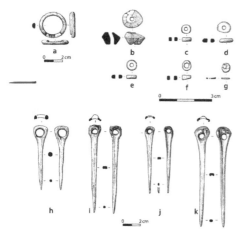

FIGURE 4.7 Wilsford Shaft: bead ring and pins (redrawn by Sveta Matskevich after Ashbee et al. 1989a, figures 43 and 45).

Ashbee views the shale ring, the amber beads, and the bone pins as votive deposits (Figure 4.7); they were items of personal adornment that could not have been merely discarded or lost (Ashbee 1989a: 137). He suggests that these objects would have been considered grave-goods in the burials of the region that date to the period when the shaft was dug. Ashbee highlights the presence of animal bone, particularly the greater parts of two young sheep, the bones of which bear butchery marks, near the bottom of the shaft. These he sees as evidence for ceremonies that took place at the shaft top (Ashbee 1989a: 137); additional animal remains found throughout the higher levels of the fill, Ashbee interprets as evidence of the reoccurrence of similar ceremonies that took place over the half century during which the shaft filled.

In the final section of his argument for the ritual significance of Wilsford, Ashbee raises the important point that even if the shaft was intended as a well (and this may indeed have had a functional meaning), the process of sinking the shaft would have been "an incursion into the unknown and the unpredictable" (Ashbee 1989a: 136). Perhaps, as Ashbee observes, the remnant 9.0 m wide depression in the surface of the ground (Figure 4.8) after the shaft had filled (i.e., which identified the site, mistakenly, as it turned out to be classified as a "pond barrow") was a reference to the location of a previous set of activities, potentially ritual and not merely to the shaft as an abandoned water well. In all of this Ashbee is careful to state that much of the activities and meanings of shaft sites "evade the strict application of archaeological inference" (Ashbee 1989a: 136).

Wilsford in Its Middle Bronze Age Context

Another way to try to understand why the people at Wilsford cut the ground in the way, and to the depth that they did, is to place those activities into the local context of the Middle Bronze Age (MBA). The landscape into which the MBA diggers cut the 30 m hole was a busy place. As more than a hundred years of modern archaeological work shows, it contains records and results of

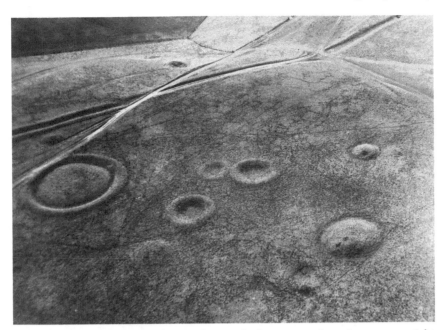

FIGURE 4.8 Wilsford Shaft: aerial view before excavation. Image copyright Edward Ashbee; used with permission.

many engagements with the ground, its stone, sediments, soils, and chalk. Some of these interventions into the ground date to centuries before the days when the diggers cut the shaft at Wilsford, back to the Neolithic. Other activities were of more recent times, the second millennium and the Early Bronze Age (EBA) (Figure 4.9). Yet other traces in the Wilsford landscape would not be made until later periods: the Iron Age and after. On the days of the second millennium when the Wilsford diggers stood on the ground surface next to their deepening hole, they could look in any direction around them and see the results of other people's efforts to move and work with dirt and stone, chalk and turves.

There were few trees around the Wilsford hole, and the diggers' views would have been unobstructed. Most of what they saw were low mounds rising up from the earth, no more than a meter in height and seldom more than five or six meters in diameter. Under almost each of these surface protrusions of earth rested the skeleton of a person whose death ritual had included the mounding of the earth and the insertion of the remains into the ground, and the placement of tools, jewelry, and pottery. Two of these mounds were close to the hole at Wilsford: one just 100 m to the south; another twice that distance to the northeast. The diggers could see a group of another four mounds, 400 m to the northwest. Within a relatively small area (i.e., 1500 m

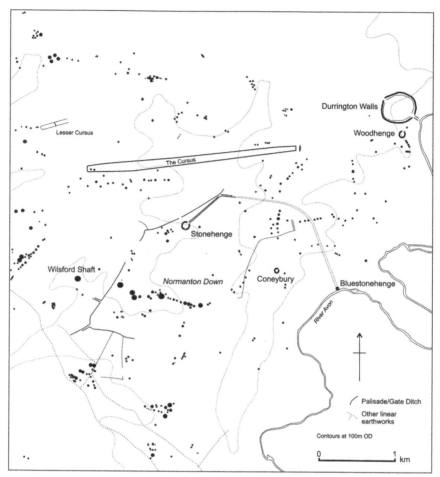

FIGURE 4.9 Wilsford landscape (redrawn by Sveta Matskevich after figure prepared by Joshua Pollard).

in any direction from the hole), there were more than one hundred of these small bumps of mounded earth risen up from the surface of the ground. Some formed clustered groups or linear arrangements; others wandered out on their own, unaccompanied.

Today we might best think of this landscape as one dominated by death. Indeed, 1200 m to the east of the Wilsford hole is a circle of massive upright stones first erected sometime over a millennium before the diggers cut their shaft (i.e., Stonehenge). Recent geophysical survey has shown the intense record of human activity throughout the landscape (Gaffney et al. 2012). In this busy and crowded landscape, the deep hole that the Wilsford diggers cut was unusual. It did not become the final resting place for a body and grave-goods; no skeleton was placed into it, though the twentieth-century diggers who excavated the shaft found some disarticulated human bone. The people doing the Middle Bronze Age digging had something else in mind, though precisely what they had intended, archaeologists have struggled to determine. What is clear is that 3,200 years ago, the people holding their antler and metal tools had been driven to break the surface of the ground in very precise and particular ways, to considerable depth.

Archaeological Context: Community, Society, *Comparanda*, Explanation

The standard way to understand the digging actions at Wilsford is to place the hole cut into the ground into its archaeological context. In terms of southern British prehistory, the Wilsford shaft sits in the Middle Bronze Age (1500–1000 cal B.C.). Recent syntheses (Brück 1999, 2000), interpretation (Barrett 1994b; Sharples 2010), and fieldwork (Barrett et al. 1991; Drewett 1982) provide a clear sense of contemporary life in this part of Britain. People lived in small farmsteads and divided the surrounding landscapes into fields where they planted, tended, and harvested cereals, and where they manipulated the breeding and death of herded animals. Small cemeteries of (mainly) crema-tion burials were located near the farmsteads.

Small groups (perhaps ten to twenty individuals) lived in the farmsteads comprising three or four buildings clustered around storage pits dug into the ground or near storage structures raised up on timber legs. Usually, a farm-stead had one larger building (round in floor-plan, with a pitched roof), built of large timber posts, set upright in holes dug into the ground, arranged in a rough circle. This main structure often had a rectangular extension built at its entrance, which we might recognize, today, as a porch. A good example of an MBA farmstead from this region is Down Farm in Wiltshire: a homestead constructed, lived in, and rebuilt in three phases of occupation lasting, in total, no more than one hundred years (Barrett et al. 1991).

Down Farm

At Down Farm, people erected two circular buildings within a wider system of fields (Figure 4.10). The larger building (Structure A) was a circle of eight posts enclosing a 64 sq. m area: on the building's southeast side was a four-posted entry porch (Barrett et al. 1991: 186). The builders of Down Farm nor-mally constructed these porches by digging holes wider than those dug for the

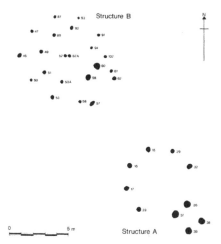

FIGURE 4.10 Down Farm Structure A and B (redrawn by Sveta Matskevich after Barrett et al. 1991: figures 5.29 and 5.30).

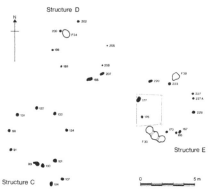

FIGURE 4.11 Down Farm Structure C, D, and E (redrawn by Sveta Matskevich after Barrett et al. 1991: figures 5.34, 5.35, 5.36).

larger, main part of the structure, and by placing wide timber posts upright into the porch holes. The construction materials used for the porch were sturdier and, perhaps, more impressive, than were those used for the rest of the building. At Down Farm, the pattern of unusually wide holes and thick posts is particularly clear in this, the first phase of construction.

Ten meters northwest of Structure A, the people erected a smaller building (Structure B), enclosing a 44 sq. m area and built with two concentric rings of posts: an inner ring (5.0 m diameter) of eight posts and an outer one (7.5 m diameter) of eleven posts. The entrance to Structure B was smaller than for Structure A, and though B had no clear porch extension, two of the holes dug for posts in B were unusually large, similar to what one might expect of a porch (Barrett et al. 1991: 186). Associated with both Structures A and B were extramural alignments of fence posts that enclosed the open space nearest to the buildings, perhaps to pen animals or maybe to mark out yards connected to the buildings, their inhabitants, and the activities taking place in each.

Some time later (after maybe no more than twenty years or so), the people at Down Farm constructed new buildings (Structures C, D, and E) in the farmstead's second phase: three round structures made of circles of holes into which the builders placed upright large timber posts (Figure 4.11). Around the southern, eastern, and northeastern edges of the small settlement, people dug a ditch (1.0 m. deep, 2.0 m wide), and used the excavated soil and chalk to make a bank along the ditch's western (interior) side. This ditch-and-bank limited access to the area of the buildings from the surrounding landscape: access was now only possible from the west and north (Barrett et al. 1991: 206).

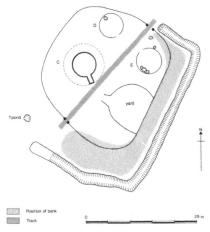

At the same time, they dug about three dozen holes (spaced at 2.5 m intervals) in a line running through the middle of the farmstead and connecting one end of the ditch to the other. Into the holes they stood timber posts to create a fenced palisade. The construction of the palisade and ditch created a 750 sq. m enclosed settlement bounded from the surrounding fields. A track ran through the middle of the farmstead (from the northeast

FIGURE 4.12 Down Farm Phase 2 (redrawn by Sveta Matskevich after Barrett et al. 1991: 5.41).

to southwest; at the track's ends stood gates at the ditch's termini (Barrett et al. 1991: 190) (Figure 4.12).

Of the three round structures inside the enclosure during this second phase of building, one (Structure C) was larger than the others (ten posts enclosing an interior with a 5.5 m diameter), and had a porch extension to the southeast; unlike the porch of Structure A of the previous phase, the holes and timber posts of the Structure C porch were no larger nor deeper than the others used to make the building. The porch faced a yard to the southeast. Neither of the other two buildings in this later architectural phase (Structures D and E) had porch extensions. Structure D (seven posts around an interior with a 5.0 m diameter) and E (eight posts encircling a 5 m diameter interior) were both smaller than Structure C. Structures D and E contained storage pits dug into their floors (Barrett et al. 1991: 206), and attached to both D and E were fences made of smaller wooden posts (Barrett et al. 1991: 198). At the southwestern end of the ditch was a small pond or water-catch hole, 1.5 m in diameter though only 0.2 m deep (Barrett et al. 1991: 198, 208).

In Down Farm's third and final building phase, the inhabitants reorganized the layout of buildings and activities more substantially (Barrett et al. 1991: 208) by digging a rectilinear grid of forty holes (almost all 10 cm deep and 10 cm in diameter) in three lines, and placing posts in them to construct a building (Structure F) 18 m long, 3.5 m wide along the eastern edge of

Structure F

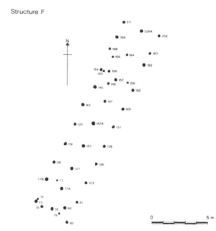

0 ━━━━━━ 5 m

FIGURE 4.13 Down Farm Phase 3, structure F (redrawn by Sveta Matskevich after Barrett et al. 1991: 5.37 modified with 5.28).

the enclosed area (Barrett et al. 1991: 198) (Figure 4.13). With its parallel lines of ten or eleven wooden posts, Structure F is unusual and difficult to interpret. The posts are placed 2.0–3.0 m apart; their arrangement at the building's northern end suggests a possible entrance and perhaps a separate room or building segment. The close spacing of F's posts would have made the interior space of the building difficult to move through (Barrett et al. 1991: 198), or at least would have resulted in a building with many small individual enclosed spaces or rooms.

Activities in the Buildings and at the Site

People ate their meals in the larger buildings at Down Farm, (i.e., the proportion of fine-ware pottery found in these structures was high), or they made and repaired their tools (particularly of flint), spun and wove textiles (i.e., loomweights were found in Structure B), or kept, used, stored, and displayed special objects made of chalk. The smaller round buildings were places for different activities: butchering animal carcasses, grinding cereal grains (as suggested by the stone rubber found in Structure A), and storing processed foodstuffs (Brück 1999: 150).

People discarded material into the ditch they dug in the second phase of Down Farm: fragments of pottery, flint flakes and cores (as well as flint tools), and a stone rubber (Barrett et al. 1991: 200, 203) (Figure 4.14). Sometime later, they added the lower jaws of six cattle, the skulls of two dogs, and the skull of a cow (Barrett et al. 1991: 203, 205). The largest amount of pottery thrown in the ditch, however, accumulated after those early, initial ditch depositions; as with the pottery discarded in the earlier periods, this later material represents large (though not complete) parts of individual vessels, mostly pots used for mundane common activities. Among these later additions were more dog skulls and one of a cow (Barrett et al. 1991), and five more stone rubbers (Barrett et al. 1991: 203). The final phase of ditch deposits contains few artifacts (only 125 sherds) when compared with the 1,245 in the second phase; only 907 flakes and cores (com-

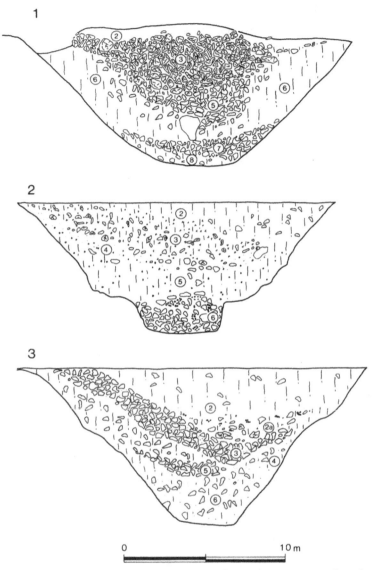

FIGURE 4.14 Down Farm Ditch sections (redrawn by Sveta Matskevich after Barrett et al. 1991: 5.32).

pared with 4,234 deposited earlier); the majority of ditch deposits from this period is burned flint (Barrett et al. 1991: 200).

The contents of the ditch provide the most reliable information for understanding the farmstead diet; animal bones had been gnawed by scavenging animals after discard, and conclusions remain tentative. By using the number of animal jaws to get an accurate picture of animal consumption, it is clear that the majority of discarded bone was of sheep; cattle was less common, and pig was very infrequent (Barrett et al. 1991: 203). The Down Farm settlers bred and managed their herds of sheep for their meat (i.e., most sheep were killed before they were two years of age) and their cattle for milk production (Barrett et al. 1991: 205).

Disposal of the Human Dead

Inhabitants of farmsteads like Down Farm cremated their dead and buried the ashes (often, though not always, in ceramic vessels) in selected places in the landscape near to but separate from the settlement. Though inhumation also occurred, cremation was most common. Aggregations of burned bone deposits formed small cemeteries no larger than needed to accommodate the extended cohabiting group of the associated farmstead. When people put the cremated skeleton into a pottery vessel, sometimes they placed the pot upside down in the burial pit: the mouth of the pot facing the ground. Other pots containing ashes were placed rightway up. Grave-goods were few in number: often it was only the pot that contained the cremation.

At Down Farm the remains of eighteen people (inhumations and cremations) were buried 145 m southwest of the farmstead, where, many centuries earlier (in the Late Neolithic), people had dug a circular ditch (15 m across) that they had filled with flint knapping debris among other material, had recut the ditch twice in later uses, and later covered it with a layer of flint (Barrett et al. 1991: 88). The Down Farm people recut part of this ditch and used it as their cemetery (Barrett et al. 1991: 211–214) (Figure 4.15).

Of the Down Farm burials, thirteen were cremations, grouped in an area to the south and southeast of an earlier Late Neolithic earthwork (Barrett et al. 1991: 211). Six of the cremations were of individual adult skeletons; four of these had been buried with sherds of globular or bucket urns, and one burial had two animal bones deposited with it. Two other cremations were double burials of adult and child: one an adult buried with a six- to nine-year-old, the other an adult with a three- to seven-year-old—the former had been buried with sherds of a globular urn. Four cremations were of indeterminate age and sex; two of these were accompanied with sherds of bucket- or globular-urns.

Of the five inhumations, one was a child (three to five years old), one a juvenile (ten to twelve years old), and three were adults: one a male, twenty-five to thirty-five years old; one a female of indeterminate age; and one of indeterminate age and sex. In addition to the cremations and inhumations, a handful of unburnt human remains (eleven bones) from the bodies of two adults and

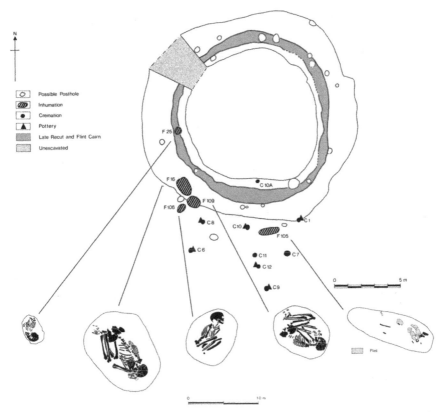

FIGURE 4.15 Down Farm cemetery and burials (redrawn by Sveta Matskevich after Barrett et al. 1991: 5.44 and 5.45).

one infant was found scattered in the northern portion of the Late Neolithic ring ditch (Barrett et al. 1991: 214). It is difficult to see any clear pattern of social structure or patterning from this burial record (Sharples 2010: fig 5.12; see Barrett et al. 1991).

Field Systems

A striking characteristic of MBA Britain is the way that people divided the previously open landscape into systems of fields, separating one from the other by linear boundaries made of stones cleared from plowed and planted areas. Field size would have accommodated farming with a traction plow (most likely pulled by cattle), in addition to less-intensive farming with spade and hoe. People probably organized the timings of planting and harvesting to increase the yields from the areas under cultivation: reducing periods when

fields were left fallow (Barrett 1994b). As cultivation of individual fields inten-
sified, soils eroded; the stone, field boundaries trapped hill-washed soils, both
preventing greater erosion and further strengthening the size and appearance
of the field borders (Barrett 1994b: 148). Individual field systems were associated with individual farmsteads, such as Down Farm. The evidence for MBA
field systems and the economic activities associated with them is common in
this and other regions of Britain (e.g., Dartmoor).

Odd Deposits: Holes and Putting Things in Them

The digging of the ditch at Down Farm (and the sequences of deposits made
into it) offers one example of the inhabitants opening up holes in the ground
and then placing objects into them. The cemetery provides a second example.
With the ditch deposits, it is not difficult to understand the inclusion of the
pottery, bone, and flint as the disposal of rubbish, though as discussed in
chapter 1 a vibrant discussion exists about deposition as potentially intentional, rule-bound behavior. With the placement of the skeletons or the cremated skeletons into the pits in the cemetery, it is equally easy to recognize
these actions as not unusual, as the locally appropriate ways to treat the
deceased.

Less easily explained is the discovery of Down Farm farmsteaders' unusual placements of objects into holes in the ground. Thus, they placed a flint
core in a posthole in Structure B (Barrett et al. 1991: 203) and other flint cores
in the postholes of the perimeter fence-palisade in the site's second phase
(Barrett et al. 1991: 203). Indeed in one posthole from the outer perimeter of
Structure B, they put four flint cores. In addition, they placed flint scrapers in
postholes in Structures A and B, as well as in the holes of the perimeter fence
posts; they put a fabricator in another posthole in A, and in Structure E they
put a whetstone in a posthole there (Barrett et al. 1991: 203).

At contemporary sites, people were placing objects in holes in the ground
in similar ways. At Black Patch in Sussex, they placed a bronze awl in the left-
hand posthole of Hut 3's porch (Drewett 1982). At Itford Hill in Sussex, someone placed the lower grinding stone of a quern-set in the bottom of a pit in
Hut E (Brück 1999: 152); at the same site, someone placed a chalk phallus
(standing straight up and erect) on the bottom of a posthole of Hut D's entrance structure (Burstow and Holleyman 1957: 176). At Crab Farm in Dorset,
they dug a pit into a ditch and then placed in it the articulated skeleton of a
pregnant sheep and a pregnant cow (Wymer and Brown 1995: 153; Brück 1999:
152). At South Dumpton Park in Kent, people dug a pit into the bottom of a
ditch and placed in it four palstaves arranged on their edges in the shape of a

fan. On top of the palstaves they put a piece of tabular flint and one fragmentary and one complete bracelet (Brück 1999: 152). Even more intriguing is the small amount of cremated human bone (9 g) that someone placed in one of the porch postholes of Structure 5 at Broom Quarry in Bedfordshire (Mortimer and McFadyen 1999; Brück 2006: 300).

Joanna Brück has called these actions "event-marking deposits" (Brück 2006: 298).³ Brück suggests that people made them "as a means of controlling the passage of time or the transformation from one social state to another (e.g., from the living to the dead)" (Brück 1999: 159). She argues that people put objects into holes in the ground (usually postholes) at critical times in the life cycle of the house, of the pit, or of the settlement (Brück 2006: 300). In this way, people celebrated the construction, repair, remodeling, and abandonment of a building by placing particular objects into the building's postholes, particularly into holes located in critical points of settlement space: boundaries, entrances, and corners (Brück 2006: 298, 300). Brück argues that people intended these depositions to maintain the household subsistence cycles and the communities' social relations (Brück 1999: 154). This may be the case, but why celebrate in this way? Why put objects into the ground? Why these objects and why these holes? Why holes at all? What are the characteristics of a hole in the ground that makes it an appropriate (and powerful enough?) place to invoke transformative acts? We could begin to find answers in these questions in the discussion of the philosophy and perceptual characters of holes examined in the previous chapter; we will return to those discussions at the end of this chapter.

Looking again at the archaeological features of the Down Farm settlements, we notice that there were pits and holes at the site in addition to the building- and fence-posts and the large eastern enclosure ditch. In phase one, the Down Farm inhabitants dug a circular hole (Pit 13) almost a meter wide and over half a meter deep (Figure 4.16). With straight sides and a flat base, Pit 13 contained few artifacts, but had two layers of fill: one of chalk fragments, the other of humus (Barrett et al. 1991: 190, fig. 5.31). In phase two, they dug a similarly sized and shaped hole (F 34) in the ground inside Structure D; they dug another pit (F 36), half the size of F 34, just beyond the outer wall of the same structure (Barrett et al. 1991: 194, fig. 5.31). They filled the hole inside the structure (F 34) first with a layer of chalk rubble (i.e., at the lower level) and then a layer of unmixed topsoil on top of it. They filled the smaller hole outside the wall (F 36) with more chalk rubble (Barrett et al. 1991: 194).

In this second phase of building at Down Farm, outside the northeastern wall of Structure E, people dug a round hole (F39: 0.75 m in diameter, 0.38 m deep) with steeply sloping sides and a rounded bottom (Barrett et al.

Pit 30 (A-C)

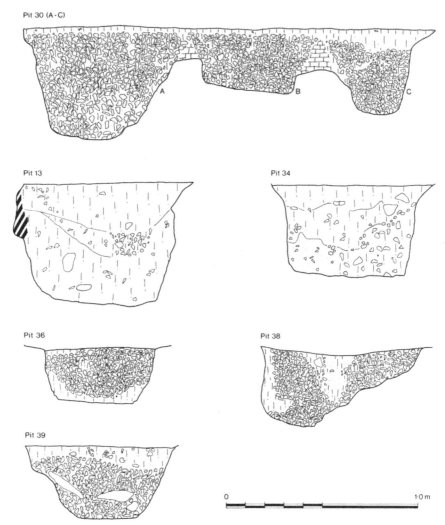

FIGURE 4.16 Down Farm pits 13, 30, 34, 36, 38, 39 (redrawn by Sveta Matskevich after Barrett et al. 1991: 5.31).

1991: 194; fig. 5.31). Just outside the southwestern wall of E, they dug three, steeply sided, flat-bottomed pits (Pit 30A–C) closely spaced in a line one next to the other: all were roughly circular with diameters between 0.75 and 0.55 m and depths ranging from 0.33 to 0.55 m (Barrett et al. 1991: 194). Probably, these three pits were used together at the same time; each was then filled with chalk rubble. To the northwest of structure E they dug another hole (F 38): 1.0 m diameter, 0.40 m deep and filled it with more chalk (Barrett et al. 1991: 194).

We could debate the functions of these holes. Why did the people dig them? Why in these particular places? What did they use these holes for? When and why did they fill them? We would struggle to move beyond anecdotal suggestion. One of the most useful ways that many archaeologists have handled them is with a rigorous discussion of acts of (potentially structured) deposition: thus Brück's intriguing comments on odd or event-marking deposits. In terms of this book's larger discussion of cutting holes and breaking the ground's surface, I suggest that the answers about functions and deposition—indeed the questions and the debates—are not necessarily relevant here. The critical point is that people in the MBA were regularly cutting holes into the ground (for one reason or another) and, eventually, putting things into those holes. Sometimes those insertions related to building construction. Sometimes they were part of the (pre)historically appropriate treatment of the dead. Other times they related to disposing of animal remains, broken pots, and disused flint tools and waste flakes. Other times, however, these actions are harder to understand in any rational, modern, Western way; this is particularly the case with the objects placed in particular postholes.

Understanding MBA Living: Social Explanation

Viewed from the long-term perspective of traditional archaeological explanation, one sees the MBA of southern Britain (as exemplified by Down Farm) in terms of diachronic changes in settlement and burial (i.e., in terms of what distinguishes the MBA from the preceding periods: the late Neolithic and the Early Bronze Age). In the earlier periods, people exploited a diverse range of subsistence resources as part of their seasonal movements through different environments. People (sometimes in large numbers) came together at particular places for short episodes (e.g., at large monumental constructions of stone and earth, but also at the source locations for raw materials, such as flint) and then these same people dispersed (Brück 2000: 281–282). It was a period defined by group and individual mobility across landscapes marked by ceremonial monuments (e.g., the earlier henges of the late Neolithic and the cemeteries of single burial mounds of the Early Bronze Age). People focused their attentions, energies, thoughts, and socio-ritual activities on these monuments (Brück 2000: 281).

In those earlier periods, people did not have strong, lasting links to particular places in the landscape (i.e., of the ground) as other people would later have in the MBA when they built structures like those at Down Farm. In the earlier periods, distinct groups of people shared access to parts of the landscape and shared rights to residences of tenure and use of landscape, ground, and its (functional and spiritual) resources. The social currency was the institution of the larger-scale group linked by lineage though birth (Brück 2000: 282). As Brück puts it, people moved around and through meaningful landscapes (Brück 2000: 282). Structuring the space of those landscapes were stone and wooden circles, complex burial structures, palisades, and grand banks and ditches. The result was that human movement was controlled through large-scale space, and the aggregation and dispersal of large groups of people across those landscapes (Brück 2000: 282).

This traditionally accepted, diachronic, and comparative perspective sees the MBA as a shift to a sedentary lifestyle, regulated by the daily activities of an agricultural existence; the enclosed settlements were foci of life within a landscape newly divided into field-systems. In social terms, this standard perspective recognizes a shift from a time dominated by ritual structures and ritual elites to a period when the social form of the household became preeminent (e.g., Sharples 2010: 235; Brück 2000).

The other significant change noted in the MBA is in the way that people treated the bodies of their cohabitants after death. Though not exclusively the case, the appropriate action was to burn the body. This is distinct from both the late Neolithic processes of excarnation, deposition, and circulation of disarticulated and articulated skeletons into stone-built burial structures (e.g., long-barrows), and the (following) Early Bronze Age practice of placing the articulated bodies (and grave-goods) into pits dug into the ground and then covering them with low mounds of dirt and stone. Furthermore, this diachronic and comparative distinction separates the EBA inclusion of objects in burials (metal body- and clothing-decoration, bone buttons, pottery vessels used for drinking or display) from the paucity of grave goods found with the MBA cremations and the mundane domestic character of the objects that are included (i.e., the globular or bucket urns, assumed to have been used for cooking and eating). The corresponding social reconstruction contrasts inequality and hierarchy of the EBA with less distinct (or absent) social distinction among the living in the MBA.

The MBA Senses of Being

John Barrett has argued that one of the consequences of the MBA emergence of landscapes of enclosed farmsteads within associated field systems was the appearance of a "place-bound sense of being" (Barrett 1994b: 147). What had been a generalized sense of community in the pre-MBA was fragmented into a pattern of more closed communities whose actions and senses of identity, relationships, resources, materials, and spiritual worlds focused on the farmstead structures and the small groups of people living in clearly defined places like Down Farm (Barrett 1994b: 147). Barrett suggests that we think of MBA society in terms of the fragmentation of landscape and of communities (Barrett 1994b: 147, 150).

Society was now constructed in smaller, more localized co-resident groups tethered to individual buildings (Brück 2000: 286), though whether we can think of these with modern Western concepts such as "houses" and "households" is less certain, probably unlikely, and assuredly ill advised. People's identity, integrity, and independence rested on the grounded position and location of a group that was bounded physically from others and segmented internally (Brück 2000: 286). Brück characterizes these communities as centripetal groups of people; the settlement and its buildings were "organizational hubs" for activities (Brück 2000: 288). Physical attachment to one particular place (Brück 2000: 288), to one specific area on the surface of the ground constituted a long-term social attachment to place.

Brück has argued that the MBA settlements, field systems, and the corresponding economy (of increased local cultivation) were the consequences of wider social transformations (Brück 2000: 76). Following Barrett, Brück takes the longer-term perspective, seeing a combination of sequential developments: the complex inhumations of individuals in the EBA, the consequent increase in the role that inheritance played in society, and the related interpersonal needs to define rights of inheritance through the control of agricultural production and human reproduction. Together these changes led to a social and political context within which emerged the MBA landscapes and settlement sites like Down Farm (Brück 2000: 276; Barrett 1991, 1994a, 1994b).

Though understood as a period of settling down (especially when compared to the preceding millennia of human behavior in southern Britain), and though the MBA-enclosed farmsteads are a clear sign of permanent residence of people in place, sites like Down Farm do not, however, argue for long-term occupational continuity at these settlements. An MBA hamlet of circular buildings may have remained in place for one or two, or even three, human generations (i.e., up to seventy-five years), but the longer-term pattern was one of shifting settlements to different places in the broader landscape of any one region.

What Is the Relevance to the Deep Hole at Wilsford?

How does this diachronic, archaeologically detailed, and traditionally informed knowledge of MBA settlement, burial, and economic and social action help us better understand the digging of the 30 m deep, straight-sided hole at Wilsford? The most obvious answer is that the new agricultural, field-system, farmstead-based economy depended on regular access to water for keeping livestock, for the potential irrigation of crops (though there is no extant evidence for this), and more generally for daily life and the domestic activities that took place at Down Farm and farmsteads like it. Indeed, as noted above, the archaeologist who excavated Down Farm identified a potential (though small) pond in the southwestern portion of the site. Similar hydro-features are known from other MBA farmstead sites and from sites dating to the preceding centuries As discussed below, the most widely followed interpretation of the function of Wilsford follows this thinking: the hole as a well to support animal grazing in the area (Bell 1989).

This may well have been the case. However, I suggest that an additional argument can be made that in its capacity as an exceptional example of breaking the surface with a perforation to great depth, the hole at Wilsford has other connections, ramifications, and consequences, less obvious initially, though perhaps more significant in terms of understanding daily life as it was lived and thought through in the MBA. This connection results from a reexamination of MBA attitudes to space, and of an extension of the work by Barrett and Brück.

Horizontality

Discussion of the spatial senses of MBA lifeways is not new. As noted above, the period is easily understood in terms of new spatial senses of being and of bounded space. The physical construction of agricultural field systems cutting up the otherwise open surfaces of the horizontally perceived landscape by making linear divisions is one manifestation of bounded space. The other is the physical and conceptual construction of the farmsteads, like Down Farm. On the one hand, farmsteads were self-contained, enclosed clusters of buildings, activities, peoples, things, and their corresponding local histories; people marked off these places from the surrounding landscape (by ditch-and-bank, palisaded fence, and formal gateways of settlement entrances and exits). At a second, intramural level, the farmsteads were internally organized and restricted zones of activities, food storage, processing and consumption, object deposition (whether the latter actions are seen as rubbish or as structured depositions), and the daily playing out of life in its locally appropriate actions and behaviors. At yet a third level, the space of the living was separated from the space of the dead: the location of a place deemed appropriate for the burial of the deceased at a distance from (though still associated with) the round buildings of the enclosed settlement.

These discussions have focused productively on the horizontal dimension. My proposal, however, is that we look anew at sites like Down Farm (and Wilsford) along the vertical dimension, and the way that the ordering, organization, and perception of the vertical played a role in how people thought about their lives, their surroundings, and their worlds, both physical and metaphysical. The crucial relevance of Wilsford and the MBA for the theme of this book is to be found where the vertical dimension collides with the land surface. Where the landed surface of living, of death, and of cultivation is met with a hole, there occurs a perforation of that physically G/grounded basis of the local MBA understanding of life in its specific and local senses of meaning and actions.

Verticality

If we agree that the horizontal division of land and social space of the MBA played a role in (or at least was part of a complex, ongoing, coming-into-being of) social action and praxis during this period, then what might we learn if we examined ways in which the people living in sites like Down Farm participated in space along the vertical dimension? As noted, it was deemed appropriate (consciously and explicitly, or implicitly and unnoticed) in the MBA to place the bodies of the deceased (many transformed by fire) into the ground. It was similarly appropriate to place fragments of pottery vessels, animal bones (some most likely as rubbish, other potentially as parts of other irregular actions, with historically specific meanings and intentions now unrecoverable), flint flakes, tools and cores into large, open pits at the boundaries of settlements: thus, the ditch at Down Farm. Also, it was appropriate to dig holes into the ground inside and outside (but close to) the buildings on MBA farmsteads. Archaeologically, we know only the final actions of placing materials into these holes: almost always chalk "rubble," and though it is not possible to be certain of the source of this chalk and soil, it is most likely that it came from the digging of other holes into the surface of the ground at the site.

In addition, it was considered appropriate in the MBA to place the bases of structurally critical components of buildings into holes that had been specially dug into the ground for them (i.e., the posts of the buildings of the farmsteads). In some cases, people made a conscious decision to place objects (flint cores, chalk objects, metal tools, and even, in at least one instance, small amounts of cremated human bone) into the holes left behind after one of these structurally supporting timbers had been removed, presumably after the building's original use (and meaning, perhaps) had expired. Often, as Brück has shown, people chose perforations of the ground surface at a particular location (of potential architectural, social, and perhaps spiritual significances) as receptacles for these objects: the flint cores in the postholes of Structure A and B and of the fence-palisade, as well as the whetstone in the Structure E posthole; and the similar actions from Black Patch, Itford Hill, Crab Farm, South Dumpton Park, and Broom Quarry.

If we step back from the traditional (as well as the more recent, and more theoretically robust) understandings of the structured, rule-bound roles of holes and hole-filling, then we may gain a new perspective on MBA daily thinking. I suggest that we accept the existing arguments (and detailed studies) both about the use of timber posts as architectural necessities and about the potential social and ritual roles of structured deposition. Both are discussions of value. What might be the consequence, however, if we suggest that what really mattered in the MBA, the thing that fashioned people's thinking as they went about building their round-structures, deposited the ashes of the deceased into the cemetery pits, tossed broken bits of pots into the ditch at the side of the site, and knelt down to put a chalk phallus into the hole left by a newly extracted (and recycled) timber post, was that each of these apparently disparate actions shared a common, deeply held, most probably subconscious connection? Each act took a person from the world supported by the ground and down into another world where different rules applied and from which altered perspectives emerged.

Does Wilsford Have a Single Function, Meaning, or Significance?

As with much (perhaps all) discussion of prehistoric constructions and artifacts, it is difficult to decide with certainty on a single function, use, or meaning. The problem that this creates, however, rests more with what archaeology attempts to achieve with its explanatory efforts than it does with actual prehistoric actions and thoughts. The authoritative detail of argument, evidence, and analysis that both Martin Bell and Paul Ashbee brought to the debate does nothing to resolve the issues of function or meaning. Two opposing explanations are offered, both equally possible. In his review of the Wilsford excavation publication, Richard Bradley suggested that both uses and meanings may have been in play (Bradley 1991). If this is the case, then we are left either unsatisfied or with a further discussion to engage. We need to move beyond the search for meaning and function, at least in the traditional way that archaeology searches for them.

The significance of the shaft may not be found in its contents (accidental or ritual) or in its potential use as a source for water. Rather the significance of the shaft may rest solely in the activities of its creation, in the digging down through the topsoil and into the white chalk (and in turn in its twentieth-century excavation, itself a project of cutting, and its politics and reputation within British archaeology; see appendix to this book). The shaft was used until it could no longer be used. Digging stopped when digging was no longer possible: when water started flowing into the bottom of the shaft in amounts that the diggers could not remove with their wooden buckets.

With the exception (perhaps) of the bucket and rope, there is nothing in the artifacts or bone found in the shaft that relates to its use. The material excavated by Proudfoot, Ashbee, and their teams all ended up in the fill of the shaft after the shaft's primary use had ceased. Pottery, flint flakes, scraps of human bone, animal bone all weathered into the hole as it filled. Might we also suggest that other finds, such as the amber and shale beads, have found their way into the hole in the same ways?

The Bronze Age significance of Wilsford may well have been in its digging, and in the *connundra*, debates, discussions, and solutions to Bronze Age engineering activities: how to get a digger (or diggers) down into and out of the shaft as it deepened; how to get the spoil excavated by those diggers up and out of the shaft; where to put the spoil; how to avoid falling chalk; what tools to use at what depth and for what purpose; where to get good tools to do the job; how to measure the diameter of the shaft with some precision so that the hole maintained its shape; how to keep people and animals from falling into the hole.

In the same way, we may see the modern 1960–1962 archaeological significance of Wilsford in the actions and consequences of its digging, and in the corresponding 1960s and 1980s interpretive disagreements and debates, indeed in the opposed proposals for the Bronze Age function of the site. The appendix to this book presents the 1960s digging process in the same detail that this chapter opened with a close replay of the MBA digging of the shaft. Twentieth-century health and safety legislation and concerns about the consequences of working at depth underground led to solutions that included scaffolding, lighting, air, a telephone, and a closed-circuit television system

FIGURE 4.17 Wilsford modern interior. Image copyright Edward Ashbee; used with permission.

(Figure 4.17). Perhaps most remarkable were the efforts expended on finding, installing, maintaining, repairing, and relying on technological solutions to continuing excavation safely and without interruption. We relive the sense of that modern process of digging down into the ground:

> At the outset, the only lighting was a 40W tungsten bulb in a plastic holder at the end of some well-worn flex and, because of the lack of cables and pipes, the generator and air compressor had been sited at the lip of the shaft with deafening effects, while field telephones had been found (but with stale batteries). Moreover, the platform had no shelter, so the mechanical hoist, supplied with a frayed cable, no shackle, and a heavy iron well-bucket, could not be controlled in the dark shaft, while there were neither safety fences nor nets to guard against objects being accidentally precipitated into the confines of the working area. As was anticipated, sudden heavy rain short-circuited the un-insulated lighting and stopped the generator, which was beyond the capacities of the contractor's workmen to restart.... The remaining 39 days were spent wrestling with the problems posed by the mal-sit-

ing of plant, inadequate lighting, continual electrical and mechanical failures, the lack of roofing, communication, and the inability of those responsible to provide a pump to stem the deep and ever-rising water. The Architect in Charge visited the site only once and did nothing, while the Ministry of Works' officials in London seemed ineffectual and unhelpful. (Ashbee 1989c: 146).

In fact, the greatest significance of Wilsford may well be the non-archaeological aspects of its excavation and interpretation: from the discussion and justification of the length of time between the completion of the excavations in 1962 and the final report, to the debate and disagreement over the Bronze Age function of the site, to the surprising lack of any subsequent discovery of a similar site. All of this attention and energies emerge out of and are drawn down into the site through its character as a hole in the ground, in the way and the depth to which it broke the surface of the landscape.

Of significance as well are the ways that the cutting of the shaft into Ground would have disrupted the existing understandings that the contemporary MBA diggers, viewers, visitors, and others held about their connections to the ground and to the ways that they understood their positions in their worlds. On the one hand, breaking the surface in this way, to this depth, was distinct from much other action and bodily work that had taken place, that was taking place, and that would take place in that local landscape: the adding to the surface of the land of dirt, soils, stones, bodies, and objects. On the other hand, cutting into the ground, making holes, putting objects into those holes (as seen clearly at sites like Down Farm) was a not-infrequent part of life (and of death, through the burial of cremated bodies in urns in cemeteries), and played a role that archaeologists have only tentatively voiced opinions about: thus Brück's discussion of odd or marking events.

The energy and essence of those G/grounded acts may best be understood in the significance that the ground surface had in contemporary senses of being and the potential conflict or threat that breaking that ground will have launched. These holes (the shaft at Wilsford and the small holes at Down Farm and other sites), seen as concavities created down into the ground would have drawn people's attention (probably subconsciously) to the actions carried out to make the holes, and to the intentional placement of objects and the more casual accumulation of materials in them. Perhaps our archaeological attentions, devoted to barrows, mounds, and stones (i.e., to convexities in the sense elaborated in the previous chapter) in this landscape have been misguided; have we elevated events and monuments to levels of significance beyond their original importance? By default, what happened in holes was important; who dug them, who did the placing, who filled them in and covered them up shared that significance, perhaps in an implicit, unstated manner. Objects placed within, labor exerted to create, also absorbed an unworldly significance through connection to the actions and consequences of breaking the surface.

Chapter 5

Cutting Bs

GORDON MATTA
CONICAL INTERS.   . 1975)

The Cut

IN THE MIDDLE of September 1975, a young American artist and two assistants picked up chisels and hammers, bow-saws, and an electric circular saw, and started cutting through the dirty, worn exterior wall of an empty seventeenth-century house in Paris's 4th arrondissement. Led by the artist, Gordon Matta-Clark, the team cut along lines they had drawn onto the 20 cm-thick plaster and wood wall (Jenkins 2011: 9). As they punched their hole through the house's northern side, Matta-Clark and his helpers threw the displaced rubble out and down where it piled onto the shattered timber joists, stone masonry, and plaster from neighboring houses that French workers had already demolished during a huge modernization project in the Les Halles district of the city.

Widening the hole in the exterior wall, Matta-Clark's team cut through the masonry and plaster, gradually expanding the perforation until it was 4.0 m in diameter; taller than the floor-to-ceiling height of the building's fourth floor (Figure 5.1). Looking up from the street, pedestrians saw the wide, precisely shaped hole but could not imagine that it was a normal architectural feature or a causal part of demolition; it was neither and both. Along the rue de Beaubourg below, drivers in their cars and delivery vans, passengers in taxis and busses, and local construction workers in adjacent buildings, looked up at the circle in the house wall and at the three men swinging hammers onto chisels and opening the wall with their saws.

From the street, people watched as every second or third hammer blow produced showers of plaster and lath spraying from the widening opening, dropping to the ground 20 m below. As the men worked, as people watched, and as the hole grew in size, the white plaster of the newly exposed edge stood out against the grime of the ancient wall, stained by time, and streaked with

FIGURE 5.1 View from rue de Beaubourg through *Conical Intersect* to the Centre Pompidou. Photo © Marc Petitjean; © 2017 Estate of Gordon Matta-Clark/Artists Rights Society (ARS), New York.

soot and rain. During breaks in the work, Matta-Clark emerged from the building to talk to the people watching from the street; he wanted to hear what they thought about the cut. The people observing the cutting team could also see, in the background, down the street, and in stark contrast, the sharp clean lines of a massive new building of fresh metal superstructure dwarfing the older houses around it. Looming over the neighboring apartments and houses, that new building that rose with symmetrical structure and order would open its doors to the public two years later as the Centre Pompidou, a spectacular monumental statement of a regenerated Paris of the last quarter of the twentieth century and of the city's (indeed the nation's) commitment to modern art.

Having finished the first hole in the exterior wall of the older building, Matta-Clark's team continued its work, turning to the templates that they had drawn on the walls, floors, and ceilings of the room immediately inside the exterior cut (Figure 5.2). Following these lines with the blade of their circular saw, the cutters perforated a bedroom wall in a billowing cloud of dust that obliterated the room in a storm of white plaster powder. As the saw's blade cut into the walls and ceilings of the room, the outlines of the cutters' bodies faded into the spewed dust and then disappeared; the saw would stop, the plaster cloud would settle, and the cutters would rematerialize goggle-eyed and mask-mouthed. In the video made of the work, it is tempting to see the

FIGURE 5.2 *Conical Intersect:* Gordon Matta-Clark with string and partial cut inside. Photo © Marc Petitjean; © 2017 Estate of Gordon Matta-Clark/Artists Rights Society (ARS), New York.

cutters in their protective gear as explorers vanishing into and returning from some other world.[1]

Using handsaws to get through the 20 cm × 20 cm wooden floor beams and the thinner wallboard and bathroom tiles, hammering their chisels into and through the paint, wallpaper, and lath of the walls, removing doors and moldings, the team cut and worked with precision perforating the interior elements of the building in a slowly emerging pattern of circles. Matta-Clark had planned the cuts so that they formed spheres of empty space in a building where for centuries walls and structure had separated room from hallway and hallway from room. To ensure the precise alignment of one circular cut to the next one on the facing wall, ceiling, or floor, Matta-Clark strung lengths of twine from points around the circumference of the cut-circle and ran the twine to outlines drawn on the new surface to be cut; the twine ensured that each hole in the wall aligned with the cuts that preceded and followed it. As it was made, each cut connected a new, empty, spherical space to the one just created (Figure 5.3). A coherent, twisting cone of empty space started to take shape as the team worked through the structural surfaces of the building's interior.

As they opened additional successively linked spaces, Matta-Clark and his assistants could gaze back down through the empty spherical voids that they had made. They looked out from the newly opened building to the street below, at the buildings across the street, and to the mounds of demolition

FIGURE 5.3 *Conical Intersect:* cutting inside the building. Photo © Marc Petitjean;
© 2017 Estate of Gordon Matta-Clark/Artists Rights Society (ARS), New York.

debris from other sixteenth-, seventeenth-, and eighteenth-century houses already knocked down. As they cut, sawed, and chiseled, the team moved up first through the interior space of the one house (27 rue de Beaubourg), and then they cut through the walls and floors of the neighboring building (number 29). Eventually, having perforated the second building's roof with a final round hole, they stopped. When they looked up and out of the roof hole, the view was of the metal armature of the Centre Pompidou and of the workers and cranes erecting its linear inside out tubular form.

In their two weeks of extreme physical labor in the dust, grime, plaster, and sawdust, Matta-Clark and his assistants had cut a single, peculiar, connected, twisting, negative space through the interior of the two buildings. The empty space took the shape of a cone, rising from its start at the 4.0 m hole in the northern wall of the first building, becoming smaller as it rose at a 45-degree angle, and cutting through the higher floors of the second building where the cone's pointed end (now 2.0 m in diameter) poked out through the tin roof.

Later, Matta-Clark said that he felt that their cutting of the conical space was as if someone had thrown a huge ball through the interior of the houses. It was as if the ball had perforated the surfaces of the buildings' walls, floors, and roof (Béar 1974: 34), thus leaving in its wake a negative cast of a cone that followed the ball's path: walls, floors, and ceilings, all rectilinear structural elements of the building interior, all perforated by the unstoppable passage of a powerful sphere. It was as if something beyond human dimensions of size and power had sliced through the bedrooms, kitchens, closets, and halls of the house.

Where the cut edge of each wall, floor, or ceiling was exposed, its edge (though cleanly cut by Matta-Clark and the team) revealed the ragged interior of its materials: splinters of wood and sawn beams, irregular jags of plaster, roughly sawn and broken stone, wallpaper torn and tattered. The team's clean and precise cuts revealed the material reality of what was otherwise hidden and internal behind wallpaper, under floorboards and tile, beneath layers of plaster and paint (Figure 5.4).

At five in the evening on the Friday that Matta-Clark's team finished cutting the twisting conical shape out of the building's roof, the work permit obtained to carry out *Conical Intersect* expired. City officials were waiting. They forced Matta-Clark and his assistants out of the property, and sealed the doorway to the site with cement and cinderblocks in a (comically vain) attempt to prevent the team (supremely skilled at cutting through building materials) from opening the site to the public on the following day. Later that night, Matta-Clark returned and used the same chisels he had hammered to carve

FIGURE 5.4 View from inside *Conical Intersect* to neighboring roof. Photo © Marc Petitjean; © 2017 Estate of Gordon Matta-Clark/Artists Rights Society (ARS), New York.

out the conical interior shape to cut through the officials' cinderblock obstacle (Simon 1985: 197).

Context of *Conical Intersect*

Matta-Clark found inspiration for the shape of the cut in *Conical Intersect* as he watched the February 1973 US premier of British artist Anthony McCall's thirty-minute film *A Line Describing a Cone* at the Artist's Space in New York (Simon 1985; Jenkins 2011: 39). McCall's film begins with a single, thin beam of white light projected through the space of the audience and onto a screen (Figure 5.5). As the film progresses, the beam gradually expands in size until it forms a circular cone of white light: a tangible object filling the space of the viewing room. As the movie viewers stand, walk about the room, and watch, they cannot escape being touched by the slowly enlarging cone of shimmering light. In its process, the film shifts the spectators from viewers of images on the screen to participants within the space of the film (Jenkins 2011: 39).[2] Matta-Clark had similar ideas for the space he wanted to make in *Conical Intersect*: a changing, growing conical presence that enlarges and moves through the area and to which viewers are drawn.

FIGURE 5.5 Anthony McCall, *Line Describing a Cone* (1973), during the twenty-four minute installation view, *Into the Light: The Projected Image in American Art 1964–1977*, Whitney Museum of American Art, 2001. Photograph by Hank Graber. Image used with permission of the artist.

Conical Intersect was Matta-Clark's contribution to the Ninth Biennale de Paris, France's international survey of artists under the age of thirty-five (Jenkins 2011: 3). In selecting the artists to invite to participate in the Biennale, the French organizing committee relied on foreign-based national commissioners to propose potential contributors. For the 1975 Biennale, the commissioner responsible for the US region was Walter Hopps, the director of the National Collection of Fine Arts in Washington (now the Smithsonian American Art Museum). One of Hopps' suggestions was Matta-Clark (Jenkins 2011: 3). The Biennale commission invited Matta-Clark to submit documentation of his previous work so that it could be shown in the gallery space devoted to the Biennale at the Musée d'Art Moderne de la Ville de Paris (Jenkins 2011: 3–4).

Matta-Clark had no interest in limiting his participation to gallery space; he preferred to make a work on-site for the Biennale, specifically in (and through) a building. After some resistance, the members of the commission agreed and, once issues of liability were resolved, they turned the matter over to the Sociéte d'Economie Mixte, which was responsible for the disposition, renovation, and restoration of the district of Les Halles. The Sociéte provided Matta-Clark with two adjoining houses on rue de Beaubourg (numbers 27 and 29) and a two-week window in which to work (Jenkins 2011: 7). The rue de Beaubourg structures had already been scheduled for demolition as part of the longer-running redevelopment of the area. Indeed at the end of the permit period, almost immediately after Matta-Clark's cut was completed, the buildings were fully destroyed.[3]

Though formally and commonly referred to as *Conical Intersect*, Matta-Clark had other names for the work at 27 and 29 rue de Beaubourg. At some point in the cutting, Matta-Clark started calling the work *Cyclopes* (Jenkins 2011: 14), with references to vision and visibility, but also alluding to size and scale and a relationship between the exterior wall hole and an eye. Through this and other nicknames that Matta-Clark and his team used, one gains traction on the artist's intentions in making the work, particularly in the context of the urban redevelopment then underway in this part of Paris in the early 1970s, and especially the construction of the Centre Pompidou.

Matta-Clark also called the work "Quel Con," or "Quel Can," or "Cal Can," which Gerry Hovagimyan, one of Matta-Clark's cutting assistants, suggests was a play on Marcel Duchamp's work *L.H.O.O.Q. La Joconde* (from 1919 and with many versions thereafter) (Figure 5.6); the Duchamp work was a modern postcard print of Leonardo da Vinci's early sixteenth-century *Mona Lisa* (Simon 1985: 197). In *L.H.O.O.Q. La Joconde*, Duchamp drew a moustache and beard on the face of the Mona Lisa. The twist that Duchamp added was that when spoken swiftly in French, L.H.O.O.Q. is pronounced *"elle a chaud au cul"* ["she has a hot ass," or more politely "there is a fire down there"] (Simon 1985: 197). Duchamp's *L.H.O.O.Q.* was a Dada-esque attack on traditional art as represented by iconic images such as the *Mona Lisa*. In Matta-Clark's informal description of *Conical Intersect*, he used Quel Can or Cal Can (meaning "what a cone" or "what a cunt") to riff off Duchamp's play on words (Jenkins 2011: 70; Simon 1985: 197), and to inject a critical energy to *Conical Intersect* directed at traditional artistic work, both of the Biennale (perhaps), but certainly of what the emerging Centre Pompidou would come to embody. Officially, *Conical Intersect* was subtitled *Étant d'art pour Locataire* [Art for the Lodger] (Jenkins 2011: 13), the intention of which Dalia Judovitz has suggested was to focus attention on the absent dwellers of 27 and 29 rue de Beaubourg (Judovitz 2010: 201): occupants who would no longer live in a building that had stood and functioned as a residence for more than two centuries; art for occupants who had been displaced.

Recording and Documentation

As part of a larger documentation of Biennale work, and at the instruction of and with equipment provided by Georges Boudaille, the organizer of the Biennale, Marc Petitjean made an eleven-minute videotape recording (*Intersection*

FIGURE 5.6 Marcel Duchamp, *L.H.O.O.Q. La Joconde* (1919) Cameraphoto Arte, Venice/Art Resource, NY; © Artists Rights Society (ARS), New York.

Conique de Gordon Matta-Clark) with still images that he and Nicholas Petitjean took and with part of an interview of Matta-Clark by Elisabeth Lebovici (Jenkins 2011: 9, 93n1).[4] In addition, Matta-Clark and Bruno Dewitt made an eighteen-minute, forty-second, silent, black-and-white 16 mm film that focused exclusively on Matta-Clark's contribution.[5]

In addition to the films and Petitjean's (and others') photographs, Matta-Clark constructed collages with his own photographs of the work, trying to reproduce and expand the experience of being in the negative spaces that the team had cut out of the buildings. Matta-Clark's photographs of *Conical Intersect* are more than documentation. With the destruction of *Conical Intersect*, the film, video, and other photographs were all that remained of the work. In many of the photo collages, Matta-Clark selected individual prints, each of which was an image of a fragment of a larger cut (usually the large hole in the exterior wall) (Figure 5.7). He then fitted the prints together to create a disjointed

FIGURE 5.7 Gordon Matta-Clark (1943–1978), *Conical Intersect* (1975). Silver dye bleach print 39 13/16 × 29 15/16 in. (101.1 × 76 cm). Whitney Museum of American Art, New York; purchase, with funds from the Photography Committee 92.71 © Estate of Gordon Matta-Clark/Artists Rights Society (ARS), New York.

visual representation of the cut. In these black-and-white photo collages, the cut is the focus of the image: the center of a photographic arrangement where each of the prints meets. Individual prints shoot out from the joined-up center of the collage, creating a jagged, rectilinear star made of the edges of the prints as they radiate out from the centrally placed hole (Sussman 2007: plate 63; Moure 2006: 189, 191, 193). In one collage, the center of the arrangement (the center of the circular cut in the wall) is itself left empty by Matta-Clark; the inner edges of the prints leave open a rectangular gap (Moure 2006: 193). In other photo-collages of *Conical Intersect*, Matta-Clark brings together multiple views of the same cut, again most often the large hole in the exterior wall of 27 rue de Beaubourg (Sussman 2007: plates 64, 65, 66). In these, the images are printed to show the edges and sprocket holes of the color negative film; masking tape holds the images in position. The result presents the viewer with multiple versions and views of the same cut in the building's walls.

In these multipart, multi-perspective, and unstable photo collages, Matta-Clark injects motion and incompleteness into the documentation of his work. Regardless of where the collage is seen (in a book or a gallery) or by whom, no single, correct position is available to the viewer. There is no one perspective or view of what Matta-Clark and his assistants have accomplished. There is no single, stationary, immobile, and agreed-upon perspective to be held of the work. No spectator of the photo collages can maintain a single position; to stand still and have one perspective is impossible. Too many views are presented in too disruptive an arrangement. Motion is unavoidable, simple observation not allowed. As the original *Conical Intersect* no longer exists, there can never be any single perspective of the work: only what is represented in the photo collages.

Politics of Modernizing Les Halles and the Centre Pompidou Construction

Twenty-seven and 29 rue de Beaubourg were two of the last buildings left standing in a massive urban redevelopment project aimed to modernize Paris' Les Halles market center. With twelfth-century origins, Les Halles had a deep history in the city and had survived into the twentieth century with its original function (Evenson 1973: 309; Muir 2011: 178). Built at the end of the seventeenth century, number 27 had one large and two narrow wings, and belonged to Mme de Lesseville. Number 29 belonged to Monsieur de Lesseville, a *conseiller au Parlement*, a position in the Paris Court of Appeals, and a stalwart of the Parisian bourgeoise of the Ancien Régime (Jenkins

2011: 94n16). By 1723, both houses belonged to Anne Antoinette Le Porguier, the widow of Pierre Le Clerc de Lesseville (Jenkins 2011: 94n16).

At the beginning of the eighteenth century, authorities identified Les Halles as a base for popular revolt and a home to disease and danger (Muir 2011: 178). In the middle of the 1800s, Les Halles was cleaned up, or "moralized" in the words of nineteenth-century French writer, traveler, and photographer Maxime du Camp (Thompson 1997: 88–89; Muir 2011: 178). These improvements included the construction of the first of a series of iron-and-glass pavilions drawn up by Victor Baltard as part of Georges-Eugène Haussmann's redesign of the city under the commission of Napoléon III; the first pavilion was built in 1858, the last not until the 1930s (Muir 2011: 179). In his 1873 novel *Le Ventre de Paris* [The Belly of Paris], Émile Zola presented Les Halles as the stomach and heart of Paris (Muir 2011: 179), describing it in multisensory detail: cut-flowers, fish, bells ringing, stalls selling cabbage soup, hot coffee, odors of seaweed, carts and donkeys, saleswomen and auctioneers, tripe, pumpkins, black radishes, dirty-coated porters, ragged children, grimy buildings and people (Zola 1873).

In the twentieth century, the Commission d'Extension called for the markets at Les Halles to be moved (in 1913, even before the last of Baltard's pavilions had been completed). In 1944 The Economic Council made the same request citing problems of public hygiene (Muir 2011: 178–179). By the 1960s, French politicians and the popular, highly negative vision of Les Halles presented a problem to be solved: an area full of foreigners and transients, particularly of North Africans, and the home for brothels and other illegal and immoral professions and activities (Muir 2011: 179). The neighborhood also contained the largest concentration of Paris' socialist voters. By 1967, in response to the Economic Council's call for proposals for the modernization of the area, six architectural firms had submitted bids for the regeneration project (Muir 2011: 179).

In 1969, the meat and produce markets were moved south to the suburbs of Rungis (Jenkins 2011: 8). Two years later, demolition work started on Baltard's pavilions and of the market in general. As work proceeded, stalls were pulled down, and trade moved elsewhere, Parisians referred to the empty space left where the markets had been as *le grand trou* or *le trou des Halles* [the big hole or the hole of Les Halles] (Muir 2011: 173) where the use of the slang *trou* [for cunt] underlined a perception of the area as a down-and-out dive. The 1960s and 1970s modernization plan for Les Halles included the construction of a new public library for the city of Paris as well as a major institute and museum dedicated to modern art; the former was the idea of Charles de Gaulle (French president from 1959–1969), the later of his successor

George Pompidou (president from 1969–1974). The Centre Pompidou, indeed the entire urban renewal project in Les Halles, were vital components of a modernization of Paris (and perhaps as well of France as a nation). As such the projects were highly political. For its part, the Centre Pompidou would stand as a major monument to French cultural prominence at the end of the twentieth century in much the same way that the Tour Eiffel stood as a monument to French engineering and industrial pre-eminence at the end of the nineteenth century (Graham 1985: 203).

It is in the context and sociopolitical consequences of the modernization of Les Halles and the construction of the Centre Pompidou that Matta-Clark carried out and understood his work, *Conical Intersect*. Many who witnessed the destruction of Les Halles in the late 1960s and early 1970s saw the urban modernization process as a symptom of the destruction and degradation of Paris as a whole (Muir 2011: 177), and as an attack on the people who had lived in the area. Peter Muir has discussed in detail the reaction and protest to the demolition of Les Halles, showing how that political conflict and energy provided the appropriate place for Matta-Clark to make his contribution to the Biennale (Muir 2011). Muir describes the destruction of the area in terms of the demolition of architecture and the dispersal of people (Muir 2011: 173), and quotes hand-lettered posters that protesters pasted to building exteriors during the modernization process:

> The centre of Paris will be beautiful. Luxury will be king. The buildings of the St. Martin block will be of high standing. But we will not be here. The commercial facilities will be spacious and rational. The parking immense. But we won't work here anymore. The streets will be spacious and the pedestrian ways numerous. But we won't walk here anymore. We won't live here anymore. Only the rich will live in our quarter. The elected officials responding to their wishes have decided. The renovation is not for us. (Muir 2011: 175; from Evenson 1973: 312)

Interpretation of *Conical Intersect*

The deep political and social history of the location where Matta-Clark made his cuts in *Conical Intersect*, the (then) contemporary politics of urban modernization in 1960s and 1970s Paris, and specifically the construction of the Centre Pompidou provide rich and controversial backgrounds against which to understand the artist's work in rue de Beaubourg. Matta-Clark's work drew its energy both from the broader history of Les Halles and from the specific projects within that modernization, such as the Centre Pompidou.

Matta-Clark spoke about his intentions and concerns for *Conical Intersect* in several interviews (Marder 1975; Béar 1976; Wall 1976; Antwerp 1977; Kirschner 1978) and he left typewritten notes and statements (e.g., Matta-Clark n.d. in Moure 2006).

Speaking to Irving Marder (then writing for the *International Herald Tribune*) while the work was in progress, Matta-Clark explained that *Conical Intersect* was closely related to the renovations taking place around the rue de Beaubourg houses, noting that "there is a lot of 'holing' going on" (Marder 1975, cited in Jenkins 2011: 11), and making direct reference to the demolition of Les Halles in preparation for a new urban landscape (Figure 5.8). As Dan Graham put it, in *Conical Intersect* Matta-Clark gives form (in a powerfully paradoxical way, via the creation of the negative cut and removed space) to the demolition of historical continuity between modern and historic Paris (Graham 1985: 203). In 27/29 rue de Beaubourg and in the, by then, other demolished buildings of Les Halles, historical discontinuity graded into lost memories and disappeared into forgotten lives and places: "buildings move from architecture to object, from object to fragment, and from fragment to memory," and it is a memory that gets lost (Muir 2011: 185).

As Muir focuses the discussion back down onto the particulars of the buildings exposed by Matta-Clark cutting *Conical Intersect*, the destruction of these two houses emerges as more than the removal of the old to make way for the new; it is the destruction and loss of the domestic, the family, the community, the home, the shelter, the safety, the feminine, and the spaces of reproduction and of the self (Muir 2011: 185). The exposures of *Conical Intersect* to the passersby on the rue de Beaubourg brought the public into the dynamism (Muir 2011: 185) of artistic practice as political statement and confrontation. For Muir, *Conical Intersect* is a plan on remembering and forgetting, a critical and violent tension between memory and history (Muir 2011: 176).

Most specifically, Matta-Clark clarified the connections that he was making between *Conical Intersect* and the emerging Centre Pompidou. Though not opened until January 1977, the design and construction of the latter was well underway in September 1975 while Matta-Clark was opening holes in the walls, ceilings, floors, and roofs of 27/29 rue de Beaubourg. The connection was visual; the opening cut through the roof of 29 provided an exterior view of the partially built Centre Pompidou. Thomas Crow and Bruce Jenkins describe the shape of the conical cut in terms of a viewing device, suggesting that it is like an inverted telescope, with the smaller, upper end of the instrument represented by the roof cut; it thus provided a viewer positioned at the lower, larger end (perhaps on the street) with a miniaturized glimpse of the Pompidou's exterior surface (Crow 2003: 96, 117; Jenkins 2011: 9, 14).

FIGURE 5.8 View from inside *Conical Intersect* to rue de Beaubourg. Photo © Marc Petitjean; © 2017 Estate of Gordon Matta-Clark/Artists Rights Society (ARS), New York.

In addition, the connection was architectural; Matta-Clark designed and placed the twisting cone in 27/29 rue de Beaubourg to match the 45-degree angle and shape of the Pompidou's exterior-escalator encased in its plastic tube as it appeared to the passersby (Jenkins 2011: 12).

Perhaps most forcefully, the connection was oppositional, inverted, and confrontational; Matta-Clark explained that *Conical Intersect* was a "non-monumental counterpart to the grandiose bridge-like skeleton of the Centre" (Antwerp 1977; Jenkins 2011: 40). Perhaps it was in the spirit of confronting or mocking the Pompidou that Matta-Clark wanted to establish a link between *Conical Intersect* and Duchamp's *L.H.O.O.Q.* in his use of "Quel Con," or "Quel Can," or "Cal Can" as alternative titles for his work. As Dalia Judovitz suggests, Matta-Clark wanted to draw attention to the place of the emerging national museum as a violent erasure of the buildings that had once stood around it in the same way that Duchamp's work had criticized and mocked traditional masterpieces like the *Mona Lisa* (Judovitz 2010: 209–211).

By exposing what is usually hidden and internal (the skeleton and organs) of 27/29 rue de Beaubourg, Matta-Clark forced a comparison with the inside out design and construction of Renzo Piano and Richard Rogers's Centre Pompidou. It is as if Matta-Clark is shouting, with a corresponding violence of action, "Look here, if you want to see the reality of inside-out architecture; it is here in what you are demolishing." Graham pushes this further with the recognition that two of the important architectural monuments of Parisian (and French) prominence (the Tour Eiffel and the Centre Pompidou) are negative structures; both reveal and celebrate their internal engineering and materials (Graham 1985: 203). With *Conical Intersect*, however, the insides are real and raw; with the Tour Eiffel and the Pompidou, the innards only appear to be open and on display to the public as polished finished products intended for posterity.

Confrontation was not only aimed at the Pompidou but also at the local context of Les Halles and what was happening under the terms of urban renewal. Speaking to Donald Wall about the choice of the particular site for the work, Matta-Clark explained that he sought locations with particular "historical and cultural identities" that have a recognizable form: "one of my concerns here is with the Non.u.mental, that is an expression of the commonplace that might counter the grandeur and pomp of architectural structures and their glorifying clients" (Wall 1976: 183; also Matta-Clark 2006: 132). With *Conical Intersect*, as with many of his other cut-architecture pieces, Matta-Clark wanted to open up and engage in a discussion about the urban landscape particularly with the monumental and centralized cultural edifices such as national collections, libraries, and, most especially, museums (Jenkins 2011: 13). He saw his works, particularly *Conical Intersect*, as interventions that could transform a building into an act of communication (Wall 1976: 183). As Judovitz points out, Matta-Clark illuminates (literally lets light into) areas of domestic space in *Conical Intersect* that are being destroyed in the name of modernist renewal and national monuments. Matta-Clark's building-cuts reveal "multiple layers of lived meaning attached to the dwelling; the light traces other people's histories" (Judovitz 2010: 211).

Reaction to Conical Intersect

The public and political reaction to *Conical Intersect* was loud and diverse, with criticism crossing the political left and right. The French Communist newspaper *L'Humanité* put an image of the work-in-progress on the front page of its Saturday, November 29, 1975, issue (the only image on the front page, laid out at the center of the page making the image, itself, appear as a hole in the front of the paper). *L'Humanité* asked *Que D'Art!* [What art! or What a work of art!] in a critique of the work as a piece of bourgeois art (Muir 2011: 185–186; Lee 1998: 76). No article accompanied the image, only a short caption that offered the caustic comment that the hole in the wall of 27 rue de Beaubourg must be art because an artist made it. From some of the people seeing the work from the street came a similar response. A student complained that as many Parisians needed places to live, would it be better to use 27 and 29 rue de Beaubourg for housing and not for art? (Béar 1976: 176). For their part, the political right and French officials who had been pushing for the modernization of Les Halls saw *Conical Intersect* as an insult (Muir 2011; Lee 1999: 185).

The workers who were busy pulling down the surrounding buildings as part of the larger urban renewal project told Irving Marder for his article in the *Tribune* that they thought that in his cutting of the walls, floors, and ceilings, Matta-Clark and his team were searching for hidden treasure, or that Matta-Clark was just a crazy American, or even a CIA agent, pretending to be a crazy American in order to cover up his real aim: to find a site for a secret missile base (Jenkins 2011: 13). A concierge from a neighboring building told Matta-Clark that she understood what he was doing: letting light and air into spaces that had never had enough of either (Béar 1976: 176) (Figure 5.9).

Matta-Clark must have found satisfaction in all of these reactions; his goal was to use the work as a communicative act to open dialogue and debate over the roles that architecture and its destruction play within urban living. He specifically chose to make the work he did in the place he made it because of

FIGURE 5.9 Gordon Matta-Clark (1943–1978), *Conical Intersect 2* (Documentation of the action "Conical Intersect" made in 1975 in Paris, France), (1975, printed 1977) Gelatin silver print, Sheet: 10 × 8 in. (25.4 × 20.3 cm). Image: 9 11/16 × 6 13/16 in. (24.6 × 17.3 cm). Whitney Museum of American Art, New York; gift of Harold Berg T.2013.191 © Estate of Gordon Matta-Clark/Artists Rights Society (ARS), New York.

the controversy that was already flaring among Parisians over the destruction of Les Halles and the Plateau Beaubourg and the mandatory displacement of the people who had lived there and over the businesses (legal and illegal, ethical or not) destroyed by a grand plan carried out in the name of modernization (Muir 2011: 173).

The place of *Conical Intersect* was already a space of tension before the cutting began: tension between the narrative of historical progress (modernization) and the narrative of the disruption of historical continuity and preservation (Muir 2011: 173). Progress required the destruction of history. As Peter Muir puts it, the tensions here are between the new and the obsolete or primordial, the rational and the irrational, the lost and the transformed, and between artistic advocacy and artistic appreciation (Muir 2011: 174). Matta-Clark's work dramatized the place and the actions that had evicted and dispersed people from their land and property (Muir 2011: 173). In the context of the Les Halles modernization and the creation of the Centre Pompidou, Matta-Clark's work symbolized memory, loss, condescension and contradiction, artistic and political naiveté, confusion and the inherent powerlessness of communities over the repossession and use of their land (Muir 2011: 174).

Matta-Clark's Cutting Oeuvre: Major Themes

Conical Intersect was but one of a series of powerful cutting works that Gordon Matta-Clark made in his short career (he died of pancreatic cancer in 1978 at the age of thirty-five). There are excellent accounts of his oeuvre, and though there is neither the space nor the need to review all of his works here, it is worth noting that Matta-Clark's output extended beyond architectural cutting to films, performances, photo collage, sculpture, and street art. The interested reader will find much of value in Graham (1985), Noever (1998), Lee (1999), Attlee and Le Feuvre (2003), Diserens (2003), Walker (2003), Moure (2006), Walker (2009), Jenkins (2011), and Muir (2011). For the purposes of our examination of the pit-houses at Măgura, I suggest that we will find most value in investigating the fundaments and intentions of Matta-Clark's cutting work; the reader is invited to investigate his other output.

Matta-Clark and Cutting

Gordon Matta-Clark was the son of two artists, Roberto Matta (1911–2002) and Anne Clark. Roberto Matta was a celebrated figure in the world of abstract expressionist and surrealist art[6] and Anne Clark was a skilled artist and designer. Formally trained as an architect (he dropped out of the program at Cornell in 1968), Gordon Matta-Clark worked as an assistant to Dennis Oppenheim and to Robert Smithson (both key figures in the changes that ran through American art in the 1960s) while they created their contributions to the seminal *Earth Art* show at Cornell in 1969. If additional flavor is needed, Marcel Duchamp was Matta-Clark's godfather (Muir 2011: 189).

In a 1977 interview, Matta-Clark spoke about the beginnings of his practice of cutting buildings, tracing them to paid work he undertook remodeling lofts in SoHo in New York City, a source of money while he pursued art work of his own. One of his early works, *Food* (1971), made in collaboration with Tina Girouard, Caroline Gooden, Suzanne Harris, and Rachel Lew, was a restaurant and performance space on Prince Street in lower Manhattan that became a meeting place for the artist community in the city.[7] Matta-Clark redesigned and rebuilt the interior space of the restaurant, to make the floor plan more suited to the performance-focused activities of *Food*. The important result for Matta-Clark was a new understanding of the ways he could transform space through the unusual alteration of a building's structural surfaces, particularly its walls and the choreography of floor space (Antwerp 1977).

From the loft remodeling and the practical redesign of *Food*, Matta-Clark began cutting buildings with less functional intent. He worked in run-down buildings on the Lower East Side and in the Bronx, in spaces frequented by junkies and dealers, in neighborhoods that were home to packs of wild dogs, and in environments of danger and crime where work was as likely to be interrupted by the police as by gangs of toughs. The deteriorating rooms in these derelict buildings were available and free to an artist without a studio or gallery sponsorship; these abandoned spaces lay outside of normal New York society and real estate valuation. Using hacksaws and hammers, Matta-Clark cut these buildings, extracted wall sections, removed them, and presented them in art galleries (e.g., at 112 Green Street, a newly created alternative art space established in 1970 by Matta-Clark, Jeffrey Lew, and Alan Saret [Fiore 2012; Barliant 2012]).

In this early work, Matta-Clark chose architecture to cut in places that were "up for grabs" (Wagner 2004: 34); dangerous locations that had appeared in the urban wastelands of New York City through the 1950s and 1960s. As Matta-Clark put it, he was drawn to the abandoned spaces that "reverberated with the miseries of ghetto lives" (Antwerp 1977: 250): once occupied residences, now open, exposed, and socially defunct; buildings that had slid into positions outside of society (Antwerp 1977: 250); spaces that had been "consigned to oblivion," of forgotten communities, and of neglected histories (Kirshner 2003: 153). In choosing buildings to cut and places to make work, Matta-Clark sought locations in which people's daily lives had submerged under daily contestation, contradiction, and the vagaries of being alive (Vidler 2006: 71). He investigated, probed, and created the possibilities that come into existence when the specific rules of social, architectural behavior crumble and decay (Walker 2009: 10).

In cutting these structures, Matta-Clark understood his work in terms of "undoing" a building; he believed that he was making gestures against the social conditions of the place, of the times, and of the people (cited in Moure 2006: 132–133). He sought out architectural structures of particular social and cultural identities, and of specific, recognizable social forms (Wall 1976: 183). In his work, he placed his activities on top of the existing in situ organization and structure of daily life (Kirshner 2003: 152). Matta-Clark's concern was with what he called the non.u.mental [*sic*]: "an expression of the commonplace that might counter the grandeur and pomp of architectural structures and their self-glorifying clients" (Wall 1976: 183). In Stephen Walker's terms, Matta-Clark's work aimed to reorganize the grounds of authority (Walker 2009: 146). As Pam Lee has seen it, his work confronted the politics of the art object (i.e., site-specific, non-museological) in relation to property (Lee 1999: xvi).

By the time he arrived in Paris in September 1975, ready to make *Conical Intersect*, Matta-Clark had made a series of building cuts, starting in 1971 with *Untitled* at the Museo National de Bellas Artes, Santiago, Chile. In 1972, he made a sequence of other works in New York City: *Bronx Floors: Threshole*; *Bronx Floors: Floor Above, Ceiling Below*; *Bronx Floors: Wall Hole*; *Bronx Floors: Double Doors*; *Bronx Floors: Four-Way Wall*; and *Bronx Floors: Boston Road Floor Hole*. He showed *Bronx Floors: Wall Hole* (1972) at 112 Greene Street. In 1973, he made *Pier In/Out*, at Pier 14 on the Hudson River and *Cooper's Cut* at

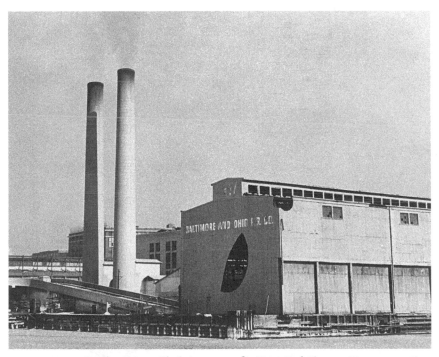

FIGURE 5.10 Gordon Matta-Clark (1943–1978), *Days End Pier 52.1* (Documentation of the action "Day's End" made in 1975 in New York, United States) (1975, printed 1977). Gelatin silver print, Sheet: 8 × 10 in. (20.3 × 25.4 cm), Image: 7 9/16 × 9 7/16 in. (19.2 × 24 cm). Whitney Museum of American Art, New York; gift of Harold Berg T.2013.186 © Estate of Gordon Matta-Clark/Artists Rights Society (ARS), New York.

155 Wooster Street in New York before traveling to Europe where he made *Infraform* in Milan, and *A W-hole House; A W-hole House: Datum Cut, Core Cut, Trace de Coeur*; and *A W-hole House: Roof Top Atrium* in Sestri, Italy. In the same year, he showed photographs and extracted pieces of *A W-hole House* at the Galleriaforma.

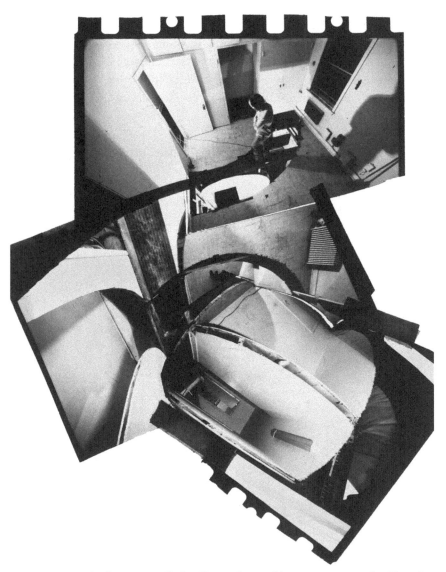

FIGURE 5.11 Gordon Matta-Clark, *Circus-The Caribbean Orange* (1978) Silver dye bleach print 39 ½– 29 7/8″ (100.3 × 75.9 cm). © 2017 Estate of Gordon Matta-Clark/Artists Rights Society (ARS), New York. Digital Image © The Museum of Modern Art/Licensed by SCALA/Art Resource, NY.

In 1974, Matta-Clark cut nine square sections from the side of a soon-to-be demolished suburban house in Lewiston, New York, to make *Bingo*.[8] More sensational and well know is *Splitting*, also made in 1974, in which Matta-Clark cut in half a soon-to-be demolished two-story family home in Englewood, New Jersey. The next year, he made *Day's End: Pier 52* at Ganevoort and West Streets in New York, a cutting project on an abandoned pier on the Hudson River (Figure 5.10). *Day's End* drew the attention of the New York City police, who served a warrant on Matta-Clark and a demand for $1,000,000 in damages (Hovagimyan n.d.). Matta-Clark escaped to Europe. In Sesto San Giovanni, near Milan, he made *Arc de Triomphe for Workers*, as part of a protest by local students, and when he arrived in Paris in the fall of 1975, he was still unsure of the legal wisdom of returning to the United States. Cutting work completed after *Conical Intersect* includes *Office Baroque* in a building across from the Steen at 1 Ernest van Dijckkaai in Antwerp (Belgium) and *Circus: The Caribbean Orange* as part of the expansion of the Museum of Contemporary Art in Chicago in 1978 (Figure 5.11).

Cutting, Action, and Performance

Matta-Clark talked about his cutting work in terms of its heavy physical process (Béar 1974: 172), and as a direct, immediate activity that did not make associations with anything exterior to it (Béar 1974: 171). The process of his works was of weighty manual performance: "putting your shoulder to part of a building, pushing it, and having it give way" (Béar 1974: 176). He saw his work as unfinished and incomplete individual pieces (Walker 2009: 105), in the same way in which he held a building to be unfinished even once the original architects, builders, and decorators had completed their contracted work. Even the photo collages that are now the sole remaining documentation of the work at a final stage were not intended as a final whole (Walker 2009: 72). Matta-Clark rejected proposals that his work or the collages contained or expressed any whole-object quality.

As Stephen Walker has argued, both the cut buildings and the photo collages provide a polyvalence of visual experiences; both have pieces missing, both are fragments, and neither pretends to offer a complete, authoritative vision of a work (Walker 2009: 107). In all of this Matta-Clark considered his work as performance, as a form of theater. The performance consisted of the actions of the cutters making the work plus the emerging, dynamic changes made to a building's structure: movement in this form of theater as a combination of metaphoric, sculptural, and social gesture. The cut (and the building being dissected) is both an act for the passerby to experience and a stage for pedestrians passing by and through (cited in Moure 2006: 132).

What Cutting Meant to Matta-Clark

For Matta-Clark, to cut a building was to create: to take an object, and to manipulate it (Béar 1974: 167). As he spoke about his Milanese work *Infraform* (1973), by cutting the masonry, Matta-Clark felt that he had shifted the object of his work from a complete building to its parts: "the cuts become more and more palpable as things in themselves" (Béar 1974: 168).

For Matta-Clark, to cut was to violate. He was intrigued by the repercussions of breaking through a surface (Béar 1974: 165). As he told Judith Kirshner in their discussion of *Circus: Caribbean Orange* (1978), the cutting works caused discrete violations of the viewers' sense of orientation (Kirshner 1978; Diserens 2003: 392; Walker 2009: 13). Matta-Clark's work disrupted the spatial experience of the spectator, and it did so in a productive manner. To make successful this transgressive violation, Matta-Clark understood that something of the original, uncut, structural situation must be maintained so that the observer could retain some measure of familiarity (Walker 2009: 53). The cut disrupted the usual, expected form of a surface, and negated spectators' expectations and understanding of what should be. Talking in 1977 in Belgium, Matta-Clark proposed that "the first thing one notices is that violence has been done. Then the violence turns to visual order and hopefully, then to a sense of heightened awareness" (Antwerp 1977: 253).

For Matta-Clark, to cut was to transform. In this, he reveals his interest in surrealist ideas of transmutation of states, situations, and realities (Malsch 1992: 206); this cannot be a surprise in an artist whose father (Roberto Matte) was a leading surrealist painter and whose godfather (Marcel Duchamp) was one of the preeminent practitioners of twentieth-century surrealism. Part of the transformations in Matta-Clark's works was a release of energy and dynamism. His cutting transformed a building from an immobile, closed, mundane architectural object into a structure that "incorporates an animated geometry" in which moved a dynamic, living but fragile relationship between the surfaces being cut and the empty spaces created (Kirshner 1978: 324).

In the void created by the cut, passersby could see revealed for the first time, internal structural elements of architecture in dynamic, kinetic motion (Kirschner 1978: 324). Matta-Clark cut so that he could make architecture into something other than a static object (GMC Wall Transcript number 1 cited in Walker 2009: 31). The transformation to dynamism is found in the cut structure itself, in the repercussions of the cut as felt by the spectators (and by the cutters, as they worked), as well as in the photography, film, and video that Matta-Clark made of the works. In filming his building dissections, he found that the movement of the lens through space provided experience that came close to the physical complexity of the work itself (Béar 1976: 176–177). In his conversation with Judith Kirshner, Matta-Clark spoke of different ways that the photographic process could interpret the cut spaces: from straight, snapshot, documentation; to time-lapse evolution of work; to voyeuristic experiencing; and finally to a more jumbled mixture of variations of finished and in-progress narrative (Kirshner 1978: 332). In making his photo collages, Matta-Clark attempted to approximate the "ambulatory getting to know" space that he and his cutting teams experienced as they made the works (Kirshner 1978: 332–333).

For Matta-Clark, to cut was to open and to liberate. Cutting a building created accessible permeable social space where once the space had been closed, aestheticized, and elitist (Vidler 2006: 69). Light enters spaces where it could not have been before (Antwerp 1977: 253). The cutting work brought into play what had been hidden (Antwerp 1977: 252; Hertz 2006: 12), and exposed what had been socially concealed (Figure 5.12). The cut released unusual amounts of information that had previously been unavailable and unknown; the cut liberated space (Béar 1974: 173). As Dan Graham realized, cutting-as-liberation results in a negative monument that aims to open history and

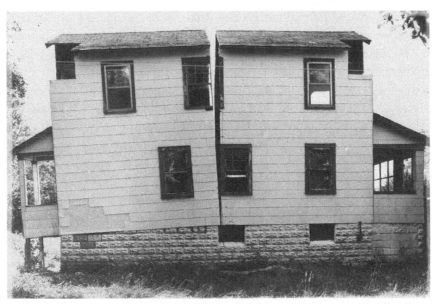

FIGURE 5.12 Gordon Matta-Clark (1943–1978), *Splitting 9* (Documentation of the action "Splitting" made in 1974 in New Jersey, United States) (1974, printed 1977). Gelatin silver print, Sheet: 8 × 10 in. (20.3 × 25.4 cm), Image: 6½ × 9⅝ in. (16.5 × 24.4 cm). Whitney Museum of American Art, New York; gift of Harold Berg T.2013.213 © Estate of Gordon Matta-Clark/Artists Rights Society (ARS), New York.

historical memory (Graham 1985; Wagner 2004: 35). In these senses, Matta-Clark's cuttings were not destructive; to pierce a surface was to liberate what lies below and behind (Attlee 2003c: 30). Through liberation, space is expanded (Noever 1998: 88; Walker 2003: 163).

For Matta-Clark, to cut was to know. He saw the act of cutting as analytical, as a probe (the essential probe) (Béar 1974: 167), as another way of knowing (Walker 2009: 162), and as a voyage of search and discovery (Walker 2009). Talking about the Humphrey House that he cut for *Splitting* in 1974, Matta-Clark spoke of getting to know the house by taking a chainsaw to it (Béar 1974: 175) (Figure 5.12). Commenting on Matta-Clark's work, Laurie Anderson put it this way, "When you pull something apart, you can really see what is there" (cited in Simon 1985: 190). For Lawrence Weiner, when Matta-Clark took buildings apart, he was doing more than removing pieces from the structure; he was clarifying an understanding of that space (Simon 1985: 199). Knowledge and clarification were of a particular type here.

With every cut and every giving way, the familiar became less so, and new questions emerged about familiar experience where before there had been none (Walker 2009: 15). In knowing through cutting, Matta-Clark argued not for solutions but for questions (Walker 2009: 9, 16): "solutions are the weakest forms at work" (Matta-Clark cited in Walker 2009: 9). Matta-Clark's search and discovery was a practice he called "living archaeology," though this was not archaeology as traditionally understood in the social sciences. Matta-Clark stood against the systematizing methods of the discipline, preferring to reveal the past as incomplete, fragmentary, and non-chronological (Walker 2009: 76). He sought not to fill in the gaps in history, but he worked to maintain the empty spaces between the histories of diverse peoples. The aim was to move beyond official history and allow other non-chronological times into experience (Walker 2009: 85). Matta-Clark's goal was to complicate existing systems; not to replace them with better ones through some disciplinary myth of progress (Walker 2003: 174). The aim of Matta-Clark's living archaeology was to illuminate the problems of mapping space and charting time; in this, complete maps and chronologies are not desirable, required, or of positive affect (Walker 2009: 83).

For Matta-Clark, to cut was to create a negative monument, a gesture against the permanence of symbolic form (Graham 1985: 202). As he told Judith Kirshner, his work was designed for collapse, failure, absence, and memory (Matta-Clark 1973a cited in Kirshner 2003: 154); was there any other way, with his building dissections cut into condemned buildings, waiting to be demolished as soon as his work was complete, when it all ended up as rubble? (Jenkins 2011: 42). Pam Lee has written about the work taking place in a "throwaway environment" (Lee 1999: 142). Matta-Clark saw his work as unfinished and incomplete (Walker 2009: 105), and that makes sense in his comments on the performative nature of what he was doing.

Matta-Clark's building dissections fit within his conception of anarchitecture:[9] "a response to cosmetic design, completion through removal, completion through collapse, completion through emptiness" (Matta-Clark 1973b). Anarchitecture was making space without building it (Attlee 2007; Jenkins 2011: 39), and it argues that structure and surface were not critically necessary terms (Wagner 2004: 28). An important part of this was Matta-Clark's opposition to use-value and function. His interest in space was particularly in making (or seeking out) voids.[10] For Matta-Clark, the value of the empty, the removed, and the void was not to be found in its possible uses (Béar 1974: 166). He thought about space in non-functional terms; the very nature of his work took issue with the functionalist attitude to space and to material culture (Wall 1976: 182). Indeed, his cutting work physically intervened into the normally accepted and normally valued function of a structure (Crow 2003: 22).

For Matta-Clark, to cut was to impregnate the void (Béar 1974: 172) with contradiction. As Stephen Walker suggests, the creation of the hole and the void reveals a space in which the cutter and the viewer occupy neither the center nor the outside (Walker 2003: 178). Drawing from the French philosopher Gilles Deleuze's understanding of elliptical space, Walker suggests that in its full sense, the ellipsis possesses two centers and constitutes a gap (Deleuze 1989: chapter 6; Deleuze 1996: part 1, 80, 85). In this sense the hole has no single location, and no clear place exists from which one can establish one's orientation. Matta-Clark's cuts were voids of neither center nor edge; they were instabilities and destabilizers.

For Matta-Clark, to cut was to create tension. A cut does opposite things synchronously (Figure 5.13). A cut destabilizes by violating expectation and experience, and at the same time clarifies by revealing hidden spaces and liberating information (Walker 2009: 42). Tension rises from a clash of familiarity (this is a building) and an emerging (or violently made present) knowledge of the possibilities of what might lie beyond and behind the surface of that structure (Walker 2009: 15). In this, Matta-Clark's cutting work creates and maintains instabilities (Walker 2009: 101). What had been simple is now ambiguous and complex. When he cut a surface, Matta-Clark intervened in the object or building (Hertz 2006: 19) in such a way that it becomes difficult (perhaps impossible) to read correctly the space created at the same time as reading correctly the original object or building that has

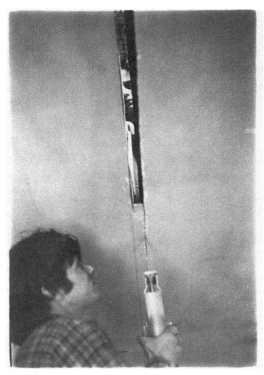

FIGURE 5.13 Gordon Matta-Clark (1943–1978), *Splitting 8* (Documentation of the action "Splitting" made in 1974 in New Jersey, United States) (1974, printed 1977). Gelatin silver print, Sheet: 10 × 8 ⅜ in. (25.4 × 21.3 cm). Image: 7 ¾ × 5 ⅜ in. (19.7 × 13.7 cm). Whitney Museum of American Art, New York; gift of Harold Berg T.2013.211. © Estate of Gordon Matta-Clark/Artists Rights Society (ARS), New York.

been dissected (Lee 1999: 158). Cutting introduces alternative views, and with that it forces a recognition that alternative views exist and are equally valid (Walker 2009: 57).

By leaving uncut enough architectural features to permit recognition at the same time as he also removed enough to violate what is expected, Matta-Clark created tremors that disoriented viewer and artist alike (Walker 2009: 13–15). As Lee argues, cuts are fundamental dislocations of both the context and the location of objects and places; in her words the cut is an "undecideable thing" (Lee 1999: 158). As is the case for a hole (as discussed in detail in chapter 3 in terms of the philosophy and psychology of holes), a cut is neither one thing nor another, neither figure nor ground, and yet it seems to be both things at the same time (Lee 1999: 158).

Part of the disorientation that comes with the building cuts results from the creation of a new complexity in depth perception (Wall 1976: 184). In his work, Matta-Clark wanted to complicate the visual area; doing so by creating concave spaces had a particularly powerful consequence due to the ways that the human visual system reacts to concavities (again, Matta-Clark was interrogating in his work much of the philosophical and psychological work carried out by others and as discussed in chapter 3): "looking through the cut, looking at the edges of the cut, should create a clearly new sense of space" (Walker 2009: 168; citing GMC *Wall Transcript, #* 15). The further paradox in his work is that Matta-Clark added complexity into space and built structures without making or building anything, but by removing matter (Béar 1974: 165): creation by destruction. The method was to rethink what was already present in a radical way (Antwerp 1977: 252). In Matta-Clark's words, the route to disorientation was to juggle syntax, to disintegrate the established sequence of parts in a substantial architectural structure (Béar 1974: 172): take a normal situation, redefine it, and then retranslate it so that it becomes multiple, overlapping readings of both past and present (Matta-Clark 2006, cited in Moure 2006: 132).

Spectating the Cut: Human Experience

The consequences of cutting were shared among Matta-Clark (with his cutting assistants); the passersby; the spectators on the ground watching the work progress; and the viewers of the photo collages, the films, and video. Matta-Clark wanted to involve the spectator, and to encourage participation in the work (Walker 2009: 89). The most direct event was when people walked through the cut buildings: at *Conical Intersect*, "when you go to the top floor and you looked down through the elliptical section in the floor that was cut out, you would look down through the fragments of a normal apartment space, but I had never seen anything like it. It looked like a pool. That is, it has a reflective quality to it and a surface—but the surface was just the accumulation of images of the space below it. It had had this strange reversal." (Béar 1976: 177).

Walking through one of Matta-Clark's building dissections, the visitor is more than spectator. All senses are engaged. Each is challenged. The normally experienced relationship of viewer to space is inverted (Hertz 2006: 20). A primary challenge is to the visitor's sense of gravity: normal positions and sensory reactions are subverted (Diserens 2003: 6; 1997: 213n5; Walker 2003). In the cutting works, and as developed in his films, such as *Sous-sol Paris* (1977), the visitor or viewer loses sight of the horizon; disorientation follows. As Stephen Walker argues, as the horizon disappears, no vanishing point is available. Only periphery remains, focus is lost, with the consequence that frustration overcomes the participant who tries to locate the cut space into a broader space system (Walker 2009: 99). The cut buildings unsettle the visitor's reliance on cardinal directionality, the existence of which becomes a question (Walker 2003: 175). Walker suggests that normally we establish our locational frameworks by relying on particular cardinal directionalities of our bodies (Walker 2003: 174–175). Critical is our relationship to gravity. With his cutting works, Matta-Clark questions the primacy of these frameworks.

Matta-Clark spoke about the Humphrey Street house of *Splitting* in this way: "at some point people's concentration breaks down and they want to find another way to look at what's happening" (Béar 1974: 171). In response to the loss of horizon, directionality, and as a reaction to being destabilized and unsettled, the visitor becomes part of the dynamics of the work, as the cuts open up unexpected possibilities of perception (Attlee 2003c: 29; 2003b: 53). New possibilities come with a new clarity that emerges in the visitors that allows— perhaps insists—that they recognize the assumptions that had underwritten (i.e., that were hidden in the covered substructure) the previous situation and understanding of building and space and being (Walker 2009: 169). Because of this disruption and new clarity, spectators and visitors impose their own meanings upon the works and onto their reactions to those works (Noever 1998: 82). Walker argues that this was part of Matta-Clark's intention: to renovate the spectator's notions of spatiality (Walker 2003: 172).[11] Part of this follows the disorientation of the viewer; part of it comes from the revelation and liberation of what was previously hidden (Hertz 2006: 12).

Matta-Clark's work aimed to invigorate human experience by opening it up to new spaces and to new senses of spatial orientation (Walker 2009: 15). The intent was to broaden the possibilities for human experience beyond what is normally accepted within traditional architecture, art, and (with his living archaeology) history and archaeology. The cuts achieve this. They destabilize the norms by which we experience space and with which we ground the vertical and horizontal framing of the world and our participation in it (Hertz 2006: 15). As James Attlee put it, Matta-Clark sliced up and reconfigured the three dimensions that we inhabit (Attlee 2003a: 69). In doing so, the possibility emerges for the undoing not only of the buildings, but more vitally of the self and the environment (Walker 2009: 162).

In all of this, Matta-Clark does more than propose alternative or extranormal dimensions of being in built and perceived space. He expands space into spheres of otherworldliness (Hertz 2006: 21). He told Judith Kirshner that in the five years running up to 1978, his sense of space had evolved beyond the senses that most people had (Kirshner 1978: 327). He was think-ing and working (and tempting people to follow him) in alternative, sensory, spatial worlds. His interest was in exploration and in the extension of the world beyond the common limits that we accept as normal.

Relevance to Măgura

What relevances do *Conical Intersect* and Matta-Clark's cutting works have for our examination of the Măgura pit-houses? As with Ron Athey's *4 Scenes in a Harsh Life* (chapter 2) and most of the work included in this book, the funda-mental connection is with the practice, action, meaning, and consequences of cutting. The essence of Matta-Clark's *Conical Intersect*, and of his best-known work, emerges from breaking building surfaces with saws, chisels, and hammers. Where Matta-Clark cut walls and floors, the Măgura diggers cut the ground (Figure 5.14). Where plaster and lath showered down from the cut to the ground below, so the soil from the pit-house was thrown up and out onto the ground around the pit. Particularly valuable for our examination are the following connections between *Conical Intersect* and Măgura: cutting as de-

FIGURE 5.14 Excavations at Măgura-Buduiasca, view to the west; Sondages 22, 20, 19 and 21, clockwise from the top left. Photo copyright D. W. Bailey.

struction; spectator-participants and their disorientation; the contents of the
visual field; and the contexts of political significance.

Cutting/Destroying

Cutting was Matta-Clark's medium as much as were the buildings or surfaces
that he perforated. Matta-Clark's cuts were more than mere perforation; their
power came from the paradox of creation though destruction. Thus, each cut
into the wall, each dissection of a floorboard, each strike of chisel piercing
roof-tin weakened and disarticulated a materially coherent structure: the
houses at 27 and 29 rue de Beaubourg. These cuts destroyed. At the same
time, each of these destructive acts was essential to the creation of the work of
art, of the entity that we refer to as *Conical Intersect*. These destructive acts
alter one object (the house) by transforming and undermining its meaning,
history, integrity, and potential future use. The cuts are violent acts; the violence leads to heightened awarenesses (Antwerp 1977). The destructive cuts,
therefore, created through unmaking.

At another level, the rue de Beaubourg houses were themselves scheduled
to be destroyed (as was all of the surrounding neighborhood) as part of the
modernization of this part of Paris. Following the destruction-thinking further,
we recognize that the very work that Matta-Clark created though destruction
as a contribution to the Ninth Biennale de Paris (*Conical Intersect*) only ever
had one future: its own destruction. The two buildings had been condemned
before the work started (and perhaps were only available because of such status),
and the teams of "professional" building destroyers moved in to pull down *Conical
Intersect* soon after Matta-Clark completed his work. In these senses, the work
is wholly empowered and enveloped by processes and acts of destruction.

While we are at ease recognizing that destruction is a primary process
of creation in Matta-Clark's work, archaeologists are less willing to examine
the role of destruction as the foundational act in the creation of pit-houses.
What happens when we step away from the traditional drive to understand
pits and pit-houses in terms of their contents and of the activities that took
place within them, after they had been created (i.e., after the ground had been
cut)? What happens when we focus on the act of digging the Măgura pit (cutting the hole into the ground's surface) in the same way that we think about
Conical Intersect?

What is being destroyed in the Măgura context? The question is unsettling; we even struggle to begin to answer it. Standard approaches to pit-houses
see them as early acts of creating a built environment, of making architecture.
Destruction has no place in the building narrative of Neolithic creations of

new ways of living. Setting aside that tradition of thinking, we see that it is the ground that is being cut; it is the integrity of the surface of the ground that is being destroyed. Some of the same important issues are in play here as in the relevance to Măgura of Ron Athey's *4 Scenes in a Harsh Life*, but also as suggested for a rethinking about the Wilsford Shaft and the holes cut and used at Down Farm. Most particular is the position of ground in the minds, spirits, and lives of the people digging the hole, watching it being dug, and talking about it being dug: ground as essential to life; ground as the appropriate place into which to put particular objects; ground as a source of material and spiritual resources; ground as boundary; and ground as vessel of powerful, perhaps mystical and dangerous essences of other worlds. Other similarities with the Athey and Wilsford discussions apply here as well. It matters when that ground is cut. It is important to understand who has the right to cut and who does not. Significant are the reactions that people had to the destruction of ground surface integrity, particularly as fear, threat, upset, and anxiety probably engulfed them.

Spectators/Participants/Disorientation

Matta-Clark intentionally brought spectators into his work. In Paris, he took time to speak with the people who stopped on the street to watch *Conical Intersect* as it took shape. He wanted to know what they thought when they watched what he was doing. Their understandings of the work were as much a part of the work as was the hole he was making. Spectators were partial collaborative participants. Their perspectives (visual, seen, observed, from the street, from other buildings, and of the films and photo collages made) were parts of what Matta-Clark and his team were making; those perspectives were not of secondary or tertiary significance.

Though these spectators (and the officials, reporters, and political commentators whose engagement was more indirect) reacted to the cutting of 27 and 29 rue de Beaubourg in different ways (in appreciation and in condemnation), those reactions had a common stimulus: the disorientation of spectators and the disruption of normal visual and physical perspectives. People were seeing things that ruptured their normal expectations not only of art works but also of the principles of architectural construction (i.e., this is not the way to make something that has walls, roofs, and floors) but also of the matching principles of architectural destruction and the accepted ways that buildings were demolished. Nothing was as it should be.

To the incorrect practices and actions (of building demolition and of making art), is added the perspectival disorientation that the angles and spaces of *Conical Intersect* present to the viewer: how could this new, open space within these buildings have been made (thus Matta-Clark's comment that it was as 'if he had thrown a steel ball through the building—an impossible action)? What function could the twisting cone have in normal architectural production? People who walked in the void of *Conical Intersect* after it was complete (as with other of Matta-Clark's cut buildings) spoke of their unease and imbalance, of an unnatural draw of gravity and visual perspective created by the cut. These disorientations and disruptions stimulated reaction (and heated opinion): some supportive, much dismissive. These viewer confusions and disruptions opened a conceptual space for reflection that was large and empty enough for the variety of reactions to find freedom of voice and opinion. Disruption and disorientation drew their strengths from the illogicality of cutting and through the paradox of creation-through-destruction. Matta-Clark destabilized the norms of our experiences, particularly the grounding devices of vertical and horizontal framing (Hertz 2006: 15) that are normally provided by a building's floors, ceiling, and walls.

As discussed in terms of Athey's *4 Scenes* and with Wilsford, archaeologists seldom fully consider the people digging pit-house holes in the Neolithic; seldom (never?) do we think about who was present, what they saw, what they thought, what role (if any) they had in the cutting of the ground, and how their conception of their world might have shifted with the cutting of the ground. I suggest that cutting the ground (i.e., in destroying the integrity of the ground surface) created the same disorientation and disruption of expectations and appropriate actions as were felt among spectators of *Conical Intersect*. Digging at Măgura or at Wilsford would have opened up not only the surface of the ground but also that same space of alternative perception that allowed for varieties of reactions and opinion as opened in Paris in 1975. *Conical Intersect* and other Matta-Clark works drew much of their impact and power from doing what was not expected (or accepted). Cutting the surface of the ground at Măgura 8000 years ago must have found similar energy and agency.

Opening up/Knowing

In much of his cutting work, Matta-Clark intended his cuts to open and liberate what was otherwise closed (Vidler 2006: 69), particularly to make fluid boundaries and borders (Walker 2009: 158), to expose to people views of what had been hidden (Hertz 2006: 12), and to release information that was otherwise unavailable (Béar 1974: 173), through a process of "spatial expansion" (Noever 1998: 88; Walker 2003: 163) (Figure 5.15). In these senses, breaking

FIGURE 5.15 Gordon Matta-Clark, *Conical Intersect* (1974). Photo © Marc Petitjean; © 2017 Estate of Gordon Matta-Clark/Artists Rights Society (ARS), New York.

the surface was less destructive than it was liberating (Attlee 2003c: 30), an act of search and discovery, and another way of knowing (Walker 2009). To cut apart a building was to analyze it (Béar 1974: 167), to see what is there, and to clarify what one finds (Simon 1985: 190, 199). The slow heavy physical process of cutting the building was a way of getting to know that place (Béar 1974: 175), though this knowing was ambiguous and complex. Buildings became at the same time more and less than what they were; where does it begin and where does it end? (Wagner 2004: 35). By cutting, Matta-Clark complicates a spectator's reading of the building: it loses legibility (Lee 1999: 158), though enough familiar elements remain to allow familiarity to reassure (Walker 2009: 13–15).

The loss of horizon (or the alteration of horizons) complicates diggers' and spectators' attempts to locate the new space created within a broader system of reference and meaning (Walker 2009: 99). The normally established relationships that are expected become unsettled. Our normal reliance on subconscious connections with cardinal directionality and with gravity loses its foundations. No longer solid, our physical relations to the ground come into question (Walker 2003: 15), and our positions relative to normal spaces are inverted (Hertz 2006: 20). With the loss of expected, familiar horizons, however, come new and unexpected vistas that the cuts open to us (Attlee 2003c: 29; 2003b: 53). These other worlds now opened, always present but previously hidden, are exposed to people, both those digging and watching. This otherworldliness is outside of the norms of the everyday (Hertz 2006: 21).

Visual Field

Matta-Clark's work forces us to confront what we often ignore or what we actively "disappear" in our archaeological investigations, reconstructions, and explanations. Archaeologists seldom give full thought to the relational contexts of what was around the hole as it was dug in the ground 8000 years ago, or to how people's perspectives of it would have been changed as the hole in the ground widened and deepened. Seldom do we think of what is in the actual experienced Neolithic periphery of a pit-house when we excavate and plot it. Our archaeological efforts are usually limited to flattened two-dimensional graphic mappings of the distribution of pits across a landscape that we compress by the pencil, site-grid, total station, paper and published illustration in plan-view.[12]

For Matta-Clark, the visible context of *Conical Intersect* included the emerging Centre Pompidou as well as the surrounding neighborhood of ancient buildings, dirty and in demolition. When Matta-Clark's work created (made unavoidable, even) a particular perspective of the Centre Pompidou, the buildings being destroyed, as well as the Tour Eiffel, it also broadened the spectator's visual field of *Conical Intersect*. Occupying that field were other buildings, in other conditions, in the process of being built, in the process of being torn down, in the stability of regular quotidian use. Differences between the physical states of these local buildings brought into play contrasts and similarities that filled-in subtle but important gaps in the presence of *Conical Intersect* in its particular built and active environments. In this sense, Matta-Clark's work was defined by what it was not, precisely what it was no longer, and what it would never be again: an occupied house (thus the subtitle *Étant d'art pour locataire* [Art for the Lodger]), and a durable piece of contemporary art available for curation and preservation. It is impossible to know *Conical Intersect* without acknowledging these other parts of one's field of vision of the work.

As archaeologists, when we excavate, plan, photograph, describe, interpret, and explain the Neolithic pit-houses at Măgura, we normally avoid expanding the visual field to similar breadth. It is not enough to draw plans showing the distribution across two dimensions of other pit-houses. The example of *Conical Intersect* suggests that we should expand our visual field more broadly to include components of a lived ground surface that existed beyond the archaeologically recoverable record. Seen in these contexts, Matta-Clark's work suggests that when we fail to broaden the visual field, we are disappearing parts of the visual landscape that are essential to Neolithic and modern understandings of pit-houses.

Part of the expanded visual field consists of archaeologically recoverable features and objects, artifacts, and traces of prehistoric behavior. We include these elements in our descriptions and reports; thus we reconstruct sizes of pit-house camps or villages and suggest population demographics and zones of activity. Beyond that, however, we provide little of the nuanced and rich detail that we see in an examination of works such as *Conical Intersect*. We relegate to the category of unrecoverable the types of elements, actions, and responses that provide the depth of our understanding of Matta-Clark's work. Indeed, in standard archaeological practice, these elements, actions, and responses are not easily excavated or recorded, if they can be located at all.

Political Context

Our appreciation of *Conical Intersect* is inseparable from the political contexts of the regeneration of Les Halles, of the creation of the Centre Pompidou, of Matta-Clark's own trajectory of work (the latter in contexts of late 1960s and early 1970s social and artistic trends), as well as the program of the

Ninth Biennale de Paris. Though the work exists without these contexts (and one can describe it in formal, descriptive detail), the resulting representation of it is empty of much of (perhaps all) the meaning that gives the work its full, rich, and provocative intentions, meanings, and consequences. The strength of *Conical Intersect* builds on the political contexts against which, along with, and from which the work struggles and emerges, escapes from, or succumbs to when the buildings are finally pulled down. Matta-Clark preferred to site/sight/cite his works so that they played against already easily recognized contexts or monuments of symbolic value (Crow 2003: 110; Wall 1976: 182), or to make work in places that were outside of society or in wastelands or derelict and dangerous places (Antwerp 1977: 250), or to choose a site for work where his interventions created acts of communication (Wall 1976: 183). He chose buildings to work in where he made non.u.ments to communities and histories that had been forgotten or neglected (Kirshner 2003: 153).

In our traditional approaches we fail to locate the corresponding political contexts at Măgura. We expend little effort in uncovering the corresponding monuments of symbolic value. Or was this place outside of society? We should seek out what may have been derelict or dangerous wasteland. We need to work through the possible acts of communication. Part of the power of *Conical Intersect* came from the work's location within a larger urban redevelopment project that was designed to modernize (read here as to sanitize and to clear of foreigners, criminality, immorality) the Les Halles neighborhood. Matta-Clark's act of destruction sits within this political context: *Conical Intersect* as a destructive-act-of-creation in a neighborhood where destructive-acts-of-moral-cleansing were in full motion. The action of cutting the ground for the pit-house at Măgura must have had a similarly significant, surrounding political context. These actions would have affected the integrity of the ground surface at Măgura. The digging of a pit would have either fit into or reacted against those actions, that context, and those communications.

Archaeology is well versed in the other Neolithic interruptions of the ground surface at sites like Măgura. We know that the clay used to make the pottery found at the site (and deposited in the house-pits) came from easily accessible local sources. We know that the ground surface was subject to frequent alterations in local hydrologic conditions as the character, course, and location of the river changed with variations in climate, rainfall, and flood events. We know that people were not practicing large-scale plant cultivation technologies at this time in this landscape: they were not yet the intensive farmers of wheat and barley, and thus clearing, planting, tending, or harvesting were not yet part of common shared understandings. We know that longer running series of pit-diggings took place on this middle terrace of the Vedea River Valley: that people understood that holes cut into the ground were of particular form and that it was appropriate to put objects into those holes and cover them up.

Some political correspondence between *Conical Intersect* and Măgura may come in response to Matta-Clark's alignment of the openings he made in the rue de Beaubourg houses: directing the spectator's visual focus to the future (i.e., the not yet completed Centre Pompidou) and the past (i.e., the Tour Eiffel). Similar directing of spectator attention would have been in play at Măgura. The digging of the pits altered two perspectives. The first is the perspective of the viewer watching the cutting of the hole as seen from the un-cut ground surface. The digging of the hole allows/insists on a viewing of what is below and within the ground: a looking down into what is normally unviewable, hidden, absent, contained. Normally, this is a view of the past, or of another world, or of another part of the viewer's world that, though known, talked about, invoked, feared, added to, or considered, was out of bounds or restrained beyond the boundary of the ground surface.

A second altered perspective is that of the digger cutting the hole, standing (or kneeling or sitting) below the level of the ground, and looking up and out. The digger's view is of an altered horizon: in fact, of both a new horizon (the edge for the hole—a horizon where below ground meets ground surface) and a more regularly experienced horizon (where the sky meets the edge of the land, itself the surface of the ground that is being cut). Here, then, digging the hole multiplies the horizons available: ground-to-sky (expected and routine) that separates the world of people, plants, animals, water, and fire; and ground-to-below-ground (unusual and normally absent) that separates that same world of the people, plants, and animals from something dark, moist, and unexplored.

If horizons separate different worlds (and parts of worlds—heavens from earth, celestial from non-celestial), then the addition of this new horizon that bounds a lower world from a grounded one must be significant. I suggest that this below-ground world and the revelation, recognition, and viewing of its horizon are part of the political contexts at Măgura. Where *Conical Intersect*'s holes directed viewers' attentions to the future and the past (and their connection via the political dynamics of the present), the Măgura pit-house holes may well have directed viewers' attentions to a world above and a world below (and their connection via the political dynamics of their present).

A further potential political context may be read in terms of the way that both cuttings manipulate spatial and temporal relationships. Like many artists working in the late 1960s and 1970s, Matta-Clark made impermanent works that prevented attempts at collection, curation, purchase, sale, and control by galleries, museums, or collectors (Kirshner 1978: 331). Often work was beyond the physical capacity of galleries (in terms of size or materials or site specificity), and often work lacked durability (either through the use of fugitive materials or through the acts of planned destruction). These works denied lasting presence or control by traditional institutions of the art world. *Conical Intersect* was one such work. Impermanence was made through destruction of the completed work.

The Măgura pits engage similar issues of permanence and control though to opposite effect. Digging the pits into the ground made permanent the otherwise transient actions of the diggers cutting the ground's surface. The acts of cutting and destroying the integrity of the ground surface (and the consequences of doing so) took physical form. These transitory acts were locked into a particular place as gestures made manifest. As Matta-Clark's uncontrollable art avoided the permanence of curation and collection, so the Măgura pits invited, even demanded, these responses. In the context of a mobile Măgura community, the establishment of locational anchors of action-to-place would have had a political significance of similar magnitude to the corresponding untethering of art work from permanence in its creation. Permanence was made from destruction of the integrity of the ground surface.

The Unavailability of Meaning

A final relevance for Măgura of *Conical Interest* is the conundrum we face in our searches for the meanings of sites, of works, and of breaks in the surface. For *Conical Intersect* we have a vast array of sources to consult, to find out what the work meant, to know what Matta-Clark intended, to learn what people in September 1975 in Paris thought about the work, and to tease out how the work fits into both Matta-Clark's oeuvre and late twentieth-century art: films, photographs, interviews, local and international press reports, and an ever-increasing library of secondary articles, books, and conference sessions on Matta-Clark in general and on this work in particular. In all of this, however, the deeper we dig, the more we learn, the less certain we are that there is any one (or even several) primary meaning or correct interpretation for the work. The more we know, the less certain we are that what we know is the single, correct understanding of *Conical Intersect*.

Matta-Clark understood his works as unfinished: both the buildings he cut and the photo collages he created of them. Pieces are missing from both; both works are fragmentary (Walker 2009: 72, 105). In his use of multiple-image photo collages and, especially, the editing of film, Matta-Clark wanted to reproduce the experience of the work by giving the viewer of the image an ambulatory experience, as if he or she was moving through the work (Kirshner 1978: 323–333). At a deeper level, Matta-Clark's interest in spaces stood against any possible function that they might have; he thought of space in non-functional ways, and his work took issue with the functionalist attitude (Wall 1976: 182). Literally, his works disabled the usual function of the buildings that he cut (Crow 2003: 22).

For Măgura we have the opposite problem (or so it seems): a clear set of data recovered through excavation and post-excavation analysis, but very little of the rich, multimedia of political, social, or economic background contexts in which to put the pit-house. For Măgura, we strain to find a corresponding set of documents (the people are long gone, preservation is moderate at best) or even applicable ethnographic or historic parallels. We read reports from sites similar to Măgura from the same period, located in this or in neighboring regions. Frustrated, we find nothing fresh in those discussions, no access to the level of social, political beings, and confrontations that made the examination of *Conical Intersect* so engaging and sumptuous. An initial reaction to working with Măgura is frustration; we hit a wall through which we cannot move, and around which we cannot find a path. The common result in archaeological interpretation is to default to terms such as house, home, storage, rubbish, ritual deposits; each of these suggestions avoids (disappears, even) the importance of the act of cuttings that Matta-Clark's work celebrated.

For both sites, therefore, meaning is unavailable. In many ways, of course, this is one of the values of the work of Matta-Clark (and of many others) and of the late twentieth-century opening up of interpretations to multiple perspectives. Archaeology has made significant progress in this direction, and some philosophical traditions within archaeology have proved to be more flexible than others. In the mainstream explanation of action in the past, however, we remain limited to a search for single meanings; certainly in the public's understanding of the past there is no room for the dynamism of multiple meanings in the same way that large parts of a public understanding of art has gained a greater appreciation and acceptance for corresponding dynamisms and multiplicities.

Matta-Clark stood against solutions and answers. His call was to question, not to solve (Walker 2009: 16). The concept he termed "living archaeology" promoted the value of the incomplete, the non-chronological, and the fragmentary. He argued that we should maintain the gaps in (pre)history, avoid the creation of complete maps of history, but seek ways to complicate coherences (Walker 2003: 174; Walker 2009: 83). At Măgura, the pits are the gaps. Our incomplete, unfinished, unattainable explanations of them are gaps as well. Our goal should not be to fill them.

Chapter 6

Cut

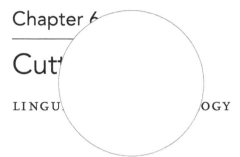

The Cut/Break

IN THE DISTANCE she could see trees, if she looked in that direction. Closer were cornfields. From her perch on a low wooden stool the woman watches a video played for her. She turns to a second woman who sits on a blanket on the ground, her legs out in front of her, her hands crossed on her lap. On the screen, a clip of a man slicing a carrot with a knife starts to play. To the left of the woman on the stool, a cassette tape player turns and beside it a man on a wooden chair is writing in a notebook he holds open with his left hand. He wears headphones and listens to the questions and answers as the tape records. While the woman on the ground watches the video, the first woman asks her, "Binti ya spas, te winike?" (Figure 6.1).

The women are speaking Tzeltal, a Mayan language that as many as half a million people speak but which many fewer use as their only language in the Mexican state of Chiapas. In English, the question asked means "What is the man doing?" The woman on the ground answers, "Ya s-bikit boj-tikla ala senoria li' ta ba mexa. Ya s-bikit boj jilele." The best English translation is "He small-cuts (i.e., cuts into small bits) the little carrot here on top of the table. He small-cuts it leaving them (pieces) behind. As for the carrot, it has been small-cut up completely." The man makes notes.

They move on to a different clip. The woman on the stool asks the same question. The woman on the ground answers. The man fills his pages. The tape records. That afternoon and again the next day, the questioner-and-note-taker team runs the same videos for other speakers of Tzeltal, and they record the responses. Working through the tape recordings and the notes, the team transcribes the answers; they check that the transcriptions are accurate by working with other locals.[1]

As an archaeologist, when I speak to someone about Măgura, and tell them that people dug holes into the earth there 8000 years ago, I ask myself

FIGURE 6.1 Penelope Brown interviewing a Tzeltal speaker in the early 1990s. Photo copyright Penelope Brown; reproduced by permission.

what does it mean? The question addresses both those long-dead, now silent, people and what they might have meant, but also what we mean today when we think of the digging of those holes. What does it mean to dig a pit in the ground, to cut the ground, or break the surface of the earth? How do we conceptualize the digging of holes in the ground and the cutting of that surface? Do all people think of these actions in the same way? If not, then what are the important differences in the ways that diverse groups of people understand cutting into and breaking the ground? What do we know about how different people think about the acts of digging into the ground, or of the events and actions of cutting or breaking in more general senses? One approach is to examine the ways that people conceive of events of material separation (a more precise description of cutting and breaking) through the ways that they talk about it. Digging a pit is breaking the surface of the ground; it is the action of cutting into a material (the ground) and of material separation. While there are very many, perhaps infinite, ways of thinking about types and actions of material separation, linguists and linguistic anthropologists have discovered that languages encode cutting and breaking events with a limited range of verb semantics. The significance for the project of assessing the pit-houses of Măgura, however, is to note the rich and intricate variations within and between language communities' uses of cut and break language, and to recognize the difficulty we would have in trying to reconstruct any one (or even several) perception that people had about cutting the surface of the ground 8000 years ago.

This chapter reveals the complexity and variations of ways in which people think about cutting, what they cut, how they cut it, and (often) what they cut it with. The discussion centers on the results obtained by a group of linguistic anthropologists studying the ways that people conceptualize acts of cutting and breaking. Detailed descriptions of several key language groups are included here with particular attention paid to variations and similarities in the ways in which different languages handle cutting and breaking. From these descriptions and discussions, I draw key features and use them to redefine pit-houses in terms of cuts made by particular utensils, in specific ways, with certain intentions and results. "Cut" is held to be distinct from "break," and the action of cutting the ground finds meaning and value in the suggestion that cuts and the object being cut find added value when invested with the concepts of the grain of the ground surface and the impact that cutting has on the integrity of the ground. Finally, I suggest a redefinition of Măgura pit-houses (and of pits for that matter for this and other periods and regions) in terms of cutting.

A Linguistic Anthropology of Cutting and Breaking

Starting in 2001, under the direction of Stephen Levinson, a group of linguists and linguistic anthropologists at the Max Planck Institute for Psycholinguistics at Nijmegen, the Netherlands, designed and carried out a major study of the varieties and commonalities in the ways that people speaking different languages semantically categorize events of material separation (Ameka and Essegbey 2007; Bohnemeyer et al. 2001; Bohnemeyer 2007; Brown 2007; Essegbey 2007; Gaby 2007; Levinson 2007; Lüpke 2007; Majid et al. 2007a, 2008; Narasimhan 2007; Taylor 2007; van Staden 2007).[2] In their research, the linguists examined the different ways that different language groups encode cutting and breaking events: cutting, breaking, slicing, chopping, hacking, tearing, ripping, smashing, shattering, and snapping are the most common (Majid et al. 2007a: 134). The team investigated whether or not different groups of people (defined linguistically) shared a universal way of thinking about cutting and breaking events. The team discovered that different languages handle cutting and breaking events in different ways, although there are important similarities across languages (Majid et al. 2007a: 133; Majid et al. 2008).

Asifa Majid and her colleagues (Majid et al. 2007a: 134) remind us that in current thinking on cross-linguistic research, two opposing positions are in play. A standard school of thought is that the categories that people associate with everyday words are largely universal across cultures and languages (Bloom 2000; E. Clark 1976; H. Clark 1973; Gleitman 1990; Piaget 1954; Slobin 1973). In opposition is the belief that semantic categories of everyday words vary in response to local economic, social, political, environmental, and cultural contexts (Bowerman and Choi 2001; Malt et al. 1999, 2003; Wilkins and Hill 1995). The latter, contextual position is the one favored by Majid and her colleagues and it is the one followed here.

Method

To examine the variation of cutting and breaking verbs across linguistic groups, the Max Planck team designed a detailed study to investigate how different people understood the events of breaking and cutting (Majid et al. 2007a, 2008). In this Event Representation Project, the researchers developed a methodology for study and applied it commonly in each of a range of field studies carried out by team members in different language communities. The team created a series of video clips showing scenes in which people cut and broke objects (Figure 6.2). The clips included varieties of objects that were cut or broken (e.g., stick, rope, cloth, plate, pot, hair, food items), of tools that did the cutting (e.g., hand, knife, scissors, karate-chop, machete, hammer), and of the action undertaken (e.g., once or repeatedly, calmly or with furious intensity). The videos included other acts of separation: opening the hand, or a teapot or book; taking the top off a pen, pulling apart paper cups, and peeling a banana).[3] Team members showed these clips to the speakers of languages in which each project worker was expert. They asked the local subjects to provide verbal descriptions in their own languages for each act of cutting and breaking that they saw in the clips. The team made audio and video recordings of the reactions and then transcribed the responses (Majid et al. 2007a: 139).

The team studied twenty-seven typologically, genetically, and geographically diverse languages from thirteen language families in twenty-three countries: Altaic (Turkish), Austronesian (Biak, Kilivila), Cariban (Tiriyo), Indo-European (Dutch, English, German, Hindi, Punjabi, Spanish, Swedish),

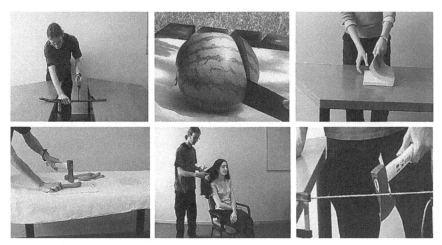

FIGURE 6.2 Examples of cutting and breaking events used in studies by Majid and colleagues (after Majid et al. 2008: figure 1).

Mayan (Tzeltal, Yukatek), Niger-Congo (Ewe, Jalonke, Kipke), Otomanguean (Otomi), Pama-Nyungan (Kuuk Thaayorre), SinoTibetan (Mandarin), Tai (Lao), West Papuan Phylum (Tidore), Witotian (Miraña), Creole (Sranan), two isolates (Chontal, Japanese), and two Papuan isolates (Touo, Yélî Dnye) (Majid et al. 2007a: 137; 2008). Subjects shown the clips ranged from industrial urban dwellers to rainforest dwelling swidden agriculturalists.

Results

This cross-linguistic methodology allowed the team to identify (dis)similarity among the semantic categories of different language communities' descriptions of cutting and breaking events (Majid et al. 2007a: 140). The events have different linguistic labels and thus are distinct from one another (i.e., the words categorize the semantic domain of cut and break events). Results of statistical analysis (Figure 6.3) (for details, see Majid et al. 2007a: 140–142; Majid et al. 2008) revealed the following. First, events of opening, taking apart, and peeling-from are distinguished from events of separation by material destruction (Majid et al. 2007a: 142). Second, verbs describing events of opening are encoded differently in different languages, and differently even within the same language (but see exceptions in Tidore and Kuuk Thaayorre by van Staden [2007] and Gaby [2007], respectively). Finally, the most important linguistically distinguished feature of the cutting and breaking events shown in the clips was whether or not the place of break or cut (i.e., of separation) could be predicted before the cutting or breaking action occurred.

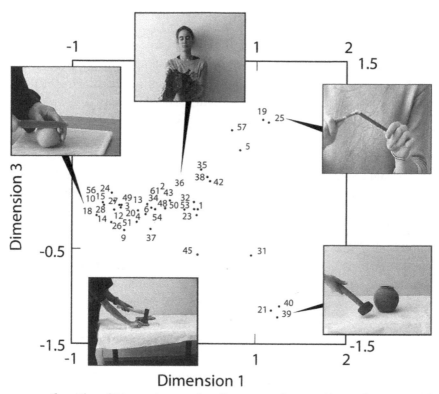

FIGURE 6.3   Plot of Dimension 1 and 3 of correspondence analysis of "cutting and breaking" verbs (redrawn by Sveta Matskevich after Majid et al. 2008: figure 4).

Cutting Versus Breaking

The difference in an event's predictability is the basis for distinguishing between cutting events/verbs and breaking events/verbs (Taylor 2007: 332). All twenty-seven languages studied made a distinction in the predictability of the event of separation: thus, in English, the outcome of a cutting event is more predictable than that for a breaking one (Majid et al. 2007b: 188–189). Some events, such as slicing a carrot with a knife, are highly predictable; the specific place where the carrot will be separated can be predicted based on where the knife is placed (Majid et al. 2008: 242). Other events, such as breaking a stick with one's hands, are highly unpredictable; the place where the break will occur is difficult to know, and it is not even possible to know whether one or many breaks will result. Other events, such as karate-chopping an object, are less predictable than cutting the carrot with a knife but more predictable than breaking a stick with your hands; these events rest in between the carrot-cutting and the stick-breaking on a spectrum of cutting and breaking predictability (Majid et al. 2008: 242).

Language-specific Diversity

In their overview of all of the languages studied, Majid and her colleagues suggest that the semantic space of cutting and breaking is highly constrained (Majid et al. 2008: 243), and that languages make similar sorts of distinctions in the cutting and breaking domain (Majid et al. 2008: 244). The important observation, however, is that there is diversity within languages spoken today in the ways that people think about cutting and breaking, perhaps more diversity than social scientists would realize, certainly more than many archaeologists would imagine. The following examples of language groups illustrate this pattern. Of most use for expanding our exploration of the surfaces that people cut are the unexpectedly diverse and unusual variations in how different communities think about and understand cutting-breaking: the varying significances placed on the object/tool of cutting-breaking, on the actor doing the cutting-breaking (and on his or her intention), on the object that is cut-broken, and on the result of the cut-break. The goal of this discussion and the examples presented here is not to find a linguistic group we can map onto the Măgura landscape, but to open up a space in which multiple and diverse local perspectives on the action of cutting the ground and of breaking its surface are given room to work with our thinking about the actions and thoughts in play 8000 years ago when people broke the ground and cut its surface in the digging of the holes for the pit-houses.

Germanic Languages

Majid and her colleagues' work on four Germanic languages (English, German, Dutch, and Swedish) showed that these languages vary both in the number of cutting and breaking categories that each language recognizes and in the relationship of those different terms to one another. Thus, English distinguishes between two large groups of verbs: *cutting* and *breaking* (Majid et al. 2007b: 189). German distinguishes three clusters of separation words: breaking (*brechen, schlagen, hacken*), cutting (*schneiden*), and tearing (*reissen*). Dutch distinguishes four clusters: breaking (*breken, hakken*), tearing (*scheuren*), cutting-with-a-single-blade (*snijden*), and cutting-with-scissors (*knippen*). Swedish has five: breaking (*bräcka, hugga*), snapping (*bryta*), cutting-with-a-single-blade (*skära*), cutting-with-scissors (*klippa*), and tearing (*slita*) (Majid et al. 2007b: 189–190). Similar attention to other, non-Germanic languages reveals the breadth of the range of numbers of verbs used in describing the events presented in the Max Planck team's sixty-one video clips. Thus, Tzeltal speakers in the highlands of Mexico use more than fifty verbs, each of which had highly specific semantics (Majid et al. 2008: 247; Brown 2007), while Yélî Dnye speakers in Papua New Guinea used only three verbs to describe all of the events portrayed in the clips (Majid et al. 2008: 247; Levinson 2007: 207).

In addition, the speakers of Germanic languages that the team studied differ in the depth of their hierarchical structure. English has the deepest structure: within its two main clusters (*cut* and *break*), there are a number of sub-clusters associated with subordinate terms such as *slice, chop, snap,* and *smash* (Majid et al. 2007b: 190). Swedish is different in hierarchy with a very flat structure consisting of five distinct clusters. Swedish speakers are more limited than English speakers; they have less linguistic room to describe an event in different ways. English speakers, on the other hand, can construe the same event in many different ways (Majid et al. 2007b: 190).

The Germanic languages studied in the project also differ in how they associate different cutting and breaking events into groups. Thus, English speakers group chopping events (e.g., separation caused by a sharp blow) with cutting events (e.g., slicing and cutting-with-scissors) (Majid et al. 2007b: 190). The other Germanic languages associate chopping with smashing events. The use of tearing is another example of this variation. German, Dutch, and Swedish have a distinct cluster for tearing events, while in English tearing events are a subtype of breaking events (Majid et al. 2007b: 190). Furthermore, the Germanic languages differ in how they distinguish cutting events. Dutch and Swedish separate cutting-with-scissors from cutting-with-a-blade, while English and German do not make a distinction based on the state of the cutting instrument (i.e., whether it is of one or two blades) (Majid et al. 2007b: 190).

For Germanic languages, cutting and breaking verbs are used and understood differently (Majid et al. 2007b: 191). Thus, English *break* subsumes finer distinctions (*snap, smash*) and is used to describe the destruction of a wide variety of objects. In German, Dutch, and Swedish, *bracken, breken,* and *bräcka* each have a much narrower application. German *bracken* and Dutch *breken* describe breaking long, thin things by hand (i.e., snapping events). Swedish *bräcka* is used for separating or cracking brittle, two-dimensional objects (Majid et al. 2007b: 191).

Germanic languages, therefore, show how categories of cutting and breaking can vary significantly even in closely related languages. As with their work on other languages in the study, Majid et al. interpret these distinctions as a factor of the predictability of the location of separation (Majid et al. 2007b: 192). They describe predictability as a spectrum ranging from events of separation by knives and scissors at one end, events in which a sharp blow causes the separation in the middle, and events of snapping and smashing at the other end (Majid et al. 2007b: 192). Thus, the study of Germanic languages shows both variation among what are otherwise closely related languages as well as similarities between the Germanic languages and other languages in terms of larger patterns, more specifically the predictability in the location of separation.

Ewe

A second case study of note from the Max Planck team's work is Ewe, a cluster of dialects spoken in southeastern Ghana, southern Togo, and across the Togo-Benin border. Here the distinction of significance among cutting and breaking verbs is agency. Following Guerssel and his colleagues (1985), Felix Ameka and James Essegbey (2007: 242) reassess the standard distinction of cutting and breaking verbs as highly agentive, agentive, non-agentive, and highly non-agentive. In this sense, cut verbs are understood to be highly agentive; break verbs, highly non-agentive. As an alternative, Ameka and Essegbey argue that the Ewe verbs possess a single core meaning with additional meanings "being encoded by constructions, i.e., form-meaning correspondences that exist independently of the verbs" (Ameka and Essegbey 2007: 242).

Highly agentive verbs invoke the instrument of cutting or breaking and the manner or purpose of the action: slash with a sharp instrument (*dza*), cut with sharp instrument (*si*), and carve (*kpa*) (Ameka and Essegbey 2007: 242). These verbs describe events that require the use of a sharp object, and they incorporate the particular manner or purpose of the action (Ameka and Essegbey 2007: 244) (Figure 6.4). Agentive verbs describe separations carried out by instruments in particular ways: cut with skill, cut cleanly, cut as if by a sharp instrument (*tso*), and all cutting events that involve a sharp instrument, though this is only seen in the southern dialects (*se*) (Ameka and Essegbey 2007: 245). Non-agentive verbs, such as snap off (*la*) and split (*dze*), describe a type

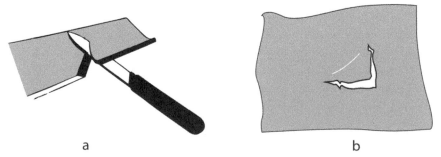

a   b

FIGURE 6.4 Ewe and the importance of agency of the cut or break: (a) agentive— cut with a sharp instrument (slash, carve), and (b) non-agentive— split (tear cloth), snap-off.

of separation, though *la* is used as a general cut verb in the inland dialects. Highly non-agentive verbs tear (*vuvu*), split (*fe*), break (*ne*), and break (*gaba*) incorporate either the type of object that undergoes a change or the nature of the change (Ameka and Essegbey 2007: 247). Highly agentive and highly non-agentive verbs behave like cut-verbs and break-verbs, respectively; agentive and non-agentive verbs sometimes behave like cut verbs and other times behave like break verbs (Ameka and Essegbey 2007: 249). Regardless, the pattern for Ewe is of variation within the types and uses of cut and break verbs.

Tzeltal

For the Mayan Tzeltal, Penelope Brown has shown that this language has a wide variety of roots that distinguish kinds of cutting and breaking events, has many cutting and breaking verbs that make culture-specific semantic distinctions, does not have any over-arching general verbs of cutting and breaking, and does not have any syntactic distinctions that provide clues to verb semantics (Brown 2007: 320). Instead the spatial and textual properties of the object being cut or broken are the key factors in finely distinguishing different cutting and breaking actions (Brown 2007: 319, 320).

Most important of these spatial and textural properties are (1) those relating to the object being cut: long, thin, hard (stick/nail; *k'as*), flexible (rope/cloth/leaf/paper; *ch'i*), round and hard (head/pot; *woch*), three-dimensional soft versus brittle (*sew* versus *top'*), small versus large object (*xet'* versus *xet*), or multi-stranded object (hair/grass/cornsilk; *jax*); (2) those referring to the spatial properties of the cutting or breaking action in relation to the object's axes or parts: cross/along the long axis (*set'* versus *sil* or *jep*), or part/whole relation (*k'ok*, *ch'uy*); and (3) those of the result and completion of the resulting effect: create a break in brittle object (*xet*) versus shatter it completely (*top'*) versus break into its inside (*woch*); make one cut or more than one (*tzep*, *p'ij* versus *sil*), or small versus large pieces (*t'ol* versus *jis*). (Figure 6.5)

Less significant in distinguishing some cut and break verbs are (4) the manner of the action: sharp blow (*boj*) versus sawing action (*tuy*), or suddenly split (*set'*) versus incremental, split/tear (*ch'i*); and (5) the type of instrument used: sharp blade (*set'*), or hands (*xet'*) (Brown 2007: 321). In other Mayan languages similar distinctions are made, though the ranking of their importance may be different. Thus, for Yukatek Mayan, one of the most significant properties of the cutting and breaking action is the instrument (for the Tzeltal, instrument is relevant for a very few verbs) (Brown 2007: 321; Bohnemeyer and Brown 2007). Brown concludes that for cut and break verbs, Tzeltal creates many "micro-distinctions"; this is especially the case for culturally

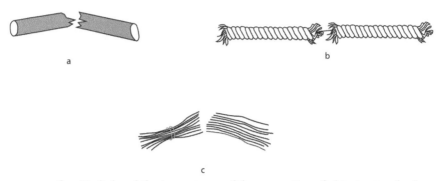

FIGURE 6.5 Tzeltal and the importance of the properties of object cut or broken between (a) long hard (stick), (b) flexible (rope), (c) and multistranded (hair, grass, corn silk).

defined actions: corn cultivation, food preparation, and firewood collection (Brown 2007: 326).

Mandarin

Mandarin is a good example of the way that the investigation of cut and break verbs supports both an argument for universality (e.g., a universal distinction between cutting and breaking verbs across different languages) and for diversity (e.g., variations within individual languages and between different languages). Mandarin follows a universal distinction between cutting and breaking verbs (after Guerssel et al. 1985; Levin and Rappaport Hovav 1995), but it differs significantly from other languages in particular ways (e.g., a distinction of cut and break in terms of semantics and argument structure) (Chen 2007: 274).

Within Mandarin, three types of cutting and breaking events are distinguished by three types of verbs: verbs that differentiate on the basis of instrument, manner, and the properties of the affected object (action verbs); verbs that differentiate on the basis of the affected object (result verbs: i.e., co-occurring with cut and break verbs to specify the resultant state); and verbs that specify both (resultative verb compounds) (Chen 2007: 283). In addition, Mandarin contains five distinct clusters of cutting and breaking verbs: (1) the most distinct cluster, cutting with scissor-like bladed instrument (jian3);[4] (2) cutting with a single-blade-like instrument (knife, machete, axe, edge of hand, wire); (3) breaking with a hammer-like instrument (hammer, pound, hit); (4) pulling on a flexible two-dimensional object (e.g., cloth, paper) with hands or a hand(-like) instrument (rip, tear); and (5) bending or pulling on a linear object (e.g., stick, carrot) with hands or a hand-like instrument (bend by hand, pluck, pull, stretch) (Chen 2007: 277). At the most general level, Chen identifies the more important distinction among Mandarin cutting and breaking action

a   b

FIGURE 6.6 Mandarin and the important distinction of (a) separation by an instrument other than a hand (e.g., hammer, knife, axe), and (b) separation with a hand or hand-like instrument (e.g., rip/tear or bending).

verbs as the distinction between separation with a hand, or hand-like instrument versus separation with instruments other than hand, or hand-like instruments (Chen 2007: 278) (Figure 6.6). However, in certain instances, it is also the case that the instrument-versus-non-instrument distinction is less important than the manner in which the break or cut is made (e.g., cutting with an axe in a swinging manner) (Chen 2007: 278). Furthermore, Mandarin has no overarching generic verb that can be used across events like slicing, hacking, chopping, trimming, and sawing (Chen 2007: 279).

Yet further distinctions are found within Mandarin's five core result verbs. These verbs are grouped into three groups: (1) be open or be apart (*kail*), be broken of long objects broken crosswise (*duan4*); (2) be in pieces (*sui4*), be in pieces, mashed, tattered or rotten, unusable (*lan4*); and (3) be broken of a non-linear object (*Po4*), general destruction of an object, be wounded (Chen 2007: 279). Result verbs differentiate cutting and breaking events along three semantic dimensions: (1) features of the affected object (e.g., linear or other), (2) state or degree of being broken (e.g., to be in pieces), and (3) duration of the separation (e.g., crosswise versus some other direction).

For Mandarin thus, the team found a rich range of variation that speakers used to differentiate their understanding of how breaking and cutting takes place, of the different materials that are cut and broken, and of the result of those actions. The pattern that is emerging across the diverse language groups that the Planck team studied is one of highly specific variation.

Jalonke

In Jalonke (a variety of Yalunka, a Central Mande language spoken in the north of Ghana), the distinction of cutting and breaking verbs takes account of four conditions of the action: (1) whether or not the agent of the separation has control over the location of the cut or break, (2) whether the object being broken or cut is whole or whether it was previously detached from some other thing, (3) whether or not the verb specifies a particular manner or instrument of cutting and breaking, and (4) whether the state change caused by the cut or break happened in a stereotypical or unexpected way (Lüpke 2007: 254). One of the emphases of importance here is the role of the agent: either willful and controlling or merely as an instigator (Lüpke 2007: 259n2) (Figure 6.7). To cut (*sege*) and pierce (*tumba*) refer to control over the location of impact; pound again (*i-din*) describes imprecise impact, for example of a hammer, and break again (*i-gira*); and cut/break into two pieces (*i-dogoti*) describes the separation of oblong, thin objects in places not under the control of the agent (Lüpke 2007: 254).

Also of note for Jalonke is the issue of whether or not an object has been cut/broken before; Lüpke does not know of another language that makes this distinction. For example, ropes and cloth that have already been detached from a larger roll or piece of fabric require one linguistic construction; leaves, twigs, fruit, and vegetables that are whole and still attached to the tree, vine, plant, or bush require a different one (Lüpke 2007: 254). In many cases, the instrument used and the manner in which it is used determine the verb employed. This is a significant factor in differentiating between cut and break verbs. Cut verbs of necessity involve particular instruments: cut in one stroke (*sege*), cut in swinging, shaving movements (*bii*), and cut/saw in several strokes with a saw or a knife with saw teeth (*xaba*). Break verbs do not specify instrument: destroy or break with hands, feet, tools, or an object (*kana*) (Lüpke 2007: 255).

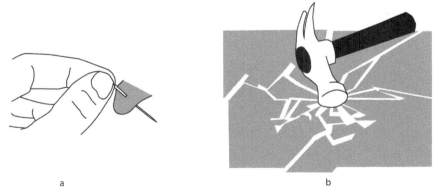

a   b

FIGURE 6.7 Janlonke and the importance in cutting and breaking of whether the agent is (a) willful and controlling (pierce) or (b) an instigator (pound with a hammer).

Hindi and Tamil

The pattern of variation continues in Bhuvana Narasimhan's (2007) analysis of Hindi (an Indo-European language spoken in North India) and Tamil (a Dravidian language spoken in South India). Narasimhan reveals similar distinctions between cutting and breaking verbs as recognized in many other languages: cutting events involve a high degree of predictability in the location of the separation; breaking verbs involve greater uncertainty (Narasimhan 2007: 195) (Figure 6.8). In addition, in Hindi and Tamil, distinctions in cutting and breaking verbs depend on several factors: the properties of what is being cut or broken; the type of instrument used to make the separation, and the manner in which the action is carried out (Narasimhan 2007: 195). Furthermore, Hindi and Tamil speakers distinguish tearing events from cutting and breaking events (Narasimhan 2007: 196). Compared to many other languages, Tamil and Hindi are unusual in their grouping of snapping and smashing events under the same verb (Narasimhan 2007: 196).

Furthermore, there are important differences between Hindi and Tamil. Thus, with the verbs for "break," the "boundaries of the category" vary in the two languages based on the properties of the instrument and the object acted upon (Narasimhan 2007: 197). For example, both Hindi and Tamil use the break verb to separate by a blunt instrument, such as a hand or a hammer, on rigid objects, such as pot, plate, or branch. In Hindi, the verb "break" (toD/) is applied to the separation of rigid objects when the break will occur where the instrument makes contact, as well as to non-rigid objects and instruments with blade-like characteristics. Tamil use of "break" (oD/ai) is more restrictive; it only applies "break" (oD/ai) to events of separation of rigid vents (Narasimhan 2007: 199). Also, Tamil is more restrictive in the properties of

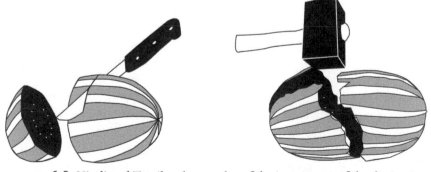

FIGURE 6.8 Hindi and Tamil and examples of the importance of the distinction between (a) predictable cutting (to carve, slash, slice with a bladed instrument) and (b) uncertain breaking (of a pot, plate, branch with a blunt instrument).

the instruments used: only blunt instruments or instruments with a flat blade-like surface.

Similar levels of distinctions are found with the use of the verb "to smash"; Hindi speakers use both the verb for "smash" (*toD/*) and a verb that means "a violent breaking of an object into several pieces" (*phoD/*) to describe the same event of smashing a plate or a pot. Where the object broken is not as brittle as a pot or plate (e.g., a carrot), Hindi speakers use a different verb for "smash" (*thakuuc(s)*); Tamil speakers do not differentiate such smashing events from other types of breaking, but label them with the verb "to break" (*oD/*) (Narasimhan 2007: 199). Other important differences are present in the two languages' uses of verbs for "cutting" and for "opening," as well as in variation of use between speakers of the same language (Narasimhan 2007: 200–202). Thus, Narasimhan's study of Hindi and Tamil found that though there are broad similarities between Hindi and Tamil verbs of "breaking," there are also important differences of a more fine-grained nature, such as the boundaries of meaning for the verbs, the pool of verbs available to describe cutting and breaking, and the finer semantic distinctions made in their use (Narasimhan 2007: 203).

Chontal

Adding more examples to the emerging pattern of variation within language groups, though with similarities in the ranges of that variation across groups, is Loretta O'Connor's study of Lowland Chontal (as spoken along the coastal plain of Oaxaca, Mexico). O'Connor documented three factors of distinction in cut and break verbs: the action that causes the separation (delivery-of-force, a cut-like class), the type of change in the object (a break-like class), and a class of verb that describes the result state as "apart" (O'Connor 2007: 222, 224–225). Delivery-of-force verbs focus on the manner of the act of separation: cut, break, separate (*tek'e*); cut, chop (*ñayk'e-*); perforate (*ñanjs'e-*); pound (*pinj-*); poke (*lyos*); and cut hair (*kegay'*) (O'Connor 2007: 224–225). Change of state verbs include break and smash (*pay'ee*); tear, split (*jas-*); shred (*ts'ajl-*); chop and dice (*telay-*); and bend or fold (*ts'ik'e-*). The verbs that focus on the result state of being-apart include break, snap apart (*tyof'ñi-*); tear apart, split apart (*jas'ñi*); divide apart (*skiñi-*); breaking apart of food (*pañi-*); and split by inserting something (*k'wañi-*) (O'Connor 2007: 225–226).

In addition, Chontal speakers perceive four major types of separation events: cut, break, separate (*tek'e*); tear, split (*jas-*); break, snap apart (*tyof'ñi-*); and break, smash (*pay'ee*) (O'Connor 2007: 223). As with Yélî Dnye, Chontal speakers distinguish events that describe ruptures with from those that go against the grain of an object (O'Connor 2007: 224). It is interesting to note the focus on the spontaneous change that occurs with the state change caused by breaking.

Tidore

For Tidore (a Papuan western outlier spoken in the North Moluccas), Mariam Van Staden reports that use of cut and break verbs is determined by several factors. The most important of these is the instrument used: break with hands or feet (*fago*); cut using scissors (*guti*); cut using a large cutting instrument (*tola*); stab, and pierce with a metal spike (*taji*) (Van Staden 2007: 298) (Figure 6.9). Also important is the manner in which the separation is caused (e.g., swaying the instrument over the shoulder) and the particular way that an instrument is held (e.g., held like a dagger or like a spear) (Van Staden 2007: 298). The result state is another factor: be scattered (*wayo*), to have a hole made (*tuso*), and to be bent or cracked but not broken (*ciko*) (Van Staden 2007: 299).

In some, less-frequent cases, the object being cut influences the use of the verb; thus *yaci* can only be used with cloth (Van Staden 2007: 299). Other

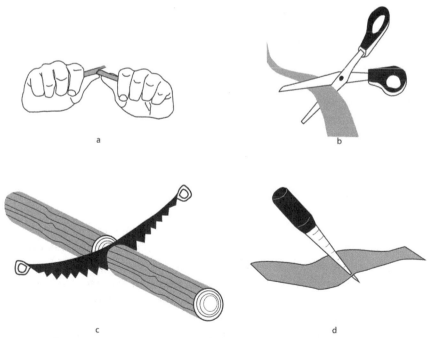

a   b   c   d

FIGURE 6.9 Tidore and examples of the importance of the instrument used in cutting and breaking: (a) break with hands/feet versus (b) cut with scissors versus (c) cut with large cutting instrument, versus (d) stab/pierce with a spike.

factors include combinations of object and manner of separation: cutting the ribs out of palm leaves in a particular manner (*noi*) and the orientation of the object or of the cut: *sepi* describes diagonal cuts; *teto* describes horizontal cuts on a plank (Van Staden 2007: 299). Significantly, Tidore forces the use of particular cut and break verbs for specific actions (e.g., cut with a kitchen-type knife, *leso*). There is no Tidore equivalent to the generic English *break*, but much variation instead, such as *yaci* for tearing cloth as mentioned above and *tawa* for opening the mouth (Van Staden 2007: 300).

Other Languages

In other languages studied by the Max Planck team, similar variations and similarities were in evidence. For Kuuk Thaayorre (spoken by a small number of people in Pormpuraaw in western Cape York, Australia) cut and break verbs include the following: break into at least two pieces (*thiik*), break so that it cannot function (*rumparr*), cut with a blade or other instrument (*yak*), chop forcefully with a blade-like instrument (*rath*), smash to pieces a brittle object with a blunt instrument (*matp*), tear partially (*thaariic*), pull apart (*thuuth*), spear to break a theme (*ke'e*), and pierce to destroy (*pican*) (Gaby 2007: 265–269).

For Sranan (an English-lexified creole developed in the plantations of Suriname in the second half of the seventeenth century), cut and break verbs include the following: break something hard and brittle (*broko*); cut with a sharp-edged or pointed instrument (*koti*); slash with a knife, axe, or machete (*kapu*); split (*prati*); smash a hard object to rubble (*panya*); tear (*priti*); saw (*sa*); and hit or beat (*naki*) (Essegbey 2007: 232–235). For Sranan, more importance is held for the nature of the separation than about the instrument: events of *koti*, a clean cut-like fracture caused by a blade or by any other way, are not distinguished from one another by different verbs, while they are distinguished from *broko*, or messy breaks (Majid et al. 2007a: 144; Essegbey 2007).

At a more general level across different language groups, Jürgen Bohnemeyer argues that while it is commonly understood that verbs of material separation are usually divided into two types (cut and break), it is also the case that some languages have a tripartite system in which cut and break categories are joined by a third group of "bipolar" verbs, distinguished as being semantically specific about the state change that separation causes and about its cause (Bohnemeyer 2007). Examples are Germanic verb-particle constructions (e.g., *zer-shmerttern*, to smash to pieces) and compound verb stems in Biak, Mandarin (*bail-duan4*, bend-broken), and Yukatek (*xíik-ch'àak*, burst-cut) (Bohnemeyer 2007: 164). In addition, Bohnemeyer shows that there are languages (e.g., Mandarin) that have neither cut nor break verbs, and in which all causative state change verbs are bipolar compounds (Bohnemeyer 2007: 172). Some languages, such as Ewe, Spanish, Sranan, and Yélî Dnye do not have cut verbs, but categorize separation events in terms of state changes and not in terms of actions with instruments (Bohnemeyer 2007: 173).

General Patterns, Principle Dimensions of Variation

In all of these examples (i.e., in all of the languages that the Majid team studied), there is clear and solid evidence of wide variations in the ways that people think about cutting and breaking across language groups. In their statistical analysis of the data from the video event descriptions for all the languages studied, Majid's team identified four principle dimensions of variation that account for about half of all variety in how people think about and describe cutting and breaking events: (1) predictable versus unpredictable place of separation, (2) tearing versus cutting/breaking, (3) snapping versus smashing, (4) and poking a hole in a piece of cloth (Majid et al. 2008: 242–243) (Figure 6.10). In addition, Majid and her team argue that across the languages that they studied, people think differently about cutting than they do about breaking. Cutting events are higher in predictability; breaking events lower (Majid et al. 2008: 246). The cutting cluster includes events with blades (knives, scissors) but also hands (chopping); the breaking cluster includes snapping and smashing events, then tearing and then poking a hole in fabric (Majid et al. 2008: 246).

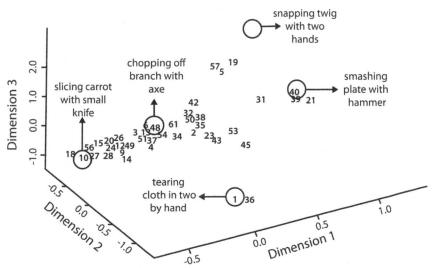

FIGURE 6.10 A three-dimensional plot of cutting and breaking events (redrawn by Sveta Matskevich after Majid et al. 2007a: figure 1).

Having noted the range of diversity within and between languages, Majid's team argued that cutting and breaking verbs (and thus actions) are specific and important human activities, important enough, or at least central enough to being human, that different languages structure differences of cutting and breaking events in similar ways. So, while there is significant variation across languages, it is also the case that cutting and breaking events are treated in a relatively coherent semantic domain across all languages (Majid et al. 2008: 246).

Stepping back from the Majid team's statistical examination and conclusions, it is useful for our examination of the prehistoric thoughts of cutting into the ground and breaking the surface of the ground to isolate the main elements of variation, regardless of the quantitative frequency or correlation of their appearance across the languages studied. In doing so, it is possible to identify four main sites of variation in how people might think about cutting and breaking.

The Key Issues

From this survey of the linguistic anthropological fieldwork and analysis carried out by Ashifa Majid and her colleagues, there emerge several commonalities within the diversity of ways that people think about cutting and breaking. At the outset it is clear that the ways in which people think about cutting and breaking are more complex than one may originally have thought, and that these complex sets of understandings vary between linguistic groups. Variation may rest in local meanings, and it would be useful to examine the potential for variation within language communities, particularly at the specific levels of individuals, subcommunity groups, and other intra-society differences (class, gender, age) as well within any one group of people at different phases, times, periods, and episodes of life lived. Basically, variation has the potential to play out over time, space, and person/people.

Across these broader and more refined variations, it is possible to identify several main sites of variation in the ways that the different groups think about cutting and breaking. For many (perhaps all) groups, people think about material separation in terms of the object that is cut or broken. What are its properties? For example, was it whole or detached before being broken (Jalonke)? Is it hard and brittle (Sranann), or is it long, thin, flexible, short, small, large, or multi-stranded (Tzeltal)? A second site of variation common across languages is the manner in which the cut or break is made. Here people pay attention to the tool that is used to separate the material and to the properties of that tool: is it the hand, the foot, a blade, or another tool (Mandarin, Jalonke, Hindi and Tamil, Tidore)? How is the instrument held (Tidore)? Part of the conceptualization of the manner of separation is qualification in the action of cutting and breaking: in one stroke or in several (Jalonke), against the grain or with it (Chontal), by sawing, splitting, or tearing (Tzeltal). Also significant is attention to the agent of cutting: does the person have control over the location of separation, and is s/he willing (Jalonke), and is that agency defined as highly agentive, agentive, non-agentive, highly non-agentive (Ewe)?

A third site of variation is the location of the cut or break and the extent to which the location of the separation can be identified: is the place of impact precise or imprecise, does the break happen as expected ("stereotypically" for the Jalonke), and is the locus predictable or not? With the final theme of variation, people attend to the result state of the object that will be or has been cut. What is the type of change that has taken place: is it open or in pieces (Mandarin)? What is the degree of its break: is the resulting condition apart (Chontal)? Is the original object now in at least two pieces (Kuuk)? Can the object still function, or has it been destroyed (Kuuk)? Has it been shattered, or made small (Tzeltal)? Indeed, Bohnemeyer's conception of bipolar verbs refers to words that are specific about the state of change of the object cut or broken.

Integrity, Materials Science, and Coherence: Levinson on Yélî Dnye

Across this range of important sites of variation and the richness of the language group's specific semantics, we can take inspiration from these detailed studies of cut and break verbs in different languages to think in new ways about what people conceptualize what they are doing and about the objects they are cutting and breaking. A particularly positive response comes from Stephen Levinson's work on Yélî Dnye, a Papuan language spoken on Rossel Island (Levinson 2007). In some ways Yélî Dnye is different from most of the other languages in the study. It is not known to be related to any other language. It has only three verbs to cover most cutting and breaking actions: one for breaking and two for cutting (with the latter distinguishing between severing across the grain, and splitting/tearing/cutting along the grain) (Levinson 2007: 208). Though there are other more specialized forms in Yélî Dnye, such as cutting open, or cutting repeatedly, they are less frequent than the three main verbs.

Levinson suggests that in Yélî Dnye people conceive of the semantic domain of cutting and breaking as an agent causing an object (or the theme) "to lose its integrity," with or without the use of a tool or instrument (Levinson 2007: 208). It is Levinson's use of the term "integrity" that is significant here. On the one hand, integrity refers to physical completeness, to an integral object, to the thing that is being broken or cut. On the other hand,

I take "integrity" to have a looser, less-tangible evocation of essence and content. In this latter sense, one gets the idea that the object that is broken or cut had some integral meaning, use, and spiritual sense that the act of breaking or cutting violates, destroys, and terminates. In the other languages studied, this sense of ending is also present in the idea promoted by verbs that designate the breaking to unusable pieces (e.g., in Kuuk Thaayorre).[5]

Levinson discusses the Yélî Dnye cutting verbs in terms of a folk "materials science" (Levinson 2007: 2010). For the Yélî Dnye, at issue is the notion of grain or more specifically of fibers in the object being broken or in the case that the cut materials consist of aligned fibers (wood, leafs, vines, cloth), and that the cut will work either against or with the grain.[6] Such materials include floorboards, baskets, thatch, planked canoes, and ropes (Levinson 2007: 212). For the Yélî Dnye, objects without grain (i.e., not built from fibers) can break incoherently in any direction. In Yélî Dnye, wood can be split along or across the grain; cloth and pottery, on the other hand, will tear, split, or break into irregular pieces (Figure 6.11). Levinson suggests that the Yélî Dnye distinctions concern the state change caused to the affected object (the thing that is cut or broken) and do not result from the type of activity that produces that change (i.e., the type of cutting and breaking). Distinct from many of the other languages studied, Yélî Dnye does not make a distinction of cutting and breaking in terms of instrument used; for example, all three verbs can work with a knife or a hammer (Levinson 2007: 212). Levinson understands coherence to be an important factor in how the Yélî Dnye think about cutting and breaking. As he puts it, cut and break verbs focus on "exotic distinctions in the mode of

FIGURE 6.11 Examples of cutting and breaking in Yélî Dnye and folk materials science: (a) breaking objects without grain (pottery), versus (b) cutting with the grain, and (c) severing across the grain or splitting/tearing/cutting against the grain (wood, rope, leaves).

severance—namely coherent severance (with the grain versus against the grain) and incoherent severance (regardless of grain)" (Levinson 2007: 216).

Relevance to Cutting the Ground at Măgura

The linguistic anthropological research of Levinson, Majid, and their colleagues is relevant to our larger project on the pit-houses at Măgura. The proposal here is not to map onto the Măgura pit-houses any one of the case studies provided by the work of the linguistic anthropologists. Nor is it to propose that we apply to Neolithic Romania a set of generalized common factors that several, many, or all language groups share. To do so would be to ignore both the political, economic, spiritual, and other local, historically particular contexts of both the ethnographic and archaeological populations under study. However, if we can show that contemporary, though linguistically distinct, groups of people today have different ways of understanding actions that we know as cutting and breaking, then it is possible also (probable even) that the people who lived in the distant past would have thought of cutting and breaking in different ways from the ways that we think and talk about them today.

Furthermore, if these distinctions hold, then we can make an additional claim: the people who dug out the pits at Măgura probably thought about the acts of digging those pits differently from the way that today we think about their digging them. If this is the case, then the unavoidable consequence is that we must broaden the horizon along which we try to understand why those Neolithic people dug those pits, what they thought when they did so, and what might have been the consequences (intentional or otherwise) of digging the pits, as well as using, living-in, filling, or covering over those holes in the ground for Neolithic understandings of living and being.

Based on what we know from linguistic research, people think of actions such as cutting in different ways, and they focus on different parts of the event, the participants, the instrument, the resulting state, and the object acted upon in different ways across different languages. This type of work also suggests that the act of digging a hole can be thought of/spoken about in a diversity of ways. And by thinking through these diversities of ways, we may find new and unexpected ways of thinking about Neolithic pits like the ones at Măgura. The value of looking at the linguistic work is to open our modern archaeological minds to the probability that Neolithic people conceptualized their actions in ways distinct from the way we conceptualize what we do today and the ways that we conceptualize what those Neolithic people thought about what they did in the past. The value to be found rests in suggesting potential ranges of thought in different places and times.

The results of the linguistic work raise important issues that provoke new thinking about the range of ways that the Neolithic people of Măgura might have thought about how they were doing what they were doing 8000 years ago when they cut the ground and broke the surface of the landscape. The first of these provocations are the different factors that may have been at the heart of how people at Măgura thought about their actions. Key elements are the act of cutting and breaking the ground, the manner of pursuing that act, the instrument(s) used, the specifics of the object being cut or broken, and the resulting state that was created by completing that action. Of particular interest is the importance that some languages place on the resultant state of an object once it is cut or broken, particularly the idea that the object has been violated (i.e., as in Kuuk and Tzeltal) or that the object that had been cut loses its integrity (as in Yélî Dnye).

But, what is it that is violated and what would have been the consequences of violation? I suggest that it is not merely the physical material of the ground, but, more provocatively, it is the metaphysical integrity of the land and ground (in the sense of Ground, noted already, in chapter 1 and discussed in more detail in chapter 9), and the result is a more specific rupture, displacement, and severance. Equally significant is the possibility that the resultant cut, ruptured, and violated state most probably would have possessed new or altered possibilities and potentialities: opportunities not available before, or not logical or previously acceptable or appropriate. The act of cutting and breaking would have opened up (in ways both physical and spiritual) the ground in senses that were dangerous and out of control, releasing energies and essences that the former integrity of the ground surface may have contained, controlled, and kept safely out of sight and out of reach.

Levinson's concept of a "folk materials" of cutting and breaking is also potent, and has similarities with current approaches to materiality in archaeology, in which the significance of objects and actions are deeply submerged in locally specific histories and personal encounters with objects, raw materials, textures, places, memories, and events. Similarly valuable are the implications for the meanings, evocations, and essences of the action itself and the manner in which it is performed, by whom, and when. Another provocative outcome of the work on Yélî Dnye is a recognition that we can conceive of a break or a cut as coherent or incoherent. The introduction of coherence (and thus of incoherence) into the grounded sense of being in the world would have been of fundamental importance to people at Măgura or elsewhere.

We have not yet discussed in significant detail the object being cut and the object being broken at Măgura: the ground (Figure 6.12). We need to address the consequences of cutting or breaking this object, and in the wake of that

FIGURE 6.12 Cătălin Lazăr excavating at Măgura-Buduiasca. Photo copyright D. W. Bailey.

discussion, we will need to investigate the importance of the ground for the human sense of being in the Neolithic. Started below, these discussions continue in chapter 9. In addition, we need to think of the Măgura pits as either cuts or as breaks. If we think of them as cuts (and thus potentially as distinct from breaks), then we will need to work through the resulting consequences for our understanding not only of those Neolithic actions but also for their Neolithic understandings of what they were doing. Questions that we will need to address are whether or not the Neolithic understanding was subconscious or whether people digging those holes actively thought in terms of event, instrument, and resulting state of object cut. Most likely, different people at the time thought of these actions and the results in different ways.

One of the refreshing understandings that emerges from a study of the linguistic material on cutting and breaking is the clear and strong recognition that the most substantial part of understanding, explaining, or even describing a pit dug 8000 years ago may dwell within the complexities of the actions, actors, manners, subjects, and objects that were brought into play when people dug the pit, broke the surface, and cut the ground. A fundamental consequence is that we need to step away from our traditional archaeological concern with the contents of the pit and with the end of a pit's life (i.e., how it was filled, with what objects, and when: that is, pit function and depositional structuring).

In an earlier paper about the surface-level houses of late Neolithic tell settlements in southeastern Europe (Bailey 2005a), I argued that we should abandon our archaeological fetishization of the contents of individual houses of tell villages and our micro-concern with activities and functions within and of the built environment. My proposal there was that we discard our concern for what a building meant and the activities that took place within it; my alternative was that we should think in nontraditional, or at least non-archaeological, ways about those three-dimensional, serial constructions that we had been calling houses. My intention here with house-pits (and pits in general) is the same. My (rhetorical) question is this: what if pit-house contents and usage (for shelter, for storage, or for rubbish discard) do not matter? Perhaps their meaning, their impact in the lives of those who knew them, radiated out from the moments, surrounding actions, manners, instruments, people, and resulting states of their creation. Their significance is found in the actions of cutting the earth and breaking the surface of the ground. By shifting our perspective in this way, the linguistic anthropology of cutting and breaking has fundamental impact on our approach to the Măgura pit-houses.

Redefining Pit-houses as Cut Ground Surfaces

In terms of cutting and breaking, pit-houses find redefinition along three lines. First, the pit-houses were cuts into (and not breaks of) the ground. Cutting is distinct; it requires an instrument for completion. In addition, cutting is an action of predictable outcome and location; breaking is not. Second, the implement, utensil, or tool that cuts and its properties are significant and it often determines meaning and the sense not only of the cutting object but also of the action of cutting as well as the effects resulting in the material that is cut: hand versus shovel versus pick versus axe versus adze versus scapula. The materiality of the object-that-cuts further invests action and flavors result: cattle bone, human hand, flint wedge flaked and polished, flexing antler driven into soils.

Third, the resulting condition and character of the surface that is cut invokes a change of state. The surface that is cut loses its original integrity: lost, disrupted, made incomplete, violated. The consequences of the loss of integrity both render what was previously possible now impossible (because the surface is no longer complete), but also creates new potentials, revealing what was hidden and offering entry into new materials and new spaces (indeed creates new surfaces available for cutting): materials and spaces of physical and metaphysical characters. The surface, to use Levinson's perspective on the Yélî Dnye, has a "grain" to it, and when we recognize this we start to think about the way that the grain of the surface is cut and, significantly, about the essence that the integrity of the surface loses once it has been cut: with ease or with resistance. Cutting across that grain is a violent counteraction that is distinct from cutting along the grain, a less confrontational and uncontested opening of the surface.

When we think of the ground having grain in this sense, we allow ourselves to see that the way that the ground is cut (i.e., with or against the grain), the objects used to cut it, and the physical human action of cutting are each central to the meaning of that action (of cutting, of digging), and the resultant state of the cut surface. In redefining pit-houses as cut surfaces in these terms, we shift our focus onto the acts of making these holes in the ground: cutting its surface. We shift the weight of attention away from filling (and the acts of filling) the holes made into the ground and away from the use or eventual abandonment of the holes. It is in their making that these features find their energy and essence.

We can push this beyond Măgura. The cutting of the deep shaft at Wilsford, the slicing of Divinity Fudge's back in Minnesota, and the sawing through the walls of 27 and 29 rue du Beaubourg in Paris each took some of their energy and impact in their making and their reception by the audience from the power that comes with cutting those surfaces. The weight of that impact came from the action of cutting, the utensils used, and the resulting altered state that the formally uncut surface obtained once it was cut. Much significance rested with the action of the cut (and all of the corresponding utensils, agents, directions, and consequences in each cutting tableau), particularly as that set of actions fueled those events as machines for attention-grabbing and thought-provocation. Any secondary or tertiary meaning or impact that each may have had through publicity, outrage, art-world acknowledgment, or archaeological attention (as at Wilsford, for example) was epiphenomenal and would not have been manifest without the original cut. It's the cut that matters.

Inter-text

Tina was a fifteen-year-old girl whose boyfriend recently broke up with her. On the way home from school, she saw him kissing another girl. When she arrived home, she immediately went upstairs to her bedroom, locked the door, and cut herself on the wrist several times with a razor blade. Although she wore long sleeves to dinner that evening, her mother spotted the wounds and brought her daughter to the emergency room, saying her daughter had tried to kill herself. Tina, however, stated emphatically that she did not want to die. "I cut myself because it made me feel better," she said.

(Peterson et al. 2008: 20)

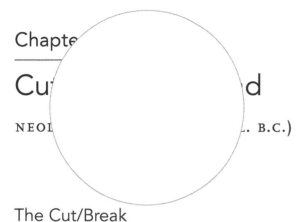

Chapter

Cu̇ d

NEOL . B.C.)

The Cut/Break

CUTTING THROUGH THE grass, she dug down into the spongy turf, into the topsoil. Under the grass the soil was dark brown, almost black. The ground was dry enough to dig. It was early fall. In the summer, this had been meadow; in the coldest months of winter, it had been much wetter; a lot of the ground had been underwater. Now, the digging was easy, and the group had been working well, marking out and then digging a curving line of narrow ditches. The ground gave itself to be opened, but even with this, she and the others were impatient and apprehensive. A large group had gathered, more people than usually got together, regardless of the time of year, or the weather, or any need to talk, or share stories, or get some help, or to brag or complain.

In not too much time, she and the other woman had opened a large hole into the surface of the ground, longer than it was wide: of a length that four of them could have lain down head-to-feet, fitting within the cutting along its longest dimension. The width of the cut into the grass and soil was much narrower; perhaps, if she lay down crossways, on what was now the bottom surface, her head would have touched one side, her toes the other. Some of the other ditches that she had dug or a few of those that others were now digging were longer, some shorter; all were about the same width. Each ditch was slightly curved; all followed a gently arcing line, one after the other, with small spaces of uncut ground-level left undisturbed, separating the end of one ditch from the start of the next. When all of the ditches had been finished they would encircle a large inner space, with enough open ground for many people, as well as for cattle and sheep and a few goats to stand; there would also be enough space left for fires to be set and fed with wood.

Now, standing in the hole that her group was digging, the woman's knees were just about level with the grass surface around her. Standing thus partially within the ground, she found that the world around and above her appeared changed; her perspective had shifted. With the first incisions into the meadow grasses and the lifting of solid turves of grass and dark brown soils, with roots and worms hanging down, the women had piled the turves around the edge of the ditch. They now scooped and shoveled more dark soil up and out, and piled it on top of the turves: a low bank of dark dirt, roots, and soil rose slowly around their ditch.

Digging deeper, they cut into a dissimilar composition of dirt and stones. They saw the difference: new colors—lighter browns, yellows, oranges. Their fingers felt the difference: sand, gravels, small areas of sticky clay. As with the darker topsoil in the layer above, this lower soil of gravel and sand was not difficult to dig into, though the stones made it heavier. They dug more slowly. While the topsoil had only been moist, this deeper level of gravel and sand was wet; she knew that if they had tried to dig here any earlier in the summer, they would have found it a bigger challenge, and she would have been standing and slipping on the gravels and on the patches of clay and mud. They would have had no chance of cutting to this depth; the ground would have been flooded with frigid water, patches of thin ice over puddles or under light drifts of snow. There was a part of the year when it was possible to cut open the ground, and there were places (these places) where it was less difficult to cut down into the soils. Now, in the early fall, with the water level much lower and the ground at its driest, they only had to remember not to step on the ground near the edge of the ditch. Both the darker topsoil and lighter sand and the ground below were easy to dig, but both also lacked the strength to prevent them from caving into the new-cut hole, especially if she stood too close to the edge of the ditch. Once they had dug into the lighter-colored gravels and sand, down to about as deep again as they had dug through the upper layer of top-soil, they stopped. The low pile of turves and dark topsoil surrounding the ditch now was topped with gravel, here and there a patch of clay. Finished with this hole, she moved on with the other partners to work on another section, farther along the circuit of holes.

Redigging and Resurfacing

Less then a year after the women had cut their elongated hole down though the brown topsoil and into the gravels and sand (perhaps the following summer or maybe in the early fall), another group of people stopped and camped at the circle of narrow, curving ditches. These people slaughtered one of the

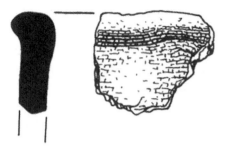

FIGURE 7.1 Fragment of Mildenhall pottery (M112) from Etton-unidentified ditch enclosure (redrawn by Svetlana Matskevich after Pryor 1989: figure 183).

young pigs that they had brought with them, and cut the meat and ligaments and innards from the carcass. They cooked over an open fire and ate. Some of the bones from the pig they threw out beyond the circuit of ditches, others (a set of ribs from one side of the dead animal) they put into the ditch that the young woman had dug the autumn before. Four bones from a cow or a bull also ended up in the ditch, as did a single foot bone from a roe deer.

Other objects (though not very many) also made it into this ditch: a scrappy piece of the rim of a pot (Figure 7.1), heavily worn as if kicked around for some time before coming to rest on the bottom of the hole. Though the sherd probably had sat exposed both to the elements and to the feet of people and animals before it ended up in the ditch, the other objects were deposited without delay. Nothing else was added. No flint tools (or flakes or cores) found their way into the ditch, though local flint outcrops were available and it is likely that their presence was one of the reasons that people came to this place. They put nothing else into the ditch other than fragments of pottery or scraps of bone.

Almost immediately after these objects found their way into the ditch, (probably) the same small group of people who had put them there then shoveled, pushed, kicked, and threw on top of the pig bones and the sherd a layer of gravel, sand, and turves from the piles that still sat around the ditch since it had been dug. As they covered the bones and the sherds and filled the ditch, they dumped in enough dirt to fill the hole about halfway toward the original, surrounding ground level. In doing so, they made a new bottom to the ditch, a new surface, clean of bone or pottery: a surface much like the one upon which they had placed the objects only moments before. Having completed this cycle of placing-and-filling, they moved away, across the lowlands in which the circuit of ditches lay, taking with them whatever animals they had arrived with the week before and which they had not killed and eaten.

Re-re-digging, Placing, and Refilling

Sometime later (a year; perhaps two or three), people came again to the circuit of ditches, bringing with them (as before) animals as well as some containers made of fired clay and some polished stone tools. As with the previous visitors, these people slaughtered, butchered, cooked, and ate some of those animals while they camped. A few of them walked over to the ditch left half-filled the year before, stepped down into it, and started digging down into that "fresh" surface of the half-filled ditch, cutting a new elongated hole down into the mix of bone, sherd, and replaced sand, gravel, and topsoil. This was the right place to cut open the ground; the soils and sediments gave way to their efforts. The earth opened up here with ease.

As had been the case in the previous year's visit, so also now, while these people stayed at the circuit, animal bones and fragments of pottery vessels ended up in this new hole, freshly cut into the bottom of the ditch. The amount of material that accumulated was not great: just over a dozen animal bones (from cattle, sheep, and pig), and some pottery (parts of two vessels—two sherds from one pot, one from another). They put the bone and the pottery into the ditch soon after the animals had been killed and the pottery broken; none of the material that ended up on the bottom of the new ditch had sat on the ground for long (if at all) to weather and be trampled. With little or no delay after the bones and sherds went into the ditch, several people covered over these objects in the ditch with topsoil, turf, gravel, and sand; they filled in the ditch that they had only just cut, and put in the bone and sherds with a mixture of the material from the original digging of the ditch (the gravels and sands and topsoils) and from their more recent second cutting of the ditch.

Re-re-re-digging, Placing, Covering, and Leaving

Again people came to the circuit of ditches: during the summer or early autumn, a year or more after the last visitors had camped there, people had dug their ditch, had placed their objects, and had then filled in the hole they had cut into that reconstructed surface, and thus covered their particular deposits. Perhaps this new group stayed longer than the others had during the earlier visits; perhaps more people came to camp here now. Regardless, while at the circuit of ditches, these people also slaughtered, butchered, cooked, and ate some of the cattle, sheep, and pigs that they brought with them. Also like the previous visitors, some of the group walked over to the ditch filled in the previous year, stepped down into the ditch and onto that most recent resurfacing, and proceeded to make fresh cuts down into that resurface left by that earlier group.

The cut that these people made was narrower than the earlier ones, and the bones, sherds, and other objects accumulated in several discrete groupings (Figure 7.2), each of which they probably put into the ditch in a separate, successive event. In the northern third of the ditch they deposited animal bone in three distinct, small concentrations (perhaps each of these three was itself a successive event of putting material into this part of the ditch). At the northern end, nearest the edge of the ditch, someone put a sherd of plain pottery and the

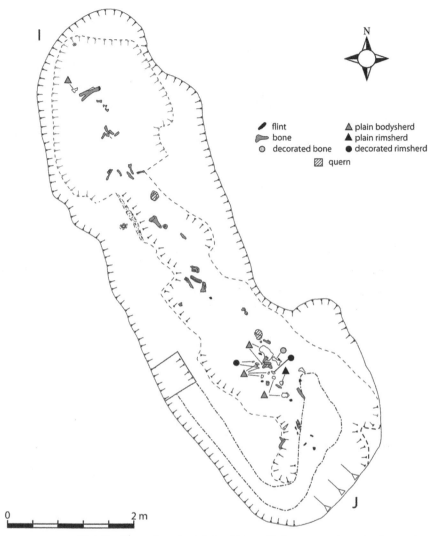

FIGURE 7.2 Distribution of material in Etton ditch segment 9 (redrawn by Svetlana Matskevich after Pryor 1998: figure 39).

shoulder bone of a cow or a bull that had been used as a tool to work with or, at least, had been marked with lines scratched into its surface (Figure 7.3). Three other animal bones ended up in this group of objects.[1] Then, someone took several handfuls of soil, gravel, and sand from the piles on the edges of the ditch and covered the material with a thin layer of dirt and stone. A step to the south someone placed a second, distinct set of material (five animal bones[2]) and then covered it over with dirt, stone, and topsoil. Two steps further to the south, someone added another small accumulation of material (another five animal bones[3]) and, without delay, he then covered them with soils.

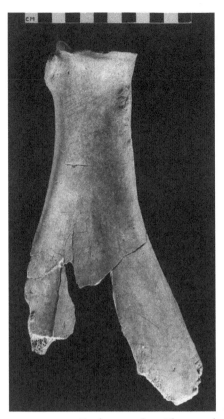

FIGURE 7.3 Cattle scapula with scored lines from Etton ditch; segment 9, layer 3 (Bone 10825). Photo copyright Francis Pryor; image reproduced with permission.

Another step to the south someone put in a piece of a quartzite saddle quern, sitting on its own (Figure 7.4); someone had broken the quern, though probably not while using it to grind anything, but by smashing it against another stone. The man (or was it a boy or a woman?) who put the fragment on this new floor of this new ditch placed it on edge, so that it stuck straight up from the floor of the new ditch, with its working surface facing the side of the ditch. A step to the south of the broken quern were two more bones, one quite large,[4] the other much smaller.[5] Two steps beyond these was another larger bone[6] sitting on its own. Like the other objects accumulating in the ditch, someone quickly covered these with handfuls of soil, gravel, and sand. Two steps to the south, someone put four larger bones[7] and a utilized, but damaged, flint flake;[8] another animal bone ended up to the west of these four.[9] All were quickly covered with dirt and stone from ground along the edge of the ditch.

Two steps to the southeast, someone placed two animal bones[10] and covered them over with soil and gravel. A step further south someone put another broken piece of a quartzite quern (Figure 7.5). Though distinct from the other fragment in the accumulation to the north (i.e., the two fragments were not of one original), this second piece was similar both in its material (quartzite) and in the way it had been broken, not in normal use, but when someone bashed it with (or against) some other stone.

Placed next to this second broken quern was a larger concentration of eight animal bones[11] and a number of pottery sherds (Figure 7.6): plain body sherds,[12] two decorated rims,[13] one plain rim sherd,[14] and five flint objects, all waste pieces, including a burnt waste flake,[15] an irregular piece of burnt workshop waste,[16] two unburnt waste flakes,[17] and an unclassifiable flint

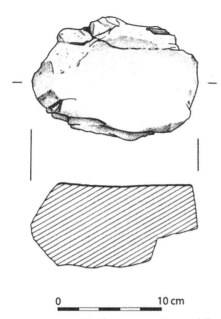

0   10 cm

FIGURE 7.4 Broken quartzite saddle quern (Other 99) from Etton ditch segment 9 (redrawn by Svetlana Matskevich after Pryor 1998: figure 232: 2).

object.[18] Having put this larger collection onto the floor of the ditch, a woman and a child covered it soon with soils and gravel. A tenth discrete assemblage was put further to the south, almost against the southern wall of the ditch. Here someone placed four animal bones[19] and five flint waste flakes.[20] These also were covered with dirt soon after being put or thrown into the ditch.

After these visitors had put these last materials into the ditch and quickly, but thinly, covered them, they left. They did not fill in the ditch with any more of the remaining gravel, topsoil, or sand that was left piled around the edges. They did not make a new surface, prepared, perhaps for some future cycle of digging-placing-and-covering. After they moved off with their animals, pots, and tools, the ditch slowly acquired a deeper covering of sediments and soils laid down by natural erosion and rainwash (French 1998: 320).

Finishing

By the time that people came again to the circuit of ditches, a winter (or two, or three) had washed soils from the ditch's walls down onto the thinly covered materials put in the ditch when the last people had camped here. These new visitors did not dig a new ditch. They did not cut down into the older fills and refills of gravels, sands, and soils. However, like the people who had been here before, they put bone, flint, and pottery into the hole. Where the previous campers had placed or tossed small groups of objects in separate, distinct piles, one after the other, each quickly covered over, these new visitors put things into this old, eroded hole in the ground without too much concern. There were no discrete clusters, no quick coverings with handfuls of gravel, soil, and clay.

Now, objects were spread out along the thin, flat bottom that ran down the middle of the ditch from one end to the other. If objects ended up in any ordered way, then it was merely that sometimes people put objects on either

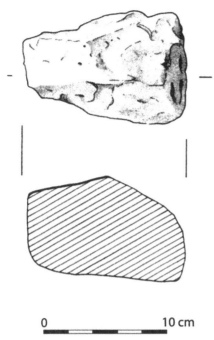

0   10 cm

FIGURE 7.5 Broken quartzite quern (Other 98) from Etton ditch segment 9 (redrawn by Svetlana Matskevich after Pryor 1998 figure 232: 1).

side of a bare, objectless area about halfway along the length of the ditch. To the far north of this empty space, near the northern wall of the ditch, someone threw an otherwise unremarkable waste flake of flint.[21] It sat on the sloping, eroded edge that ran down to the bottom of the ditch. A fragment of a plain pottery sherd ended up a little lower down that slope.[22] Nearby, on the ditch's flat bottom had tumbled a serrated flint flake.[23] Several other scraps of pottery, bone, and flint were half a step to the south. Two steps farther south were another waste flake[24] and other plain body sherds.[25] A bit to the south, were another waste flake,[26] but also a leaf-shaped flint arrowhead.[27] Close by, someone had discarded a utilized flake[28] and four more plain body sherds.[29] Other fragments of bone, flint, and pottery accumulated nearby.

A little farther to the south, someone had strewn another loose set of material: a flint waste flake,[30] a serrated flake,[31] and another plain body sherd.[32] Half a step to the east had ended up some waste products from flint working,[33] and another waste flake.[34] The last loose grouping of material put into this northern half of the ditch was deposited one step farther to the south: a flint core,[35] three waste flakes,[36] a flint piercer,[37] (Figure 7.7), and two undecorated body sherds.[38]

Two or three steps to the south, across the space empty of objects, was a greater density of material: a decorated body sherd,[39] a decorated rim sherd[40] (Figure 7.8), two plain rim sherds,[41] undecorated body sherds,[42] waste flakes,[43] and unclassified animal bones. Farther to the south was another undecorated body sherd,[44] and farther south still, almost against the end wall of the ditch, were more undecorated body sherds,[45] scraps of flint,[46] waste from flint working,[47] and waste flakes.[48] Throughout the ditch, people had distributed animal bone (much more than had been put into the ditches

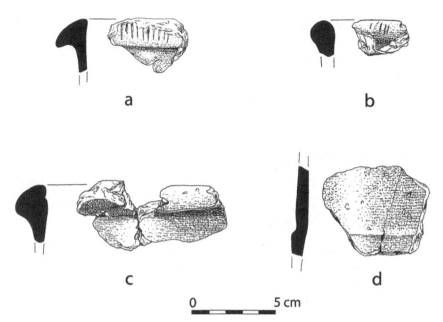

FIGURE 7.6 Selection of Mildenhall pottery from Etton ditch segment 9: a) M108, b) M109, c) M110, d) M111 (redrawn by Svetlana Matskevich after Pryor 1998: figures 182, 183).

in its earlier fillings), almost all of which was from cattle, though individual bones from a few pigs were included as was one bone from a sheep or a goat. All of the bone that they put into the ditch when they stayed at the circuit at this time were scrappy small pieces. After the last sherd, waste flake, and cattle bone had been placed or thrown into the ditch, the group moved on, leaving their camp at the circuit, and leaving the material at the bottom of the ditch uncovered. With time, and with the rains that came with the lengthening fall and the winter, dirt and soil slowly covered over the material.

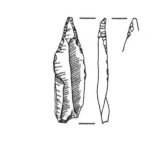

FIGURE 7.7 Flint piercer from Etton ditch segment 9 (redrawn by Svetlana Matskevich after Pryor 1998: figure 225: 89, pp. 247–248).

The next time that people stopped at the ditches, they paid the little hole in the ground little attention at all. They tossed some bone from their meals into it

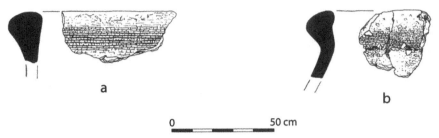

FIGURE 7.8 Decorated Mildenhall rim sherds (a, M105; b, M107) from Etton ditch segment 9 (redrawn by Svetlana Matskevich after Pryor 1998: figure 182).

(mostly cattle); the number of bones is less than half a dozen. Five sherds of pottery vessels ended up in the ditch, all but one are rim-sherds, and most were put into the ditch soon after the original vessels broke. More unusual is that the visitors left almost two dozen pieces of flint resulting from working the stone, as well as two tools. No one dug a new ditch or filled in the old one.

Questions

How can we understand these sequences of digging-placing-tossing-filling-redigging-tossing-placing-refilling? Is it enough to view all of these actions in simple terms of garbage disposal, of getting rid of the leftover bits and pieces from other activities that took place at this camp for the short periods when people stayed there? To be sure, there is nothing simple about rubbish, what it means, how it is constructed as a category, how it might create and maintain (and thus display) relationships and boundaries of people, places, and thoughts. As discussed in chapter 1 in the debate about structured deposition, and as we will see in more detail below, one of the most widely accepted interpretations of the Etton cycles of digging, depositing, and filling is that they are records of people's ritual actions, purportedly related to ceremonies and conceptions of liminal spaces and transitions of life, death, and human identities: that the objects were structured deposits. To equip ourselves for that debate, and to allow ourselves a chance to understand these sequences of actions, requires that we make a fuller investigation of the traces of activities, the archaeological features, patterns, and materials recovered and recorded at this site. What was this place? When and how did it come into being? What happened here in addition to the activities focused on the ditch segments as described above?

What was Etton?

The ditch segment described above in detail (Segment 9 in the archaeologists' site report; Pryor 1998) was only one of many holes that the diggers cut, filled, and redug at Etton, and the objects placed in the ditches are only one part of the material that archaeologists recovered from their own 1980s scientific cuttings of the ground at Etton (Figure 7.9). The site is acknowledged as one of the best excavated and analyzed sites of its type (i.e., a Neolithic causewayed enclosure), and a review of the analyses and conclusions of the excavation team (Pryor 1998) and of subsequent reanalysis and comment (Edmonds 1999; Pollard 2008) should provide the most detailed and precise understanding available of what people were doing at this place, at this time, and why they were doing it.

The earliest evidence for human activity at Etton dates to the first half of the fourth millennium B.C. (4000–3750 cal. B.C.) (Pryor 1998: 352), and the excavation team divided the earliest activities at the site into two stages (Phase 1 and 2), with Phase 1 divided into sub-phases: A, B, and C. In terms of ceramic tradition, Phases 1A and 1B represent a regional variant (Mildenhall wares) of the Hurst Fen pottery tradition. Material from Phase 1C is of the late Neolithic and was identified by Fengate-style wares, and that from Phase 2 is of the Peterborough and Grooved Ware traditions. Phase 3 dates to the Beaker Period and the Early Bronze Age, and Phase 4 to the Iron Age. Phase 5 is of Iron Age and Romano-British date. The discussion in this chapter focuses only on the first sets of activities at the site (Phases 1A–C), that is, those that are contemporary with the ditch segment activities as described in the first half of this chapter.

The Site in Its Setting

The ditches, pits, and activity areas at Etton are located in a landscape at the edge of the Fens of eastern England in a flat, low-lying plain, in what is now the lower Welland Valley in Maxey Parish, Cambridgeshire. In the Neolithic, this land was subject to intermittent flooding (Pryor 1998: 364, 373) with stream-systems running through it (Armour-Chelu 1998b: 272) and would not have supported plant cultivation. The river meander that partially surrounds Etton on its northern and western sides effectively cuts off the site from the higher, drier Maxey Island (Pryor 1998: 372). To the south, southeast, and southwest of the enclosure is a large area of floodplain (Pryor 1998: 372). In the years of Neolithic activity, the landscape in which the site is located would have been wet during all but the summer months. Through the years

FIGURE 7.9 The causewayed enclosure at Etton during excavation: top, ditch segment 5, view to the southwest toward causeway E, after excavation; bottom left, exploratory excavations in 1981; bottom right, excavation of ditch segment 1. Photo copyright Francis Pryor; image reproduced with permission).

of prehistoric use of the site, the water table would have risen, particularly though Phases 1 and 2, and by the end of the late Neolithic and with the early Bronze Age (Phases 2 and 3), the site would have been too wet to have been of any use for cultivation.

Site Description

The Neolithic site of Etton consists of an oval-shaped ring of narrow ditch segments (of which Segment 9 is a typical example), each of which was longer than it was wide: lengths vary from 10–90 m; widths range from 3–5 m; and depths vary less—no greater than 1.25 m (Figure 7.10). The fourteen ditch segments that were excavated (a southern part of the site could not be studied before gravel quarrying destroyed it) form a curving line of features that bounded a central area of 1.75 ha (or 4.32 acres)—187 m from east-west and 150 m from north-south (Pryor 1998: 1). Into the land surface of this interior space, people dug small pits, placed objects inside those pits, and then quickly

FIGURE 7.10 Plan view of the ditch segments and interior filled-holes at the Etton causewayed enclosure at Etton (redrawn by Svetlana Matskevich after Pryor 1998: figure 103).

backfilled them. In some areas of the enclosure people lit, fed, and tended large fires, some of which reached very high temperatures (up to 600° Celsius); in other parts of the interior they corralled livestock. The excavators found no evidence for buildings or other structures that might have functioned as residences or shelters for the medium or long term.

The ditch segments were separated one from another by narrow "causeways" where the ground was left uncut at its Neolithic surface. Three of these causeways were probably entrance and exit points for the interior (i.e., they are wider than the others): one to the north (causeway F), one to the east (M), and one to the west (B). A fourth access causeway may have been to the south in the unexcavated area. The northern entrance causeway (F) was the widest (c. 25 m). At its center, two parallel slots in the ground (each 8 m long, and 5 m apart) would have held large timbers (the slots' steep-sided, flat-bottomed ditches were packed with gravel to support the wood in the vertical) and formed a substantial gateway (Pryor 1998: 98–99, 356). The line of the western timber of the entry extended to the south in a straight line of fencing running another 40 m toward the center of the site (Pryor 1998: fig. 103).

Eastern and Western Ditch Segments

The excavators distinguished the nine ditch segments (nos. 6–14) to the east of the gateway at causeway F from the five (nos. 1–5) to the west. With variations in size, shape, contents, and the practice and frequency of digging-filling-redigging, the western ditches differ from Segment 9 (as described in detail above) and the other eastern ditches (Pryor 1998: 21; figure 12): for example, the western ditches are both shorter and longer than those to the east, including the unusually long (90 m) Segment 5 (Pryor 1998: 66; figure 10). In addition, the western segments differ in the absence of evidence for the careful object placement and for sand and gravel (re)fillings that are so evident in the eastern segments. This distinction, however, is not absolute: while Segments 3–5 in the west were not recut, Segments 1 and 2 were recut as many as seven times (Pryor 1998: 66; French 1998: 319–321). Related is the fact that the western ditches were left open for longer periods of time than were the eastern ones (Pryor 1998: 26).

Most clearly, however, the western ditches are distinct in terms of their contents, particularly the large amount of preserved organic remains (more than 4,800 pieces of worked wood), as well as in terms of the surprisingly low number and infrequently deposited fragments of pottery, bone, and flint (Pryor 1998: 21, 365). Non-wood remains that ended up in the western segments are limited in number and type: two sets of articulated cattle bones (ribs in Segment 1; neonatal bones in Segment 2) and disarticulated individual animal bones in several segments, small numbers of pottery sherds throughout (though also a complete Mildenhall bowl in Segment 1; Figure 7.11), fragments broken from stone axes (Segments 1 and 5), and a red deer antler crown and antler working debris (Segment 5).

The major category of material from the western ditches is wood and organics (other than bone and antler) and their presence here (and not in the eastern ditches) is best explained by the waterlogged conditions of the western ditches (Pryor 1998: 21). It is possible (likely in fact) that the earliest deposits in the western ditches (Segments 1–4) were made into already waterlogged conditions, and that the other western ditch (Segment 5) would have been wet and muddy when in use (Pryor 1998: 21; Charles French personal communication). Furthermore, it is likely that the western ditches (most clearly Segments 1 and 5) were parts of, or took advantage of, a running stream (Pryor 1998: 22, 26).

The preserved organics in the western segments are striking: in Segment 1, a 300 sq. mm birchbark mat, resting under the complete Mildenhall bowl noted above (M3; Taylor 1998: fig. 175), and a broken wooden axe haft (Wood 409) (Pryor 1998: 21; Taylor 1998: 148–152, 158–159, figures 160–162); a heap of sloe stones, a piece of twine made from vegetable fiber (Taylor 1998: 157, figure 174), and a sheet of birch bark (Wood 1271) in Segment 2 (Pryor 1998: 25; Taylor 1998: 156–157, figure 172); a timber plank with clear axe-cutting marks in Segment 5 (Wood 3950; Taylor 1998: 147, figures 157–158); and substantial debris from woodworking activities in Segments 3, 4, and 5 (Pryor 1998: 25, 26, 29). In terms of all the wood from the western ditch segments, the 4,833 objects and debris from working wood or managing wood resources (Taylor 1998: 157) far outnumber the 400 pieces of natural wood recovered (i.e., that showed no sign of human activity). However, only 19 of the more than 5,200 wooden pieces recovered were artifacts, fragments of artifacts (e.g., the axe-haft), or pieces of prepared timber. The majority of wood from Segments 1–6 (almost 3,600 pieces) consists of woodworking byproducts: woodchips, trimmed and untrimmed straight roundwood, and other debris (Taylor 1998: 116, Table 10).

This unusually high proportion (4:1) of worked-to-natural wood in the ditches (Taylor 1998: 157) and the composition of the wood inventory argue strongly that working of small roundwood took place in and around the western ditch segments; it also reveals something about what people were doing and how they were doing it at the site. Of the woodworking debris, blade-like

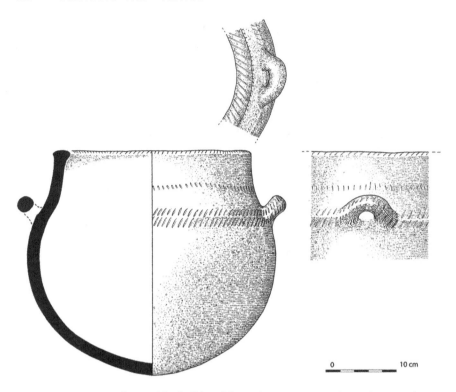

FIGURE 7.11 Complete Mildenhall bowl from Etton causeway A, section 1 (redrawn by Svetlana Matskevich after Pryor 1998: 175).

wood chips dominated the assemblage; these longer narrow chips were produced by an oblique axe blow used to cut rods from a growing coppice (Taylor 1998: 158; Brooks and Agate 1975: 75). The less frequent (but still numerous) shorter, squatter chips resulted from secondary, final working of wood (Taylor 1998: 158) that was being made into screens, hurdles, and biers as needed for the activities taking place in the enclosure's interior (Taylor 1998: 158) or that ended up as fuel for fires. Only one piece of wood (the oak timber from Segment 5) would have been suitable for use in a building or other structure (Taylor 1998: 147, 158). Finally, detailed examination of the wood assemblage (e.g., the way that growth rings were truncated at the time of their cutting) and the presence of the sloe stones suggests that much of the wood cutting and working took place in late summer and autumn (Taylor 1998: 159).

Enclosure Interior: Fires, Animal Corrals, and Filled Pits

Divided into two large sections by a ditch or fence running south from the northern entrance causeway (F), the large area of the enclosure interior contained almost one hundred filled-pits dated to Phase 1, as well as areas where fires burned or where livestock were corralled.[49] Analyses of phosphate concentrations and of the magnetic susceptibility of soils of the interior distinguished an eastern from a western half of the enclosed area (Gurney and Pryor 1998: 77–79, figures 81–85). The resulting pattern strongly suggests that people at Etton penned or at least corralled livestock in the western part of the enclosure (Pryor 1998: 80), most particularly in the southwest (Pryor 1998: 355). Similarly clear in terms of magnetic susceptibility of areas of the interior are locations of high temperature fires: an area of intense activity in the southeast, distinct from an area of less intense activity to the northwest. Concentrated activity related to high temperature was also detected in eastern ditch Segments 8–12, as well as for an area of the interior to the west of these segments (Challands 1998: 73–77; figures 77–79). The excavators suggest the areas of particularly high readings in the eastern interior represent the intense burning required (200–600° Celsius) for animal "cremations" (Challands 1998: 76), the remains of which ended up both in filled-pits and in ditch segments. Indeed, many objects that ended up in the ditches had been burned (Edmonds 1998: 260; Pryor 1998: 68) (e.g., Segment 6). The fills of Segments 10–12 had particularly high magnetic susceptibility readings and may represent the deposition of the material that was burned close by in the enclosure interior where high readings were recovered as well (Challands 1998: 76). Another area of high readings was in the central and central-western part of the interior, most probably reflecting the deposition of burned bone in filled-pits in that zone (Challands 1998: 76).

Filled-pits

Most striking of the features at Etton are small filled-pits (on average 0.62 m in diameter and 0.20 m in depth), steep-sided, and flat-bottomed, that people dug into the ground surface of the interior. There were no filled-pits in the areas excavated outside of the segmented ditches, and one senses that the enclosure and its ditches were places specifically designated for digging holes, putting objects into the holes, and then covering those holes up again. Though the pits occur across all areas of the interior, the majority is in the eastern half. Filled with combinations of pottery, bone, charcoal, and flaked or ground stone, the pits had been positioned with care; no one pit cut into another. It is likely either that the individual locations of these pits were marked on the ground in some way that has not survived, or that the people digging and filling them had a clear memory or map (mental or otherwise) of their precise locations. Regardless, it was important to the people digging and filling these pits that the cuts they made into the ground did not interfere with one another. During Phase 1, ninety-five individual pits were dug and filled in the enclosure's interior; in Phase 2 only five were dug and filled; and in Phase 3, only two (Pryor 1998: 88–112, Table 6).

While there is no single pattern apparent in the places that people chose to dig and fill these pits, two trends emerge (Pryor 1998: figure 103). First, and least definite, is that many filled-pits were dug outside of but near to the edges of the ditch segments, on the interior sides of the enclosure space. With very few exceptions, this pattern only occurs in the eastern half of the enclosure interior. The second pattern is of clusters of filled-pits, often of two or three (though sometimes as many as a dozen) dug near one another. Clusters of filled-pits are most clearly represented in two tightly grouped sets: one to the southwest of entrance-causeway F, the other to the west of causeway N. The dense cluster south of F consisted of eleven filled-pits dug into an area 25 × 16 × 12 m (Figure 7.12). Here, two separate groups of pits had been dug and filled: one group of six pits[50] (Pryor 1998: figure 107) was just to the south of a second group of five pits.[51] Less is known about the cluster near causeway N, as excavation was limited to only two of the eight pits there.

FIGURE 7.12 Cluster of filled-pits (Cluster F), 3.0 m southwest of causeway F; scale 1.0 m. Photo copyright Francis Pryor; image reproduced with permission.

FIGURE 7.13 Complete, used, greenstone axe (Other 63) from Etton filled-pit F263; scale 0.10 m units. Photo copyright Francis Pryor; image reproduced with permission.

All of the filled-pits in the two concentrations near causeway F contained pottery, flint, and animal bone, though pits F264 and F268 lacked flint. A more notable exception is filled-pit F263, which contained pottery, flint, and bone, as well as a complete polished, used, greenstone axe (Pryor 1998: figure 108; Edmonds 1998: 262, figure 237, no. 9) (Figure 7.13). For the cluster of eight filled-pits to the west of causeway N, only two were excavated; both contained pottery and flint, though neither contained bone (Pryor 1998: 103, Table 8). Excepting the axe in pit F263, the fills of these two clusters of pits present the general pattern detected in all pit-fills from the site's interior (i.e., for Phases 1–3 at the site, inclusive): soils mixed with fragments of animal bone, flint debris, charcoal, and pottery. Eighty-four percent of the 123 filled-pits from Phases 1–3 contained pottery, 79 percent contained flint, and 32 percent bone (Pryor 1998: Table 8). Focusing only on pits securely identifiable as Phase 1 (i.e., that contained Mildenhall and Fengate pottery), almost all pits (89 percent) contained flint, less than half contained charcoal (38 percent), a similar proportion contained unburned animal bone (34 percent); none contained animal bone that had been burned or human bone, in any condition (Pryor 1998: Table 8).

While it is possible that some Phase 1 pits did not contain Mildenhall or Fengate pottery (and thus are not included in the sampling used here), it must be significant that none of these early pits contained burned animal bone. If animals were "cremated" at the site as the excavators suggest, then evidence for it does not come from the filled-pits of the interior. Another significant pattern is the mutual exclusion of animal bone and charcoal in filled-pits from Phase 1: of the thirty-three filled-pits that contain charcoal or bone, only one contains both. It is highly likely that different pits had different uses and meanings, and that while some pits were deemed appropriate contexts into which to place ash but not animal bones, others were understood to be appropriate places to deposit animal bone (the remains, perhaps, from meals), but not the ashy remains from fires, regardless of whether or not the function of those fires was for cooking.

Exceptions to the general pattern of pottery-flint-bone-charcoal fills for Phase 1 interior pits are few, though noteworthy for the other materials included in them. Pit F263 (noted above) near causeway F contained the greenstone axe. Pit F786 contained a quartzite axe *polissoir* (Pryor 1998: 103; Edmonds 1998: 266, figure 239) (Figure 7.14). Pit F711 contained a complete but heavily used quartzite saddle quern[52] (Edmonds 1998: 259, figure 235) placed on its edge with a stone rubber[53] placed below it (Middleton 1998: 235; Pryor 1998: 258, figures 111, 112, 234: 9) as well as Mildenhall pottery, bone, and flint debris. Pit F713 (3 m south of pit F711) contained a broken fragment of a heavily worn, quartzite saddle quern[54] (Pryor 1998: 103, 258, figure 234: 8).

Seven other querns or rubbers were found at Etton from these early phases (all from Phase 1A or 1B contexts; Pryor 1998: figure 114) (Figure 7.15): four came from ditch segments and one from a filled-pit. In addition to the two heavily damaged quern fragments[55] left in Segment 9 as described in the first part of this chapter and the three from F711 and F713 just mentioned, the others include the following: a complete quartz cushion quern/pounder[56]

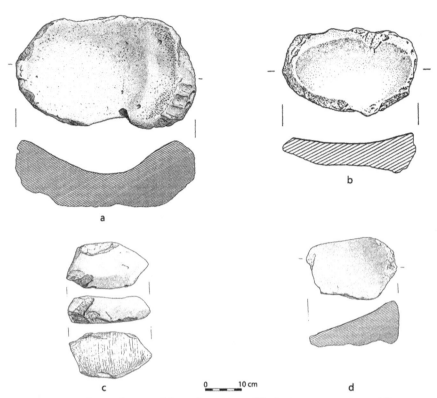

FIGURE 7.14 Ground-stone objects from Etton filled-pits: a, quartzite saddle quern, heavily used (Other 94 from pit F711); b, quartzite axe *polissoir* (Other 83 from pit F786); c, stone rubber (Other 95 from pit F711); d, quartzite saddle quern, heavily used and broken (Other 192 from pit F713) (redrawn by Svetlana Matskevich from Pryor 1998 figures 111, 112, 234, 235, 239).

(Segment 10); a fragment of a dolorite saddle quern,[57] a heavily worn quartzite rubber,[58] and a large fragment of a slightly used quartzite saddle quern,[59] all from Segment 13; a lightly used quartzite cushion quern from F40, at the edge of causeway I.[60] Of the ten querns or rubbers found at Etton, all but one were either broken or worn, and most of the latter were heavily worn.

With the exception of the greenstone axe in pit F263 near causeway F, none of the polished stone objects from the filled-pits of the interior is a complete tool: one is a fragment from a ground stone axe[61] found below the buried soil on the gravel surface (Edmonds 1998: 264; figure 237: 13); another is a fragment of a ground stone axe[62] from pit F857 (Edmonds 1998: 264, figure 237: 16); a third was a small indeterminate flake[63] from F795 (Edmonds 1998:

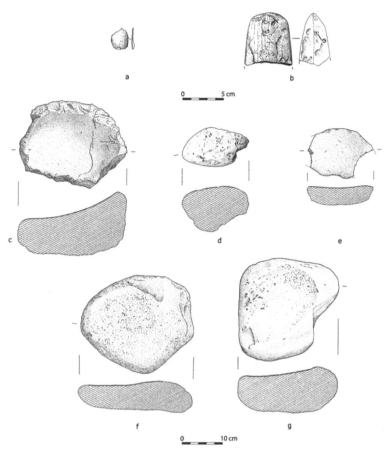

FIGURE 7.15 Ground-stone objects from Etton found in filled pits and ditch segments: a, Other 1 and b, Other 2 from ditch segment 1; c, dolorite saddle quern, fragment from segment 13—Other 152; d, quartzite rubber, heavily worn from segment 13—Other 166; e, quartzite saddle quern, fragment, used from segment 13—Other 167; f, quartzite cushion quern, lightly used from pit F40 in segment 1—Other 209; g, complete quartz cushion quern/pounder from segment 10—Other 206) (redrawn by Svetlana Matskevich from Pryor 1998 figures 232, 233, 236).

264, figure 238: 1); a fourth was a large fragment of a ground stone axe[64] from F866 (Edmonds 1998: 264, figure 238: 18); a fifth was a flake[65] from the edge of an axe (Edmonds 1998: 264, figure 238: 22) from pit F1054 that was a filled-pit that also contained a fragment of a stone axe[66] (Edmonds 1998: 265, figure 238: 23); a sixth was a broken flake[67] from a polished stone implement from pit F839 (which was not a filled-pit) (Edmonds 1998: 265, figure 238: 24). At least at first sight, it is hard to see these fragments as anything other than deposition through discard of no-longer useful materials; in any event, flint and ground stone objects (excepting the greenstone axe) that end up in the filled-pits are fragmentary and few in number. If there is a significant observation about the axe and axe-fragments, it is that the raw material was not local; it would have been brought to the enclosure (e.g., the greenstone axe was made of material that originated in the Lake District; Edmonds 1999: figure 52).

Interpretation of Filled-pits

The excavators suggest that the "small filled pits of Phase 1 represented individual people and that the contents of the pit referred to a person's skills, achievements, or social position. The ditch segment (and the deposits within it) nearest to a particular 'small filled pit' would represent that individual's family or kin group" (Pryor 1998: xix). It is difficult to find any support for this suggestion. There is no direct evidence, such as human bone in any pit, either for the pits with the broken pieces of polished objects in them, or for any of the other filled-pits at the site.

In his contribution to the excavation's final report, Mark Edmonds makes a bolder case for the connection of the pits containing fragments of ground stone tools such as axes to individual lives (living or deceased) (Edmonds 1998). Edmonds argues that ground stone may have had a particular currency in expressing or standing in for an individual, for example through the effort required to make the ground-stone tool or the particular history of obtaining the raw material used in its construction. This may be the case, though it is not clear why the same reasoning does not apply to the other materials and objects (e.g., pottery, bone, ash, and charcoal) each of which may well also have had its own particular local set of process-, material-, extraction-, and use-histories; meanings; energies; and connections evident to individuals or groups who visited the site.

For the few pits that contained unusual objects such as the axe fragments or the querns (most of which were broken, perhaps intentionally), there may be a stronger case for relating their contents not to individual people but to specific activities (e.g., grinding, pottery production, and decoration). However, the fact that such a connection would have been made through broken and fragmentary materials suggests that any connection is not a straightforward or (from a twenty-first-century perspective) a rational one. Even if such connections are valid, it is not clear that these activities would have been associated with individual people (or to groups of people), and not to some idea or essence of meaning that resided in the activity itself; no clear connection to people or person is present.

Other Materials: Flint, Human Bone, Animal Bone

The regular inclusion of pottery and flint in the filled-pits suggests that these materials might help us understand why people dug and filled these holes. Though evidence for the working, use, and discard of flint is infrequent in the first two sub-phases of the site's use (Phase 1A and 1B), significant flint working, tool use, discard, and deposition are evident in Phase 1C. A number of patterns is clear. First, the flint that ends up in the ditches and the pits is of a material from local sources (Middleton 1998: 238), and one of the probable reasons that people visited this place in the Neolithic was to exploit those sources. Second, though no knapping floors were present, people did work flint in the enclosure's interior (but not in the ditch-segments) (Middleton 1998: 217), because entire knapping sequences are present. Third, the remains of the flint-working ended up in the filled-pits and in the surface soil of the interior (Middleton 1998: 241). Fourth, some of the flint that ended up in the ditch-segments had been burnt, particularly the material in Segments 9–11 (Pryor 1998: 254–255). Fifth, the flint assemblage contained an unusually high number of implements (especially scrapers and serrated flakes) compared to other contemporary sites of this type (Middleton 1998: 241). Sixth, during Phase 1C, concentrations of flint working, use, discard, and deposit mark out the northeastern section of the interior as foci for activity (Middleton 1998: 241).

Most significant is a seventh pattern: that flint that entered filled-pits and ditch segments was unabraided and unworn, and thus had not been exposed on the ground surface for long periods of time before it entered the filled-pits and the ditch segments (Middleton 1998: 216). Analysis of the pottery from Etton revealed the same pattern: the majority of sherds (from the eastern ditch-segments) was unabraided (Pryor 1998: 362) and the pottery from Phase 1 features (including the filled-pits) was fresh and showed no signs of weathering or trampling (Taylor 1998: 118; Pryor et al. 1998: 211; Pryor 1998: 363). It is also significant that not all parts of a pot were placed in the pits and the ditches: rim-sherds and decorated pieces were more frequent than were undecorated body sherds (Pryor et al. 1998: 211).

These patterns in the conditions of the material that ended up in the pits and in the ditches are important for the information that they provide about how and why the pits and ditches were filled, especially in terms of what people brought with them when they came to the enclosure (polished- and ground-stone objects or parts of them; and pottery) and what they acquired and made while there (flint tools). Significantly, they tell us about pit-filling (a secondary activity) but not about pit-digging (a primary one); they do not help us understand why these people thought it appropriate to dig holes into the ground in the interior (and not outside). A fuller discussion below addresses this latter task.

Animal Bone

At a general level, analysis of animal remains from Etton suggests that the fauna from the site do not represent a "domestic" assemblage (Armour-Chelu 1998a: 275). Cattle, sheep, and pig made up the range of animal remains, with cattle in the majority (in terms of counts of bone and meat provided) with sheep and pig less frequent and each of the latter two species of equal importance to each other (Armour-Chelu 1998a: 276–277). Similar proportions of material (cattle dominate; sheep and pig equal and less frequent than cattle) were found in both the ditch and the filled-pits of the interior. The disproportionately high number of meat-yielding cattle bones and the groups of ribs and vertebrae (four of cattle, two of pig, and one of sheep) and partial skeletons that ended up in the ditch segments suggest that people feasted while at the site (Armour-Chelu 1998a: 284).

Also of note for the same reasons are the two cattle skulls (both domestic, and thus distinct from the two auroch skulls from late Neolithic Phase 2), the skull of a fox, and the skull of a roe deer; all of these were found in ditch segments. The presence of skulls is not expected in an assemblage that represents the exploitation of animals for meat alone. If the pattern of faunal remains from the ditches reflects feasting, then the animal bone from the interior features of the site reveal a different though complementary and also non-domestic pattern.

Though the excavation report does not provide information about which bones were found in which pits or data that distinguishes phases for the site (i.e., it groups animal bones from Phases 1 and 2 together), animal bone placed in the filled-pits includes a wider range of skeletal elements, including non–meat-bearing bones such as teeth and the extremities of long bones (Armour-Chelu 1998a: 282). Also of significance (though also without precise phase identification) is the high proportion (perhaps 95 percent) of bone from the filled-pits that was burned at a high temperature (up to 600° Celsius) (Armour-Chelu 1998a: 282). Based on an examination of Phase 1 pits (i.e., pits with Mildenhall and Fengate pottery in them), none of this burned bone was deposited in the pits of the site interior during Phase 1 (Pryor 1998: Table 8).

Human Bone

While large amounts of animal bone ended up in both the filled-pits of the interior and the ditch segments (on both western and the eastern sides), human bone was deposited only in the ditch segments, and the total assemblage is small: fourteen bones (Amour-Chelu 1998a: 271–272). Crania or parts of crania (e.g., frontal bone) are most frequent (43 percent). Femurs and parts of femurs are less frequent (29 percent); present also are scapula and parts of scapula (14 percent) as well as one humerus and one tibia. Of the skulls, only the cranium from Segment 6 was complete.

The patterns of importance are that the deposition of human bone at Etton is limited to ditch segments, that the amount of bone deposited is low, and that no complete (or even partial) skeletons were left at the site.[68] If death and its celebration, expression, or manipulation were in play at the site, then corporeal-skeletal death was not part of the digging-and-filling of the filled-pits of the interior. Considering the human bone from the ditch segments, it is more interesting to observe that the condition of the bone informs about what was happening (or at least how what was happening was happening) at the enclosure. Half of the human bone showed signs of canid gnawing (Figure 7.16), and all human remains bore evidence of damage from exposure

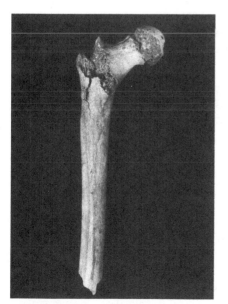
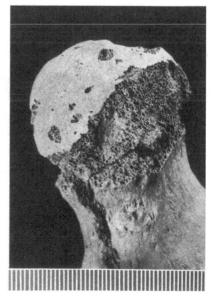

FIGURE 7.16 Human femur (Bone 5267) with evidence of canid gnawing from Etton ditch segment 3, layer 3. Photo copyright Francis Pryor; image reproduced with permission.

to "abrasive environments" (Armour-Chelu 1998b: 272) such as trampling. Furthermore, the condition of the human bone complements the limited amount of human bone and the disparate, disarticulated parts of the body represented. Armour-Chelu suggests that the patterns of bone damage are consistent with the practice of the excarnation of the corpse before burial (Armour-Chelu 1998b: 272).

The condition of the human bone is unusual compared to the other material that ended up in the ditches at Etton, most of which was not abraided, gnawed, or damaged. These patterns in the different conditions of materials deposited in the same contexts are intriguing. Two possibilities emerge. One is that the individual parts of the post-life body (indeed perhaps even the post-life body itself) were not subject to any special treatment and had no particular meaning or currency for the living. If this were the case, then the human remains in the ditches may be nothing other than refuse that ended up in the ditches, intentionally thrown in or not, after the bones had been kicking around on the surface. The second possibility is that after death and excavation, people carried around with them parts of a skeleton with other materials, tools, and objects, and that when and where appropriate, these people placed these individual bones in particular places. If this were the case then it appears that the ditch-segments at Etton were one such appropriate place.

The condition of the human bone (weathered, worn, fragmentary, trampled) and thus its distinction from the condition of the animal bone that ended up in the pits and the ditches (not abraided, gnawed, or damaged) suggests that the former possibility is the most likely (i.e., that people did not care much for the bones of the dead). If the other option is in play (i.e., the cared-carried-deposited thesis), then even here the paucity of human bone in the ditch segments suggests that if the placement of human bone into the holes that people cut into the ground at Etton was an activity that took place when people came to the site, it was not a primary activity. It may have been one of many activities, and people may have carried out similar activities of bone placement during visits to other contemporary sites by these same people.

Condition of Materials: Ported with Intention

Etton provides an example of community behavior through which fragments of people and certain categories of material culture and debris from particular activities were placed into the ground together, if not always in the same place (i.e., in direct physical connection), at least in the same larger, but spatially contained part of the land (i.e., the pits and the ditch segments of the enclosure). Taking a taphonomic perspective on all of the material that ended up in the filled-pits and the ditch-segments from Phase 1, a clear pattern emerges. Flint, pottery, and animal bone were deposited without delay, soon after the productive, consumptive, or other activities that produced/employed them had taken place. On the other hand, deposits of human bone and ground- or polished-stone occurred at some time after the end of the person's life or the object's use-currency. In the case of all but two of the ground stone objects (the greenstone axes and one of the querns), they were deposited in a broken or well-used state: at a point in their lives when they were no longer of use for their original, functional purposes. Either they were being specially curated (and thus had some extra-normal value) or they had so little value that they had been left to be kicked around, exposed, and weathered. The human bone reveals the same pattern: it ended up in a pit or ditch some considerable time after the death of the individual.

Were the events of deposition of the fragmented human bone and the ground- and polished-stone one of the primary reasons that people visited Etton? Was the digging and filling of holes primarily related to these materials (and what they meant to the people who episodically came to this place)? Did people bring these objects to this place, and bring with them particular meanings and restrictions about what they could do to them and where they could do it? Were the activities that were related to making flint tools, butchering animals, and using pottery of secondary (perhaps supporting) importance to what people were doing at this site when they came here? Were these latter activities and materials more of the mundane and of the quickly disposable nature? The objects are important, but also important (perhaps more so) is the act of cutting open the earth and making as deemed appropriate a hole in the surface of the ground into which the materials were placed and then which was filled quickly and sealed to reform the ground surface.

The Function of the Site

But, what was Etton? The detailed excavation report provides clear information about what happened there and when it happened. Harder to infer are what significances did this place and these activities have for the people who visited the site, dug the holes and ditches, put objects into them, and then covered them over. What lay behind these activities? The patterns in the conditions of materials, the cuttings of the ground surface, the deposits in the pits and the ditches, and the filling of the ditches and pits tell us a great deal about what people did when they came to and stayed at the site. Etton is perhaps one the best excavated and published of the many causewayed enclosures from the British Neolithic. Much has been written about the functions or meanings of these sites in their fourth millennium cal. B.C. contexts (Evans 1988b, 1988a; Evans et al. 1988; Edmonds 1999: 80–105, 110–129; Oswald et al. 2001; Pollard 2008; Whittle et al. 2011).

In the more critical discussions of causewayed enclosures in general, several common proposals for use recur: places of gathering, of death, and of exchange. Earlier suggestions that they were settlements or defended positions are now less well supported in the light of recent excavations: Windmill Hill (Whittle et al. 1999); Hambledon Hill (Healy 2004); Briar Hill (Bamford 1985), though see the extended discussion by Alasdair Whittle and colleagues (Whittle et al. 2011). Arguments that causewayed enclosures were places-of-gathering may have found original support in suggestions about the labor that would have been required to dig the ditches with which causewayed enclosures were constructed. In concert with the labor-gathering suggestions, it is likely that causewayed enclosures would then have been ideal locations for people to get together, to exchange materials and goods, to resolve disputes, to find mates, to slaughter animals, to feast, to tell stories, to recite legends, to invoke memories, to celebrate and perform, to invoke rituals, to establish alliance, and to do any range of other things that required the co-presence of groups of people, from a single community or from several otherwise unconnected groups.

At a more specific level are proposals that enclosure sites were action places in large-scale exchange networks, particularly of axes (Edmonds 1998, 1999). Edmonds has written evocatively about the roles that flaked and polished stone axes could have played in marking Neolithic individuals' identities (Edmonds 1998: 267–268). He argues that the "circulation of the axes may have been keyed into the reproduction of relations of affiliation and authority between dispersed groups" (Edmonds 1998: 267). Furthermore, Edmonds sees some axes as "harnessed, broken, and/or burnt within important rites of passage" (Edmonds 1998: 268). He notes that the Etton axes (how many, which ones?) have break marks and evidence of burning (Edmonds 1998: 268). Etton, for Edmonds at least, would have been part of that circulation and those rites. Unfortunately, the evidence for axes is very thin on (or in) the ground at Etton in Phase 1: one complete greenstone axe in pit F263; three fragments from filled-pits; and five from the ditch segments (Edmonds 1998).

The location of some causewayed enclosures in landscapes (at Flag Fen, Windmill Hill, and other sites such as Etton) that are not obviously useful for agriculture has led some to argue that these places were marginal, and that such marginality of land correlates with liminality in metaphysical senses of what happened at these sites (Bradley 1990: 172; Thomas 1991: 36; Edmonds 1993; Whittle et al. 1993: 172). The potential role of the ditches as boundaries at Etton (and at other contemporary enclosure sites) is another frequent proposal: the horizontal separation of what lies and happens within the circuit of ditches from what happens beyond.

The Evidence from Etton

The archaeological work at Etton is particularly valuable for its precision and multidisciplinary breadth. What does that work tell us about the function of the site? How does it add to and refine the proposals for the functions of other contemporary sites of similar form? Strongest of the Etton conclusions is the case against the use of the site for settlement or long-term habitation. In addition to the absence of large postholes for architectural elements, the analysis of insect remains produced no evidence for the "decomposer fauna" that would result from collections of discarded domestic rubbish (Robinson 1989). In addition, the geomorphological record documents a place that would have been habitable only for parts of the year when the ground was dry (Pryor 1998: 361). Furthermore, the examination of the Etton faunal remains revealed them as atypical of a domestic assemblage: small-scale exploitation of some species, such as sheep, pigs, and some cattle (Pryor 1998: 361), with clear evidence for localized feasting, documented by the partial skeletons of some pig and sheep, and the selection of particular cattle parts for meat (Pryor 1998: 361). The patterns revealed by the phosphate analysis of the interior soils and the evidence for high concentrations of dung beetles in some features (e.g., pit F505) supports the use of part of the interior as a corral for animals, and it is most likely that the people who came to the enclosure brought animals with them, and kept them in the site's interior.

As has become common in the last twenty-five years of British archaeological thinking and as proposed for other British prehistoric sites, so also at Etton has great pressure been placed of the assumption that the materials that ended up in the pits and ditches were placed there according to rules and rituals, as structured deposits (see fuller discussion in chapter 1). In addition to the excavation report, and particularly Edmond's contributions to it, Josh Pollard has recently reviewed and refined this proposal with specific attention to Etton (Pollard 2008). Pollard argues that longer-running episodes of placing objects in the ditches at the site functioned to reanimate the ditches and, in turn, the site (Pollard 2008: 51). He offers the nuanced suggestion that the inclusion of material (particularly animal bone) helped release, insert, or reactivate generative "energies and potencies" of the animals for the pits and the ditches and how people understood and used them (Pollard 2008: 52).

Pollard suggests that the combination of different materials (bone, pottery, flint, ash) in individual Etton deposits created "new material relations" that thus condensed "multiple identities of the makers and consumers of these objects, their connections and energies" (Pollard 2008: 58). Together these actions of deposit and mixture contributed to a stronger sense of community cohesion for people who spent most of the rest of the seasons away from the enclosure, moving in small, dispersed groups (Pollard 2008: 58). Furthermore, putting these materials into the Etton pits and ditches "forced an evocation of memory," of history of actions and places (Pollard 2008: 58). Actions, contents, and meanings of these deposits, Pollard thus suggests, prompt us to see enclosures as laboratories (after Turnbull 2000) where the messiness and complexity of the material world was worked through and negotiated. Etton and other monuments like it were spaces that facilitated the gathering of substances as well as the gathering of people. They were spaces for creating and negotiating material relations as well as social relations (Pollard 2008: 59).

More dramatic are the excavators' proposals for the ritual function of Etton (Edmonds 1998: 266–267). They suggest that rites of passage played a large role in what people did at the site (Pryor 1998: 367). From this perspective, the site was a place of transition, particularly between life and afterlife, where such periods of time and transition are understood as dangerous periods. If this were the case, then the enclosure would have been a place of safety within which people could perform and administer the requisite rites for the journey from life to post-life. The excavators propose that the filled-pits and the backfilled ditch deposits are the evidence for these rites (Pryor 1998: 367), though the limited number of human remains weakens this proposal for a death connection. Other proposals for Etton as a ritual space include the claim (otherwise unsupported) that several of the few non-vessel fired clay objects (of unclear obvious function) from Segment 7 were fertility objects and that birth as well as death was celebrated at the site (Pryor 1998: 367). Edmonds puts it best: "at certain times, passage across the threshold of these sites may have constituted a movement between arenas of value—from the everyday world of dispersed communities to the more socially charged atmosphere that attended encounters with others" (Edmonds 1998: 266–267; Edmonds 1999: 110–129).

Etton as Surface: Cut, Resurfaced, and Recut

All of these thoughts, activities, and functions may well have been in play on late summer and early fall days in the early fourth millennium B.C. at Etton. Without other supporting evidence, however, it is hard to find merit in proposals for dangerous transitions, fertility rites, or associations of filled-pits-as-people. The evidence for human remains is weak; the associations between person and objects in pits are frail. Paradoxically, even with the amount of detailed analyses and these broader comparisons, it is difficult to find surety in any interpretation of this place. In most cases, the explanations and proposals rely on limited evidence (though studied in intricate detail). One observation, however, is clear. With the documentation of object placements and their coverings with backfill in ditch or in pit, to date, all of the thinking about the site has privileged the *use* of the pits and the ditches: the focus has been on objects and their deposition, with the conclusion that the latter followed a structured pattern.

Seen through the eyes of the philosophers of holes and surfaces (as discussed in chapter 3), we realize that the archaeological analysis and interpretation of Etton have focused primarily on what Casati and Varzi recognized as the filling of a hole, in their words an action of secondary (or at least other, non-original) importance. From this perspective, the archaeological discussions have missed the primary, original actions and events that made the place what it was: the breaking of the surface by the cutting of holes into the ground. Is it the case that the activities reconstructed from pit- and ditch-fill (object breakage, animal and human death, feasting, burning) are nothing more than the filling of the holes and ditches? Are they just after-events, disarticulated from the distinct and (potentially) more important actions of cutting the ground that created the pits and made (and remade) the ditches?

If we separate the objects and their deposition (structured or haphazard) from the acts of cutting the surface of the ground and the re-cuttings of the re-made surfaces (created by many of the ditch re-filling activities; what excavators often disclaim as "backfilling") (Figure 7.17), one can see deposition as separate in timing and in importance, though undoubtedly of another significance rightfully to be taken up on its own. Deposition of objects, though not unimportant for other sets of particular references and meanings, may have nothing to do with the original and early human actions at Etton. If this is the case, then a reformed conception of the site would start with the acts, meanings, consequences, and significances of breaking the surface of the ground. When we shift our thinking in this way, new questions arise. Why was re-cutting not appropriate in the interior (where no filled-pit was cut by

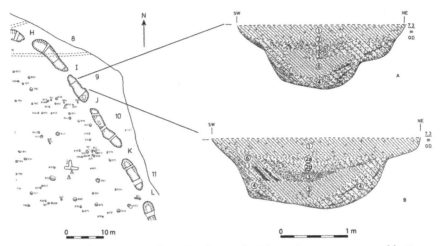

FIGURE 7.17 Segment 9 at Etton in plan and with sections (top, 203 and bottom, 204) showing sequences of digging, resurfacing, and redigging (redrawn by Svetlana Matskevich after Pryor 1998 figures 73A and B).

any other filled-pit), while re-cutting was the norm in the cycles of ditch segment cut-fill-cut? Were these two different practices or spheres or deployments of these cutting surfaces? How does attention to cutting distinguish the interior pits from the ditch segments?

Cutting Etton

If we think about Etton in terms of cutting the surface of the ground and of the potential disruptive consequences that may have resulted, then we gain a sharper focus and, unexpectedly, find connection with some of Edmonds' and the excavators' initially less supportable proposals, particularly their arguments for the structured insertion of particular objects into the ground: those materials that were brought to the site from other places, specifically human bone, ground and polished stone, and probably pottery. In his unconventional, soothing, narrative approach to causewayed enclosures (including Etton), Mark Edmonds (1998) recognizes (even if he only acknowledges it in passing) that the making of these pits and ditches (i.e., the diggings into the surface) deserves our attention: "the practice of breaking the earth and planting cultural remains is something that we should think about.... What ideas were implicated in activities such as cutting and filling pits of pits" (Edmonds 1999: 29–30). Edmonds also breathes life to the actions of pit- and ditch-making-as-cutting in his equally brief (but evocative) comment about the "features cut with antler picks and the shoulder blades of cattle, with digging sticks and stones" (Edmonds 1999: 101). More evocative is his narrative mis en scène in which he fleshes out the real-time digging of an enclosure: "Many had begun to cut the ground.... Already the earth was white.... They worked carefully, antler and axe following the edge where the loose earth met the chalk.... Others followed with bone and basket, collecting the spoil and heaving it up to form the inner face of the line" (Edmonds 1999: 106–108). He continues with a similarly brief suggestion (unfortunately not expanded upon in his text) that digging could have the "qualities of performance" (Edmonds 1999: 103).

Edmonds also includes a brief reference to the participation of individuals in the shared acts of digging as collaboration that "created a sense of the collective" (Edmonds 1999: 102). With this, Edmonds delivers us back to the standard treatment of these sites and what people were doing and thinking while there (i.e., enclosures as gathering places). The discussion returns to the mundane and the functional: digging in terms of labor output and a discussion of digging "gangs" (Edmonds 1999: 101–102). Despite the glimpse of a new way to think about this site, digging remains unexplored in terms of surface cuttings, and unexamined remain the potentials that breaking the surface might have for opening up new understandings of how people lived their lives at the place with those actions.

Perhaps a fresh significance of Etton is its position (physical and spiritual) as a place where people opened up the ground by digging holes into it. That objects then ended up within these holes may be secondary in importance not only to the original breaking of the surface of the ground in this place and in these ways but also secondary to the covering of those objects and the recreation of a new, constructed surface with the Neolithic refilling and back-filling. In this case, the liminality to which Edmonds and other members of the team refer may not have been about movement across the horizontal dimension (thus, the linked ditches as boundaries between the world-out-there and the place-in-here, within the "enclosure"). Perhaps the threshold (if this concept even approaches the appropriate senses) was between the ground upon which people moved, lived, acted, met, and on which animals roamed and were corralled, on the one hand, and the space below the surface of the ground, on the other. That latter space was hidden, covered, and closed off. In this sense, cutting open and breaking the surface of the ground by digging ditches (and making the voids that became the "filled-holes" in the interior) should be seen as the provision of a portal into (and out of) both worlds: below and above the ground level.

The Texture of Etton Ground

Chapter 6's report on the linguistic anthropology of cutting and breaking, and most particularly Stephen Levinson's discussion of the Yélî Dnye conception of breaking and cutting, recognizes the potential significance of the character of an object that is cut, specifically in terms of its grain. The implication drawn in that discussion was that cutting against the grain differs from cutting with the grain: that one (the former) was contested and less easily achieved than the other. Might the shape, location, and layout of the peripheral ditches be better understood in these terms? If so, then the thin, curved line of the ditch segments at Etton reveals a cutting with the grain of the ground surface. Perhaps the positions and shapes of the ditches refer to an easier, less contested, unresisted slipping into and out of different worlds. Thinking this way about the potential grain of the ground surface and the corresponding difficulty and ease of cutting (along or against) may help us to understand both the cutting-filling-re-cutting of the ditches, but also about the absence of re-cutting or intercutting of the interior "filled-pits" at Etton.

In the ditches, the sequences of cutting and then filling created new surfaces that could be cut again and mark the ditched parts of the site as appropriate for multiple movements into and out of other worlds, of truly liminal spaces. In addition, the cycle of cutting, filling, and not re-cutting that defines the interior's "filled-pits" suggests that these may not have been understood as places where repeated movements between worlds was deemed feasible, or desirable. Different eases of breakage in differently textured ground surfaces refer to different potentials for the manifestation of liminality. Regardless, by shifting our attention to the sequences of cutting-re-surfacing-re-cutting (or in the case of the "filled-pits" of cutting-and-filling-and-leaving), the objects that ended up in the ditches and pits fade into less significant position, or at the least, to a position of different significances. Placing objects into the ground may have been important, though perhaps that importance now rests more with the place/world that the objects end up in, and less with the individual objects themselves and any specific reference those objects may have with individuals, identities, or distant relationships among the people who came to this low-lying part of this landscape.

Relevance to Măgura

While there is no value in drawing a direct analogy between Etton and Măgura as homogenous contexts for behavior or belief, there is benefit in thinking again about Măgura in terms of a place where the ground surface was cut open and through which access to another world may thus have been made possible. What is striking about the Etton examples, for the ditch segments at least, is the cycle of cutting-filling-and-re-cutting. For whatever reasons the people who cut those ditches (originally, but also with successive actions of breaking the reconstructed surfaces) understood that it was appropriate to cut the surface in these ways in the particular places where they continued to do so over many different visits to the site. Perhaps this was an understanding that was shared by different groups of people. Breaking the surface of the ground followed particular patterns of appropriate actions in much the same way as others have proposed for the structured patterning in the placement of objects into pits and ditches in the Neolithic at Etton and at other contemporary sites.

Both the ditchs and the filled-holes are clear examples of the reconstruction of a ground surface after initial cutting into that original surface. Present here was the need to remake a surface by filling in a ditch in such a particular way and to a partial level that that ditch was made ready to be cut (and filled) again. It is as if the ground surface, both inside a ditch cut but also across the original uncut land surface, had a charge and energy that was depleted when cut (perhaps as if energy released from below) and then needed to be recharged or repaired in such a way that the potency of and in the ground was re-established. Pollard made a similar proposal about generative "energies and potencies" invoked in the making of Etton. It is possible that replenishment and recharging were made possible through the action of resurfacing. It may well be that cutting took its power and meaning from the resident energy and essence which the ground contained and which the surface skin of the ground protected and restrained. Perhaps breaking the surface caused a release, escape, and even harvesting of that energy. If these proposals have merit, then the positioning of the ditches (and the filled-pits) where they were cut at Etton may well have followed particular knowledges about the distribution of these energies in the same way that the people coming to this landscape had particular knowledges of other resources (such as flint). In standard archaeologies, the latter, standard sets of knowledges (i.e., about raw material sources) are more comfortable and frequently seen: locating, mapping, and using as stimulus for the movement of people and the differential valuation of actions (flint mining) and of materials (the materiality of specific types of flint).

The holes (at Etton or at Măgura; Figure 7.18) do not make sense, in the terms that Casati and Varzi propose, except in reference to, and (literal) dependence from, the surfaces that define them. The holes cut into the ground at Etton (both in the interior and in the perimeter ditches) only made sense in relation to the ground into which they cut and which defined them. Even the

FIGURE 7.18 Excavations of Complex 35 at Măgura-Buduiasca. Photo copyright D. W. Bailey.

holes and what they contained may not have mattered as much as did the ground surface and how it signified to the people of those places and of those times. In these ways, our discussion edges closer to a metaphysics of the land surface (or even a topographical metaphysics), in which is contained a richer thinking about how people at Etton and Măgura understood their positions in their worlds, literally, as grounded, and subsequently the effects that resulted from actions that punctured that ground.

On their own, these proposals make little sense and find even less traction in a standard archaeological approach to the Neolithic landscapes and activities of Etton. In light of the cutting performances and actions of Ron Athey and Gordon Matta-Clark, however, greater potential is present. The release of highly charged and metaphysically (and medically) charged material (i.e., blood) in the case of Athey's cutting of the back of Darryl Carlton brought with it tremendous and far-reaching reaction and consequence. Much of the violence of that reaction can be traced back to the disruption of what many people believed was acceptable and appropriate: the skin surface of an HIV-positive man. The transformation of the spectators into witnesses and participants in Athey's surface transgression of Carlton's back may have been mirrored in the ways that the cutting of the Etton pits and ditches implicated people at that site. Similarly, Matta-Clark's opening up of the rue de Beaubourg houses created senses of curiosity, wonder, outrage, and fear in the passers-by and those who walked within the cut buildings. I suggest that the same reactions would have been in play around (and in) the ditch segments at Etton and at Măgura. The same potential rests with the cutting of the surface at Wilsford. In all of this is the action of breaking the surface through cutting, which provokes the reaction and stimulates response. Cutting these surfaces in these ways disrupts the stability of the status quo in deep and dangerous ways.

Chapter 8

Cutting

LUCIO FONTA   D.
1950S AND 19

The Cut/Break

LATE IN 1952, members of the Italian architecture, design, and art history communities opened their new issues of the journal *Spazio* (volume 7–December 1952–April 1953). Subtitled *Rassegna della arti e dell 'architettura*, the periodical was the creation of editor Luigi Moretti (1907–1973), a collector of fine art, and the owner of a gallery in Rome (also called Spazio). A practicing civil architect, Moretti promoted debates and exhibitions about the connections among art, architecture, painting, film, and theater. Opening this issue of *Spazio*, the reader flipped past ads for Carpano (a vermouth), LN (a linoleum manufacturer), Air France (and its claims as "The Highway to Paris!"), Patek Philippe (the Swiss horologists), the Sicilian Tourist Board, Alfa Romeo (advertising the delicious new Alfa 1900 coupe), the Aurora 88 (a "beautiful and dependable" pen), Olivetti (with its Lexikon typewriter), and other full- and half-page notices in black-and-white or color for art galleries, construction firms, industrial mineral suppliers, aluminum window manufactures, local airlines (e.g., Linee Aeree Italiane), swimming pool contractors, kitchen appliance distributors, domestic floor installers, pivoting window manufacturers, toothpaste companies, furniture designers, and perfumiers.

Over the first seventy-three pages of the issue, the reader skimmed or read more deeply about the critical academic opinions about sculptor Roger Fry (and the African primitive stimuli to his work), and on the statue of Hermes in the temple of Hera at Olympia before she came to three more philosophical articles on structures of architectural space, spatial aesthetics, and the aims of the New Abstraction in modern art. There followed articles reviewing the interior design of an art gallery (the Palazzo Bianco in Genoa), the recent Venice Biennale, an Art Nouveau exhibition in Zurich, the architectural design of the recently completed Astrea House and the church at Recaro-Terme, as well as critical reviews of a hotel, a family apartment, a holiday retreat bungalow, and an art school.

When the reader turned from page 73 to 74, her eyes would have fixed on an unexpected and disorienting image: a black-and-white photograph without obvious subject (Figure 8.1). Dominating from the page's top-left corner, the image is a chaotic spread of vibrating light streaks and dark spaces. In the right three-quarters of the photograph were fuzzy, vibrating, open-ended, thin hook-shapes of bright light repeated ten or more times and partially overlapping one another. The brightest light-vibrations are in the center of the image, almost in movement, as if traveling from fainter hooks of light in the right portion of the photograph toward brighter ones to the left. On the left of these advancing tremors of light, a black, empty, vertical area separates the space of light-hooks from the image's left-hand portion: a smooth vertical surface interrupted with many small, short shadows cast from tiny protrusions raised from, or perforated through, its vertical plane. In the image's bottom-left corner, emerging from a round shade or a deflector is a bright light, the source of the hooked vibrations.

The page 74 photograph (and one other, even less clearly recognizable image on the same page) was the work of Lucio Fontana (1899–1968), one of

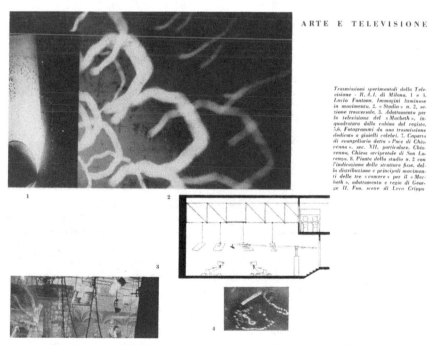

FIGURE 8.1 Page 74 from *Spazio* volume 7 (December 1952–April 1953).

Italy's most important postwar artists.[1] The image and others on the same *Spazio* page illustrate editor Moretti's short text "Arte e Televisione" (Moretti 1952), a comment on an experimental transmission of the Italian public television broadcaster Radiotelevisione Italiana (RAI) made in May 1952 (Gottschaller 2008: 35–36; Whitfield 2000: 188). RAI had invited Fontana to participate in the experiment, and he had responded with at least two works.[2]

As Christine Mehring has shown, the early development of television in Europe understood the training of artistic and technical personnel and experimentation to be of higher importance than did the early American broadcasting industry that focused more tightly on commercial success and expansion (Mehring 2008: 41). Indeed, Moretti's comment in *Spazio* suggested that television was a particularly powerful platform and medium for the arts. The 1952 RAI transmission was not public, but an in-house broadcast seen by a small group of people (Petersen 2000: 54). Fontana's photographs and Moretti's *Spazio* article are the only documentation of the event.

To make his contribution to the RAI experiment, Fontana had presented his recent works (made three years earlier) that he then had called *Concetto Spaziale* [Spatial Concept], and which now are more commonly called *buchi* (literally "holes"). In the RAI work, Fontana positioned one of his *buchi* on a stool (49 B 1—arguably one of the first *buchi* that he made[3]) and then shone light (from the bottom-left of the image in *Spazio*) through the holes. The intended result were slivers of light projected onto the studio walls opposite which produced the multiple vibrating hooked shapes that the reader saw in the photograph. Though full details of the broadcast do not exist, Pia Gottschaller suggests that Fontana included three of his *buchi* in the RAI transmission (Gottschaller 2008: 35–36).

Fontana's RAI projections of light through his *buchi*, the photographs of the event, and the dissemination of the photograph to a wider audience in *Spazio* mark one of many times that the artist made works by combining his *buchi* with light sources. Similar images appear in other publications, including an article in *Domus* published in June 1952 (Ponti 1952) (Figure 8.2). As Stephen Petersen has shown (and as the contents of the archives of the Fondazione Fontana illustrate), the artist made many photographic combinations of *buchi* and projected light. In some of his gallery installations, Fontana exhibited *buchi* (as well as later works, such as some of his *pietre*) with small, battery-powered light bulbs installed at the rear of the work to provide the light source. In March 1953, in Milan, the Italian architect, publicist, and art critic Agnoldomenico Pica published *Fontana*, a short pamphlet containing eight of Fontana's *buchi* photographed with oblique lighting raking across the works (Pica 1953).

What the *Spazio* image showed in its dancing vibrations of hooked light, another photograph of three other works arranged in Fontana's studio (and

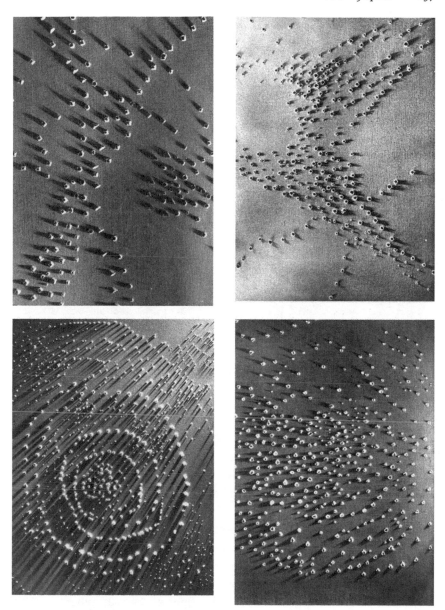

FIGURE 8.2 Four *buchi* as published in *Domus* (1952). © 2017 Artists Rights Society (ARS), New York/SIAE, Rome.

the photographs published in Pica's 1953 pamphlet) expand and refine. This photograph was taken in Fontana's studio in 1952 or soon after (Figure 8.3). The artist arranged three of his *buchi* to combine the perforations in the works, the light source placed behind one, and the raised bumps on the surface of the third work. At the right of the photo, one *buco* (52 B 3) stands perpendicular to

FIGURE 8.3 Installation photograph in Fontana's studio by Attilio Bacci. Left: Lucio Fontana, *Spatial Concept* (52 B 1), 1952. Oil on paper, 80 × 80 cm. Nello Baroncelli Collection. Right: Lucio Fontana, *Spatial Concept* (52 B 3), 1952. Oil and glitter on cardboard, 80 × 80 cm. Guido Azario collection, Biella. Bottom: Lucio Fontana, unknown work. © 2017 Artists Rights Society (ARS), New York/SIAE, Rome.

the floor with a light shining through the work's holes and directed to the left. In front of this wall of light dots and emissions, another work (title unknown as it has not survived) was laid flat on a stool or tripod, parallel to the studio floor. Onto this second work the light flowing from 52 B 3 to the right cast streaks of brightness (particularly on its lower right-hand corner), and caught the small raised protrusions sitting on the flat work's surface. From the photograph, it is not clear whether these protrusions are the edges of holes punctured from the back of the work, or whether they are materials added to the surface. The result is the same; the protrusions catch the light and throw shadows to the left and across the work. The third *buco* in the photograph (52 B 1) stands perpendicular to the floor and at right angles to the other two. This work has many raised protrusions: results of holes being punched through its surface from the back. The light source from the right, behind 52 B 3, hits the protrusions of 52 B 1 and sends another series of shadows to the left.

Two other photographs are worth describing here: both are of the same *buco* (49 B 2), and both were reproduced by Stephen Petersen in his discussion of Fontana's experimental use of photography (Petersen 2000: figures 2 and 3). In the first image, Fontana photographed[4] (Figure 8.4) the *buco* with obliquely angled light pouring over the surface of the work from the upper left. As the light meets each protruding paper lip raised from one of the holes punctured through the work, the light casts shadows to the right. In addition, as the light runs along the surface of the work, slight modulations of the rumbled paper of the *buco* surface create a landscape of valleys and hills. As the light crosses the voids created by the holes punched through from the front, the light creates darkness and empty spaces in the surface. In all, the light travels across, through, and around the *buco* and stimulates new senses and shapes of space, not only of the surface of the works but also of the space and shape of the studio or gallery in which 49 B 2 was lit and photographed.

At first sight, the other photograph Petersen published (Figure 8.5) appears as if it is an image of yet another *buco*: the distribution of holes; the

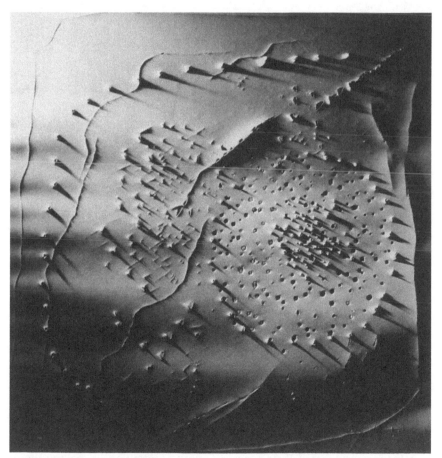

FIGURE 8.4 Lucio Fontana, *Spatial Concept* (49 B 2) (1949) pierced paper, (size unknown). © 2017 Artists Rights Society (ARS), New York/SIAE, Rome.

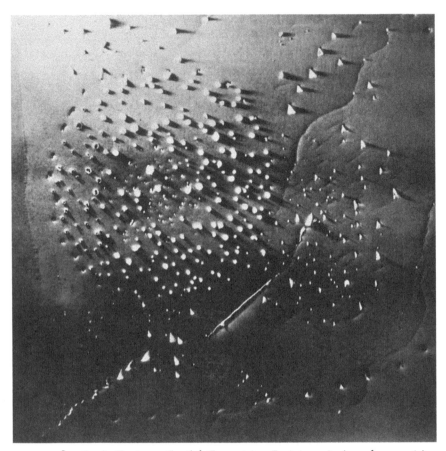

FIGURE 8.5 Lucio Fontana, *Spatial Concept* (49 B 2) (1949) pierced paper (size unknown). © 2017 Artists Rights Society (ARS), New York/SIAE, Rome.

raised paper tears; the resulting protrusions; the position, size, and orientation of the hills and valleys (some now look to us like rivers in an aerial photograph or map) are distinct from those illustrated in the first photograph. In truth, these two photographs are of the same work (49 B 2): one image taken from one side of the work, the second from the other. The perforations and creases are the same; the use of light and the photography of the work created two different works existing in two separate spatial environments.

Lucio Fontana's *Buchi*

Fontana's *buchi* are striking works and we gain much from examining more closely the conditions of their genesis, Fontana's intention in making them, and the effects the works had on viewers. My proposal in bringing Fontana and his work into the discussion of the Măgura pit-houses rests on two strong connections: that much of the power of the *buchi* and of Fontana's other works (particularly the later and better known *tagli*, discussed in detail below) is a consequence of the artist's perforations of these works' surfaces; and that *buchi* do what they do because Fontana broke their surfaces (i.e., their affective power derives from the action and consequence of hole making and viewing). Second, Fontana's work and the philosophy behind it rests on the ways that light and space (and thus perceptions and experience of one's environment) are heavily affected by the perforations he made in the surfaces of his works, the consequent opening up of other worlds that followed, and on his larger effort (seen across his *oeuvre*) to turn away from the materiality of artistic production and to explore the expanded potentials of light, time, space, and what he called fourth-dimensional art.

My proposal is that Fontana's *buchi* (and the often overlooked use of light and photography in their completion) provide significant surfaces of traction for archaeologists studying pit-houses for the following reasons: in Fontana's intention, *buchi* were to be transformations of space and time; in their creation of spatial spectacles, *buchi* negated the value of the material (in art and beyond); in their display and photographic reproduction, *buchi* created a series of endless possibilities of, and avenues into, worlds beyond the expected and the everyday; and, finally, in the ephemerality of their display, *buchi* were not intended as complete end-products with a simple meaning or function; they opened up other, never-ending worlds of perception.

Genesis, Production and Intention of Fontana's Buchi

Between 1949 and his death in 1968, Lucio Fontana made many buchi,[5] and though less well known than his *tagli* (the canvases that he slashed with a Stanley knife) of which he made over 1,500, it is from the *buchi* that we find most clearly the core of the artist's revolutionary thinking and contribution to twentieth-century art. The literature on the genesis of the *buchi* is substantial, and Anthony White has written with authority about the artist's thinking and intentions with these works (White 2011: 173). In a 1949 untitled study in ink on paper (surviving only in a documentary photograph), Fontana sketched out a plan for his *buchi* (Figure 8.6). At first sight the sketch is chaotic and senseless. As White explains, however, the drawing reveals Fontana's intentions for the display and observation that eventually will take form in his *buchi*. The scribbles in the sketch illustrate a room in which he depicted triangular or rectangular panels that had been perforated with round holes. Stretching out from many of the holes, Fontana drew lines, representing streams or beams of light, traveling through the panels and then shooting out across the room before hitting either the walls opposite or the ceiling above.

Fontana's 1949 sketch shows the shared, primary roles that light and holes were to play in his *buchi*. The holes (and the light cast through them) animated and gave shape to the ambient character of light and space (White 2011: 173). Here, in its strongest sense, is Fontana's desire to connect artwork-as-material-object with space in environmental terms. The works that Fontana planned (as seen in this sketch) presage the intention and action of his RAI works that Moretti published and discussed in the 1952 issue of *Spazio*. We see the same intentions and actions in the

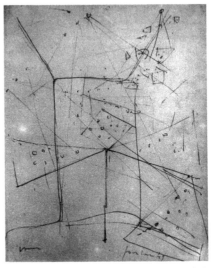

FIGURE **8.6** Lucio Fontana, *Untitled*, (1949) Of unknown size, materials, or location. © 2017 Artists Rights Society (ARS), New York/SIAE, Rome.

photographs of the lit-through-and-across *buchi*. Thus illuminated and positioned, these works are art in action; *buchi* are not static art trapped in and on material supports through which a few holes had been punched. On the contrary, *buchi* are dynamic, multipart, performative works that engage, enter, traverse, and create space in the studios or galleries in which they were positioned. With his *buchi*, Fontana activated the punctured canvases with light and with its particular, powerful characteristics and qualities.

Making Buchi

In 1949, with two decades of experience and success as a sculptor, Fontana started making a *buco* as a new type of work by perforating flat surfaces with metal awls: first through paper (which was then mounted on canvas) and then directly onto and through canvas. The three earliest *buchi* (49 B 1, 49 B 2, and 49 B 3) are all on heavy paper lined onto canvas that was then mounted onto wooden stretchers (Gottschaller 2012: 22). For these early examples, Fontana made his perforations from both the front and the rear of the paper/canvas (though 49 B 1 has holes only made from the rear), and he made the holes in recognizable patterns (e.g., clear concentric circles).

Fontana exhibited these early works first in a 1952 group show by the artist and his Spatialist colleagues at the Galleria del Naviglio in Milan and then again later that year in a one-man show in May and June at the same gallery (Gottschaller 2012: 25). At the solo show, the works were lit from behind and would have presented similar visions as did those in the *Spazio* article and in the other photographs made from 1952 and 1953 (White 2011: 194). Battery-powered light sources on the back for the canvas were used in the *buchi* shown in Venice at the Gianna Prize exhibition (White 2011: 193).

In a masterful technical study, Pia Gottschaller has tracked the development of Fontana's *buchi*, showing that in his pre-1951 work, the artist worked with white or monochromatic canvases, arranging the holes in straight and waving lines moving in various directions, following a range of patterns, and using holes of different sizes and shapes (round, square, triangular, rectangular) (Gottschaller 2012: 25). After 1951, Fontana started to use color paint, and in some examples, he added particles of glitter (i.e., *lustrini*) and sand to make the surfaces of the *buchi* active reflectors of light. Also at this time, he made holes more frequently round in shape; rectangular- and triangular-shaped ones started to drop out of use (Gottschaller 2012: 25). Fontana then took a break from making *buchi*, and when he returned to the form in 1955, he arranged the perforations only in geometric patterns and clusters, and he started to use quick-drying PVA-based house paints to give the works matte surfaces (Gottschaller 2012: 27). From 1960, patterns of the holes in the works were more regularly ordered, usually in horizontal, vertical, or curvilinear lines (Gottschaller 2012: 28).

Method

To make the *buchi*, Fontana used canvases already coated (on both front and back) with a matte chalky primer and stapled to wooden stretchers (Gottschaller 2012: 30–31). Before making the holes, Fontana applied another layer of primer to stiffen the canvas and to fill in as much of the fabric's weave as possible. The stiffer the canvas, the greater the possible precision of the shape and stability of the punctures. In addition, the more Fontana filled the weave with paint, the less like a traditional artist's canvas the work appeared (Gottschaller 2012: 31). Choice of canvas material also contributed to surface stiffness; Fontana chose thinly woven linen to help create the illusion of the canvas surface as one continuous plane (Gottschaller 2012: 29–30).

Gottschaller's study of Fontana's method and the contents of his studios revealed that the artist used metal *punteruoli* (similar to awls) to hole the canvases (Figure 8.7). Five *punteruoli* found in his studio had round steel spikes sharpened to fine points; some had wooden handles. Two had spikes of 0.5 mm diameter and three of 1.2 mm diameter; all five would have been used to make the round holes in the *buchi* (Gottschaller 2008: 71). Fontana controlled the size of the holes by controlling the depth through the canvas that he thrust the *punteruoli*: the deeper the thrust, the larger the hole (Gottschaller

2008: 70). The choice and preparation of the canvas, as well as the size and sharpness of the tools (blunt points required more force and left bulges in the surfaces), were decisions made to avoid torn edges to the punctures, and thus to create a flat surface interrupted only by perforation.

FIGURE 8.7 A selection of awls from the studio of Lucio Fontana in Comabbio, Italy. Photo copyright Pia Gottschaller; reproduced with permission.

For a period of time (from late 1959 to late 1960), Fontana signed his *buchi* with an impression of his thumb; first he applied some viscous material to the bottom-right corner of the work and then he pushed the pad of his thumb into that material (Gottschaller 2012: 32–33). On other *buchi*, he signed the back of the work with an ink thumbprint directly onto the white priming layer; on yet others, Fontana made his thumb print on a separate piece of paper that he then adhered to the rear of the work (Gottschaller 2012: 33).

Buchi *and the Experience of Space*

As noted above in the context of the photographed *buchi* (and as seen in the 1949 sketch prefiguring *buchi* creation), Fontana created and displayed (performed even) these works in combination with precisely placed and directed light; light was the element that activated the *buchi*. By perforating the pictorial plane of the canvas in such a way as to leave exaggerated relief rims of paper (in the first works) and canvas (thereafter), Fontana created a three-dimensional space where there had once been a blank two-dimensional surface. Fontana intentionally painted that surface in a way that would erase any reference to the weft and weave of the canvas support. With the oblique lighting, the holed surfaces created sets of spaces that had not existed before. For the viewers of the work (both witnessing originals in person and arrangements reproduced in photographs), the holes altered the viewers' experiences not only of the work but also of the spaces around them in the gallery.

With his *buchi*, Fontana played with, created, disrupted, and manipulated space, and the viewers' experiences of it. Part of the intention of these disruptions was to deny the received understanding of the pictorial surface of the canvas as a traditional artistic medium. Most of this disruption occurred (outside of and beyond the materially bounded limits of the work) in the newly created, connected (and illuminated) space joined together by the *buchi*'s holes and the light shooting through them: light that dragged over the ragged perforation-lips, which cascaded and draped itself over parts of the work, and which volleyed out into the space of the gallery, onto and among the people in that space, and onto the other works present.

Writing about the illuminated *buchi* in the June 1952 issue of the Italian architecture and design journal *Domus*, Lisa Ponti suggests that in the movement "from art object to effect" one finds an "enlargeable, three-dimensional spatial spectacle": a movement from matter to light (Ponti 1952 in White 2011: 181). Similarly, Stephen Petersen suggests that we think of *buchi* in terms of their animated surfaces, brought to life by the application of light (and specifically not of paint), and of the way that the holes "exploit the materiality of light" (Petersen 2000: 53, 56). In this, Petersen sees the influence of early twentieth-century photography, particularly the writings of the Hungarian photographer, painter, and visual theorist László Moholy-Nagy (1925, 1947). Petersen sees an origin for Fontana's pierced works in the photographic process' position as "the quintessential dialogue between light and paper" (Petersen 2000: 56). For Moholy-Nagy, writing in the first half of the twentieth century, light was a new creative means on a par with (though fundamentally distinct from) forms such as painting and music (Petersen 2000: 56).

More directly, Petersen reminds us that Moholy-Nagy urged artists to create "light modulators," and that people should then light these modulators (of paper, metal sheets, plastics, and other materials) and photograph them in different positions (Petersen 2000: 53). The connection between Moholy-Nagy's modulators and Fontana's *buchi* is strong. Picking up both on Ponti's turn of phrase (the spectacular) and on Petersen's photographic thinking, Anthony White has suggested a link between Fontana's lit-*buchi* and the phantasmagoria of nineteenth-century lantern shows that also harnessed projected light through semipermeable surfaces to create visions of other worlds (White 2011).

As Petersen argues, both Fontana and Moholy-Nagy understood that photography is not a process that merely documents a work; on the contrary photography completes, transforms, and extends that work into endless alternative possibilities (Petersen 2000: 54). The inclusion of Fontana's *buchi* in the 1952 RAI experimental transmissions, and the photographs from that experimentation, as well as from other light-and-photography extensions of the *buchi*, illustrate Fontana's desire to create luminous spectacles. In this sense, Fontana's creation of the *buchi* sits tightly within these contemporary mid-twentieth-century understandings of visual spectacle and photography. In order to fully understand the *buchi* and Fontana's intentions in making them, however, requires a closer examination of Fontana's particular philosophy of art. This examination begins with the work that the artist was making in the four or five years before he created his *buchi* and with Fontana's position within the Spatialist movement.

Fontana's Early Spatial Art

Fontana's training and early work was as a sculptor working in clay and bronze; he produced works ranging from funerary monuments (both in Argentina where he was born), to competing for and winning competitions and tenders for civil architecture projects in Italy. In 1947, the year in which he settled in Italy for good, Fontana made a work in bronze titled *Sculptura spaziale* [Spatial Sculpture] (47 SC 1) (Figure 8.8). This work revealed a new direction in the artist's output and thought, a direction one can start to detect in his work from as early as the 1930s: a move away from figurative and representational work and toward the

FIGURE 8.8 Lucio Fontana, *Sculptura spaziale* [Spatial Sculpture], (47 SC 1) (1947) bronze 57 × 51 × 24 cm. © CNAC/MNAM/Dist. RMN-Grand Palais/Art Resource, NY. Photo: Christian Bahier/Philippe Migeat.

abstract. Half-a-meter high and the same measure across, *Sculptura spaziale* appears at first sight as an imprecise circle made by joining together small blobs of material, and ends up as a wobbly arch leaning to one side.

Gottschaller describes the work in richer tones, recognizing in the circle of blobs, two figures (one seated and one standing) linked and surrounded by the otherwise undefined loop of sculptural material (Gottschaller 2012: 17). The circuit marks a border in which Fontana positioned the two individuals. The work inspires a sense of "uneasy gravity" in its attempt to balance the empty space inside the circle with the material of the sculpture itself; a larger lump of material at the upper right-hand section of the circuit threatens to tip over the piece (Gottschaller 2012: 17). With *Sculptura spaziale* Fontana was working to connect the material object of the artwork with the surrounding environment, and in doing so to collapse the traditional definitions and boundaries of an art object (White 2011: 138).

In February of the following year, Fontana pushed these efforts strongly forward in a radical, provocative work: *Ambiente Spaziale a Luce Nera* [Spatial Environment in Black Light] (Figure 8.9). As installed in the Galleria del Naviglio in Milan, this work eviscerated the separation of art object and art

FIGURE 8.9 Lucio Fontana, *Ambiente spaziale* (1949) papier mâché Private Collection/© Luisa Ricciarini/Leemage/Bridgeman Images.

spectator, through the arrangement of the work in the gallery space, and through his use of light to connect object and viewer. The work was made of nine connected, papier mâché, curvaceous but unrecognizable forms hung from the gallery ceiling. The work had a central opening and what one might call arms, though in truth the viewer would have struggled to identify any clear representational referents (Gottschaller 2012: 18; White 2001). Fontana painted the papier-mâché with polychrome fluorescent paint, and illuminated the otherwise dark room with ultraviolet light. As a result, the work generated its own glowing aura that spread out from the hanging forms and filled the gallery and covered the visitors in one connected, newly created spatial environment (White 2011: 151): light and form at work.

As Gottshaller has argued, Fontana wanted to create a work (indeed a new space) that would unsettle the spectator; as visitors engaged the work, they could find neither visual or visceral referents for their experience, nor for the work itself (Gottschaller 2012: 18). As a consequence, in order to find traction with the work and their connection to it, viewers had to look within themselves, and through the space that they shared in common with the work. As a precursor to the lit-*buchi* (that Fontana was probably already thinking about making), the artist's use of the fluorescent paint and the ultraviolet light in *Ambiente Spaziale a Luce Nera* caused the work to shoot out light into the gallery space that connected the work of art, the spectator, and the space of the gallery into a newly created shared environmental space (White 2011: 134, citing Ballo 1971: note 54).

Another relevant work from the period when Fontana was planning and producing his first *buco* is *Struttura al Neon par la IX Triennale di Milano* [Neon Structure for the Ninth Milan Triennale] (51 A 1) (Figure 8.10). *Struttura al Neon* further reveals the artist's desire to expand the artistic creative space beyond its traditional, material definition. Made of 200 m of neon tubing, the work was suspended from the ceiling above the stairway and landing at the 1951 *Triennale delle Arti Decorative e Industriali e dell'Architecttura Moderna* [Triennale of Decorative Arts, Modern Industries, and Modern Architecture]. The neon tubing was a tangled loop that curled and flowed in an organic, unrestrained swirl of flying light (Gottschaller 2012: 18).

Positioned above the heads of Triennale visitors as they walked up or down the stairs, the work cast its light down upon their heads. As with *Ambiente Spaziale* at the Naviglio, *Struttura al Neon* connected spectators with the artwork and with the surrounding architectural and environmental space (White 2011: 159). The movement of the Triennale visitors up and down the stairs energized their connections with the work and with the space it inhabited and illuminated; as they went up or down or crossed the landing, the viewers'

FIGURE 8.10 Lucio Fontana, *Neon Structure for the 9th Triennale of Milan*, 1951 (2010), twentieth–twenty-first century, environmental installation, crystal glass-tube, diameter 18 mm, white neon light 6500? K, 250 × 1000 × 800 cm. Bridgeman Images. © 2017 Artists Rights Society (ARS), New York/SIAE, Rome.

relationships to the suspended work shifted, and their experiences of it changed when seen either above their heads or at eye-level (White 2011: 165, 168). The work transformed and expanded the space of the stairway and the landing, and integrated the visitor into a light performance (White 2011: 168). At the time, Fontana commented that he wanted to get away from the materialism of artworks, that he wanted to make neither a sculpture nor a painting, but rather a luminous shape in space (Gottschaller 2012: 18, citing Campiglio 1999: 217).

In his other works from this period in his career, Fontana explored and violated the limits of art and its materiality, with particular effort expended to break the boundaries in standard architectural structures and people's perceptions of them. Two examples will suffice. Fontana was invited to design ceiling

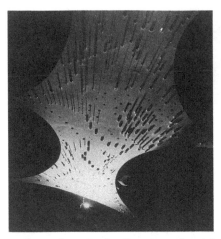

FIGURE 8.11 Lucio Fontana, *Spatial Ceiling* at the Breda Pavilion at the 31st Milan Fair (53 A 1) (1953) destroyed, 1000 × 600 cm. © 2017 Artists Rights Society (ARS), New York/SIAE, Rome.

decorations for two temporary cinemas to be used in the 31st Milan Fair, held in 1953. For the first, *Spatial Ceiling* (53 A 1) (Figure 8.11), as installed in the Breda Pavilion, Fontana created a 6 × 10 m panel suspended high above the movie watchers' heads. Fontana perforated the panel with holes and created corresponding protruding lips that extended out from the visible side of the panel that the moviegoers would have seen. In a way identical to the *buchi* as activated in the RAI transmission and as he photographed and displayed in galleries in 1952 and 1953, the *Spatial Ceiling*'s hole-protrusions created long, sharp shadows, darknesses, and intervals of light, as the cinema's electrical ceiling illumination cut across the panel. As Anthony White suggests, the panel reflected light, but also the sound of the movies being played; these multisensory extensions into, across, and down from the ceiling space of the Breda cinema created new environmental connections through space and with spectators (White 2011: 183). For a second ceiling, at the other temporary Milan Fair cinema (the Sidercomit), Fontana punctured a metal surface and installed red, white, and blue neon lighting. The result was another reflective, disrupted surface that emitted its light down onto the movie watchers and enveloped them into another newly created spatial environment (White 2011: 183).

Spatialism, Light, and Fourth-dimensional Art

In a treatment longer then possible here, the discussion of Fontana's philosophy of art practice should continue from the *buchi* and other works (such as his ceiling installations that the artist was making when he started to puncture paper and canvas), through most of his output from the early 1950s until his death in 1968. That discussion would include his *pietre* (1951–1958), *gessi* and *inchiostri* (1956–1959), *tagli* (1958–1968), *olii* (1957–1968), *venezie* (1961), and *fine di dio* (1963–1964). While I will turn below in detail to his *tagli*, it is important first to explore the art movement (i.e., Spatialism) that Fontana founded and led, and about which he wrote and talked as he elaborated on his intentions for his work and in the work of his fellow Spatialists.

Fontana titled many of his works (particularly his *buchi* and *tagli*) as *Concetto spaziale* [Spatial concepts]. Giving each of thousands of works this same title, the artist declared his aversion to making paintings or sculpture as easily classified representational works: he was making spatial concepts, connecting the artwork with space (Gottschaller 2008: 23; White 2011: 173). Fontana's use of the term *"Concetto spaziale"* may have come from two possible sources. The first is Enrico Prampolini's title (*construzione spaziale-paesaggio*) for a 1919 oil painting with a vortex-based composition (Gottschaller 2008: 32). It is also possible that it came from the futurist artist Fillia's (aka Luigi Colombo) 1932 abstract aero-paintings, such as *Aeropittura* (1932) (Lista 2000). The source of the term is perhaps not critical. More important are the declarations on Spatialism that started to appear in a series of manifestos that Fontana and his colleagues and followers authored.

In 1946, while still living in Argentina, Fontana participated in founding[6] a new private academy of arts in Buenos Aries (Academia di Altamira, Escuela Libre de arte Plásticas) as a focus for an alternative art education (Gottschaller 2008: 23; White 2011: 134). Under Fontana's influence, a group of ten young artists at the Academia di Altamira drafted and signed[7] (Fontana was not a signatory) the *Manifesto Blanco* [The White Manifesto] (Arias et al. 1946), a c. 1,200-word call to make synthetic art work. The manifesto became a cornerstone of *Spazialismo*.

Manifesto Blanco called for the rejection of traditional artistic materials, and for the creation of a "physical-psychic unity" (through the synthesis of the physical elements of art), particularly through the combination of color, sound, movement, time, and space (White 2011: 134). In this new art, movement was elevated as a vital condition of matter; artists were to acknowledge the essential role of movement in artistic production, and to recognize that time was a requisite element of art (Gottschaller 2012: 25). The authors of the *Manifesto Blanco* found explicit inspiration in the Baroque masters, recognizing that they had enriched the plastic arts with the concept of time.

Following the ideas that emerged from the *Manifesto Blanco*, a small group of Spatialist artists published the *Primo Manifesto dello Spazialismo* (*First Spatial Manifesto*) in May 1947. Here Fontana (now a co-signatory) and his colleagues questioned the position of art as durable, fixed creation; they declared that "art is eternal but cannot be immortal" (i.e., that artists should no longer prioritize materials for their longevity) (Gottschaller 2012: 16). The new synthetic Spatialist works were to involve dynamic movement through time and space (White 2011: 134–135), and as such, the use of radio and television as vehicles to transmit artistic expressions was central to Spatialism (Gottschaller 2012: 17). As the group declared in their 1952 *Manifesto del Movimento Spaziale per la Televisione* [Manifesto of the Spatialist Movement for Television], Spatialism seeks "an aesthetics whereby a painting is no longer a painting, sculpture is no longer sculpture, and the written page quits its typographical form" (Ambrosini et al. 1952, cited in Celant 1994).

As the *Manifesto Blanco* had argued, the stimulus for an integration of time, movement, and the immortality of the art work had come from seventeenth- and early eighteenth-century Baroque practices; as important was the influence of the early twentieth-century advances in theoretical physics and its investigations of time and space (Gottschaller 2012: 19). The integration of the arts and sciences was essential in the Spatialist propositions (White 2011: 149), specifically in the development of what Spatialists identified as four-dimensional art. Four-dimensional art resulted from a combination of artists and scientists, and the *Manifesto Blanco* called on scientists "to direct part of their investigations toward the discovery of this luminous malleable substance and toward the creation of instruments capable of producing sounds that will permit the development of four-dimensional art" (Arias et al. 1946: 185). Four-dimensional art was intended to connect to the human experience and to the ways that art reflects and expands that experience (Gottschaller 2012: 19).[8]

In the *Manifesto Tecnico dello Spazialismo* [Technical Manifesto of Spatialism] Fontana and his co-signatories[9] (Whitfield 1999: 187) gave the fourth dimension firmer form: art based on novel media and techniques such as neon, ultraviolet light, and television (Fontana 1951 in Celant 1994). In a 1963 interview with Bruno Rossi, Fontana pushes further, defining (and complicating an understanding of) the fourth dimension as space-time: "the Nothing, the Infinite, the discovery of Nothing" (Rossi 1963: 48). As Fontana told Grazia Livi in 1962: "by making a hole in the picture I found a new dimension in the void. By making holes in the picture, I invented a fourth dimension" (Gottschaller 2008: 31, citing Livi 1962: 55). *Buchi* can be seen as part of Fontana's exploration of *spatializmo*.

If time and space and the amorphous fourth dimension were important elements in the theory of Spatialism, then light and its use by the artist was vital to the movement's creation of work. In the *Manifesto Tecnico dello Spazialismo*, Fontana explicitly defined the role of light in the work. Here, with his colleagues, he wrote of the art of the future as art of "luminous forms traversing spaces" and of the triumph of the *fotogramma* (cited in Petersen 2000: 55). Fontana believed that with the movement of light, one would move beyond the third dimension; for him light was a carrier toward infinity (Gottschaller 2008: 30).

With his *buchi*, Fontana exploited the canvas as if it were material culture and not the pictorial field as traditionally used (i.e., as if it were a physical support). Fontana used the punctured surface of the *buchi* as a context in which to explore variations in the interaction of light with environment and with spectator, and thus he both created and questioned the relationships among the work and the space around it (White 2011: 181). In his *buchi*, we can see *spatializmo* emerging and at work. In the *buchi*, light plays a major role, and forms the main theme though much of the work that Fontana completed until his death in the late 1960s. One of these series of works, his *tagli*, deserves closer attention here.

Tagli—Attese

In the autumn of 1958 Fontana started to make a new type of work (Gottschaller 2012: 58), which he called *tagli* (literally, cuts) (Figure 8.12).[10] To make a *taglio*, Fontana coated the back of a canvas with Cementite, a commercial primer normally applied to building walls and surfaces (Gottschaller 2012: 69). Once the canvas was dry, Fontana removed the keys from the wooden support, treated both sides of the fabric with water, reinserted the keys, and tapped them in with a hammer to tighten the frame and stretch the cloth (Gottschaller 2012: 71). Taking up a wide brush, he painted a white ground on the front surface, and set the canvas outside his studio to dry (Gottschaller 2012: 71).

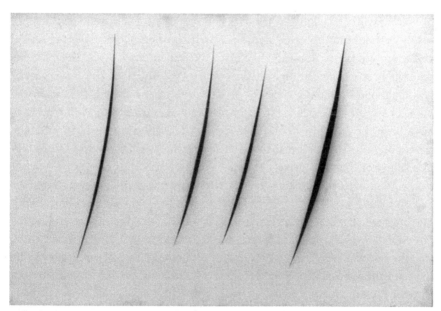

FIGURE **8.12** Lucio Fontana, *Spatial Concept #2* (1960) oil on canvas, support, 50.48 × 73 cm. Albright-Knox Art Gallery/Art Resource, NY. © 2017 Artists Rights Society (ARS), New York.

Before bringing the canvas back inside, Fontana contemplated what color to paint. Placing the canvas on an easel, and using house paint poured into a dish or bowl, he worked in a zigzag pattern beginning at the top-left corner with a wide, thick brush holding liberal quantities of paint (Gottschaller 2012: 81). Next, he turned the canvas 90 degrees on the easel and repeated the zigzag motion. Placing the wet canvas on a table, he painted the thin sides where the canvas wrapped around the support. If the weather was fine, he then took the canvas back outside to dry (Gottschaller 2012: 72). Before the paint had dried fully, Fontana added another coat; with each coat, the patterns of the fabric and the traces of the bristles became less distinct, resulting in a cleaner, smoother, more opaque, and more abstract surface (Gottschaller 2012: 71).

Leaving this final surface coat longer to dry, Fontana would take lunch at a local *trattoria* (Gottschaller 2012: 72, citing Alviani 2007). When he returned to the studio, he asked his assistant Takahashi to clean the brushes and finish for the day, and to leave him to continue the work without any distractions. Next Fontana cut the painting. With the canvas on an easel next to the window, and a Stanley knife in his hand, Fontana pushed the tip of the blade into and through the painted surface, pulling down and across the painting, opening up a long, straight slit (Gottschaller 2012: 72). In the earliest *tagli*, Fontana made multiple parallel cuts, most straight, some curved to the left at their ends; soon, though, he cut each canvas with no more than a few incisions, often only with one (Gottschaller 2012: 87, 131n32, citing Crispolti 2006: 442).

By cutting into the paint before it was fully dried (Gottschaller 2012: 82, citing Brambilla Barcilon and Matalon 1978: 3), Fontana reduced the difficulty of slipping the blade through the layers of paint and cloth and he increased the likelihood of making a clean cut, with little if any flaking or cracking of paint along the edges of the incision (Gottschaller 2012: 82). Variation may have been the rule over the longer term; some canvases were cut after the paint had fully dried (Vigo 2006), and Fontana may have worked in this way to produce as many as ten *tagli* in one day (Gottschaller 2012: 82).

Another benefit of cutting the surface while it was still damp and flexible was that it allowed Fontana to shape the opening in the canvas more easily. Having made the cut, the artist then used his hand to open the cut, easing the cut edges of the canvas, and pressing them inward (Whitfield 1999: 31) so that they curved away from the front of the work and formed a concave shape, back into the work (Gottschaller 2012: 73). Moving to the back of the cut canvas, Fontana next attached strips of the stiff black gauze (*telletta*) made from material that tailors used to face suits (Gottschaller 2012: 73; Vigo 2006). Using a commercial adhesive (Vinavil), he attached each strip across the back of the opening of the cut, placing the black cloth strips at right angles to the opening (Gottschaller 2012: 73, 88). The black *telletta* tented over the rear of the cut, not touching the edges of the opening, and created a concave space reaching back into the work (Gottschaller 2012: 87). For some *tagli*, Fontana used a single piece of *telletta* (Gottschaller 2012: 88), for others he used several thinner strips.

Technically, the *telletta* added stiffness and strength to the painted canvas around the cut, reducing the chance that it would sag or slacken as a result of the cut severing the thread of the fabric (Gottschaller 2012: 87). More significantly, when looking into the opening from the front and thus at the black background of the cut's interior, the spectator's attention did not rest on the wall behind the work, but plunged into an undefined space of darkness, brought into contrast with the monochromatic paint of the surface; the intention was to create a perception of absolute blackness and not a view of fabric or of wall (Gottschaller 2012: 87–88). Fontana's final act was to sign the back of the work: either *concetto spaziale* or *attessa* or *attesse* (literally "anticipation"; see discussion below) and often with the addition of a word or two or a phrase—perhaps the name of a friend or a political event, a trip or the name of Fontana's dog Blek (Gottschaller 2012: 73, 89).

Genesis of Tagli

His most numerous works (Fontana made over 1,500 of them between 1958 and 1968), *tagli* first appeared formally as a last-minute addition to the artist's February 1959 show at the Galleria del Naviglio in Milan, a show that was dedicated to another of the artist's forms: *inchiostri* (Gottschaller 2012: 58–59), works made with washes of ink and perforation. Fontana experts disagree on the origins and inspiration for the *tagli* (Figure 8.13) The anecdotal claim (by Jan van der Marck) that Fontana had slashed one of his otherwise normal canvases in anger is discounted by most (Gottschaller 2012: 59, citing Crispolti and van der Marck 1974: 15; and as supported by White 2008: 102, 109).

More likely, the original idea to cut a painted canvas emerged more gradually from variations on earlier works. In this sense, a possible early version of a *taglio* can be identified in an *olio* (57 O 2) made in 1957 (*olii* are cut and perforated works using large amounts of paint). This *olio* has abnormally large, rough openings and gashes in its surface, made with an awl though, and not a knife. In the lower left-hand corner of the work, two of the holes were so close together that the canvas in between tore and made a longer area of cut (Gottschaller 2012: 59). Perhaps this unintended tear was a provocation to make long, linear openings rather than smaller perforations.

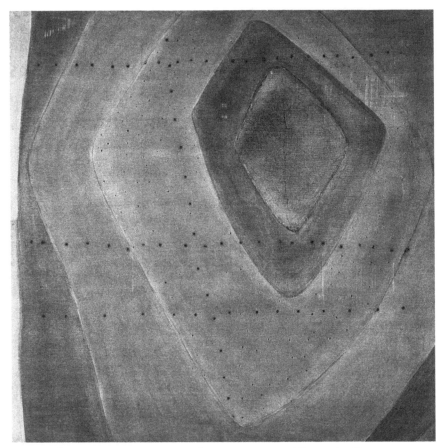

FIGURE 8.13 Lucio Fontana, *Spatial concept*, (1957) aniline and collage on canvas, 149 × 150 cm. Italy, twentieth century. Private Collection/De Agostini Picture Library/Bridgeman Images. © 2017 Artists Rights Society (ARS), New York.

Another possible precursor to the *tagli* is found in Fontana's *gessi* (produced from 1954–1958): *gessi* were made with *gesso* (the gypsum- or chalk-based layer of the pastels applied) (Gottschaller 2012: 52) (Figure 8.14). Though not long (no greater than 1.0 cm), the perforations in Fontana's *gessi* are closer to linear rips than they are to holes: torn or lacerated more than poked, and these may have prompted Fontana to make the larger, longer cuts that he eventually did in cutting the surfaces of the *tagli* (Gottschaller 2012: 52). Most likely, the inspiration for making *tagli* rests in the *inchiostri* (i.e., aniline-covered canvases perforated with holes that often form outlines of irregular shapes). As Gottschaller shows, the first twenty of the *tagli* that Fontana made were conversions of *inchiostri* into *tagli* (Gottschaller 2012: 130n7).

Regardless of the original source for the idea to make long linear cuts into the surfaces of canvases, Fontana refined his designs during the first few

FIGURE 8.14 Lucio Fontana, *Concetto Spaziale (Spatial Concept)* (54 G 4) (1954) pastel and collage on canvas, 82 × 65 cm. © 2017 Artists Rights Society (ARS), New York/SIAE, Rome.

years that he made them. The early examples have a greater number of linear cuts in them than do the later ones (Gottschaller 2012: 61), they were made with slashes of different lengths, and the incisions were both straight and curved (Gottschaller 2012: 61). Early *tagli* were cut into canvases of different sizes (up to 100 × 136 cm), weights, and materials (e.g., jute, burlap, linen). Early cuts were small and at an angle (Whitfield 1999: 31), and had frayed edges: the result of being cut either with an unsharpened blade or of being made into a surface covered by inflexible, probably brittle, and dried primer.

Most of the damage of these early cuts is located near the bottom of the cut where Fontana brought the Stanley knife blade to a sudden stop (Gottschaller 2012: 65).

The early *tagli* did not satisfy fully the artist's intentions: to create a break in the surface that showed no interruption in the expected tension in the plane of the painted canvas (Gottschaller 2012: 64, 66). Quickly, Fontana refined his methods and adjusted his selection of materials. By 1960, Fontana was following a standard that he would use until his death in 1968: one to five cuts made into monochromatic backgrounds, on a variety of cloth supports (jute but also burlap and linen), and with a clear shift in 1959 from fine, regular-weave linen to medium-weight canvas (Gottschaller 2012: 63, 69; Whitfield 1999: 34). The heavier fabric allowed greater tension in the surface (Gottschaller 2012: 69) and provided the rigidity that the artist was seeking.

Fontana tried a wide range of colors: white, orange, yellow, ochre, red, pink, green, turquoise, blue, purple, brown, gray, black, silver, and gold (Gottschaller 2012: 63). Similarly, by adding extenders such as chalk or *gesso* to the paints he created richly monochromatic surfaces; water added to the paint helped create smooth surfaces with the minimum of visible brush strokes and striations (Gottschaller 2012: 81). The changes and refinements may have had several intentions: one result was that the cleaner, clearer, finer cuts left the spectator's perception of the work unhindered by the mess of material distraction (Gottschaller 2012: 65).

Genesis Within the Context of Contemporary Art Practices and Artists

While the stimulus for Fontana's work with *tagli* has roots in the artist's earlier work, Anthony White has argued for the impact of contemporary trends in European art, particularly developments in Italy at the end of the 1950s (White 2011: 208). Most strong, perhaps, is the connection to the Informel movement of painters, who had attacked, though ultimately failed to disrupt, the standard production and reception of mechanical, formulaic art (White 2011: 214). In their reactions to the alienation that they saw in post-war European industrial society, Informel artists such as Mattia Moreni emphasized the process of artistic creation in their work, highlighting the individuality of spontaneous gestures (White 2011: 211).

White identifies two other potential influences on Fontana. The first is Yves Klein's 1957 Milan exhibit of monochrome paintings and his arguments for painting as object (White 2011: 216); Fontana's transformation in much of his work of painting to sculpture fits well with Klein's philosophy. The second possible influence is Jackson Pollock's 1958 Rome retrospective, particularly his 1949 work *Out of the Web*, from which Pollock had cut away sections of the

FIGURE 8.15 Jackson Pollock, *Out of the Web Number 7* (1949) oil on masonite, 121.5 × 244 cm. © 2017 Artists Rights Society (ARS), New York.

canvas to show the Masonite support behind (White 2011: 208) (Figure 8.15). Fontana would have been attracted to this example of cuts that disrupted the surface of the work, and would have attempted to work with the figure while also negating it (White 2011: 227).

Fontana on His Tagli

In making the cuts into the painted canvas and, especially, in using the *telletta* to create the dark, tented space behind, Fontana aimed to open up a space behind the surface of the work into which the viewer could enter (Gottschaller 2012: 58). In his use of the linear cuts, Fontana extended his conception of hole as used in *buchi* and other perforated works (Gottschaller 2012: 58). Perhaps more than his other series of works, in his *tagli*, Fontana moved furthest from decorative art and closest to the existential nature of the gesture; the shape created by the gesture and the absent movement of the cut stood without reference to other images but retained an ontological potency (Gottschaller 2012: 58).

One of the keys to unlocking Fontana's intentions and thoughts about his *tagli* is his use of *attessa* as a subtitle to the works. Like his other output, Fontana called each of his *tagli* a *concetto spaziale*; here though he added the term "*attessa*" if the work had a single cut and *attesse* if the work had several (Gottschaller 2012: 60). Fontana may have come across the term in the work of the Italian sculptor Arturo Martini who had used it as a subtitle in the late 1920s (Gottschaller 2012: 60). *Attessa* translates from the Italian as "expectation" or, more accurately in Fontana's intention, as "anticipation"

(Gottschaller 2012: 60). As Gottschaller suggests, the emphasis for Fontana was on the state of waiting, and not on an event that one is expecting to happen (Gottschaller 2012: 60, 130n5).

Ugo Mulas has written about Fontana's sense of anticipation as part of the artist's creative process in making the *tagli*, writing that the time between preparing the canvas and cutting it sometimes stretched to weeks (and thus suggests variations in the artist's methods and the potential need to cut while surface paint was still wet), using the interval to think about what to do with the canvas, only cutting when he is certain what he wants to do. For Fontana, the time before the cutting was a critical moment in his creation of *tagli*, a time for conceptual concentration and the anticipatory sensation (Gottschaller 2012: 82 citing Fossati 1973: 100ff.).

Fontana understood the cuts of the *tagli* as a "formula" that gave "the spectator an impression of spatial calm, of cosmic rigor, of serenity in infinity" (Fontana, quoted in Crispolti 2006: 105). For Fontana a central goal was to evoke the idea of the infinite cosmos (Gottschaller 2012: 64); indeed he saw a *taglio* as a statement of belief in infinity (Livi 1962: 56, cited in Gottschaller 2012: 89). Talking with Grazia Livi in the early 1960s, Fontana explained, "My *tagli* are primarily a philosophical expression, an act of faith in the Infinit, an affirmation of spirituality. When I sit down in front of one of my *tagli*, to contemplate it, I suddenly feel a great expansion of the spirit, I feel like a man liberated from the slavery of the material, like a man who belongs to the vastness of the present and the future" (Gottschaller 2012: 87, citing Livi 1962: 56). For Fontana, the *tagli* (though also many of his other series of works as well) illuminated the role of time in the viewer's perception of the works. To see a *taglio* was to retrace the event of cutting and of perforating the painted canvas. As Gottschaller explains, with these works Fontana folded time and space into one entity, and thus, in his *tagli*, Fontana found the fullest exploration of his various series within the *concetto spaziale* (Gottschaller 2012: 58).

Fontana, *Buchi, Tagli,* and Măgura

Provocations of relevance for our thinking about the Măgura pit-houses lurk within Fontana's *buchi, tagli,* and almost every other of his series of works: disrupting and confusing surfaces, involving the spectator, enfolding light and time, referencing movement and gesture, making space manifest, invoking the void, and accessing worlds beyond.

Fontana's works created three-dimensional space where once there had been only the two-dimensional. He sought freedom from what he saw as "the slavery of the material" (Gottschaller 2012: 87, citing Livi 1962: 56). On top of this, the three-dimensional spaces that he made employed the most paradoxic of all forms: the hole. Casati and Varzi's thinking on the troubles and potential impossibilities of defining a hole loom large here. Fontana's making the two-dimensional into the three-dimensional through the choice of a negative space is rich with complexity and evocation of philosophic contemplation that reaches both the metaphysic and the scientific. There could be no further escape from the restraints of the physically manifest than the nonmaterial of the hole as Fontana pushed them into his *buchi* or cut them into the *tagli*.

In holing the *buchi* and slicing the *tagli*, Fontana denied the standard understandings of the pictorial surface of the canvas as a traditional and un-problematic medium for artistic practice and as a visual destination for art spectators' viewing. He wanted to destroy the accepted divisions between what one was supposed to look at and how people perceived those visual targets: from complete canvas to holed or cut surface. Fontana made viewers face the questions not only of what is the work (i.e., what does it mean?): more destabilizing, they questioned. What is the front? What is the back? Where does it start? And where does it end? The pits that people cut into the ground at Măgura held the same potential. They would have thrown into confusion understandings of where this world ended and other worlds began, even perhaps of what space was up and which is down, perhaps even of whether or not the concepts of up or down exist anymore or at least in the same way as they had before the hole was dug. The same applies to the reactions to Wilsford, to Athey, to Matta-Clark, and to Etton.

When Fontana created *buchi* and *tagli*, he "made holes, infinity passes through them, light passes through them, there is no need to paint" (Fontana quoted in Crispolti 1998: 146). His concern with the science of light and time and deeper metaphysical conceptions took the viewer beyond the here and now, beyond the material (of the canvas or of the world as we think that we know it to be). The connection of work, spectator, environment (of gallery, of theater, of stairway), created ephemeral, inclusive worlds that engaged people, objects, and places in new, improbable ways that were difficult to record for later (re)visits by analyst or spectator: light beams piercing *buchi*, touching works, walls, and viewers; connections made from within and behind to without and beyond. Light was the active agent powering these connections, and these connections were dynamic and momentary; after the creation and installation of these works, the only non-ephemeral traces that survive are the first-hand oral or written accounts and the photographs (as in *Spazio*). The holes cut into the ground surface at Măgura would have had the potential to work in the same ways: to introduce the potential for the deeper metaphysical connections with other worlds. What would have been the local analogies to the light that emerged through Fontana's surfaces and created an ephemeral environmental connection between that other world, previously hidden, covered, and out of sight and the people, animals, and world that have lived on (and within) that previously unbroken surface?

As archaeologists, we worry about preservation and recording, often to the point that the records become the facts, and the original actions are abandoned, ignored, or most often intentionally disappeared. At Măgura, the opening up of the ground similarly would have posed comparable questions and would have forced related thoughts about the links between what is here now (on the ground surface) and what is there, beyond the material world of the surface and of the ground as we normally perceive it as a static canvas. Excavation photographs, plan-drawings, stratigraphic sections, and dislocated artifacts are the non-ephemeral traces that remain. So also are the *buchi* and the *tagli* on the museum wall or the page of the *catalogue raisonné*. Both artwork in contemporary galleries and excavation plans in archives and publications are disarticulated from the movement, space, gesture, light, and connection of the events and people that made them. Art and excavation reports, in truth however, are failed representations of original events; our elevations of gallery object and academic volume are illusions. Trace-actions, light emissions, shadows and Spatialist connections of briefly connected environments—all are (at best) lost, and at worst ignored.

In response therefore, to look at the works that have survived is to observe the original gestures of the cutting and holing and, with knowledge of the original light agents, it is an observation of the physical gestures of perforating and cutting, as well as of the more distant, and long-faded light that activated the environmental connection. Movement, light, and time: movement of cutting, light that connected and created, time of that action and that light in an absent past. The gesture of cutting the soil with a stone adze. The gesture of slicing the painted canvas with a Stanley knife. With a deep examination of Fontana's works, words, and of his conversations about his work, we come to recognize that in their current fixed immobility in the studio, gallery, and museum, the *buchi* and *tagli* are absent of the dynamism and its constant reference to the bodied, handed movements that made them: the piercing, the slicing. Fontana held that matter exists in movement and only in movement. The same applies to what happened at Măgura. The pits at Măgura, now static in photograph and drawing, archaeological plan of record, measurement and sampling, are also equally dynamic. We need to recognize that (now-absent) dynamism. In fact, the pits possess a double dynamism: of the original movements and gestures of their making eight millennia ago, and in a dynamic of our archaeological excavations of the last decade.

The daylight that reaches down into the hole in the ground (Figure 8.16). The light of the bulb running through the *buchi* hole. The darkness of the *telletta*-tented void drawing the curiosity of the spectator's eye. The dark, moist opening in the ground that the digger peers into. There is an energy (of dark questioning) that comes back out of the depth of the *taglio's* cut openings and that assaults the viewer with questions and an unknowing; there would have been an energy (of similar questionings) that came back out of the holes dug into the Măgura ground. There is a Măgura correspondent to Fontana's light: an energy that was there at that time, and which is only remembered/present in its absence and in the epiphenomenal construction of the hole itself in the same way that Fontana's lights—both dark void and electric bulb are only present in the edges for the *buchi* holes and the *tagli* cuts. This movement is dynamism embodied, standing beyond the rational control of action or, especially, of understanding and explanation today as well, perhaps, as then. Fontana and the Spatialists called for a march toward movement in the "passage from abstraction to dynamism" (in the *Manifesto Blanco*): art as gesture and performance. What of the Măgura pits in an archaeology as gesture and performance: gesture and performance then (6000 cal. B.C.) and now (our 2001 excavations)?

FIGURE 8.16 Cutting exploratory sondage at Măgura-Buduiasca. Photo copyright D. W. Bailey.

The gesture with which Fontana negated the canvas also opened up new sculptural possibilities in the void and emptiness of a canvas backspace that had not existed before he pushed in the awl or pressed the point of the Stanley knife through the paint and canvas. The destruction of that clean, monochrome surface created a space of emptiness and void. Fontana wanted the viewer who looked at a *taglio* to see pure blackness, and not the physical reality of black tailor's fabric (Gottschaller 2012: 88). Opening the canvas provided access to a world that had not existed before, a world that the viewer had perhaps not imagined to exist. Opening Mǎgura's ground surface also provided access to a world that had not existed before, and which, before the act of opening, the digger holding the antler pick tool may not have known to exist.

To deliver the invitation to enter that other, newly opened world of dark void, of the space beyond, Fontana took pains to develop a method to remove distractions and reminders of the conceit he was practicing: materials were selected and the canvas surface was painted to remove reference to canvas and to brush(ing); he cut the *taglio* at the right time and with the appropriate method and tool to avoid the fraying of edges and thus to remove reference to the this-worldly construction of the act of cutting and opening. The viewer slipped in with her eyes, into that space beyond the surface and beyond the easy safety of standard representational art. When the digger opened up the ground at Mǎgura, 8000 years ago she opened up a dark void of space into which slipped the eyes of the people watching by the side of that hole. She cut the edges with the same attention to careful detail to promote the passage from one world (of the surface) to another (of the subterranean).

Both Fontana's *tagli* and the Mǎgura pits are invitations to "break through the limits of consciousness in the search for what lies beyond form" (Gottschaller 2012: 89) of the art world's canvas of standard artwork production and of 8000-year-old grounded perceptions of reality. The pits evoke the faith in infinity that Fontana intended for his holes. In the digging of holes in the ground at Mǎgura, there lurks the same *attessa* as in Fontana's *tagli*. The Mǎgura pits are manifestations of anticipations, of evocations of infinities. Both the Mǎgura pits and Fontana's holes violate the limits of being in the grounded world of the terraced valley of the Vedea River and the art world of post–WWII Italy.

Cutting Absolute Worlds

GROUNDED FRAMES OF REFERENCE

Introduction

THE PRECEDING CHAPTERS examined the surfaces cut in several modern art practices and in two prehistoric landscapes, and then investigated the philosophy of holes and surfaces, the visual perception of concavities, as well as the linguistic variety in people's conceptions of breaking otherwise coherent objects. This chapter turns back to the pit-houses at Măgura, and examines the surface that people cut 8000 years ago: the ground. The investigation focuses on the ways that those people thought about their places in the word, particularly in terms of their frames of spatial reference: how they understood where they were, where objects were, and where other people were. Examination follows the social anthropologist Tim Ingold and his thoughts about groundedness, and the linguistic anthropologist Stephen Levinson and his discussion of spatial frames of reference. Here, the intention is to push the disparate and juxtaposed artistic output, archaeological examples, and philosophic discussions toward a new understanding of lived reality in that valley in southern Romania, 8000 years ago. The result is an attempt to sense those people's (mostly) silent conceptions of their places on, in, and of the ground: the goal is not to explain what ground or space meant to them (e.g., to do a landscape archaeology; to write about catchments, territories, access maps, and privacy), but to open up less quantifiable, more metaphysical engagements of how those peoples sensed their lives and, particularly, to consider what would have been the consequences of breaking the surface of the ground by cutting holes into it. The proposal is that people's relationships to Ground (as proposed in chapter 1) and specifically to ground surface was fundamental to Măgura ways of being, and that any action that disrupted that surface was of greater significances than archaeologists have previously recognized.

Ingold and Grounded Living

In his discussions of landscape, routes, wayfaring, and the human engage-ment with environment, Tim Ingold defines ground not as a material surface, but as "a textured composite of diverse materials that are grown, deposited, and woven together through a dynamic interplay across the permeable inter-face between the medium and the substances with which it comes into con-tact" (Ingold 2015c: 130). Ground is dynamic, flexible, open, changing, always in constitution, and much more than a single surface to be easily defined, mapped, or understood. Ingold distinguishes between the ground as a back-ground against which things stand out, and the ground as the focus of action itself (Ingold 2004: 331). He urges us to hold the ground as important, per-haps fundamental to an understanding of what it means to be human in the world. Ground is alive and always present, yet equally quiet and foundational. Ingold suggests that people apprehend the world around them from within, particularly through the processes of "ordinary wayfinding" (Ingold 2000b: 241). By foot, people make their way across the ground. They move through rela-tional fields as they incorporate "embodied capacities of movement, awareness, and response" (Ingold 2004: 332). Citing Chis Tilley, Ingold suggests that "through walking...landscapes are woven into life, and lives are woven into the landscape, in a process that is continuous and never-ending" (Ingold 2004: 332; Tilley, 1994: 29–30).

Significantly, Ingold argues that the world has no surface. He suggests that surfaces are not of the world, but in the world, "formed on the interface, not between matter and mind, but between solid or liquid substance and the gas-eous medium (air) in which humans live and breathe, and which affords move-ment and sensory perception.... The surfaces of the land...are in and not of the world, woven from the lines of growth and movement of inhabitants" (Ingold 2000a: 241; 2015b: 71). In this sense, Ingold argues that the ground is not a boundary but a vaguely defined zone of intermingling and admixing in which life is lived (2008: 8; 2015c: 119). Of the ground, he sees mutual perme-ability and binding (2015c: 120). Following the geographer Torsten Hägerstrand, Ingold suggests that the environment does not have insides or outsides, only openings and ways through (Hägerstrand 1976; Ingold 2008: 12). Ingold's dis-cussion of the surface of the ground loosens our definitions of ground-surface and helps us to recognize the fluidity and messiness of what previously we had seen as simple and distinct: ground not as an impermeable interface (between earth and sky), but a relation "between binding and unbinding of the world" (Ingold 2015b: 121) that comes from wind, weather, movement, medium, and substance (Ingold 2015b: 119). For Ingold, we live not on the ground but in it.

Ingold shows that this dynamic, unbounded sense of living-in-the-ground is distinct from a modern cartographic, navigational understanding, where the ground is a hard, easily defined (and improperly understood) surface upon which one travels and lives one's life. Ingold argues that in modern industrialized communities, footwear has come to separate people from the ground, and thus from the center of their worlds (Ingold 2000a: 209). The introduction of (and the industrialized world's cultural and moral insistences on) shoes and boots, sandals and sneakers, has prevented people from thinking with their feet (Ingold 2004: 323); modernity has reduced our connections to the ground to an extent that walking has become "the operation of a stepping machine" (Ingold 2000a: 209).

As a consequence, our perceptions of the environment and of our places in it suffer from a "head over heels" bias: we overvalue cognition at the expense of locomotion (Ingold 2004: 331). Chairs and stools have the same intrusive, deadening effect as do shoes and boots and have widened our separation from ground: "the chair enables the sitter to think without involving the feet at all" (Ingold 2015a: 39). The making of the modern (and prehistoric) built environment starting from the Neolithic (in Eurasia at least via architecture, floors, carpets, tiles, sidewalks, paved roadways, and many other constructions) has maintained and increased the distance between our bodies and the ground (Figure 9.1). Other inventions in the technologies of moving (e.g., cars, bicycles, horses, planes) further weaken the possibility of a grounded existence and of a connected knowledge of the world. Following the work of Neil Lewis,

FIGURE 9.1 Examples of technologies that distance body from ground and constitute groundlessness.

Ingold calls this the groundlessness of modern living (Ingold 2004: 321, 323; Lewis 2001: 68).

A Grounded Living

If Ingold and Lewis are correct (and I think that they are), and if we live groundless lives in modern (and historic), Western, industrialized worlds, then what might constitute a grounded living in other places and at other times where and when shoes, chairs, cars, and horses are absent? What consequences would such a grounded way of living have had for the ways that people understood themselves, for how they understood their places in their worlds, for how they understood ground as a (meta)physical surface (i.e., as Ground), and for what would have been the consequences and intentions of breaking the surface of the G/ground. I suggest that people who lived in-the-ground, to use Ingold's phrase and sense, and thus who lived a grounded life, understood their relations to the world around them in ways distinct from how people in groundless societies (such as ours) understand those connections. To explore grounded perspectives on self and environment requires further investigation, and will further help expand our thinking about the Măgura pit-houses. Such an exploration requires several steps away from traditional viewpoints (it even may require that we shut our eyes) to G/ground in the ways that we conceptualize the space in which we live in modern, industrialized, Western communities.

Ingold starts that discussion, for example, by suggesting that living in close proximity to the earth's surface (i.e., living a grounded life) prevents people from taking a global perspective (Ingold 2000a: 209); grounded people saw things differently, they recognized different horizons, and saw the same horizons from different perspectives. The distinction of significance, then, is in the ways that people understood the world around them, their places in that world (or worlds), and their spatial relations to other objects, topographic features, landmarks, and other people in those shared worlds. To explore the possibilities for these other (potentially grounded) spatial ways of knowing and being, I suggest, comes from examining variations in the spatial frames of reference that people of different communities hold. To do this, we turn to the work of linguistic anthropologist, Stephen Levinson (Levinson 2003).

Levinson and Spatial Frames of Reference

People think about their positions in the space around them in different ways. A particularly powerful way to identify and uncover this diversity is to study how people in different language groups talk about where they are, where other people and objects are, where they have been, and where they are going. Elaborating, refining, and broadening the work of psychologists Laura Carlson-Radvansky and David Irwin (1993: 224), the linguistic anthropologist Stephen Levinson identifies three separate ways that people talk about (and thus conceptualize) spatial position (i.e., their spatial frames of reference) that account for all variation across human groups: the relative frame of reference, the intrinsic frame, and the absolute frame (Levinson 2003).

Frames of reference are spatial representation schemes, driven by human actions and systems such as the senses, communication, and action (Levinson 2003: 286). Although they may relate to different pathways of neural processing (Levinson 2003: 322), spatial frames of reference are not essential, ready-made, natural conceptual systems (Levinson 2003: 313), but "bio-cultural hybrids" that come from a complicated interaction among perception, internal neuroanatomy, and cultural tradition (Levinson 2003: 322). Across the globe, not every language uses all three frames of reference, though some do. As we will see in more detail below, some languages use one frame predominantly (the absolute or intrinsic; though the use of the relative appears to require the use of the intrinsic). Some use two frames (intrinsic and relative; intrinsic and absolute) (Levinson 2003: 53). Though his primary research is linguistic, Levinson argues that people use their particular frame of reference across not only language but also through nonverbal communication (such as gesture), non-linguistic social memory, and spatial reasoning (Levinson 2003: 112).

What distinguishes one frame of reference from another? Indeed, why are there different frames of reference at all? How do they develop in different language groups, and how do different groups of people prefer or select one and not another? Significantly, Levinson has shown that there is no clear correlation between a group's economic basis (e.g., hunting, gathering, farming) or mobility pattern (e.g., settled, mobile) and the way that a group organizes spatial positioning and spatial navigation through their frame of reference (Levinson 2003: 212). Levinson suggests that socialization and language learning combine to construct special mental faculties that coordinate people's understanding of spatial orientation (Levinson 2003: 129). Critically, we can recognize this spatial understanding though the study of how people use language and gesture.

Spatial frames of reference are not static; they change over time as local linguistic and cultural context changes. One of the exciting consequences of Levinson's work is the stimulation for archaeologists to look at the ways that past peoples thought about their spatial positions relative to other people, objects, and landmarks. A critical result of Levinson's work is the realization that the Western, industrialized perception of space (identified below as a relative frame and the one that archaeologists normally lay onto all past behaviors) may well not have been the way that many ancient and prehistoric people understood their spatial worlds.

Relative Frame of Reference

The relative frame of spatial reference is viewer-centered, and understands the locations of people, objects, and places in relation to planes or axes that the relative thinker imagines to run through her body: left/right, back/front, up/down (Levinson 2003: 43). Thus, to describe the spatial relationship illustrated in Figure 9.2, the relative thinker would tell you that "he is to the left of the cactus" (Levinson 2003: fig. 2.2). Thinking and speaking with the relative frame, it is the location and position of the viewer who is understanding and expressing where the "he" is, and which determines a person's understanding and expression of that relationship in space. In the example illustrated, the viewer is standing at one specific place and in one particular way such that she is looking at the cactus so that the cactus is in front of her body and so that the "he" is to the left of that cactus understood in terms of the left and right sides of her body. For the relative thinker, understanding and expressing the spatial location of someone or something find their bases in the position of the speaker's body and the direction of her gaze (i.e., the position of her head) (Levinson 2003: 43–44).

In twenty-first-century industrialized societies, almost all (indeed perhaps all) of us live in cultures in which our awareness of spatial behavior is organized by relative coordinates; we are most familiar with this way of thinking and less with the others (Levinson 2003: 112). One of Levinson's major contributions to an anthropology of diversity is to show not only that the relative frame is only one of three ways of understanding spatial relations but also, surprisingly, to demonstrate that a relative frame of reference is "entirely dispensable" (Levinson 2003: 46); there are language communities that do

RELATIVE

"He is to the left of the cactus."

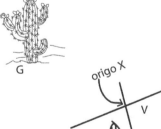

FIGURE 9.2 Relative frame of reference (redrawn by Svetlana Matskevich after Levinson 2003: figure 2.2).

not use the relative frame at all (e.g., Guugu Yimithirr in northern Australia), or who only use it in very limited ways (Levinson 2003: 46). Furthermore, Levinson reminds us that even in Western traditions where the relative frame appears to dominate, it is not a constant or essential part of lives; children only master concepts basic to the relative outlook (such as left or right) as late as eleven or twelve years of age (Levinson 2003: 46). These concepts (and thus perhaps also the entire relative perspective) are slowly constructed within locally existing cultural, political, and social contexts.

Using a relative frame of reference, people reach their understandings of direction though the alignment of their bodies and of their eyes (i.e., their gaze), and thus this frame of reference is viewpoint dependent (Levinson 2003: 135, 260). Spatial understanding in the relative frame corresponds to our visual experience (Levinson 2003: 256). To make a map (mental or otherwise), relative thinkers link up the views that they hold based on what they can see at a particular moment from their specific, bodied, position in space (Levinson 2003: 278). As Levinson put it, a relative framer "imports the observer's bodily axes and maps them onto the ground object thus deriving named angle" (Levinson 2003: 76). Especially useful in this process are familiar landmarks; when determining where to go or where they have been or when they explain location to someone else, relative framers physically look for a familiar landmark and usually point at it (Levinson 2003: 270, 274). The relative system, therefore, correlates visual and physical motor systems: gaze-plus-pointing (Levinson 2003: 259, 279).

When relative spatial thinkers conceptualize themselves moving, they imagine themselves navigating along a strip-map (Levinson 2003: 265, after Tolman 1948). They build a virtual space as if it were a scratch pad (Levinson 2003: 264), flatten the three-dimensional world into two-dimensions that are in front of their bodies, and then align that scratch pad with the trunks of their bodies (Levinson 2003: 261). Making the world relative to one's body has been and remains one of the most powerful (and easy) ways in which the organization of people and shared cultural environments (e.g., writing systems, traffic rules) are deemed to be natural (Levinson 2003: 279) and through which an egocentric sense of being has come to dominate much modern, historic, and ancient life.

Intrinsic Frame of Reference

As Levinson shows, the relative frame is not the only way that people understand their place in their worlds, however, and fieldwork and synthetic analyses define two other frames: intrinsic and absolute. Thinking with an intrinsic frame of reference, one's understanding of the locations of people, places, and things finds its base in the conceptual properties of an object's shape, canonical orientation, characteristic motion, and use (Levinson 2003: 42). Thus, an

INTRINSIC

"He is in front of the cactus."

F

FIGURE 9.3 Intrinsic frame of reference (redrawn by Svetlana Matskevich after Levinson 2003: figure 2.2).

intrinsic thinker would tell us about the spatial relationship in Figure 9.3 by saying, "He is in front of the cactus" (Levinson 2003: fig. 2.2). The cactus determines where the "he" is. The cactus has a front and a side and a back, and the person who understands and expresses where the "he" is understands the cactus to have a front and to know that the "he" is positioned to the cactus to be on that side. The intrinsic frame of reference is an object-centered coordinate system (Levinson 2003: 41), where the object has properties (sided-ness, front- and back-ness, for example) that a person uses to understand and express location.

Where the relative frame of reference rests fully on the position of the viewer-speaker-thinker, is egocentric, and maps the world from the position of the viewer-speaker-thinker, the intrinsic thinker projects out their maps and understandings from the object (Levinson 2003: 81), or from one of the named "facets" of the object; thus the "he" is to the side of the cactus, because the speaker understands that the cactus, as an object, has something that he calls sides, and thus that the "he" is to the side of the cactus. In this sense, then, the intrinsic frame of reference is an allocentric system (Levinson 2003: 54); it is based not on the person, but on something other, and importantly some thing that is out of the body. The intrinsic frame, therefore, is viewpoint independent, and the origin of the spatial relation within it is not the ego (Levinson 2003: 54).

Absolute Frame of Reference

Levinson's third frame of reference is the absolute, and it is the one that appears to us as the least familiar. People who understand spatial relationships with an absolute frame think and talk about locations not in terms of their particular positions (i.e., where and how their body is positioned as in the relative frame), or by the sides of an object that they are talking about, as in the intrinsic frame; they think about location by making intricate, comprehensive references to a set of angles and coordinates that run unbounded across space. These angles or coordinates are neither based on the person's position (to the left or the right) or to the person's viewpoint (in front of the tree) (Levinson 2003: 114), nor based on the facet of an object (the side of the cactus). Rather, an absolute thinker makes reference to arbitrary fixed bearings such as the cardinal directions of which north or east is an example (Levinson 2003: 48).

To describe the spatial relationship in Figure 9.4, therefore, the relative thinker would tell us, "He is north of the cactus" (Levinson 2003: fig. 2.2). In this case, the person talking about where the "he" is understands that the cactus, the "he," and the speaker herself (and every item, person, and place in the world, for that matter) are located in relation to one another in reference to a set of positions defined by a north/south/east/west system. As with the intrinsic frame, there is no reference (or need to reference) the thinker, viewer, or speaker's location (Levinson 2003: 48).

In this sense the absolute frame of reference (like the intrinsic one) is allocentric; it does not rely on the fixed viewpoint of a person (Levinson 2003: 91); it locates people, objects, and places without reference to the location of viewer or speaker (Levinson 2003: 48). As allocentric systems, the absolute and the intrinsic frames of reference stand both outside of and within the person: coordinates are outside of and independent of the person (north of the rock-shelter is north of the rock-shelter for you, me, and for other members of our

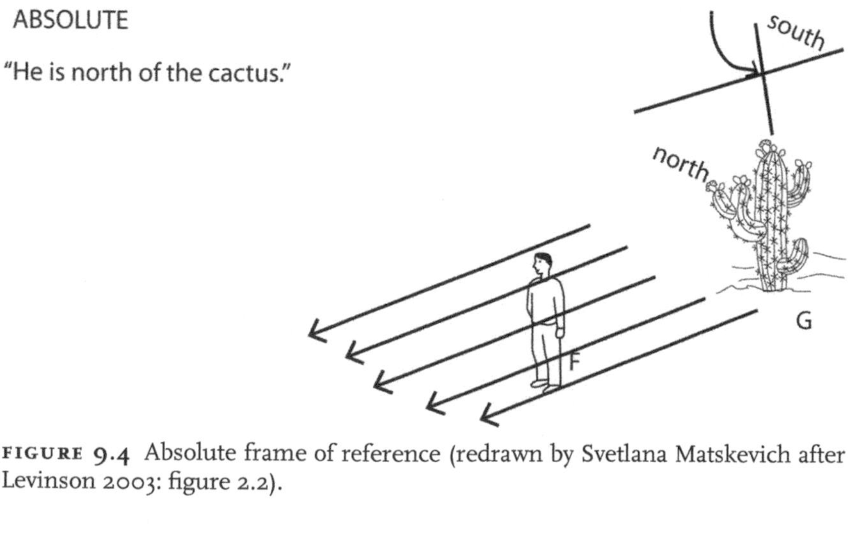

ABSOLUTE

"He is north of the cactus."

FIGURE 9.4 Absolute frame of reference (redrawn by Svetlana Matskevich after Levinson 2003: figure 2.2).

community). At the same time knowledge of these coordinates is inside the person (you, me, and our peers); in an absolute system we share our coordinated understanding of north.

Clearly, one of the simplest ways for those of us living in the industrialized west to imagine an absolute system is in reference to cartographic, cardinal directions such as north/south/east/west. These are not always the coordinates in play, however, and for our efforts to think about 8000-year-old pithouses, it may be more useful to think in less immediately familiar terms. Often absolute thinking communities base their directional coordinates on natural sources that they select and that they then make abstract, elevating them to a vital set of coordinate directions. Possible natural sources include seasonal winds, mountain inclines, coastal alignments, river drainage directions, and star-settings (Levinson 2003: 90). Thus, instead of understanding that the "he" is north of the rock-shelter, one might therefore say that the "he" is downriver from the shelter or upwind from it.

In an absolute system, local landmarks can become the basis for the coordinate system, particularly within a small region. Furthermore, some absolute systems map one coordinate system on top of another. Levinson offers the example of Austronesian island languages in which an east-west axis is fixed in reference to the monsoons, while a second axis is defined by a dimension that runs from mountain to sea. In these spatial systems, one axis works in contrast to the other. As people move around an island, one axis remains constant and the other rotates (Levinson 2003: 90; see Ozanne-Rivièrre 1977, 1987; Wassmann and Dasen 1998).

On Bali, for example, the monsoons determine one axis (which is fixed), but the location with respect to the central mountain determines the other, and varies continuously as one moves around the island (Wassmann and Dasen 1998; Levinson 2003: 49) (Figure 9.5). More specifically, people orient to Gunung Agung, Bali's central volcano where the Hindu gods of the island are said to live. The directional term *kaja* means toward the mountain, and *kelod* means toward the sea. As Wassmann and Dasen warn, when people translate *kaja* into English or Indonesian, they equate the word with "north," and usually do so from a South Bali perspective, where most of the populace live, and thus mistakenly impose that southern perspective over the whole island (Wassmann and Dasen 1998: 692). Furthermore, the *kaja-kelod* axis varies depending on where on the island one stands at any particular moment: for someone standing in the north of the island, *kaja* (toward the mountain) will be the "south"; standing in the south of the island, the same term will be the "north" (Wassmann and Dasen 1998: 692). There is another axis of importance on Bali: *kangin-kauh* between the direction in which the sun rises

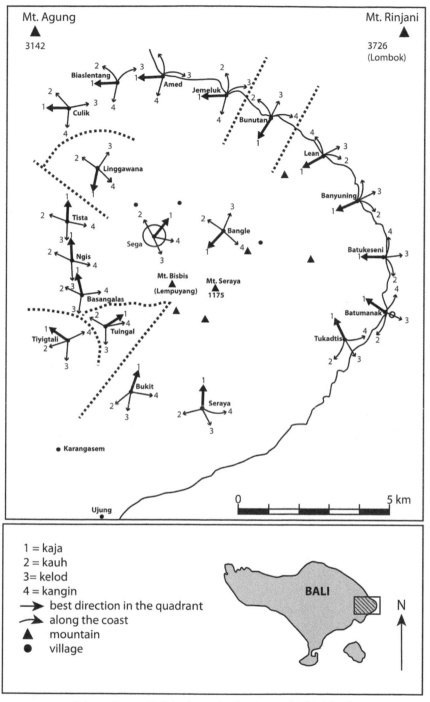

FIGURE 9.5 Orientation on Bali (redrawn by Svetlana Matskevich after Wassmann and Dasen 1998: figure 2).

(*kangin*) and its opposite (*kauh*). While this *kangin-kauh* axis is fixed regardless of where one stands on the island, the other axis (*kaja-kelod*) varies as one moves (Wassmann and Dasen 1998: 692). The riverine systems of Alaska provide an intermediate example; here, one absolute referencing system works within an individual drainage basin, and then resets when people move from one basin into another (Leer 1989).

Regardless of the coordinate and axes in play, absolute speakers have the ability and information that they need to understand and speak about the world only once they understand their heading and their direction in terms of location based on the coordinates (Levinson 2003: 289). Where a relative thinker always has her body to refer to when making positional decisions, an absolute thinker needs to have the coordinate system in his mind all the time. Because of this, in an absolute system, people position themselves physically and conceptually as if they possessed mental compasses that they continuously calibrate and recalibrate. They figure out heading from, and direction to, those other locations through continuous "dead reckoning" calculations that run ceaselessly in the background of their minds (Levinson 2003: 289). In an absolute system, these constant reckonings keep accurate a person's mental maps by knowing a person's fixed bearings to other locations as one moves.

Levinson describes absolute systems as conceptually simple and logically elegant (Levinson 2003: 48), and as such they are distinct from intrinsic systems that are complicated by the multiplicity of object types and by the different degrees of asymmetrical shapes that different objects have (the latter making the naming of facet-variation problematic) (Levinson 2003: 48). Absolute systems are distinct from relative ones in that the latter entail psychological difficulties in learning left/right distinctions and can be highly ambiguous across different referents (e.g., what do we understand "to the right of" or "in front of" to mean) (Levinson 2003: 48–49).

As an example of a language that is more or less completely absolute, Levinson offers Guugu Yimithirr, as spoken by the inhabitants of the Hopevale township, located north of Cooktown, Northern Queensland, Australia (Levinson 2003: 118–128). Guugu Yimithirr is a richly absolute system; it has no relative terms, and only a very restricted set of intrinsic expressions (Levinson 2003: 118). The subjects of Levinson's study maintained mental maps of a relatively large terrain (45,000 sq. km), and were able to compute their locations within that area "more or less at the speed of conversational response" (Levinson 2003: 128). As absolute speakers, they had the (to us, uncanny) ability to point with otherwise unexplainable precision to unseen places, often located at great distance from the speaker-pointer (Levinson 2003: 289). The Hopevale speakers of Guugu Yimithirr based almost every description of spatial location on something similar to our understanding of the cardinal directions of north/ south/east/west (Levinson 2003: 114). For example, one would say the following: " 'George is just north of the tree,' or, to tell someone to take the next left turn, "go north," or, to ask someone to move over a bit, "move a bit east," or, to instruct a carpenter to make a door jamb vertical, "move it a little north," or, to tell someone where you left your tobacco, "I left it on the southern edge of the western table in your house," or to ask someone to turn off the gas camping stove, "turn the knob west" (Levinson 2003: 114).

The Significant Distinction of an Absolute Frame of Reference

Of particular interest is the recognition that an absolute frame of reference is incommensurable with a relative one (Levinson 2003: 290); they do not mix, because they represent radically different ways of understanding and communicating about locations of people, objects, and places in the world. An important part of this difference is that where relative speakers will depict characteristics such as shape in viewer-based descriptions, absolute speakers do so by using fixed coordinates (Levinson 2003: 289). Levinson writes of the absolute system and its central feature of absolute reckoning in terms of "disembodiment" (Levinson 2003: 267), calling it a "decorporealized orientational system" (Levinson 2003: 260). As distinct, the relative frame of reference is body-centric: the human body is the source of notions of orientation and direction. One of the greatest values of Levinson's work is the recognition that there are other ways of thinking about spatial orientation besides the relative (or body-centric) one that dominates modern Western lives. Of greater significance, however, is his argument that our traditions of studying language (and I would add culture and human behavior, particularly of the past) have focused almost exclusively on the relative, body-centric perspective. Levinson calls this a major ethnocentric error of modern social sciences (Levinson 2003: 14).

One of the significant incompatibilities between relative and absolute frames of reference centers on the role that vision plays in people's thinking about their worlds. Absolute spatial coordinates are not fundamentally consistent with our visual experience (Levinson 2003: 256); the absolute frame is viewpoint-independent (Levinson 2003: 135). In fact, for the absolute spatial thinker, visual memory is a confusing and nonsensical distraction. As Levinson illustrates, a relative spatial thinker sees (and understands without second thought) that a coffee pot to the left of a cup becomes a coffee pot to right of cup when the observer stands on the other side of the table. For an absolute spatial thinker, a coffee pot to the north of cup remains to the north of the cup regardless of the viewer's position on any side of the table or, in fact, in any place in the world (Levinson 2003: 274). A consequence of this distinction-in-the-visual is that relative spatial thinkers are unable to point with accuracy at places that are out of sight, yet absolute thinkers do so with extraordinary precision and without hesitation (Levinson 2003: 279). People of these two frames of spatial reference conceive of the world in radically different ways.

Levinson identifies a second, kinesthetic, incompatibility between relative and absolute frames of reference. For a relative thinker, gesture is locked into the viewer-speaker-thinker's egocentric strip maps; kinesthetic information coordinates the body (left, right, front, back) in its movement and its conceptions (Levinson 2003: 279), particularly in the use of arms and fingers to point out directions and locations in coordination with the gaze. For an absolute thinker, gestures are a "more fully fleshed semiotic system," are not guided or restricted by the gaze, and often are large and involve full limb/arm movement (Levinson 2003: 290).

Because the absolute thinker's spatial memory is not a view-centered system and is allocentric, he struggles to follow the egocentric consistencies that make many tasks simple for a relative thinker: for example, setting a table requires a conception that forks go to the left and knives to the right, and is more complicated for an absolute thinker (Levinson 2003: 91). More significant is the cognitive costs of the absolute thinker's never-ending, continuous dead-reckoning calculations that an absolute, coordinate-based frame of reference requires. As Levinson puts it, the absolute thinker's individual, internal reckoning calculator can "never go on holiday"; if it does, then the absolute individual would literally be lost, without an understanding of the directions and experiences that she would need to make communication and living possible (Levinson 2003: 243, 273). One other difference may be significant in distinguishing absolute from relative; to exist within the absolute requires a person to have access to local knowledge, to know (as learned and subconsciously maintained) the coordinate system in use.

A Different Past

Perhaps most significant of Levinson's work on spatial frames of reference and his discussion of the absolute frame of reference is the possibility that many peoples in the past, particularly in a non-industrialized, non-Western past, thought about, talked about, and conceptualized the worlds around them in a way that is not based on the body. The majority (perhaps all) of traditional, recent, and current archaeological work has assumed (indeed even without thinking that there were other options) that what Levinson defines as a relative frame of reference was the dominant (and only) way that people saw their worlds. Across the social sciences, Levinson's work opens our perspectives on human behavior, particularly by "demoting the body as a source of spatial concepts" (Levinson 2003: 14). Indeed, he identifies three unsupportable assumptions in the standard (and dominant) ways of studying spatial thinking: human spatial thinking is always relative, human spatial thinking is primarily egocentric in character, and human spatial thinking is anthropomorphic (Levinson 2003: 10).

These ethnocentric errors that Levinson identifies more generally for the social sciences applies with a vengeance to archaeology, particularly to the archaeology of prehistoric peoples, and perhaps even more dramatically to the peoples living in Europe before the social, economic, technological, and political changes that gradually took form after 6000 cal B.C., indeed in the set of transformations still referred to in the oversimplified terminology of Childe as the Neolithic Revolution (Childe 1925). Regardless of one's support or critique of arguments for the adoption of a new language in Europe at this time (i.e., Renfrew's idea for the Indo-Europeanization of southeastern Europe with the spread of a farming economy; Renfrew 1987), there is great potential in rethinking European prehistory in terms of non-relative frames of spatial reference. What if people thought about the world with an absolute frame of reference, or an intrinsic one? How would such a potential shift in our approaches to those past lives and thoughts change how we think we know what happened then, why it happened, and how it happened?

We can push this further. One step is to think about people in the past not as relative, egocentric, body-oriented, viewer-defined beings, but as intimately integrated into, and of, their worlds in terms, for example, such as described for an absolute framer.[1] A second step is to think about those absolute thinkers as living grounded lives in Ingold's sense. Taking these two steps (leaps perhaps) into the unfamiliar, I suggest helps us understand the local reality at a time when people were cutting the surface of the ground at Măgura. In addition, moving in this direction, we may start to think in richer, more nuanced, and previously obscured ways, about each of the archaeological and artistic examples discussed in the preceding chapters.

Măgura: Absolute and Grounded

One consequence of thinking with Ingold's concept of a grounded existence and with Levinson's sense of an absolute frame of spatial reference is that

FIGURE 9.6 View to the west from Măgura-Buduiasca, just before dawn. Photo copyright D. W. Bailey.

when we look again at the Măgura pit-houses we see a different landscape and we become aware of new significances and consequences of people breaking the ground surface by cutting holes into it (Figure 9.6). More is in play here than merely digging a hole in the dirt. By cutting into that ground 8000 years ago, men, women, and children inserted themselves into the field or zone of energy and groundedness that was vital to their knowledge of who and what they were. Breaking the surface of the ground was an unbinding and a release of what made up the groundedness of being, in Ingold's terms (Ingold 2015b: 122) like fire that releases substance in volatile form though smoke and heat, cutting the surface would have released what, before, had been bound into the known, shared, accepted, and unquestioned coordinates of living.

In breaking that ground surface, those people altered that Grounded base of living and of understanding life and one's place in it. In a Grounded world, digging a hole into the surface of the ground is a disruptive act. The proposal here is that the people living in that place and breaking the surface of their world lived the grounded, depersonalized lives that Ingold illuminated. Thinking in Levinson's terms of absolute frames of spatial reference, we see (perhaps for the first time) the affect that manipulating the ground by cutting holes into and through it would have had on people's physical and metaphysical interweavings with the ground. If people's understanding of where they were (physically and spiritually), of their place in the world, was based on constant, subconscious reckonings and re-reckonings of person and grounded coordinates (uphill, downhill, to-the-coast, from-the-coast), then any breaking of the fabric of those coordinates would have had fundamental impacts (at the least disruptions) on how people positioned themselves in their worlds. In these senses, we should think about life at that time as more powerfully bound into the earth than archaeologists have previously allowed. Life was about the ground and all that was on, in, through, under, and above it. If we must locate this way of living into the standard sequence of understanding European prehistory, then it might be best to conceptualize what was happening at Măgura at 6000 cal B.C. as the symptoms of a bleeding out of a very long phase of human action and belief in which people understood the world as grounded.

What was slowly emerging from this time onward (in this region and at other times in other regions) are the phenomena that the standard archaeological perspective views in terms of agriculture, permanent built environments (physical, social, and political), and other material and behavioral components that make up the received understanding of the Neolithic. These symptoms indicate the end of a grounded way of knowing the world and the beginning of an understanding of life that rested not on the ground but on the body of the individual person; hence anthropomorphic figurines, self-contained buildings with segmented built internal areas, the horizontal concentrations of structures, and accompanying manifestations of a shift in the values and energies away from those associated primarily with the ground. Where Ground had powered life-understandings, now the body gradually took over as the central vehicle for expression and action: life gradually took on a corporeal basis (Figure 9.7). In Levinson's terms, the shift was from an absolute frame of knowing to a relative one. Fading from relevance was a sense of being in which other worlds, not visually present or physically manifest, were ontologically central within a local, shared, continuously calibrating, coordinate understanding of existence. With this, there also slowly dissipated a metaphysics of invisible worlds and self-locations: connections among people, places, and things that ran over potentially infinite distances that were not yet measured (nor would they have been measurable) in relation to corporeal existence, but which ran on the energies of deep-seated, subconscious coordinates of trust and shared understandings.

While this disappearing absolute grounded life was rich in unbounded complexity, it also had limitations; the material and mental manifestations

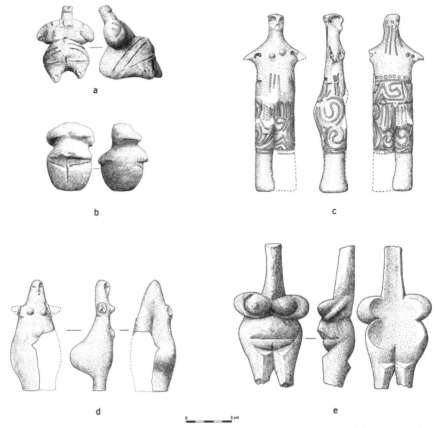

FIGURE 9.7 Symptom of the emergence of a bodied way of being in the Neolithic—figurines.

that archaeologists have summarized as "Neolithic" are symptoms of the ways that people enabled themselves to remove those restrictions and move beyond those limitations. The world seen with the corporeal, relative worldview accelerated with newly expanding conceptions of identity where the person (and groups of similar individuals) came to be central to emerging systems of symbolism, economies, and material manifestations of what it meant to exist (Figure 9.8). These corporeal systems were more easily expressed and understood in the physical manifestations of material culture (from pottery to the built environment to body ornaments and prestige raw materials), and had the potential for more effortless circulation and recognition well beyond the local limitations of the more intimately shared, continuously calibrated, ways of knowing that had worked within an absolute, grounded, non-bodied conception of being.

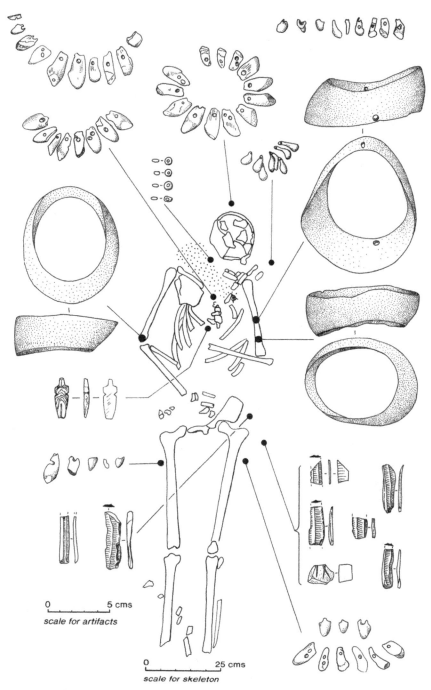

0   5 cms
scale for artifacts

0   25 cms
scale for skeleton

FIGURE 9.8 Symptom of living a relative/corporal existence in the Neolithic—grave with gravegoods, especially pots, prestige metals, body ornaments.

People, Ground, and Surfaces at Măgura

The proposal that, once, we thought with our feet opens for us other ways of thinking about what once the ground might have meant to us as a species. If once we drew other, various sets of information from our foot-to-dirt contact, then we are left to wonder not only what those thoughts and perspectives were, and through what realms of knowledge they reached (physical but also metaphysical and spiritual), but also what might it have meant to live in a world of regular, unmediated, physical contact with the ground. Enhance this connection to ground with Ingold's suggestions about the living of and within the earth (distinct from cartographic, navigational livings of the global perspectives of modernity) and we begin to understand that for the people at Măgura (or Etton or Wilsford) the ground was something of more complex dimensionalities (perhaps unbounded in any way that we can conceive today) and more riven with energies and essences than we think in our twenty-first-century lives and also than we have imagined in our modern archaeological treatments of the non-industrialized, ancient, and prehistoric past.

Beyond Ground: Breaking Surfaces and Transformation

If we accept that the ground of Măgura was integrated into the lives of the people who lived of it (on it, through it, and with it), and if we believe that cutting the surface of that ground had significances and consequences that we struggle to visualize when we approach those pit-houses from the traditional interpretive direction, then how might we now think anew about the other examples included in the preceding chapters. In each case-study a surface was broken: the skin of Darryl Carlton, the architectural fabric of numbers 27 and 29 rue de Beaubourg, the paper and canvas of Fontana's *buchi* and *tagli*, the ground of Etton and Wilsford.

In each of those breakages and cuttings, previously coherent surfaces were punctured, sliced, dug into, and split open. Consequences of those surface breakages were the disruptions of what had been accepted coherences of appropriate and acceptable action and product. Skin is not to be cut, at least not in this way, in this place, by this person, for this purpose. What is released from under that skin is not safe or appropriate, but is dangerous and frightening when released into the open (out from under its retaining, boundary layer) and disseminated among other people. Walls, floors, and ceilings are not to be cut, at least not in this way, by these people, in this place, for these reasons. What is exposed from under the wallpaper and plaster threatens sensible ways in which architecture is normally to be used, viewed, and visited. The views exposed (and the precarious perches made available) to the public and the gravitational and structural dangers threaten how the architecturalized world is supposed to be seen, and how the built environment is expected to behave in its distinctions of inside from out, of private from public, of old and decrepit from new and future-forward. Canvas is not to be punctured or sliced, interrogated with light, and then promoted as ephemeral artistic product of a fourth dimension. The result forces its way into standard knowledge and connoisseurship, traditionally presented in galleries, museums, and lecture-halls, and the consequent threat to long-established regimes of monetary and aesthetic hierarchies at the core of European artistic production. Ground is not to be opened with scapula shovels, antler picks, and stone adzes, especially not to such depths (as at Wilsford) or (as at Etton) unless the location and texture of the ground to be cut gives itself to the act of breakage through an ease of opening (perhaps though its possession of a surface materials' "grain") and unless that opened ground is then refilled and resurfaced, made ready for future cutting-filling-and-(re)cutting.

In each of these acts of opening, cutting, and breaking surfaces new possibilities of knowing are revealed, previously hidden worlds are exposed, otherwise contained energies are released. There are possibilities of knowing the world in a new way. Possibilities of reordering what had been accepted and in control. Possibilities of accessing other worlds and energies. Each of these surfaces once bound, through cutting open and breakage, is newly unbound and liberated; consequences are neither predictable nor rationally positioned. Each of these openings feeds on the energies that come from the paradoxic status that holes possess: outside of normal understanding, both something and nothing, thus unmanageable and undefinable. Each of these openings attracts visual perceptual attentions in ways that overvalue their coming into being and everything that happens to them, in them, and around them. Each surface broken is an understanding of the world disrupted. Each of these case studies, like the surface-cuttings at Măgura, finds its power in the act of surface breaking and its significance in the way that it suggests to us the presence of (at least) two worlds: like the absolute opposition to the relative frame of spatial reference, so also do each of these other examples of surface breaking suggest other tensions between world views accepted and world views contested and feared.

What to Do with Pit-houses?

What are we to think of pit-houses at the end of this journey through the philosophy of holes, the psychology of perceiving concavities, the linguistic anthropology of cutting and breaking, the recognition of grounded living and the absolute frame of reference, as well as the practice, intention, output, and impact of the performance art of Ron Athey, of the anti-architecture of Gordon Matta-Clark, and of the punctured and sliced canvases of Lucio Fontana? Throughout, I have retained the term "pit-house." Does that term remain of use, or should we pull it apart (cut it, perhaps) and replace it with a more nuanced concept that more fully represents what was in play when people, at Măgura for example, cut the ground surface?

Moving in one direction, one could argue to retain the term because it is highly likely that pit-houses once functioned as facilities in which people sat, ate, slept, made and modified objects, ejaculated, talked, laughed, burped, spat, and did a range of other activities that we associate with our modern Western conception of "house" and domesticity. We could break the use of the word *house* (and the domestic) as impositions from a heteronormative, industrialized understanding; we could perhaps locate a less charged term. If we opted for replacement, then we would need to build a new definition that accommodated the following actions and consequences.

First, these facilities were holes, and as such they are philosophically and materially complex entities, the creation and experience of which would have had significant consequences in how people think (most probably subconsciously) about the making of the hole, the actions that take place within the hole, the objects placed in it, and the people who make, use, fill, and resurface that hole.

Second, the existence of a hole depends on (and, literally, from) a surface, and thus to understand that hole requires an understanding of that surface and the role (and the significance of that role) that that surface played in the way that people understood (again, most probably, without thinking) that physical, but also the metaphysical and spiritual, world in which, on which, and through which they lived.

Third, in the archaeological case under study, the surface that is broken with a hole is the ground, and thus actions of breakage implicate complicated and nuanced sets of relationships among people, objects, and environments that live through the ground surface, and that the holing of the surface of the ground in a g/Grounded existence would have had significant local meanings and consequences that we (as archaeologists) will struggle to understand, or even recognize.

Fourth, the people who holed that g/Grounded land surface conceptualized their spatial relationships in their worlds by way of absolute and not relative or corporeal references, and thus the consequences of breaking that surface will have been of a degree fundamentally beyond one that we can imagine from our Western, industrialized perspectives.

What are we to do? If we accept that the facilities that we study, excavate, interpret, write about, and continue to call pit-houses are cloaked in sets of complexities and 8000-year-distant meanings, functions, and positions in that Măgura reality, then how do we seek to understand them? One answer is to ignore (or turn away from) the enriched thought that comes with discussions of holes, surfaces, g/Groundedness, convexities, cutting verbs, and distinctions in frames of reference. That option is to continue to assume that the concept that we drape over the broken surface of the ground is good enough, is easily knowable, and fits within the accepted understanding of the emergence of sedentism in the Neolithic of southeastern Europe. It is the safe option: supportable, comprehendible, solid, teachable, reassuring. The other option, and the one pursued in this book, is to explore less stable worlds of investigation that, though still within accepted traditions of Western academic and scientific rhetoric (visual anthropology, philosophy, art history, psychology), refuse to produce an easy, simple definition or statement of function or of meaning.

To opt for the latter course is to welcome the challenge of the unknown and to recognize the limitations of much standard archaeological research and fieldwork. It is not to discard that work; indeed the stimulation to take the

FIGURE **9.9** Backfiling Măgura-Buduiasca, after final season of excavation. Photo copyright D. W. Bailey.

journey of this book was prompted by fieldwork, analysis, and attempts at explanation that sat comfortably at the core of traditional, rigorous archaeological investigation. The option taken here is to seek disruptions and unexpected
juxtapositions in our work and in our thinking about our work, in the field
and outside of it. The intention is to move beyond the boundaries of archaeology (as well as of art history) in order to produce something (this book and its
chapter title pages and page headers) that has the same provocation to thought
and questions as did Athey's cutting of Carlton's back, Matta-Clark's breaking
of the rue de Beaubourg houses, and Fontana's punching and slicing of his
canvases. Thus the insertion of holes into particular chapter titles; the book
and its contents become something other than the standard reading of its subject: pit-houses. I suggest that the breaking of the ground surfaces at Etton
and at Wilsford, the cutting of the ground 8000 years ago at Măgura, had the
same provocation as did our re-cutting of those re-filled and re-made surfaces
in the first decade of the twenty-first century (Figure 9.9); they are incitements
to us as a team in the field and in those late-night *ţuica*-fueled discussions in
Cristi's lab at the museum in southern Romania. All of these provocations are
connected; they share the recognition that breaking surfaces matter. On these
pages. In that distant ground. In Paris on the rue de Beaubourg. At Etton and
Wilsford. In Minneapolis at Patrick's Cabaret. In Fontana's studios.

Inter-text

Recommended Code of Practice

1. Excavate to maximum depth achievable leaving 6 inches of soil above the last coffin buried.
2. Ensure that the length and width of the excavation are sufficient to allow the construction of the walls of a cell or compartment and allow the coffin free passage at the committal.
3. Construct a solid foundation in the bottom of the grave by either the preparation of footings around the perimeter of the bottom of the grave or by inserting a preformed concrete foundation slab. Alternatively a layer of dry mix concrete can be spread over the bottom of the grave.
4. Construct 4.5 inch brick walls around the inside of the grave (alternatively a proprietary preformed concrete sleeve can be lowered into the grave).
5. Ensure that there are no gaps in the mortar between bricks.
6. Carry out the interment with the coffin coming to rest within the brick cell or compartment formed.
7. Seal the top of the cell or compartment by bedding concrete slabs of at least 2 inches in thickness onto mortar ensuring that no gaps exist.
8. Backfill remaining depth with soil.

(Institute of Cemetery and Crematorium Management 2004)

Recutting Wilsford (A.D. 1960–1962)

In July 1960, Edwina Proudfoot and a team of laborers dug into green meadow grasses with steel shovels and spades not far from Normanton Gorse. Trained as a teacher and archaeologist, holding a degree from Edinburgh University, and having worked as Stuart Piggott's assistant, Edwina's 1960 remit from the Ancient Monuments Inspectorate of the Ministry of Works was to salvage archaeological information from a damaged site. Listed as Wilsford 33a, the site stood out as a raised circular bank around a shallow depression (0.5 m deep) into the ground surface. Archaeologists classified the site as a pond barrow.[1] In 1954, fearing that cattle would fall and be trapped in the depression, the local farmer had bulldozed the circular bank into the shallow hole. Edwina's team started by laying a grid over the site and then cut four rectangular trenches over what remained of the bank and depression (Proudfoot 1989b: 15). Cutting down through the first meter of soils and sediments, the diggers recovered no finds (Proudfoot 1989a: 37). The archaeologists expected to find human remains, probably an articulated skeleton and accompanying grave goods of amber, stone, and gold. Funerary features were expected in barrow excavations, though little was known about the contents of pond barrows.

Seventy-five cm down from the modern ground surface, the diggers traced a raw edge of bedrock chalk that ran around the depression's edge. As they dug, they defined a circular hole in the chalk, and noticed that the hole's shape was like the top of a funnel. As they dug, the area available for them to excavate became smaller and smaller. At 1.0 m below ground level, the diggers reached a small circle of dark soil (the narrowest, lowest point of the funnel-shaped hole). They found a few unworked pieces of natural flint, material that had accumulated when rainwater had washed material into the original open hole. The soil became compact and difficult to cut with the diggers' tools (Proudfoot 1989b: 16). Nothing was as it should be, or as the diggers expected. They found no sign of the expected artifacts or features of Bronze Age burials. The hole in the ground that they stood in was now deeper than they had expected.

From 1.10 to 3.50 cm Below Surface

As the chalk edges of the funnel-shaped hole increased in steepness, the team dug through the brown silts of the central area and the compact, weathered chalk surrounding them. As they cut down below 1.0 m, they recovered a pony bone (*Equus caballus*). Cutting through chalky soil at 1.8 m, the team found a flint waste flake (Proudfoot 1989a: fig. 39: 2; 40). Along the side of deepening hole pieces of oak charcoal (*Quercus* sp.) appeared (Proudfoot 1989a: 43). Next, the team uncovered a large number of pottery sherds, including material from ten vessels. Sixteen sherds dated to the second century A.D., including two fragments of Samian ware (Proudfoot 1989a: 37, 39). Undiagnostic body sherds were heavily worn by ancient exposure on the surface and washed into the pit by rainwater (Proudfoot 1989a: 39). All of the material from this depth dated to the early Iron Age (fifty-two sherds from four vessels) (Proudfoot 1989a: 39; fig. 37) and to the Middle Bronze Age (Deverel-Rimbury wares: twenty-seven sherds from a globular urn, two barrel urns, and one indeterminate form; Proudfoot 1989a: 38; fig. 37). Cutting through rain-washed sediments at 2.4 m, they recovered a flint end-scraper (Proudfoot 1989a: fig. 39:1; 40).

Digging through 3.0 m, they found several hundred animal bones (sheep/goat, cattle, dog), and twelve fragments of human remains. Most bone surfaces bore marks of butchery and gnawing. Marks on a horse bone suggest that the animal had been skinned (Grigson 1989: 114) and suggest that these were domestic rubbish (Proudfoot 1989a: 42). None of the bones were articulated (Henderson 1989: 115). A few bones (including horse, cattle, and dog) lacked marks from animal gnawing, and had been buried quickly, either by people or covered by rain and erosion (Hendersen 1989: 115). Human bone at these depths consisted of two infants and one individual less than ten years old (Henderson 1989: 126). No evidence remained for formal or ceremonial burial. Highly fragmented, the bone bore no traces of burning. Cutting down below 2.0 m, the team found two fragments of separate left femurs of adult male adults (Henderson 1989: 126). Dates from samples at this depth show that this material was no older than the Early Iron Age (the sixth and fifth centuries B.C.) (Proudfoot 1989a: 42). Digging to 3.0 m, the team removed unworked flints and coarse pieces of chalk, and then naturally accumulating charcoal from hazel, oak, and alder that had weathered into the depression.

From 3.4–12.0 m Below Ground Surface

After thirty days of digging with shovel and trowel the team had reached a depth of 3.5 m (Proudfoot 1989b: 15), and they hoped soon to reach the bottom.

They cut down below 4.0 m. Here the diggers found a few animal bones (seventeen fragments): remains of prepared joints of sheep/goat (i.e., two sets of vertebrae held together by ligaments when thrown into the hole). Lacking any clear pattern of association, the bones probably resulted from domestic activities at the mouth of the shaft (Grigson 1989: 115). Another two weeks cutting into the pit brought the diggers to 6.0 m, into clean, un-rainwater-stained material, where equally sized pieces of the chalk were common (Ashbee 1989e: 26). Searching for the bottom, the diggers probed down with a metal rod. They felt no resistance; the bottom of the hole was not near. At a depth of 7.5 m, the diggers lashed together four ladders, one above the other, to create an extended, rickety route out of the hole (Proudfoot 1989a: 15). Up above, on the surface, they built a platform of wood and steel scaffolding. A powered-hoist lifted out large latrine buckets of material.

Digging deeper, they noticed a difference in the fill. Below 7.5 m, they cut through rubbly, loose material of black soil and chalk (Ashbee 1989e: 26). On the vertical sides of the hole was evidence of weathering (exposure to frost) from a time when the hole had been open for a substantial period (Ashbee 1989e: 31). The diggers found cattle and sheep skulls, and feet bones—casually discarded refuse from animal butchery or food preparation. Cutting through 8 m, they found a well-burnished (i.e., used) broken awl made of a sheep's tibia (fig. 46:6, 47:2; Ashbee 1989b: 49). A meter deeper, they found a bone pin, also broken (fig. 45:5), and a single fling waste flake (Ashbee 1989b: 51). Cutting a little deeper, they recovered an ox skull and vertebrae of one animal, with butchery marks suggesting that people had skinned the animal before throwing the bones into the hole (Grigson 1989: 112).

At 9.0 m, they dug past a hole in the shaft's wall where a block of flint had fallen out and into the open shaft (Ashbee 1989e: 31). Between 9.0 and 12.0 m, they found particularly clear gouges in the wall left by falling flint. This part of the hole also had been open to the elements (Ashbee 1989e: 31). With their trowels, the diggers found a white-patinated flint waste flake and a flake of cracked, burned flint (Ashbee 1989b: 51). A similar flake was found when the diggers reached 10.5 m (Ashbee 1989b: 50). They noticed how close-packed was the chalk rubble filling at this depth and how it contained concentrations of charcoal flecks (Ashbee 1989e: 26).

From 12–21 m Below Ground Surface

As the diggers cut down to 12 m, they found fewer nodules of flint, and dug through cleaner fill, only coming across occasional charcoal flecks (Ashbee 1989e: 26). The shaft's walls no longer were frost-weathered (Ashbee 1989e: 31);

at this depth the original hole had been filled soon after it had been cut. As they dug, the archaeologists noted the grooves left by the original antler picks that had first cut the shaft, and the traces from the broad-bladed bronze axes that smoothed the rougher, antler-picked walls (Ashbee 1989e: 33). In some places, the patterns of axe marks suggested vertical, horizontal, or oblique blows; others suggested striking the chalk with the tip of the axe blade (Ashbee 1989e: 34).

As they cut down to 13 m, the team found a pair of hind feet and forefeet (Grigson 1989: 108) of a one-year-old sheep/goat, a second pair from an animal between thirteen and twenty-four months old (Grigson 1989: 112), and two sheep skulls (both young, one a male), broken into hundreds of pieces. If the skulls and feet were of the same animal, then this was evidence of animals butchered for their fleeces, and of bones discarded (Grigson 1989: 112). A sample from one of the sheep skulls yielded a date of 3130 +/− 60 (OxA 1215) [1397 +/− 69 cal. B.C.]; these bones had entered the hole in the Middle Bronze Age.

At 13.5 m, the diggers were cutting though fewer flint nodules, bits of chalk, or animal bone fill and more soil (Ashbee 1989e: 26). At 14.5 and 16 m the team found single flint flakes, unassociated with other materials (Ashbee 1989b: 51). Digging down through 18 m, they recovered scattered fragments of a Middle Bronze Age (1400–1100 cal B.C.) Deverel-Rimbury barrel urn, 50 cm tall with a 40 cm diameter rim and a 20 cm diameter base (fig. 41:1; pp. 44, 108). By the start of the 1961 season, the archaeologists had dug to a depth that required a more sophisticated system to get diggers and material in and out of the hole. The team improved lighting, air, communication (i.e., diggers could now talk to the surface with a telephone) (Ashbee 1989c: 144). At the surface, the team installed a stronger platform that covered the top of the hole, blocking out any natural light for the team below, and removing any visual connection between members on the surface and in the hole. Even with these improvements, the diggers struggled. Inadequate lighting, electrical and mechanical failures, dead batteries for the telephones, and an inability to clear rainwater combined to limit the number of digging days in the 1961 season to fourteen of a possible fifty-three. A closed-circuit television system allowed the surface team to follow the digging in real time. Even with improvements like these made for the 1962 season, digging was halted in late July when the water pump seized and the electrical generator fused (Ashbee 1989c: 147). When work resumed, the team cut down to 21 m and found larger pieces of chalk rubble (up to 15 × 15 cm). Now using picks and forks, the diggers loosened tightly compacted fill. At 22 m, they found an ox pelvis and skull, just below a broken bone pin with unpolished point and abraded shaft (Ashbee 1989b: 48–49), and another flint flake (Ashbee 1989b: 51).

Below 21 m

Digging deeper, the team reached depths that had been underwater for long periods; material and shaft walls were stained by oxidized iron compounds (Ashbee 1989e: 35). As they dug the staining became less frequent. The material was looser, the digging easier (Ashbee 1989e: 30). The animal bones uncovered now were scatters of sheep, cattle, and (a few) pigs: probably culinary refuse that had been thrown in from the surface (Grigson 1989: 115). The team cut into the waterlogged layers. Between 23.3 and 24 m they found five sherds of pottery, all of different wares (Ashbee 1989b: 45). Digging to 25.3 m they recovered fragments of a small globular vessel, originally 20 cm tall with a base 11 cm in diameter (Ashbee 1989b: 44; fig. 41:2). At 26.6 m, the diggers found a shale, D-cross section ring, one side of which had been ground flat and notched four times (Ashbee 1989b: 46; figs. 43:1, 44:1). Digging down to 26.9 m, they found the remains of two neonatal or fetal sheep and two sets of sheep vertebrae: one an adult, the other younger (Grigson 1989: 108). Digging below these, the team cut through 1.5 m of sterile soil (Grigson 1989: 107).

As they reached 27 m, the diggers benefited from equipment improvements made before the start of the season; even so, digging at this depth required a fifteen-minute trip down into and, later, up out of the hole (Ashbee 1989c: 147). As the diggers cut down to 28.2 m, they found fragments of wood preserved and trapped in rubble packed at the shaft's sides (Ashbee 1989e: 30). They came down upon a mass of humus with grass and seeds, as well as small pieces of wood, twigs, and beetle remains (Ashbee 1989e: 30). At 28.3 m, they recovered an oval-shaped, translucent brown, amber bead (figs. 43:4, 44:4), worn on one side, with clear marks of the drill that produced it.

Against the shaft's side the diggers found a heavily worn and weathered oak timber, pointed at one end and beveled at the other, half a meter long and 20 cm wide (Ashbee 1989b: 53, 59; figs. 59, 60). Digging through the next 1.8 m, they found almost four thousand pieces of wood, most (70 percent) shapeless scrapes and pieces. Several (curved and with worn edges) were scoops. The other pieces were from containers (at least forty-nine), mostly circular-based, stave-built buckets (Ashbee 1989b: 51, 58) with a diameter of 25 to 35 cm (Ashbee 1989b: 59). Almost eight hundred pieces (64.1 percent) of the container pieces were bucket staves, a few with holes that once held rope or with handles (Ashbee 1989b: 53–54), most heavily worn and well used. Looking at a smaller (20 cm dia.; 7.5 cm tall), thin-walled bowl, the team saw traces left by the tool that had cut it when it was originally turned (Ashbee 1989b: 59). The diggers recovered 250 pieces of withes (i.e., organic fibers twisted into cordage) that had once been parts of the containers or baskets (Ashbee 1989b: 59), and fragments of plant fiber cord made of three strands twisted together in the reverse direction (i.e., a Z-twist) (Heal 1989: 62).

Digging to 28.8 m, the team found two sherds of different fabric (Ashbee 1989b: 45), a heavily battered flint core (Ashbee 1989b: 50–51), and a flint waste flake (Ashbee 1989b: 51). Just below, they found another waste flake, a fresh, sharp-edged, single-platform prismatic flint core (Ashbee 1989b: 50–51), a well-used 10-cm long sheep or deer bone needle. Just below this, they found seven freshly struck flint flakes, eleven fragments of freshly struck flakes, two flint spalls (Ashbee 1989b: 51), and just a bit lower, a single sherd, and two freshly struck flint flakes (Ashbee 1989b: 51). At the same level, the diggers found a highly polished, translucent brown, amber, circular bead (Ashbee 1989b: 46), and another heavy-used bone needle made of sheep or roe deer tibia or metapodia. Digging just 10 cm deeper, they found another needle made from sheep or roe deer metatarsal. Just below this, they recovered three sherds of different fabrics (Ashbee 1989b: 45–46), yet another worn bone needle, made of horse or cattle (Ashbee 1989b: 47), and a smaller (3 cm) bone needle; all of the needles had been well used. More flint was in the centimeters immediately below: a freshly struck flake, two lumps of fire-cracked flint (Ashbee 1989b: 51), and a waste flake. Ten centimeters deeper, they found nine freshly struck flint spalls (Ashbee 1989b: 51). Next, the diggers came down on three complete lamb skeletons: one neonate, probably stillborn, and one, perhaps aborted, fetus, possibly evidence for sheep breeding/birthing at the surface when these lambs entered the hole (Grigson 1989: 106–107, 115). Also present were the remains of other sheep/goats, of dog, and of cattle (Grigson 1989: 107). Bone breaks and cut marks suggest domestic (culinary) activities that had taken place around the mouth of the shaft.

Digging down to 29.8 m, they found two more translucent brown beads: one biconical, worn and damaged, and larger than the other beads; the second bead was smaller. Ten centimeters deeper, they found a fragment of a bone pin and a waste blade (Ashbee 1989b: 51). Cutting down to 30 m, the diggers found a deciduous incisor of a juvenile human (Henderson 1989: 126), another waste flake, a freshly struck spall, and six lumps of fire-cracked flint (Ashbee 1989b: 51). Ten centimeters lower, the diggers found the only flint tool in the shaft: a double-ended scraper rough-out (Ashbee 1989b: 51). Below this, the diggers could dig no deeper. With the shaft now emptied of fill material, artifacts, chalk, flint, and bone, the diggers could see what had stopped their prehistoric predecessors: a fissure in the chalk through which water still flowed. Excavation concluded in August 1962. On the twenty-eighth of the month, a photographer from the Inspectorate of Ancient Monuments recorded those shaft sections of particular interest: the juncture of weathered upper part and the unweathered lower part; places where Bronze Age diggers had smashed off flint nodules sticking out of the wall; traces of axe-dressing, and of vertical striations left by falling rubble from weathering (Ashbee et al.1989a: 142). Over the last five days of August, Edward Cripps made latex impressions of marks left by antler picking and axe-dressing[2] (Ashbee et al. 1989b: 144). On September 17, the now re-emptied shaft was back-filled at the request of Mr. A. M. Hosier, the tenant farmer, in order to bring the land back under cultivation. Geoffrey Dimbleby and Ian Cornwall, as well as Tom Margerison, the science correspondent for the *Sunday Times*, argued to keep the site open. Regardless, the authorities ruled that the shaft was both too dangerous and too expensive to keep a deep hole open and properly protected. A twice-excavated hole in the landscape disappeared.

Endnotes

CHAPTER 1

1. Preliminary results from the project have appeared and a final synthesis is in progress. Readers interested in learning more should consult the following: Bailey et al. (2002); Bălăşescu (2014); Bălăşescu et al. (2005); Balasse et al. (2012, 2013); Evin et al. (2015); Howard et al. (2004); Lazăr and Soficaru (n.d.); Macklin et al. (2011); Macphail (et al. 2005); Mărgărit et al. (2014); Mills (2009); Mirea (2011a, 2011b); Pannett (2009, 2011); Thissen (2008, 2009, 2012, 2013); Van As (2010); and Walker and Bogaard (2011).
2. For full details about Zadubravlje, see Minichreiter (1992, 1993). For a synthetic overview of pit-house and pit architecture in Starčevo northern Croatia in general, see Minichreiter (2001).
3. The focus on English-language works is noted, and a similar review of works in local central and east European languages as well as French and German is eagerly anticipated.
4. The other primary institutions were subsistence, government, language, the family, religion, and property (Morgan 1877: 12).
5. Note, however, that Greenfield and Jongsma are careful in their use of terminology, referring to "pit-complexes" and "pit-features" and "semi-subterranean Starčevo-Criş structures," "simple semi-subterranean huts," and "pit-dwellings" (Greenfield and Jongsma 2008: 114–115, 125).
6. A fuller discussion of the debate can be found in the appendix to Chapman's article.
7. Readers interested in a fuller discussion of structured deposition, its origins, growth, and influence will find Garrow's paper of particular value.

CHAPTER 2

1. Details of the performance come from published descriptions (Shank 2002: 222; Johnson 2013a) and from a video of a similar performance of the work at the Los Angeles Theatre Center earlier in 1994.

2. For further details about the NEA controversy and the role that Athey's Minneapolis performance played in it, see Johnson's excellent chapter (2013a), Carr (1994: 16), Vance (1994: 107–108), Carlson (1996: 158–159), Blocker (2004: 111–115), Johnson (2008), Shank (2002: 224), and Congressional Record (1994).

3. A doctor or a nurse's reactions to the cuttings may be different, may be sanitized of the emotion of cutting into the body: that is part of the necessity of their training and experience that allows them to complete every day actions that would upset and frighten members of the public, who are unsanitized of emotion.

CHAPTER 3

1. The difference between concave and convex change was highly significant ($F(1, 10)$ = 40.34, P < 0.0001). There was no significant effect of change direction (introduction vs. removal), and no significant interaction (P > 0.25 in both cases).

CHAPTER 4

1. For a critical discussion of the excavation and post-excavation analyses, see Bradley (1991).

2. The interpretation of pond-barrows (of which Wilsford is traditionally associated) as ritual in function can be traced back to their earliest excavation; in 1740 William Stukeley wrote about one to the south of Wilsford, "the use of it seems to have been a place for sacrificing and feasting in memory of the dead, as was the ancient custom" (Stukeley 1740: 45).

3. Note that Brück originally called these "odd deposits" (Brück 1999).

CHAPTER 5

1. For a video of *Conical Intersect*, see http://vimeo.com/10617205.

2. For a 2011 project about the film, see http://vimeo.com/29428835.

3. Matta-Clark had also thought about making his work in the then-under-construction Centre Pompidou, though French authorities rejected his proposal (Muir 2011: 188n13).

4. To see this film go to http://www.exquise.org/video.php?id=2161&l=uk.

5. For a 2001 version of the Petitjean video, see http://www.exquise.org/video.php?id=2161&l=uk (accessed June 2, 2014). For the Bruno and Matta-Clark film, see http://vimeo.com/10617205 (accessed June 2, 2014). Both are excellent and the latter includes a vivid soundtrack and conversations between Matta-Clark and an interviewer.

6. Readers interested in Roberto Matta's work and career should consult Dolin (2005) and Flahutez (2004).

7. The aim was to make a restaurant that was also a performance piece; thus the kitchen was open to the dining area; see Waxman (2008) and see the film (*Food*) made by photographer Robert Frank.

8. The bulldozer drivers delayed their final work twelve hours to give Matta-Clark the time he needed to complete the work.

9. For more on anarchitecture, see Noever (1998), Attlee and Le Feuvre (2003), Attlee (2007), and Walker (2009, 2011).

10. For one of his most intriguing examples of the latter, see *Reality Properties: Fake Estates* (1973), in which he bought at auction in New York City useless, plots of abandoned, unusable land in the city.

11. As James Attlee has noted, Matta-Clark's desire to create altered states of perceptions and disoriented experiences has connections to Guy Debord's work (Attlee 2003a: 310).

12. Note of course the exceptions, still seen as alternatives, such as Sue Hamilton and her team's phenomenological work in Tavriole, Italy (Hamilton et al. 2006).

CHAPTER 6

1. This mise en scène was provided by Penelope Brown and Asifa Majid based on Penelope's fieldwork from the early 1990s (for details about her results, see Brown 2007).

2. The project was directed by Stephen Levinson and the researchers were members of Levinson's Language and Cognition Group at Max Planck Institute.

3. Here are descriptions of the sixty-one video stimuli used in the study as designed by Bohnemeyer, Bowerman, and Brown (see Bohnemeyer et al. 2001)—regular font = spontaneous events with no agent; bold = showing an agent; italic = open, take apart, and peel. 1. Tear cloth into two pieces by hand; 2. Cut rope stretched between two tables with single downward blow of chisel; 3. Hack branch off tree with machete; 4. Chop cloth stretched between two tables with repeated intense knife blows; 5. Break stick over knee several times with intensity; 6. Chop multiple carrots crossways with big knife with intensity; 7. *Push chair back from table*; **8. Piece of cloth tears spontaneously into two pieces**; 9. Slice carrot lengthwise with knife into two pieces; 10. Slice carrot across into multiple pieces with knife; 11. *Pull two paper cups apart by hand*; 12. Cut strip of cloth stretched between two people's hands in two; 13. Cut rope stretched between two tables with blow of axe; 14. Make single incision in melon with knife; 15. Saw stick propped between two tables in half; **16. Forking branch of twig snaps spontaneously off; 17. Carrot snaps spontaneously; 18. Cut finger accidentally while cutting orange**; 19. Snap twig with two hands; 20. Cut single branch off twig with sawing motion of knife; 21. Smash carrot into several fragments with hammer; **22. Take top off pen**; 23. Chop cloth stretched between two tables into two pieces with two blows of hammer; 24. Cut rope in two with scissors;

25. Snap twig with two hands, but it doesn't come apart; 26. Cut carrot crossways into two pieces with a couple of sawing motions with knife; 27. Cut hair with scissors; 28. Cut fish into three pieces with sawing motion of knife; 29. *Peel an orange almost completely by hand*; 30. *Peel a banana completely by hand*; 31. Smash a stick into several fragments with single blow of hammer; 32. Cut carrot in half crossways with single karate-chop of hand; 33. Open a book; 34. Chop cloth stretched between two tables with single karate-chop of hand; 35. Break yarn into many pieces with fury; 36. Tear cloth about half-way through with two hands; 37. Cut carrot in half lengthwise with single blow of axe; 38. Break single piece off yarn by hand; 39. Smash flower pot with single blow of hammer; 40. Smash plate with single blow of hammer; 41. *Open a hinged box*; 42. Break vertically-held stick with single karate-chop of hand; 43. Cut carrot crossways into two pieces with single blow of chisel; 44. *Open canister by twisting top slightly and lifting it off*; 45. Poke hole in cloth stretched between two tables with a twig; **46. Rope parts spontaneously, sound of a single chop**; 47. *Open hand*; 48. Chop branch repeatedly with axe, both lengthwise and crosswise, until a piece comes off; 49. Cut rope in two with knife; 50. Chop rope stretched between two tables in two with repeated blows of hammer; 51. Split melon in two with single knife blow, followed by pushing halves apart by hand; 52. *Open mouth*; 53. Break stick in two with single downward blow of chisel; 54. Cut carrot in half crosswise with single blow of axe; 55. *Open teapot/take lid off teapot*; 56. Cut cloth stretched between two tables in two with scissors; 57. Snap carrot with two hands; 58. *Open eyes*; 59. *Open scissors*; 60. *Open door*; 61. Break rope stretched between two tables with single karate-chop of hand.

4. It is interesting to note another moment of diversity here: that Mandarin has as its most distinct group cutting with scissor-like, two-bladed instruments sets in similarity to four other of the twenty-eight languages studied by Chen (Dutch, Swedish, Tidore, and Otomi) but in distinction from the twenty-three others (Chen 2007: 277).

5. John Chapman and Bisserka Gaydarska have written extensively on the potentials of breaking objects in the Neolithic, though in other terms and with other methodologies (Chapman 1999, 2000c; Chapman and Gaydarska 2007).

6. Similar attention to grain and axis of cutting or breaking is present in Chontal (see above).

CHAPTER 7

1. Bone inventory numbers 10824, 10823, and 10822.
2. Bone inventory numbers 10821, 10818, 10817, 10819, 10820.
3. Bone inventory numbers 10813, 10812, 10814, 10815, 10816.
4. Bone inventory number 10810.
5. Bone inventory number 10743.

6. Bone inventory number 10742.

7. Bone inventory numbers 10741, 10738, 10740, 10737.

8. Flint inventory number 5902.

9. Bone inventory number 10739.

10. Bone inventory numbers 10736, 10735.

11. Bone inventory numbers 10733, 10677, 10675, 10672, 10671, 10676, 10674, 10673.

12. Pottery inventory numbers 2632, 2631, 2637, 2640, 2638, 2635, 2636, 2633,

13. Pottery inventory numbers 2641 (M 109), 2639 (M 108, includes 3523).

14. Pottery inventory number 2634 (M 110).

15. Flint inventory number 5900.

16. Flint inventory number 5903.

17. Flint inventory number 5898, 5901.

18. Flint inventory number 5899.

19. Bone inventory numbers 10670, 10669, 10668, and 10667.

20. Flint inventory numbers 5897, 5893, 5896, 5894, and 5895.

21. Flint inventory number 5365.

22. Pottery inventory number 2144.

23. Flint inventory number 5352.

24. Flint inventory number 5606.

25. Pottery inventory numbers 2141, 2139, 2138, 2333.

26. Flint inventory number 5604.

27. Flint inventory number 5603.

28. Flint inventory number 5605.

29. Pottery inventory numbers 2146, 2145, 2334, 2140.

30. Flint inventory number 5607.

31. Flint inventory number 5602.

32. Pottery inventory number 2332.

33. Flint inventory numbers 5364.

34. Flint inventory number 5600.

35. Flint inventory number 5357.

36. Flint inventory numbers 5355, 5356, 5359.

37. Flint inventory number 5358.

38. Pottery inventory numbers 2147, 2148.

39. Pottery inventory number 2142 (M359).

40. Pottery inventory number 244 (M105).

41. Pottery inventory numbers 2443 (M106), 2442 (M107).

42. Pottery inventory numbers 2198, 2197, 2150, 2437, 2440, 2444, 2438, 2448, 2449, 2149, 2445, 2451, 2452.

43. Flint inventory numbers 5360, 5361, 5368, 5369, 5362, 5370.

44. Pottery inventory number 2337 (M114).

45. Pottery inventory numbers 2195, 2196, 2446, P2450, 2196, 2447.

46. Flint inventory number 5363.
47. Flint inventory number 5364.
48. Flint inventory number 5367.
49. In addition to these features, the excavators recorded undiagnostic pits or post-holes, hollow "scoops" of indeterminate origin (human or natural), and other indistinct ditches and gullies (Pryor 1998: 82).
50. Feature inventory numbers 227–231, 570.
51. Feature inventory numbers 263–264, 266–268.
52. Site inventory number Other 94.
53. Site inventory number Other 95.
54. Site inventory number Other 192.
55. Site inventory numbers Other 1, 2.
56. Site inventory number Other 206.
57. Site inventory number Other 152.
58. Site inventory number Other 166.
59. Site inventory number Other 167.
60. Site inventory number Other 209.
61. Site inventory number Other 85.
62. Site inventory number Other 89.
63. Site inventory number Other 104.
64. Site inventory number Other 120.
65. Site inventory number Other 181.
66. Site inventory number Other 205.
67. Site inventory number Other 208.
68. Different patterns are evident at other Neolithic causewayed enclosures.

CHAPTER 8

1. For the most authoritative English introductions to Fontana and his work, see Gottschaller (2008, 2012), White (2011), and Whitfield (1999).
2. There is no extant copy of the broadcast that he called *Immagini luminose in movimento* [Luminous Images in Movement].
3. In the *catalogue raisonné* and at the Foundazione Lucio Fontana in Milan, the artist's works are labeled with the year of creation (49 for 1949), the type of work (B for a *buco*, for example), and the number of that work in the sequence that it was made in that year (1 for the first one).
4. It is unclear if Fontana himself took the image or if a photographer did.
5. Fontana produced *buchi* in two periods: 1949–1953 and 1955–1968.
6. In collaboration with fellow artists Jorge Romero Brest and Jorge Larco (Gottschaller 2008: 23).

7. Signatories were Bernardo and Pable Arias, Enrique Benito, César Bernal, Rodolfo Burgos, Horacio Cazenueve, Luis Coli, Marcos Fridman, Alfredo Hansen, and Jorge Rocamonte (Gottschaller 2008: 24).

8. After the *Manifesto Blanco* of 1946 came the following: *Primo Manifesto dello Spazialismo* [First Spatial Manifesto] (1947); *Secondo Manifesto dello Spazialismo* [Second Spatial Manifesto] (March 1948); *Terzo Manifesto dello Spazialismo* [Third Spatial Manifesto] (April 1950); *Proposta di un Regalamento del Movimento Spaziale* [Proposal for a Set of Rules of the Spatial Movement] (March 1950); *Manifesto Tecnico dello Spazialismo* [Technical Manifesto of Spazialismo] (1951); the *Manifesto del Movimento Spazialista per la Televisione* [Manifesto of the Spatialist Movement for Television] (1952).

9. Signatories were Anton Giulio Ambrosiani, Albero Burri, Roberto Crippa, Mario Deluigi, Bruno De Toffoli, Gianni Dova, Enrico Donati, Lucio Fontana, Giancarlo Carozzi, Virgilio Guidi, Beniamino Joppolo, Guido La Regina, Milena Milani, Dilani, Berto Morucchio, Cesare Peverelli, Tancredi (Parmeggianai), and Vinicio Vinello.

10. It is unlikely that the sequence described here (which I have based on a number of accounts, such as those by Pia Gottschaller) was used in every case, and the reader should not assume that the experts I cite and from whose work I have drawn inspiration would agree with my reconstructed set of actions.

CHAPTER 9

1. The move to the relativistic, egocentric, body-oriented is the argument I made in *Prehistoric Figurines* (Bailey 2005b) as well in subsequent articles and chapters (e.g., Bailey 2008, 2012): that one of the unintended, but fundamental, consequences of making, decorating, handling, arranging, imagining with, displaying, breaking, and discarding miniature, three-dimensional representations of the human body (i.e., Neolithic figurines) was the emergence of a corporeality in prehistoric, ancient, and historic Europe. In Levinson's terms we could also call this a shift away from an allocentric (probably absolute) understanding of the world to a relative one.

APPENDIX NOTES

1. For more on pond barrows, see Grinsell (1941: 89; 1953: 23), Ashbee (1960: 25–26), and Colt Hoare (1810: 22) and see the excellent review in Ashbee et al. (1989c: 4–8) and Ashbee (1989d).

2. Plaster casts made from the latex originals are stored in the Salisbury and South Wiltshire Museum.

Bibliography

Abbe, Mary. 1994a. Bloody performance draws criticism. *Star Tribune* (Minneapolis) March 24: 1A.

Abbe, Mary. 1994b. Walker seems surprised at reaction to mutilation show. *Star Tribune* (Minneapolis) March 29: 1E.

Abbe, Mary. 1994c. Walker survives dispute, remains on NEA grant list. *Star Tribune* (Minneapolis) July 25: 1B.

Alhazen, I. 1030. [Ibn Al-Haytham] [1989]. Book of optics. In A. I. Sabra (ed. and trans.), *The Optics of Ibn al-Haytham* (Vol. 1), 123–145. London: Warburg Institute. (Original work published ca. 1030.)

Alviani, Getulio. 2007. Interview with the author. Transcript of a taped interview. Milan, July 20.

Ambrosini, Burn, Crippa, Delia gi, De Toffoli, Donati, Dova, Fontana, Giancarozzi, Guidi, Joppolo, La Regina, Milena Milani, Morucchio, Peverelli, and Tancredi, Vianello. 1952. *Manifesto del Movimento Spaziale per la Televisione* [Manifesto of the Spatialist Movement for Television] (trans. Stephen Sartarelli). Reprinted in Germano Celant (ed) *The Italian Metamorphosis*, 716–717. New York: Guggenheim and Abrams.

Ameka, Felix K. and Essegbey, James. 2007. Cut and break verbs in Ewe and the causative alternation construction. *Cognitive Linguistics* 18(2): 241–250.

Antwerp. 1977. Interview with Gordon Matta-Clark, Antwerp, September 1977. In *Gordon Matta-Clark*. Antwerp: International Culutreel Centrum. Reprinted in Gloria Moure (ed) *Gordon Matta-Clark: Works and Collected Writings*, 249–257. Madrid: Ediciones Polígrafa.

Arias, Bernardo, Cazeneuve, Horacio, Ridman, Marcos, Arias, Pablo, Burgos, Rodolfo, Benio, Enrique, Bernal, César, Coll, Luis, Hansen, Alfredo and Rocamonte, Jorge. 1946 [1971]. *Manifesto Blanco*. (trans. Guido Ballo). In Guido Ballo (ed) *Lucio Fontana*, 185–189. New York: Praeger.

Armour-Chelu, Miranda. 1998a. The animal bone. In Francis Pryor (ed) *Etton: Excavations at a Neolithic Causewayed Enclosure near Maxey, Cambridgeshire, 1982–7*, 273–288. London: English Heritage.

Armour-Chelu, Miranda. 1998b. The human bone. In Francis Pryor (ed.) *Etton: Excavations at a Neolithic Causewayed Enclosure near Maxey, Cambridgeshire, 1982–7*, 271–272. London: English Heritage.

Ashbee, Paul. 1960. *The Bronze Age Round Barrows in Britain*. London: Littlehampton.

Ashbee, Paul. 1963. The Wilsford shaft. *Antiquity* 37: 116–120.

Ashbee, Paul. 1989a. Archaeological conclusions. In Paul Ashbee, Martin Bell, and Edwina Proudfoot (eds.) *Wilsford Shaft: Excavations 1960–62*, 133–138. London: English Heritage.

Ashbee, Paul. 1989b. The artefacts from the shaft's lower infill. In Paul Ashbee, Martin Bell, and Edwina Proudfoot (eds.) *Wilsford Shaft: Excavations 1960–62*, 43–67. London: English Heritage.

Ashbee, Paul. 1989c. The excavation's plant and its use. In Paul Ashbee, Martin Bell, and Edwina Proudfoot (eds.) *Wilsford Shaft: Excavations 1960–62*, 144–146. London: English Heritage.

Ashbee, Paul. 1989d. Pond barrows in Wiltshire and Dorset. In Paul Ashbee, Martin Bell, and Edwina Proudfoot (eds.) *Wilsford Shaft: Excavations 1960–62*, 139–142. London: English Heritage.

Ashbee, Paul. 1989e. The shaft, its infill and character. In Paul Ashbee, Martin Bell, and Edwina Proudfoot (eds.) *Wilsford Shaft: Excavations 1960–62*, 26–36. London: English Heritage.

Ashbee, Paul, Bell, Martin, and Proudfoot, Edwina. 1989a. Appendix C. Photographs taken on August 28, 1962. In Paul Ashbee, Martin Bell, and Edwina Proudfoot (eds.) *Wilsford Shaft: Excavations 1960–62*, 142. London: Historic Buildings and Monument Commission for England.

Ashbee, Paul, Bell, Martin and Proudfoot, Edwina. 1989b. Appendix D. Latex impressions. In Paul Ashbee, Martin Bell, and Edwina Proudfoot (eds.) *Wilsford Shaft: Excavations 1960–62*, 144. London: Historic Buildings and Monument Commission for England.

Ashbee, Paul, Bell, Martin, and Proudfoot, Edwina. 1989c. General introduction. Paul Ashbee, Martin Bell, and Edwina Proudfoot (eds.) *Wilsford Shaft: Excavations 1960–62*, 1–14. London: Historic Buildings and Monument Commission for England.

Ashbee, Paul, Bell, Martin, and Proudfoot, Edwina. 1989d. *Wilsford Shaft: Excavations 1960–62*. London: Historic Buildings and Monument Commission for England.

Athey, Ron. 1997. Dissections: sex work: a breakdown. *Honcho* April: 70–72.

Athey, Ron. 2013. Deliverance: the "Torture Trilogy" in retrospect. In Dominic Johnson (ed.) *Pleading in the Blood: The Art and Performances of Ron Athey*, 100–109. Chicago: University of Chicago Press and Intellect.

Attlee, James. 2003a. Flame, time and the elements. In James Attlee and Lisa Le Fevre (eds.) *Gordon Matta-Clark: The Space Between*, 69–89. Tucson: Nazraeli Press.

Attlee, James. 2003b. In other words . . . Matta-Clark and language. In James Attlee and Lisa Le Fevre (eds.) *Gordon Matta-Clark: The Space Between*, 45–53. Tucson: Nazraeli Press.

Attlee, James. 2003c. The Matta-Clark situation. In James Attlee and Lisa Le Fevre (eds.) *Gordon Matta-Clark: The Space Between*, 25–44. Tucson: Nazraeli Press.

Attlee, James. 2003d. Skyhooks and dragon buildings about hot air—what can it do. In James Attlee and Lisa Le Fevre (eds.) *Gordon Matta-Clark: The Space Between*, 55–67. Tucson: Nazraeli Press.

Attlee, James. 2007. Towards anarchitecture: Gordon Matta-Clark and Le Corbusier. *Tate Papers* 7: 1–17.

Attlee, James and Le Feuvre, Lisa (eds.). 2003. *Gordon Matta-Clark: The Space Between*. Tucson: Nazraeli Press.

Attneave, Fred. 1954. Some informational aspects of visual perception. *Psychological Review* 61: 183–193.

Augusta Chronicle. 1997. Exhibit gets bad reviews. *The Augusta Chronicle* (July) 23: 1.

Bailey, Doug. 1990. The living house: signifying continuity. In Ross Samson (ed.) *The Social Archaeology of Houses*, 19–48. Edinburgh: Edinburgh University Press.

Bailey, Doug. 1996. The life, times and works of House 59 from the Ovcharovo tell, Bulgaria. In Tim Darvill and Julian Thomas (eds.) *Neolithic Houses in Northwest Europe and Beyond*, 143–156. Oxford: Oxbow.

Bailey, Doug. 1999a. The built environment: pit-huts and houses in the Neolithic. *Documenta Praehistorica* 26: 153–162.

Bailey, Doug. 1999b. What is a tell? Spatial, temporal and social parameters. In Joanna Brück and Melissa Goodman (eds.) *Making Places in the Prehistoric World*, 94–111. London: UCL Press.

Bailey, Doug. 2000. *Balkan Prehistory: Incorporation, Exclusion, and Identity*. London: Routledge.

Bailey, Doug. 2005a. Beyond the meaning of Neolithic houses: specific objects and serial repetition. In Doug Bailey, Alasdair Whittle, and Vicki Cummings (eds.) *(un)settling the Neolithic*, 95–106. Oxford: Oxbow.

Bailey, Doug. 2005b. *Prehistoric Figurines: Representation and Corporeality in the Neolithic*. London: Routledge.

Bailey, Doug. 2008. The corporeal politics of being in the Neolithic. In J. Robb and D. Borić (eds.) *Past Bodies*, 9–18. Oxford: Oxbow.

Bailey, Doug. 2012. Figurines, corporeality and the origins of gender. In D. Bolger (ed.) *Companion to Gender Prehistory*, 244–264. Oxford: John Wiley.

Bailey, Doug. 2013. Cutting the earth/cutting the body. In A. Alfredo González-Ruibal (ed.) *Reclaiming Archaeology: Beyond the Tropes of Modernity*, 337–345. London: Routledge.

Bailey, Doug. 2014. Art//archaeology//art: letting-go beyond. In Ian Russell and Andrew Cochrane (eds.) *Art and Archaeology: Collaborations, Conversations, Criticisms*, 231–250. New York: Springer-Kluwer.

Bailey, Doug. 2017a. Disartulate-repurpose-disrupt: art/archaeology. *Cambridge Archaeological Journal* 27(4): 691–701.

Bailey, Doug. 2017b. Art/archaeology what value artistic-archaeological collaboration? *Journal of Contemporary Archaeology* 4(2): 246–256.

Bailey, Doug, Andreescu, Radian, Howard, Andy, Macklin, Mark, and Mills, Stephen. 2002. Alluvial landscapes in the temperate Balkan Neolithic: transfers to tells. *Antiquity* 76: 349–355.

Bailey, Doug, Zambelli, Jean, and Cochrane, Andrew. 2010. *Unearthed: A Comparative Study of Jōmon Dogū and Balkan Figurines*. Norwich: Sainsbury Center for Visual Arts.

Bălăşescu, Adrian. 2014. Neolithic fauna from Măgura "Buduiasca" (Vădastra Culture). *Buletinul Muzeului Judeţean Teleorman. Seria Arheologie* 6: 19–30.

Bălăşescu, Adrian, Radu, Valentine, and Moise, Dragoş. 2005. *Omul di Mediul Animal între Milenile VII–IV î.e.n. la Dunărea de Jos*. Muzeul National de Istorie României, Seria Cercetări Pluridisciplinare. Târgovişte: Editura Cetatea de Scaun.

Balasse, Marie, Bălăşescu, Adrian, Hedges, Robert, Bogaard, Amy, Walker, Angela, Ughetto-Monfrin, Joël, Mirea, Pavel, Andreescu, Radian, Mills, Stephen, and Bailey, Doug. 2012. Early herding at Măgura *Buduiasca* (6th mil BC, Southern Romania): integrating zooarchaeology, palaeobotany and stable isotope analyses. Unpublished paper presented to the Department of Archaeology, Cambridge University.

Balasse, Marie, Bălăşescu, Adrian, Janzen, Anneke, Ughetto-Monfrin, Joel, Mirea, Pavel, and Andreescu, Radian. 2013. Early herding at Măgura-Boldul lui Moş Iănuş (early sixth millennium BC, Romania): environments and seasonality from stable isotope analysis. *European Journal of Archaeology* 16: 221–246.

Ballo, Guido. 1971. *Lucio Fontana*. Westport, CT: Praeger.

Bamford, Helen. 1985. *Briar Hill. Northampton*. Northampton: Northants Development Corporation.

Barenholtz, Elan and Feldman, Jacob. 2003. Visual comparisons within and between object parts: Evidence for a single-part superiority effect. *Vision Research* 43: 1655–1666.

Barenholtz, Elan and Feldman, Jacob. 2006. Determination of visual figure and ground in dynamically deforming shapes. *Cognition* 101: 530–544.

Barenholtz, Elan, Cohen, Elias H., Feldman, Jacob, and Singh, Manish. 2003. Detection of change in shape: an advantage for concavities. *Cognition* 89: 1–9.

Barliant, Claire. 2012. 112 Green Street. *The Paris Review* (July 25). https://www.theparisreview.org/blog/2012/07/25/112-greene-street/ (accessed June 7, 2014).

Barrett, John C. 1991. Synthesis. In John Barrett, Richard Bradley, and Martin Green (eds.) *Landscape, Monuments and Society: The Prehistory of Cranborne Chase*, 223–226. Cambridge: Cambridge University Press.

Barrett, John C. 1994a. Defining domestic space in the Bronze Age of southern Britain. In Mike Parker Pearson and Colin Richards (eds.) *Architecture and Order: Approaches to Social Space*, 87–97. London: Routledge.

Barrett, John C. 1994b. *Fragments from Antiquity: An Archaeology of Social Life in Britain, 2900–1200 BC*. Oxford: Blackwell.

Barrett, John C., Bradley, Richard, and Green, Martin. 1991. *Landscape, Monuments and Society: The Prehistory of Cranbourne Chase.* Cambridge: Cambridge University Press.

Bataille, Georges. 1930. L'art primitif. *Documents* 7: 389–397.

BCFE 1994. *Boston Coalition for Freedom of Expression Quarterly Report.* Boston: Boston Coalition for Freedom of Expression.

Béar, Liza. 1974. Gordon Matta-Clark: Splitting the Humphrey Street building. *Avalanche* (December): 34–37. Reprinted as Gordon Matta-Clark: Splitting the Humphrey Street Building, an Interview by Liza Béar, May 1974, in Gloria Moure (ed.) 2006. *Gordon Matta-Clark. Works and Collected Writings,* 165–177. Madrid: Ediciones Polígrafa.

Béar, Liza. 1976. Gordon Matta-Clark: dilemmas. A radio interview. WBAI-FM. New York. In Corinne Diserens (ed.) *Gordon Matta-Clark,* 175–177. New York: Phaidon.

Bell, Martin. 1989. Environmental conclusions. In Paul Ashbee, Martin Bell, and Edwina Proudfoot (eds.) *Wilsford Shaft: Excavations 1960–62,* 128–132. London: English Heritage.

Bertamini, Marco. 2001. The importance of being convex: An advantage for convexity when judging position. *Perception* 30: 1295–1310.

Bertamini, Marco. 2006. Who owns the contour of a visual hole. *Perception* 35: 883–894.

Bertamini, Marco. 2008. Detection of convexity and concavity in context. *Journal of Experimental Psychology: Human Perception and Performance* 34: 775–789.

Bertamini, Marco and Croucher, Camilla J. 2003. The shape of holes. *Cognition* 87: 33–54.

Bertamini, Marco and Farrant, Tracy. 2005. Detection of change in shape and its relation to part structure. *Acta Psychologica* 120: 35–54.

Binford, Lewis. 1983. *Working at Archaeology.* New York: Academic.

Blocker, Jane. 2004. *What the Body Cost: Desire, History and Performance.* Minneapolis: University of Minnesota Press.

Bloom, Paul. 2000. *How Children Learn the Meaning of Words.* Cambridge, MA: MIT Press.

Bohnemeyer, Jürgen. 2007. Morpholexical transparency and the argument structure of verbs of cutting and breaking. *Cognitive Linguistics* 18(2): 153–178.

Bohnemeyer, Jürgen and Brown, Penelope. 2007. Standing divided: dispositional verbs and locative predications in two Mayan languages. In Felix K. Ameka and Stephen C. Levinson (eds.) *Linguistics* 45(5/6): 1105–1151.

Bohnemeyer, Jürgen, Bowerman, Melissa, and Brown, Penelope. 2001. Cut and break clips. In Stephen C. Levinson and N. J. Enfield (eds.) *Field Manual 2001, Language and Cognition Group, Max Planck Institute for Psycholinguistics,* 90–96. Nijmegen: Max Planck Institute.

Bowerman, Melissa and Choi, Soonja. 2001. Shaping meanings for language: Universal and language-specific in the acquisition of spatial semantic categories.

In Melissa Bowerman and Stephen C. Levinson (eds.) *Language Acquisition and Conceptual Development*, 475–511. Cambridge: Cambridge University Press.

Bradley, Richard. 1975. Maumbury Rings, Dorchester: the excavations of 1908–13. *Archaeologia* 105: 1–97.

Bradley, Richard. 1990. *The Passage of Arms*. Cambridge: Cambridge University Press.

Bradley, Richard. 1991. Review of Paul Ashbee, Martin Bell, and Edwina Proudfoot. 1989. *Wilsford Shaft: Excavations 1960–61* (London: Historic Buildings and Monuments Commission for England) *Antiquity* 57(2): 231.

Bradley, Richard, Over, L., Startin, Dudley W.A., and Weng, R. 1978. The excavation of a Neolithic site at Cannon Hill, Maidenhead, Berkshire, 1974–75. *Berkshire Archaeological Journal* 68: 5–19.

Brambilla Barcilon, Pinin and Matalon, Stella. 1978. Techniques employees par le peintre Lucio Fontana et problèmes de conservation concernant son oeuvre. In *5éme Reunion Triennale, Zagreb*, 78/6/3/1–7. Paris: Comité pour la Conservation, International Council of Museums.

Bronić, I. Krajcar and Minichreiter, Kornelija. 2007. C14 dating of the early Neolithic settlement Galovo near Slavonski Brod in Northern Croatia. *Nuclear Instruments and Methods in Physics Research A* 580: 714–716.

Brooks, Alan and Agate, Elizabeth. 1975. *Hedging: A Practical Conservation Handbook*. Wallingford: British Trust for Conservation Volunteers.

Brophy, Kenneth and Noble, Gordon. 2012. Within and beyond pits: deposition in lowland Scotland. In Hugo Anderson-Whymark and Julian Thomas (eds.) *Regional Perspectives on Neolithic Pit Deposition: Beyond the Mundane*, 63–76. Oxford: Oxbow.

Brown, Penelope. 2007. "She had just cut/broken off her head": cutting and breaking verbs in Tzeltal. *Cognitive Linguistics* 18: 319–330.

Bruce, Labruce. 2013. Athey-ism, collaboration, and *Hustler White*. In Dominic Johnson (ed.) *Pleading in the Blood: The Art and Performances of Ron Athey*, 118–123. Chicago: University of Chicago Press and Intellect.

Brück, Joanna. 1999. Houses, lifecycles and deposition on Middle Bronze Age settlements in Southern England. *Proceedings of the Prehistoric Society* 65: 145–166.

Brück, Joanna. 2000. Settlement, landscape and social identity: the Early-Middle Bronze Age transition in Wessex, Sussex and the Thames Valley. *Oxford Journal of Archaeology* 19(3): 273–300.

Brück, Joanna. 2006. Fragmentation, personhood and the social construction of technology in Middle and Late Bronze Age Britain. *Cambridge Archaeological Journal* 16(3): 297–315.

Burl, Aubrey. 1981. *Rites of the Gods*. London: Dent.

Burstow, George P. and Holleyman, George A. 1957. Late Bronze Age settlement on Itford Hill, Sussex. *Proceedings of the Prehistoric Society* 23: 167–212.

Campiglio, Paolo. 1999. *Lucio Fontana: Lettere 1919–1968* (with text by Loredana Parmesani). Milan: Skira.

Carlson, Marvin. 1996. *Performance: A Critical Introduction*. London: Routledge.

Carlson-Radvansky, Laura A. and Irwin, David. A. 1993. Frames of reference in vision and language: where is above? *Cognition* 46: 224–344.

Carr, Cynthia. 1994. Washed in the blood: congress has a new scapegoat. *Village Voice* July 5: 16.

Casati, Roberto and Varzi, Achille. 1994. *Holes and Other Superficialities*. Cambridge, MA: MIT.

Casati, Roberto and Varzi, Achille. 2004. Counting the holes. *Australasian Journal of Philosophy* 82: 23–27.

Casati, Roberto and Varzi, Achille. 2012. Holes. In Edward N. Zalta (ed.) *The Stanford Encyclopedia of Philosophy* (Winter 2012 Edition). http://plato.stanford.edu/archives/win2012/entries/holes/ (accessed February 10, 2017).

Celant, Gerald. 1994. *The Italian Metamorphosis*. New York: Guggenheim and Abrams.

Challands, Adrian. 1998. The magnetic susceptibility survey. In Francis Pryor (ed.) *Etton: Excavations at a Neolithic Causewayed Enclosure near Maxey, Cambridgeshire, 1982–7*, 73–77. London: English Heritage.

Chapman, John. 1990. Social inequality on Bulgarian tells and the Varna problem. In Ross Samson (ed.) *The Social Archaeology of Houses*, 49–92. Edinburgh: Edinburgh University Press.

Chapman, John. 1999. Where are the missing parts? A study of artefact fragmentation. *Pamatky Archeologicke* 90: 5–22.

Chapman, John. 2000a. *Fragmentation in Archaeology: People, Places and Broken Objects in the Prehistory of Southeastern Europe*. London: Routledge.

Chapman. John. 2000b. Pit-digging and structured deposition in the Neolithic and Copper Age. *Proceedings of the Prehistoric Society* 66: 61–87.

Chapman, John. 2000c. "Rubbish-dumps" or "places of deposition"? Neolithic and Copper Age settlements in Central and Eastern Europe. In Anna Ritchie (ed.) *Neolithic Orkney in its European Context*, 347–362. Cambridge: McDonald Institute for Archaeology Research.

Chapman, John and Gaydarska, Bisserka. 2007. *Parts and Wholes: Fragmentation in Prehistoric Context*. Oxford: Oxbow.

Chen, Jidong. 2007. "He cut-break the rope": encoding and categorizing cutting and breaking events in Mandarin. *Cognitive Linguistics* 18(2): 273–285.

Childe, V. Gordon. 1925. *The Dawn of European Civilization*. London: Kegan Paul.

Childe, V. Gordon. 1929. *The Danube in Prehistory*. London: Kegan Paul.

Clark, Eve V. 1976. Universal categories: on the semantics of classifiers and children's early word meanings. In Alphonse Juilland (ed.) *Linguistic Studies Offered to Joseph Greenberg on the Occasion of His Sixtieth Birthday*, 449–462. Saratoga, CA: Anma Libri.

Clark, Herb H. 1973. Space, time, semantics, and the child. In Timothy E. Moore (ed.) *Cognitive Development and the Acquisition of Language*, 27–64. New York, NY: Academic Press.

Clarke, Grahame and Piggott, Stuart. 1965. *Prehistoric Societies*. New York: Alfred Knopf.

Clarke, Grahame, Higgs, Eric S., and Longworth, Ian H. 1960. Excavations at the Neolithic site of Hurst Fen, Mildenhall, Suffolk, 1954, 1957 and 1958. *Proceedings of the Prehistoric Society* 26: 202–245.

Cohen, Elias H., Barenholtz, Elan, Singh, Manish, and Feldman, Jacob. 2005. What change detection tells us about the visual representation of shape. *Journal of Vision* 5(4): 3, 313–321.

Coles, John M. and Harding, Anthony F. 1979. *The Bronze Age in Europe*. London: Routledge.

Comşa, Evgen. 1959. La Civilisation Criş sur le territoire de la R. P. Roumaine. *Acta Archeologica Charpatica* 1(2): 173–184.

Comşa, Evgen. 1994. Aşezarea Starčevo-Criş de la Dulceanca. *Analele Banatului* 3: 13–40.

Congressional Record. 1994. Cliff Stearns in Congressional Record 140.81 House, 23 June 1994. http://webarchive.loc.gov/congressional-record/20160315160251/ http://thomas.loc.gov/cgi-bin/query/B?r103:@FIELD(FLD003+h)+@ FIELD(DDATE+19940623) (accessed October 14, 2015).

Crispolti, Enrico. 1998. Spatialism and Informel. The fifties. In Enrico Crispolti and Rosella Siligato (eds.) *Lucio Fontana*, 123–145. Rome: Palazzo delle Esposizioni.

Crispolti, Enrico. 2006. *Lucio Fontana: Catalogo Ragionato di Sculture, Dipinti, Ambientazioni*. Milan: Skira.

Crispolti, Enrico and Van der Marck, Jan. 1974. *Lucio Fontana: Catalogue Raisonné* (Volumes 1 and 2). Brussels: La Connaissance, Exclusivité Weber.

Crow, Thomas. 2003. Gordon Matta-Clark. In Corinne Diserens (ed.) *Gordon Matta-Clark*, 7–132. New York: Phaidon.

Darvill, Tim. 2012. Sounds from the underground: Neolithic ritual pits and pit-clusters on the Isle of Man and beyond. In Hugo Anderson-Whymark and Julian Thomas (eds.) *Regional Perspectives on Neolithic Pit Deposition: Beyond the Mundane*, 30–42. Oxford: Oxbow.

Deleuze, Giles. 1989. *Cinéma II: l'Image-temps* [The Time-Image] (trans. Hugh Tomlinson and Robert Galtea). New York: Continuum.

Deleuze, Giles. 1996. *Francis Bacon: Logique de la Sensation*. Paris: Éditions de la Différence.

De Winter, Joeri and Wagemans, Johan. 2004. Contour-based object identification and segmentation: stimuli, norms and data, and software tools. *Behavior Research Methods, Instruments and Computers* 36(4): 604–624.

De Winter, Joeri and Wagemans, Johan. 2006. Segmentation of object outlines into parts: a large-scale integrative study. *Cognition* 99: 275–325.

Diserens, Corinne. 1997. Gordon Matta-Clark: the reel world. Unpublished paper given at *Documenta X*. Kassel, Germany.

Diserens, Corinne. 2003. Preface. In Corinne Diserens (ed.) *Gordon Matta-Clark*, 6. New York: Phaidon.

Dolin, Bryan. 2005. Matta's lucid landscape. In Thomas Mical (ed.) *Surrealism and Architecture*, 53–59. London: Routledge.

Doyle, Jennifer. 2013. Sex with Ron. In Dominic Johnson (ed.) *Pleading in the Blood: The Art and Performances of Ron Athey*, 124–129. Chicago: University of Chicago Press and Intellect.

Drewett, Peter. 1982. Later Bronze Age downland economy and excavations at Black Patch, Sussex. *Archaeological Journal* 136: 3–11.

Edmonds, Mark. 1993. Interpreting causewayed enclosures in the past and the present. In Christopen Tilley (ed.) *Interpretive Archaeology*, 99–142. London: Berg.

Edmonds, Mark. 1998. Polished stone axes and associated artefacts. In Francis Pryor (ed.) *Etton: Excavations at a Neolithic Causewayed Enclosure near Maxey, Cambridgeshire, 1982–7*, 260–267. London: English Heritage.

Edmonds, Mark. 1999. *Ancestral Geographies of the Neolithic: Landscape, Monuments and Memory*. London: Routledge.

Edwards, Ben. 2012. Social structures: pits and depositional practice in Neolithic Northumberland. In H. Anderson-Whymark and J. Thomas (eds.) *Regional Perspectives on Neolithic Pit Deposition: Beyond the Mundane*, 77–99. Oxford: Oxbow.

Essegbey, James. 2007. Cut and break verbs in Sranan. *Cognitive Linguistics* 18(2): 231–240.

Evans, Chris. 1988a. Acts of enclosure: a consideration of concentrically organized enclosures. In John Barrett and Ian A. Kinnes (eds.) *The Archaeology of Context in the Neolithic and Bronze Age: Recent Trends*, 65–79. Sheffield: Department of Archaeology, University of Sheffield.

Evans, Chris. 1988b. Monuments and analogy: the interpretation of causewayed enclosures. In Colin Burgess, Peter Topping, Claude Mordant, and Margaret Maddison (eds.) *Enclosures and Defenses in the Neolithic of Western Europe*, 47–74. Oxford: British Archaeological Reports.

Evans, Chris, Rouse, Amanda J., and Sharples, Niall. 1988. The landscape setting of causewayed camps: recent work on the Maiden Castle enclosure. In John Barrett and Ian A. Kinnes (eds.) *The Archaeology of Context in the Neolithic and Bronze Age: Recent Trend*, 73–84. Sheffield: Department of Archaeology, University of Sheffield.

Evenson, Norma. 1973. The assassination of Les Halles. *Journal of the Society of Architectural Historians* 32(4): 308–315.

Evin, Allowen, Flink, Linus Girdlan, Bălăşescu, Adrian, Popovic, Dragomir, Andreescu, Radian, Bailey, Doug, Mirea, Pavel, Lazăr, Cătălin, Boroneanţ, Adina, Bonsall, Clive, Vidardottir, Una Strand, Brehard, Stéphanie, Tresset, Anne, Cucchi, Thomas, Larson, Gregar, and Dobney, Keith. 2015. Unravelling the complexity of domestication: a case study using morphometrics and ancient

DNA analyses of archaeological pigs from Romania. *Philosophical Transactions of the Royal Society B* 370: 1–7.

Feldman, Jacob and Singh, Manish. 2005. Information along contours and object boundaries. *Psychological Review* 112(1): 243–252.

Fiore, Jessamyn. 2012. *112 Greene Street: The Early Years (1970–1974)*. New York: Radius.

Flahutez, Fabrice. 2004. Biologie cellulaire et fonctions mathématiques dans l'œuvre de Roberto Matta. *Art Présence* 51: 32–37.

Fontana, Lucio. 1951. *Manifesto Technico dello Spazialismo: Noi Continuiamo l'Evoluzione del Mezzo dell'artt* [Technical Manifesto for Spazialism: We Continue the Evolution of the Medium of Art] (trans. Stephen Sartarelli) reprinted in Celent, Germano. 1994. *The Italian Metamorphosis*, 717–718. New York: Guggenheim and Abrams.

Fossati, Paolo (ed.). 1973. *Ugo Mulas: La Fotografia*. Turin: Einaudi Letteratura.

Foster, Sally. 1989. Analysis of spatial patterns in buildings (access analysis) as an insight into social structure: examples from the Scottish Atlantic Iron Age. *Antiquity* 63: 40–50.

French, Charles. 1998. Soils and sediments. In Francis Pryor (ed.) *Etton: Excavations at a Neolithic Causewayed Enclosure near Maxey, Cambridgeshire, 1982–7*, 311–332. London: English Heritage.

Gaby, Alice. 2007. Describing cutting and breaking events in Kuuk Thaayorre. *Cognitive Linguistics* 18(2): 263–272.

Gaffney, Chris, Gaffney, Vince, Neubauer, Wolfgang, Baldwin, Eamonn, Chapman, Henry, Garwood, Paul, Moulden, Helen, Sparrow, Tom, Bates, Richard, Löcker, Klaus, Hinterleitner, Alois, Trinks, Immo, Nau, Erich, Zitz, Thomas, Floery, Sebastian, Verhoeven, Geert, and Doneus, Michael. 2012. The Stonehenge Hidden Landscapes Project. *Archaeological Prospection* 19(2): 147–155.

Gamble, Clive. 1998. Palaeolithic society and the release from proximity: a network approach to intimate relations. *World Archaeology* 29: 426–449.

Gamble, Clive. 1999. *The Palaeolithic Societies of Europe*. Cambridge: Cambridge University Press.

Garrow, Duncan. 2006. *Pits, Settlement and Deposition During the Neolithic and Early Bronze Age in East Anglia*. Oxford: British Archaeological Reports.

Garrow, Duncan. 2012. Odd deposits and average practice: a critical history of the concept of structured deposition. *Archaeological Dialogues* 19(2): 85–115.

Gelfand, Lou. 1994. NEA joins fray over report on Athey performance. *Star Tribune* (Minneapolis) June 26: 23A.

Gibson, Bradley S. 1994. Visual attention and objects: one versus two or convex versus concave? *Journal of Experimental Psychology: Human Perception and Performance* 20: 203–207.

Gibson, James J. 1979. *The Ecological Approach to Visual Perception*. Boston: Houghton Mifflin.

Gleitman, Lila. 1990. The structural sources of verb meanings. *Language Acquisition* 1: 3–55.

Gottschaller, Pia. 2008. *The Act of Creating Space: Lucio Fontana*. Munich: Siegl.

Gottschaller, Pia. 2012. *Lucio Fontana: The Artist's Materials*. Los Angeles: Getty Museum.

Graham, Dan. 1985. Gordon Matta-Clark. *Kunstforum International* Oct.–Nov.: 114–119. Reprinted in Caroline Diserens (ed.) 2003. *Gordon Matta-Clark*, 199–203. New York: Phaidon.

Greenfield, Haskel and Jongsma, Tina. 2008. Sedentary pastoral gatherers in the early Neolithic: architectural, botanical, and zoological evidence for mobile economies from Foeni-Salaş, south-west Romania. In Doug Bailey, Alasdair Whittle, and Daniela Hofmann (eds.) *Living Well Together? Settlement and Materiality in the Neolithic of South-East and Central* Europe, 108–130. Oxford: Oxbow.

Greenfield, Haskel and Jongsma, Tina. 2014. Subsistence and settlement in the early Neolithic of temperate SE Europe: a view from Blagotin, Serbia. *Archaeologia Bulgarica* 18(1): 1–33.

Grigson, Caroline. 1989. Large mammals. In Paul Ashbee, Martin Bell, and Edwina Proudfoot (eds.) *Wilsford Shaft: Excavations 1960–62*, 106–120. London: English Heritage.

Grinsell, Leslie. 1941. The Bronze Age round barrows of Wessex. *Proceedings of the Prehistoric Society* 7: 73–113.

Grinsell, Leslie. 1953. *The Ancient Round Barrows of England* (2nd edition). London: Methuen.

Guerssel, Mohamed, Hale, Kenneth, Laughren, Mary, Levin, Beth, and White Eagle, Josie. 1985. A crosslinguistic study of transitivity alternations. In William H. Eilfort, Paul D. Kroeber, and Karen L. Peterson (eds.) *Papers from the Parasession on Causatives and Agentivity at the 21st Regional Meeting*, 48–63. Chicago: Chicago, Linguistic Society.

Gund, Catherine. 2013. There are so many ways to say Halleluja! In Dominic Johnson (ed.) *Pleading in the Blood: The Art and Performances of Ron Athey*, 55–63. Chicago: University of Chicago Press and Intellect.

Gurney, David and Pryor, Francis. 1998. The phosphate surveys. In Francis Pryor (ed.) *Etton: Excavations at a Neolithic Causewayed Enclosure Near Maxey, Cambridgeshire, 1982–7*, 77–79. London: English Heritage.

Hägerstrand, Torsten. 1976. Geography and the study of the interaction between nature and society. *Geoforum* 7: 329–334.

Hamilton, Sue, Whitehouse, Ruth, Brown, Keri, Combes, Pamela, Herring, Edward, and Thomas, Mike S. 2006. Phenomenology in practice: towards a phenomenology for a "subjective" approach. *European Journal of Archaeology* 9(1): 31–71.

Heal, Veryan. 1989. Some conserved wooden artefacts. In Paul Ashbee, Martin Bell, and Edwina Proudfoot (eds.) *Wilsford Shaft: Excavations 1960–62*, 60–62. London: English Heritage.

Healy, Francis. 2004. Hambledon Hill and its implications. In Ros Cleal and Joshua Pollard (eds.) *Monuments and Material Culture. Papers in Honour of an Avebury Archaeologist: Isobel Smith*, 15–38. East Knoyle: Hobnob.

Heathfield, Adrian. 2013. Illicit transit. In Dominic Johnson (ed.) *Pleading in the Blood: The Art and Performances of Ron Athey*, 206–222. Chicago: University of Chicago Press and Intellect.

Henderson, Julian. 1989. Human bones. In Paul Ashbee, Martin Bell, and Edwina Proudfoot (eds.) *Wilsford Shaft: Excavations 1960–62*, 126–127. London: English Heritage.

Hertz, Betti-Sue. 2006. Double triangle: the madness of the unexpected. In Briony Fer, Betti-Sue Hertz, Justo Pastor Mellado, and Anthony Vidler (eds.) *Transmission: The Art of Matta and Gordon Matta-Clark*, 11–23. San Diego: San Diego Museum of Art.

Hillier, Bill and Hanson, Julienne. 1984. *The Social Logic of Space*. Cambridge: Cambridge University Press.

Hoare, Richard Colt. 1810. *The Ancient History of South Wiltshire*. London: William Miller.

Hoffman, Donald D. and Richards, Whitman. 1984. Parts of cognition. *Cognition* 18: 65–96.

Hoffman, Donald D. and Singh, Manish. 1997. Valence of visual parts. *Cognition* 63: 29–78.

Hovagimyan, Gerard H. n.d. *Gordon Matta-Clark (a Remembrance)*. Unpublished manuscript, https://www.academia.edu/6408483/Gordon_Matta-Clark_A_Remembrance (accessed November 22, 2016).

Howard, Andy, Macklin, Mark, Bailey, Doug, Mills, Stephen, and Andresscu, Radian. 2004. Late-glacial and Holocene river development in the Teleorman Valley on the southern Romanian Plain. *Journal of Quaternary Science* 19(3): 271–280.

Hulleman, Johan and Olivers, Christian N. L. 2007. Concavities count for less in symmetry perception. *Psychonomic Bulletin and Review* 14: 1212–1217.

Hulleman, Johan, Winkel, Wilco Te, and Boselie, Frans. 2000. Concavities as basic features in visual search: evidence from search asymmetries. *Perception and Psychophysics* 62: 162–174.

Humphreys, Glyn and Müller, Hermann. 2000. A search asymmetry reversed by figure-ground assignment. *Psychological Science* 11: 196–201.

ICA Panel Discussion. 1995. *Spanner in the Works*. Panel discussion at the Institute of Contemporary Arts, London, *TheatreForum* 6: 66–68.

Ingold, Tim. 2000a. Globes and spheres: the topology of environmentalism. In Tim Ingold (ed.) *Perception of the Environment: Essays on Livelihood, Dwelling and Skill*, 209–218. London: Routledge.

Ingold, Tim. 2000b. To journey along a way of life: maps, wayfinding and navigation. In Tim Ingold (ed.) *Perception of the Environment: Essays on Livelihood, Dwelling and Skill*, 219–242. London: Routledge.

Ingold, Tim. 2004. Culture on the ground: the world perceived through the feet. *Journal of Material Culture* 9: 315–340.

Ingold, Tim. 2007. Materials against materiality. *Archaeological Dialogues* 14(1): 1–16.

Ingold, Tim. 2008. Bindings against boundaries: entanglements of life in an open world. *Environment and Planning A* 40(8): 1796–1810.

Ingold, Tim. 2015a. Culture on the ground: the world perceived through the feet. In Tim Ingold (ed.) *Being Alive: Essays on Movement, Knowledge and Description*, 33–50. London: Routledge.

Ingold, Tim. 2015b. Earth, sky, wind and weather. In Tim Ingold (ed.) *Being Alive: Essays on Movement, Knowledge and Description*, 115–125. London: Routledge.

Ingold, Tim. 2015c. Landscape or weather-world. In Tim Ingold (ed.) *Being Alive: Essays on Movement, Knowledge and Description*, 126–136. London: Routledge.

Ingold, Tim. 2015d. Rethinking the animate, reanimating thought. In Tim Ingold (ed.) *Being Alive: Essays on Movement, Knowledge and Description*, 67–75. London: Routledge.

Institute of Cemetery and Crematorium Management. 2004. Policy relating to Shallow Depth Graves (Institute of Cemetery and Crematorium Management). London: Institute of Cemetery and Crematorium Management.

Jenkins, Bruce 2011. *Gordon Matta-Clark: Conical Intersect*. London: Afterall.

Johnson, Dominic. 2008. Perverse martyrologies: an interview with Ron Athey. *Contemporary Theatre Review* 18(4): 503–513.

Johnson, Dominic. 2010. Ron Athey's visions of excess: performance after Georges Bataille. *Papers of Surrealism* 8: 1–12.

Johnson, Dominic. 2013a. Does a bloody towel represent the ideals of the American people? Ron Athey and the culture wars. *Pleading in the Blood: The Art and Performances of Ron Athey*, 64–93. Chicago: University of Chicago Press and Intellect.

Johnson, Dominic. 2013b. Introduction: towards a moral and just psychopathology. In Dominic Johnson (ed.) *Pleading in the Blood: The Art and Performances of Ron Athey*, 10–40. Chicago: University of Chicago Press and Intellect.

Jones, Amelia. 2013. How Ron Athey makes us feel: the political potential of upsetting art. In Dominic Johnson (ed.) *Pleading in the Blood: The Art and Performances of Ron Athey*, 142–178. Chicago: University of Chicago Press and Intellect.

Judovitz, Dalia. 2010. *Drawing on Art: Duchamp and Company*. Minneapolis: University of Minnesota Press.

Keane, Simone, Hayward, William, and Burke, Darren. 2003. Detection of three types of changes to novel objects. *Visual Cognition* 10: 101–129.

Keidan, Lois. 1995. Ron Athey comes to London. *TheaterForum* 6: 64–65.

Killacky, John. 2014. Inside the culture wars maelstrom of the 1990s. *Flynn Center* https://flynncenter.tumblr.com/search/athey/ (accessed June 15, 2014).

Kirshner, Judith. 1978. Interview with Gordon Matta-Clark by Judith Russi Kirshner, February 13, 1978 (Museum of Contemporary Art, Chicago). Reprinted in Gloria Moure (ed.) *Gordon Matta-Clark: Works and Collected Writings*, 317–335. Madrid: Ediciones Polígrafa.

Kirshner, Judith. 2003. The idea of community in the work of Gordon Matta-Clark. In Corinne Diserens (ed.) *Gordon Matta-Clark*, 147–160. New York: Phaidon.

Klíma, Bohuslav. 1954. Palaeolithic huts at Dolní Věstonice, Czechoslovakia. *Antiquity* 28: 4–14.

Klíma, Bohuslav. 1963. *Dolní Věstonice: Vyzkum Táboriste Lovcù Mamutù v Letch 1947–1952*. Prague: Academia.

Klíma, Bohuslav. 1983. *Dolní Věstonice: Táboriste Lovcù Mamutù*. Prague: Akademia Nakladatelstvi Ceskoslovenske Akademie Ved.

Knusal, Chris. n.d. Report on the human bone from the Southern Romania Archaeological Project 2003. Unpublished report in the possession of the author.

Koenderink, Jan J. 1984. What does the occluding contour tell us about solid shape? *Perception* 13: 321–330.

Koukouli-Chrysanthaki, Chaido I., Aslanis, Ioannis, Vaisov, Ivan, and Valla, Magdalini. 2005. Promachonas-Topolniča 2002–2003. *Archaiologiko Ergo sti Makedonia kai Thraki* 17: 91–110.

Lappin, Joseph S. and Craft, Warren D. 2000. Foundations of spatial vision: from retinal images to perceived shapes. *Psychological Review* 107: 6–38.

Lazăr, Cătălin and Soficaru, Andrei D. n.d. Preliminary report of the human bone from Teleor 003. Unpublished report in the possession of the author.

Lee, Pamela M. 1998. On the holes of history: Gordon Matta-Clark's work in Paris. *October* 85: 65–89.

Lee, Pamela M. 1999. *Object to Be Destroyed: The Work of Gordon Matta-Clark*. Cambridge, MA: MIT Press.

Leer, Jeff. 1989. Directional systems in Athabaskan and Na-Dene. In Eung-Do Cook and Keren D. Rice (eds.) *Trends in Linguistics* (vol. 15), 575–622. Berlin: Mouton.

Levin, Beth, and Rappaport Hovav, Malka. 1995. *Unaccusativity: At the Syntax-Lexical Semantics Interface*. Cambridge, MA: MIT Press.

Levinson, Jerrold. 1978. Properties and related entities. *Philosophy and Phenomenological Research* 39 (1): 1–22.

Levinson, Stephen C. 2003. *Space in Language and Cognition: Explorations in Cognitive Diversity*. New York: Cambridge University Press.

Levinson, Stephen C. 2007. Cut and break verbs in Yélî Dnye, the Papuan language of Rossel Island. *Cognitive Linguistics* 18: 207–218.

Lewis, David and Lewis, Stephanie. 1970. Holes. *Australian Journal of Philosophy* 48(2): 206–212.

Lewis, Neil. 2001. The climbing body, nature and the experience of modernity. In Phil MacNaghten and John Urry (eds) *Bodies of Nature* 58–80. London: Sage.

Lewis-Williams, David. 2002. *The Mind in the Cave*. London: Thames and Hudson.

Lista, Giovanni. 2000. The cosmos as finitude: from Boccioni's chromogony to Fontana's spatial art. In Jean Clair (ed.) *Cosmos: From Goya to de Chirico, from Friedrich to Kiefer. Art in Pursuit of the Infinite* 96–123. Venice: Palazzo Grassi.

Livi, Grazia. 1962. Incontro con Lucio Fontana. *Varità* 6(13): 52–57.

Lunch, Lydia. 2013. Joyce: the violent disbelief of Ron Athey. In Dominic Johnson (ed.) *Pleading in the Blood: The Art and Performances of Ron Athey*, 194–197. Chicago: University of Chicago Press and Intellect.

Lüpke, Friederike. 2007. "Smash it again, Sam": Verbs of cutting and breaking in Jalonke. *Cognitive Linguistics* 18(2): 251–262.

Macklin, Mark, Bailey, Doug, Howard, Andy, Mills, Stephen, Robinson, Ruth, Mirea, Pavel, and Thissen, Laurens. 2011. River dynamics and the Neolithic of the lower Danube catchment. In Stephen Mills and Pavel Mirea (eds.) *The Lower Danube in Prehistory: Landscape Changes `and the Human-Environment Interactions*, 9–14. Bucureşti: Editura Renaissance.

Macphail, Richard, Haită, Constantin, Bailey, Doug, Andreescu, Radian, and Mirea, Pavel. 2005. The soil micromorphology of enigmatic Early Neolithic pit-features at Măgura, southern Romania. *Studii de Preistorie* 5: 61–78.

Majid, Asifa, Boster, James S., and Bowerman, Melissa. 2008. The cross-linguistic categorization of everyday events: a study of cutting and breaking. *Cognition* 109: 235–250.

Majid, Asifa, Bowerman, Melissa, Van Staden, Miriam, and Boster, James S. 2007a. The semantic categories of cutting and breaking events: a crosslinguistic perspective. *Cognitive Linguistics* 18–2 (2007): 133–152.

Majid, Asifa, Gullberg, Marianne, van Staden, Miriam, and Bowerman, Melissa. 2007b. How similar are semantic categories in closely related languages? A comparison of cutting and breaking in four Germanic languages. *Cognitive Linguistics* 18(2): 179–195.

Malsch, Friedemann. 1992. Gordon Matta-Clark. *Kunstforum International* 117 (March/April): 172–183. Reprinted in Corinne Diserens (ed.) *Gordon Matta-Clark*, 204–207. New York: Phaidon.

Malt, Barbara, Sloman, Steven, and Gennari, Silvia. 2003. Universality and language specificity in object naming. *Journal of Memory and Language* 49: 20–42.

Malt, Barbara, Sloman, Steven, Gennari, Silvia, Shi, Meiyi, and Wang, Yuan. 1999. Knowing versus naming: similarity and the linguistic categorization of artifacts. *Journal of Memory and Language* 40: 230–262.

Marder, Irving. 1975. The art of putting holes in houses. *International Herald Tribune* 20 (October): 9.

Mărgărit, Monica, Bălăşcu, Adrian, and Mirea, Pavel. 2014. Processing of *Ovis Aries/Capra Hircu* bones from the Starčevo-Criş I level at Măgura-Buduiasca (Boldul lui Moş Ivănuş) settlement. *Buletinul Muzeului Judeţean Teleorman. Seria Arheologie* 6: 7–18.

Matta-Clark, Gordon. n.d. *Articles and Documents 1942 to 1976*. Weston, CT: Estate of Gordon Matta-Clark.

Matta-Clark, Gordon. 1973a. Letter to Carol Goodden and "The Meeting," and letter to Carol Goodden and "The Mob (Again)," December 10. Weston, CT: Estate of Gordon Matta-Clark.

Matta-Clark, Gordon. 1973b. Notecard: # 1153 c. 1973, EGM–c. Weston, CT: Estate of Gordon Matta-Clark.

Matta-Clark, Gordon. 2006. Gordon Matta-Clark's Building Dissections. Typewritten statement, undated. In Gloria Moure (ed.) *Gordon Matta-Clark: Works and Collected Writings*, 132–133. Madrid: Ediciones Polígrafa.

Meadows, Phillip J. 2011. What angles can tell us about what holes are not. *Erkenntnis* 78(2): 319–331.

Megaw, J. Vincent S. and Simpson, Derek D. A. 1979. *Introduction to British Prehistory*. Leicester: Leicester University Press.

Mehring, Christine. 2008. Television art's abstract starts: Europa circa 1944–1969. *October* 125: 29–64.

Middleton, Robert. 1998. Flint and chert artefacts. In Francis Pryor (ed.) *Etton: Excavations at a Neolithic Causewayed Enclosure near Maxey, Cambridgeshire, 1982–7*, 215–250. London: English Heritage.

Mills, Stephen. 2009. High-resolution study and raster interpolation of early Neolithic pit features at Măgura-Buduiasca, Teleorman County, Southern Romania. *Buletinul Muzeului Județean Teleorman. Seria Arheologie* 1: 55–66.

Minichreiter, Kornelija. 1992. *Starčevačka Kultura u Sjevernoj Hrvatskoj*. Zagreb: Dissertationes et Monographiae.

Minichreiter, Kornelija 1993. Arhitektura starčevačkog naselja kod Zadubravlja. *Arheološka istraživanja u Slavonskom Brodu i Brodskom Posavlju, Izdanje Hrvatskog Arheološkog Društva* 16: 97–111.

Minichreiter, Kornelija. 2001. The architecture of Early and Middle Neolithic settlements of the Starcevo culture in Northern Croatia. *Documenta Praehistorica* 28: 199–214.

Minichreiter, Kornelija. 2007a. *Slavonski Brod, Galovo, deset godina arheolo kih istraivanja* [Slavonski Brod, Galovo, Ten years of archaeological excavations]. Zagreb: Monografije Instituta za Arheologiju i Zagreb.

Minichreiter, Kornelija. 2007b. The white-painted Linear A phase of the Starčevo Culture in Croatia. *Prilozi Instituta za Arheologiju u Zagrebu* 24: 21–34.

Minichreiter, Kornelija. 2008. Radna zemunica 291 u naselju starčevačke culture na Galovu u Slavonskom Brodu. [Working pit 291 in the Starčevo culture settlement at Galovu u Slabonskom Brodu] *Prilozi Instituta za Arheologiju u Zagrebu* 25: 5–14.

Minichreiter, Kornelija and Botić, Katarina. 2010. Early Neolithic burials of Starčevo culture at Galovo, Slavonski Brod (Northern Croatia). *Documenta Praehistorica* 37: 105–124.

Miracco, Renato. 2006. *Lucio Fontana: At the Roots of Spatialism*. Rome: Gangemi.

Mirea, Pavel. 2005. Consideraţii asupra locuirii Starčevo-Criş din sud-vestul Munteniei. *Cutură şi Civilizaţie la Dunărea de Jos* 22: 37–52.

Mirea, Pavel. 2011a. Between everyday and ritual use: "small altars" or "cult tables" from Măgura-Buduiasca, Teleorman County (I): the early Neolithic finds. *Buletinul Muzeului Judeţean Teleorman. Seria Arheologie* 3: 41–58.

Mirea, Pavel. 2011b. A Neolithic microlandscape: the story of Complex 40 from Măgura-Buduiasca (Teleor 003), Teleorman County, Southern Romania. In Stephen Mills and Pavel Mirea (eds.) *The Lower Danube in Prehistory: Landscape Changes and the Human-Environment Interactions*, 241–256. Bucureşti: Editura Renaissance.

Moholy-Nagy, László. 1925 [1969]. *Malerie, Fotographie, Film (Painting, Photography, Film*, (trans. anon). London: Albert Langen.

Moholy-Nagy, László. 1947. *Vision in Motion*. Chicago: Paul Theobald.

Moretti, Luigi. 1952. Arte e televisione. *Spazio* 7: 74, 106.

Morgan, Lewis Henry. 1877 [1964]. *Ancient Society or Researches in the Lines of Human Progress from Savagery Through Barbarism to Civilization*. Cambridge, MA: Harvard University Press.

Morphy, Howard. 1992. From dull to brilliant: the aesthetics of spiritual power among the Yolngu. In Jeremy Cootes and Anthony Shelton (eds.) *Anthropology, Art and Aesthetics*, 181–208. Oxford: Clarendon.

Mortimer, Roger and McFadyen, Leslie. 1999. *Investigation of the Archaeological Landscape at Broom, Bedfordshire: Phase 4*. (Report 320). Cambridge: Cambridge Archaeological Unit.

Moure, Gloria (ed.). 2006. *Gordon Matta-Clark: Works and Collected Writings*. Barcelona: Ediciones Polígrafa.

Muir, Peter. 2011. Gordon Matta-Clark's Conical Intersect: "luxury will be king." *Journal for Cultural Research* 15(2): 173–192.

Myers, Julia. 1995. An interview with Ron Athey. *TheatreForum* TF 6 (Winter–Spring): 60–65.

Nakayama, Ken and Shimojo, Shinsuke. 1992. Experiencing and perceiving visual surfaces. *Science* 257: 1357–1363.

Nakayama, Ken, He, Zijiang J., and Shimojo, Shinsuke. 1995. Visual surface representation: a critical link between lower-level and higher level vision. In Stephen M. Kosslyn and Daniel N. Osherson (eds.) *Visual Cognition. An Invitation to Cognitive Science*, 1–70. Cambridge, MA: MIT Press.

Narasimhan, Bhuvana. 2007. Cutting, breaking, and tearing verbs in Hindi and Tamil. *Cognitive Linguistics* 18(2): 195–205.

Nelson, Rolf and Palmer, Stephen E. 2001. Of holes and wholes: the perception of surrounded edges. *Perception* 30: 1213–1226.

Noever, Peter (ed.). 1998. *Anarchitecture: Works by Gordon Matta-Clark*. Los Angeles: MAK Center for Art and Architecture.

Norman, J. Farley, Phillips, Flip, and Ross, Heather E. 2001. Information concentration along the boundary contours of naturally shaped solid objects. *Perception* 30: 1285–1294.

O'Connor, Loretta. 2007. "Chop, shred, snap apart": verbs of cutting and breaking in Lowland Chontal. *Cognitive Linguistics* 18(2): 219–230.

Odendaal, Johannes. 1997. An ethological approach to the problem of dogs digging holes. *Applied Animal Behaviour Science* 52(3–4): 299–305.

Opie, Catherine. 2013. Flash: on photographing Ron Athey. In Dominic Johnson (ed.) *Pleading in the Blood: The Art and Performances of Ron Athey*, 142–151. Chicago: University of Chicago Press and Intellect.

Osborne, Peter J. 1969. An insect fauna of Late Bronze Age date from Wilsford, Wiltshire. *Journal of Animal Ecology* 38: 555–566.

Osborne, Peter J. 1989. Insects. In Paul Ashbee, Martin Bell, and Edwina Proudfoot (eds.) *Wilsford Shaft: Excavations 1960–62*, 96–99. London: English Heritage.

Oswald, Alastair, Barber, Martyn, and Dyer, Carolyn. 2001. *The Creation of Monuments: Neolithic Causewayed Enclosures in the British Isles*. Swindon: English Heritage.

Ozanne-Rivièrre, Françoise. 1977. Spatial reference in New Caledonian languages. In Gunter Senft (ed.) *Referring to Space: Studies in Austronesian and Papuan Languages*, 83–100. Oxford: Clarendon Press.

Ozanne-Rivièrre, Françoise. 1987. L'expression linquistique de l'espace: quelques exemples oceaniens. *Cahiers du Lacito* 2: 129–155.

Palmer, Stephen. 1999. *Vision Science: Photons to Phenomenology*. Cambridge, MA: MIT Press.

Palmer, Stephen and Rock, Irwin. 1994. Rethinking perceptual organization: the role of uniform connectedness. *Psychonomic Bulletin and Review* 1(1): 29–55.

Pannett, Amelia. 2009. The lithic assemblage from Teleor 003: preliminary analysis and interpretations. *Buletinul Muzeului Judeţean Teleorman. Seria Arheologie* 1: 67–74.

Pannett, Amelia. 2011. Lithic exploitation in the Neolithic of the Teleorman Valley, Southern Romania: preliminary discussion of results. In Stephen Mills and Pavel Mirea (eds.) *The Lower Danube in Prehistory: Landscape Changes and the Human-Environment Interactions*, 167–172. Bucureşti: Editura Renaissance.

Pannett, Amelia. 2012. Pits, pits and plant remains: trends in Neolithic deposition in Carmarthenshire, South Wales. In Hugo Anderson-Whymark and Julian Thomas (eds.) *Regional Perspectives on Neolithic Pit Deposition: Beyond the Mundane*, 126–143. Oxford: Oxbow.

Pasupathy, Anitha and Connor, Charles E. 1999. Responses to contour features in macaque area V4. *Journal of Neuro-physiology* 82: 2490–2502.

Pasupathy, Anitha, and Connor, Charles E. 2001. Shape representation in area v4: Position-specific tuning for boundary conformation. *Journal of Neurophysiology* 86: 2505–2519.

Petersen, Stephen. 2000. From matter to light: Fontana's *Spatial Concepts* and experimental photography. *Art on Paper* 4(4): 54–55.

Peterson, John, Freedenthal, Stacey, Sheldon, Christopher, and Andersen, Randy. 2008. Nonsuicidal self-injury in adolescents. *Psychiatry (Edgmont)* 5(11): 20–26.

Piaget, Jean. 1954. *The Construction of Reality in the Child*. New York: Basic.

Pica, Agnoldomenico. 1953. *Lucio Fontana e lo Spazialismo*. Venice: Cavallino.

Piggott, Stuart. 1965. *Ancient Europe*. Edinburgh: Edinburgh University Press.

Piggott, Stuart. 1973. The Wessex Culture, and the final phase of bronze technology. *Victoria County History of Wiltshire* 1(2): 352–407.

Piggott, Stuart. 1975. *The Druids*. London: Thames and Hudson.

Piggott, Stuart. 1978. Nemeton, temenos, bothros: sanctuaries of the ancient Celts. *Academia Nazionale del Lincei* 237: 127–154.

Pollard, Joshua. 2001. The aesthetics of depositional practice. *World Archaeology* 33: 315–333.

Pollard, Joshua. 2008. Deposition and material agency in the Early Neolithic of Southern Britain. In Barbara J. Mills and William H. Walker (eds.) *Memory Work: Archaeologies of Material Practices. The Archaeology of Ritual, Memory and Materiality*, 41–59. Santa Fe, NM: School for Advanced Research.

Ponti, Lisa. 1952. Idee di Lucio Fontana. *Domus* 271: 33.

Popescu, Dorin, Constantinescu, Nicolae, Diaconu, G., and Teodorescu, Victor. 1961. Şantierul Arheologic Târgşor. *Materiale şi Cercetări Arheologice* 7: 631–644.

Proudfoot, Edwina. 1989a. The artefacts from the shaft's infill: the artefacts from the pond barrow and weathering cone. In Paul Ashbee, Martin Bell, and Edwina Proudfoot (eds.) *Wilsford Shaft: Excavations 1960–62*, 37–43. London: English Heritage.

Proudfoot, Edwina. 1989b. The pond barrow and weathering cone. In Paul Ashbee, Martin Bell, and Edwina Proudfoot (eds.) *Wilsford Shaft: Excavations 1960–62*, 15–25. London: English Heritage.

Pryor, Francis (ed.). 1998. *Etton: Excavations at a Neolithic Causewayed Enclosure near Maxey, Cambridgeshire, 1982–7*. London: English Heritage.

Pryor, Francis, Cleal, Ros, and Kinnes, Ian. 1998. Discussion of Neolithic and earlier Bronze Age pottery. In Francis Pryor (ed.) *Etton: Excavations at a Neolithic Causewayed Enclosure near Maxey, Cambridgeshire, 1982–7*, 209–212. London: English Heritage.

Renfrew, A. Colin. 1987. *Archaeology and Language: The Puzzle of Indo-European Origins*. London: Pimlico.

Resnikoff, Howard L. 1985. *The Illusion of Reality: Topics in Information Science*. New York: Springer.

Richards, Colin and Thomas, Julian. 1984. Ritual activity and structured deposition in the latern Neolithic Wessex. In Richard Bradley and Julie Gardiner (eds.) *Neolithic Studies*, 189–218. Oxford: British Archaeological Reports.

Robinson, Mark. 1989. Seeds and other plant macrofossils. In Paul Ashbee, Martin Bell, and Edwina Proudfoot (eds.) *Wilsford Shaft: Excavations 1960–62*, 78–89. London: English Heritage.

Robles, Jennifer J. 1994. Disturbing viewers is one of the things art can do. *Star Tribune* (Minneapolis) April 3: 21A.

Ross, Anne. 1967. *Pagan Celtic Britain*. Chicago: Academy.

Ross, Anne. 1968. Shafts, pits, wells: sanctuaries of the Belgic Britons? In John M. Coles and Derek D. A. Simpson (eds.) *Studies in Ancient Europe*, 255–285. Leicester: University of Leicester Press.

Rossi, Bruno. 1963. L'Astronauta dell'arte. *Settimo Giorno* 16(4): 744.

Royce, Graydon. 1994. Why does he do this? *Star Tribune* (Minneapolis) August 1: 10A.

Sandahl, Carrie. 2001. Performing metaphors: AIDS, disability and technology. *Contemporary Theatre Review* 11(3): 49–60.

Schwarz, Klaus. 1960. Spätkeltische Viereckschanzen, Ergebnisse der topographischen Vermessung und der Ausgrabungen 1957–59. *Jahresbericht der Bayerischen Bodendenkmalpflege* 1: 7–41.

Schwarz, Klaus. 1962. Zum Stand de Ausgrabungen in der spätkeltischen Viereckschanze von Holzhausen. *Jahresbericht der Bayerischen Bodendenkmalpflege* 3: 21–77.

Schwarz, Klaus. 1975. Die Geschichte eines Keltischen Temenos im Nördlichen Alpenvorland. *Ausgrabungen in Deutschland Gefördert von er Deutschen Forshungsgemeinshaft 1950–1975, Teil 1, Vorgeschicte Romerzeit*, 324–358. Mainz: Verlag des Römisch-Germanischen Zentralmuseums.

Shank, Theodore. 2002. *Beyond the Boundaries: American Alternative Theatre*. Ann Arbor: University of Michigan Press.

Shanks, Michael. 1992. *Experiencing the Past: On the Character of Archaeology*. London: Routledge.

Shanks, Michael and Tilley, Christopher. 1987a. *Re-Constructing Archaeology: Theory and Practice*. Cambridge: Cambridge University Press.

Shanks, Michael and Tilley, Christopher. 1987b. *Social Theory and Archaeology*. Cambridge: Polity.

Sharples, Niall. 2010. *Social Relations in Later Prehistory: Wessex in the First Millennium BC*. Oxford: Oxford University Press.

Simon, Joan. 1985. Interviews. Reprinted in Corinne Diserens (ed.) 2003. *Gordon Matta-Clark*, 190–199. New York: Phaidon.

Singh, Manish and Fulvio, Jacqueline M. 2005. Visual extrapolation of contour geometry. *Proceedings of the National Academy of Sciences* 102(3): 939–944.

Slobin, Dan I. 1973. Cognitive prerequisites for the development of grammar. In Charles A. Ferguson and Dan I. Slobin (eds.), *Studies of Child Development*, 175–208. New York: Holt, Reinhart and Winston.

Souvatzi, Stella. 2007. *A Social Archaeology of Households in Neolithic Greece: An Anthropological Approach*. Cambridge: Cambridge University Press.

Stone, Rosanne A. 1996. Speaking of the medium: Marshall McLuhan interviews Allucquére Rosanne Stone. In Duncan McCorquodale (ed.) *Orlan: Ceci est Mon Corp, Ceci est Mon Logiciel*, 42–51. London: Black Dog.

Stroll, A. 1988. *Surfaces.* Minneapolis: University of Minnesota Press.

Stukeley, William. 1740. *Stonehenge, A Temple Restor'd to the British Druids.* London: Innys and Manby.

Sussman, Elizabeth (ed.). 2007. *Gordon Matta-Clark: "You Are the Measure."* New York: Whitney Museum of American Art.

Taylor, John R. 2007. Semantic categories of cutting and breaking: some final thoughts. *Cognitive Linguistics* 18(2): 331–337.

Taylor, Maisie. 1998. Wood and bark from the enclosure ditch. In Francis Pryor (ed.) *Etton: Excavations at a Neolithic Causewayed Enclosure near Maxey, Cambridgeshire, 1982–7*, 115–160. London: English Heritage.

Teodorescu, Victor. 1963. Cultura Criş în Centrul Munteniei (Pe Baza Săpăturilor Arheologice de la Târgşorul Vechi). *Studii şi Cercetări de Istorie Veche* 14(2): 251–268.

Thissen, Laurens. 2008. The Ceramics of Teleor 003/Măgura-Buduiasca, a Neolithic Site in S Romania. Unpublished report.

Thissen, Laurens. 2009. First ceramic assemblages in the Danube catchment, SE Europe. *Buletinul Muzeului Judeţean Teleorman. Seria Arheologie* 1: 9–30.

Thissen, Laurens. 2012. Starčevo-Criş pottery from Teleor 003, S. Romania. *Buletinul Muzeului Judeţean Teleorman. Seria Arheologie* 4: 5–46.

Thissen, Laurens. 2013. Middle Neolithic ceramics from Teleor 003, Southern Romania. *Buletinul Muzeului Judeţean Teleorman. Seria Arheologie* 5: 25–124.

Thomas, Julian. 1991. *Rethinking the Neolithic.* Cambridge: Cambridge University Press.

Thomas, Julian. 1999. *Understanding the Neolithic.* London: Routledge.

Thomas, Julian. 2012. Introduction: beyond the mundane. In Hugo Anderson-Whymark and Julian Thomas (eds.) *Regional Perspectives on Neolithic Pit Deposition: Beyond the Mundane*, 1–12. Oxford: Oxbow.

Thompson, Victoria E. 1997. Urban renovation, moral regeneration: domesticating the Halles in Second-Empire Paris. *French Historical Studies* 20(1): 87–109.

Tilley, Christopher. 1994. *A Phenomenology of Landscape: Places, Paths and Monuments.* Oxford: Berg.

Tolman, Edward C. 1948. Cognitive maps in rats and men. *Psychology Review* 55(4): 109–145.

Trescott, Jacqueline. 1994. Art on the cutting edge: bloody performance renews funding debate. *The Washington Post* (March 31): C1.

Tringham, Ruth. 1971. *Hunters, Fishers, and Farmers of Eastern Europe 6000–3000 BC.* London: Hutchinson.

Tucholsky, Kurt. 1930. Zur soziologischen Psychologie der Löcher' (signed Kaspar Hauser), *Die Weltbühne* (March 17): 389. The social psychology of holes (trans. Harry Zohn). Reprinted in Harry Zohn (ed.). 1990. *Germany? Germany! The Kurt Tucholsky Reader*, 100–101. Manchester: Carcanet.

Tudor, Ersilia and Chichideanu, Ion. 1977. Săpăturile Arheologice de la Brăteştii de Sus, Judeţul Dâmboviţa. *Valachica* 9: 119–151.

Turnbull, David. 2000. *Mason, Tricksters and Cartographers: Comparative Studies in the Sociology of Scientific and Indigenous Knowledge.* Amsterdam: Harwood.

USA Today. 2014. "Shy" student held in mass stabbing at Pa. school. *USA Today* (April 10). https://www.usatoday.com/story/news/nation/2014/04/09/pa-school-stabbings/7498911/ (accessed April 20, 2014).

Van As, Abraham. 2010. How and why? The Neolithic pottery from Teleor 003, Teleor 008 and Măgura-Bran, Teloerman River Valley, Southern Romania. *Buletinul Muzeului Judeţean Teleorman. Seria Arheologie* 2: 29–44.

Vance, Carole. 1994. The war on culture. In Ted Gott (ed.) *Don't Leave Me This Way: Art in the Age of AIDS*, 91–111. London: Thames and Hudson.

Vandekerckhove, Joachim, Panis, Sven, and Wagemans, Johan. 2007. The concavity effect is a compound of local and global effects. *Perception and Psychophysics* 69: 1253–1260.

Van Staden, Mariam. 2007. "Please open the fish": verbs of separation in Tidore, a Papuan language of Eastern Indonesia. *Cognitive Linguistics* 18(2): 297–306.

Vasić, Miloje. 1936. *Preistoriska Vinča.* Volume 2. Belgrade: Izdanie Državne Štamparije.

Vidler, Anthonys. 2006. "Architecture-to-be": notes on architecture in the work of Matta and Gordon Matta-Clark. In Briony Fer, Betti-Sue Hertz, Justo Pastor Mellado, and Anthony Vidler (eds.) *Transmission: The Art of Matta and Gordon Matta-Clarke*, 59–73. San Diego: San Diego Museum of Art.

Vigo, N. 2006. Interview with the author. Transcript of a taped interview. Milan (October 2).

Wagner, Anne M. 2004. Splitting and doubling: Gordon Matta-Clark and the body of sculpture. *Grey Room* 14: 26–45.

Wainright, Geoff J. 1973. Prehistoric and Romani-British settlements at Eaton Heath, Norwich. *Archaeological Journal* 130: 1–43.

Wake, Andrew, Spencer, Joshua, and Fowler, Gregory. 2007. Holes as regions of spacetime. *The Monist* 90: 372–378.

Walker, Angela, and Bogaard, Amy. 2011. Preliminary archaeobotanical results from Teleor 003/Măgura-Buduiasca. In Stephen Mills and Pavel Mirea (eds.) *The Lower Danube in Prehistory: Landscape Changes and the Human-Environment Interactions*, 151–160. Bucureşti: Editura Renaissance.

Walker, Stephen. 2003. Baffling archaeology: the strange gravity of Gordon Matta-Clark's experience-optics. *Journal of Visual Culture* 2(2): 161–185.

Walker, Stephen. 2009. *Gordon Matta-Clark: Art, Architecture and the Attack on Modernism.* New York: I. B. Tauris.

Walker, Stephen. 2011. The field and the table: Rosalind Krauss' "expanded field" and the Anarchitecture group. *Architectural Research Quarterly* 15: 347–358.

Wall, Donald. 1976. Gordon Matta-Clark's building dissections. An interview by Donald Wall. *Arts Magazine* (May): 74–79. Reprinted in Corinne Diserens (ed.) 2003. *Gordon Matta-Clark*, 181–186. New York: Phaidon.

Wassmann, Jurg and Dasen, Pierre R. 1998. Balinese spatial orientation: some empirical evidence of moderate linguistic relativity. *Journal of the Royal Anthropological Institute* 4(4): 689–711.

Waxman, Lori. 2008. The banquet years: FOOD, a SoHo restaurant. *Gastronomica: The Journal of Food and Culture* 8(4): 24–33.

White, Anthony. 2001. Lucio Fontana: between utopia and kitsch. *Grey Room* 5: 54–77.

White, Anthony. 2008. Industrial painting's utopias: Lucio Fontana's "Expectations." *October* 124: 93–124.

White, Anthony. 2011. *Lucio Fontana: Between Utopia and Kitsch*. Cambridge, MA: MIT Press.

Whitfield, Sarah. 1999. *Fontana*. London: Hayward Gallery.

Whitfield, Sarah. 2000. *Lucio Fontana*. Berkeley: University of California Press.

Whittle, Alasdair. 1991. Wayland's Smithy, Oxfordshire: excavations at the Neolithic tomb in 1962–3 by Richard J. C. Atkinson and Stuart Piggott. *Proceedings of the Prehistoric Society* 57(2): 61–102.

Whittle, Alasdair. 1996. *Europe in the Neolithic: The Creation of New Worlds*. Cambridge: Cambridge University Press.

Whittle, Alasdair. 2007. On the waterfront. In Alasdair Whittle (ed.) *The Early Neolithic on the Great Hungarian Plain: Investigations of the Körös Culture Site of Ecsegfalva 23, County Békés*, 727–755. Budapest: Institute of Archaeology, Hungarian Academy of Sciences.

Whittle, Alasdair, Healy, Francis, and Bayliss, Alex. 2011. *Gathering Time: Dating the Early Neolithic Enclosures of Southern Britain and Ireland*. Oxford: Oxbow.

Whittle, Alasdair, Pollard, Joshua, and Grigson, Caroline. 1999. *The Harmony of Symbols: The Windmill Hill Causewayed Enclosure*. Oxford: Oxbow.

Whittle, Alasdair, Rouse, Amanda, and Evans, John. 1993. A Neolithic downland monument in its environment: excavations at the Easton Down long barrow, Bishops Cannings, North Wiltshire. *Proceedings of the Prehistoric Society* 59: 197–239.

Wilkins, David P. and Hill, Deborah. 1995. When "go" means "come": questioning the basic-ness of basic motion verbs. *Cognitive Linguistics* 6: 209–259.

Wolfe, Jeremy M. and Bennett, Sara C. 1997. Preattentive object files: shapeless bundles of basic features. *Vision Research* 37: 25–43.

Wolfe, Jeremy M., Yee, Alice, and Friedman-Hill, Stacia. 1992. Curvature is a basic feature for visual search tasks. *Perception* 21(1): 465–480.

Wymer, John J. and Brown, Nigel. 1995. *Excavations at North Shoebury: Settlement and Economy in South-East Essex 1500 BC–AD 1500*. Chelmsford: East Anglian Archaeology.

Young, Alison. 2005. *Judging the Image: Art, Value, Law*. London: Routledge.

Zola, Émile. 1996 [1873]. *Le Ventre de Paris* [The Belly of Paris] (trans. Ernest A. Vizatelly). Los Angeles: Sun and Moon.

Index